MW00940872

ADDICTION:
THE HIDDEN EPIDEMIC

To Brita!

Best wishes,

Pam Killeen

ADDICTION:
THE HIDDEN EPIDEMIC

*Common Sense Solutions
for Our #1 Health Problem*

PAM KILLEEN

Library of Congress Control Number:		2010907245
ISBN:	Hardcover	978-1-4535-0374-4
	Softcover	978-1-4535-0373-7
	Ebook	978-1-4535-0375-1

This book was printed in the United States of America.

To order additional copies of this book, contact:
Xlibris Corporation
1-888-795-4274
www.Xlibris.com
Orders@Xlibris.com
79666

CONTENTS

PART I

PART II

DEDICATION

To Abram Hoffer, MD, PhD (1917-2009), your vision lives on.
And to all those struggling with addiction—there is a better way.

AUTHOR'S NOTE

The information in this book is for educational purposes only. If you have been diagnosed with a medical condition and/or are taking medications of any kind, you should consult a qualified health care professional before following any suggestions in this book. In addition, it is important to keep in mind that the approaches discussed in the book should be used in conjunction with psychological counseling or spiritual support.

FOREWORD

Dr. Chris Reading

Ms. Pam Killeen has asked me to review her wonderful new book *Addiction: The Hidden Epidemic* and to record my impression. As a retired orthomolecular psychiatrist I am all too familiar with the ravages of addictive behaviors, which is an important component of not only criminal and other psychiatric pathology, as well as affecting millions of people who resort to chemicals—legal and illegal—to find some relief from debilitating mood disorders. Her book is crammed with references to countless studies showing how the chemicalization of our society has produced in Aldous Huxley's words "a kind of painless concentration camp for entire societies . . . distracted from any desire to rebel by propaganda or brainwashing . . . enhanced by pharmacological methods."

She points out that contrary to popular opinion legal drugs, such as alcohol, nicotine and thousands of prescription and OTC drugs, such as opioids, stimulants, tranquilizers and sedatives are the main reasons why patients are admitted to emergency departments of hospitals.

The author correctly points out that one of the major factors responsible for addiction is the "rise of the pro-addiction diet": that is, a commercialized diet that has been robbed of the nutrients that are necessary for the body to manufacture the various feel good neurotransmitters such as serotonin. The tragedy is that cheap industrially processed foods have become the main part of our diets. About 90% of our food dollars are spent on these nutrient-deficient foods.

In order to help solve our addiction epidemic, we must return to basics—and that means returning to the nutrient-dense foods that kept our ancestors both physically and mentally healthy. As a nutritional psychiatrist, I have witnessed patients improve their mental health as they introduce these natural foods into their diets.

She records how hypoglycemia—an illness and forerunner of diabetes, obesity, and Syndrome X—and which has been declared by the American Medical Association to be non-existent in 1973, is now a major contributor to the development of epidemic of addiction and mental illnesses today.

Addiction: The Hidden Epidemic offers a thorough exploration into the causes and solutions for our most prevalent health problem. We can no longer ignore the devastating effects of mood disorders and addiction on society and must recognize the common sense solutions Ms. Killeen proposes in her book. If you know someone struggling with a mood disorder or addiction, the information and extensive resources in this book will help guide them to the answers they need. This book is also a must-read for every therapist working in the recovery field.

Dr. Chris M Reading, BSc, Dip Ag Sc, MB, BS, FRANZCP, FACNEM
Orthomolecular Psychiatrist and author of research articles including the book *Trace Your Genes to Health* with special diets for schizophrenia, autism, hyperactivity, OCD, bipolar disorder, etc.

Carolyn Dean, MD, ND

Dr. Abram Hoffer says that sugar and consequent nutrient deficiency triggers addictions. Law enforcement says it's due to bad people behaving badly. Dr. Bruce Alexander, a psychologist who retired after thirty-five years at Simon Fraser University in British Columbia, says since addiction is stimulated by environmental factors drug policies don't work.[1] Alexander is convinced that "The only way we'll ever touch the problem of addiction is by developing and fostering viable culture."

In the late 1970s, Alexander ran a series of elegant experiments he calls "Rat Park." The conclusion he reached was that drugs, even hard drugs like heroin and cocaine, do not cause addiction; the user's environment does. Like a lot of research that goes against the prevailing grain, Alexander's work was mostly ignored. People were so convinced that drugs cause addiction they couldn't see any other cause.

It turns out that all the animal drug experiments were carried out in confined Skinner boxes where a surgically implanted catheter is hooked up to a drug supply that the animal self-administers by pressing a lever. There is no lack of experiments showing that lab animals readily became slaves to such drugs as heroin, cocaine, and amphetamines, which was the proof that drugs are irresistible and addictive. When Alexander did his own drug experiments he built a paradise for rats and called it Rat Park. He created a plywood enclosure the size of 200 standard cages. Floors were covered with cedar shavings; there were boxes and tin cans for hiding and nesting, climbing poles, and no lack of food. Most important, because rats live in colonies, Rat Park housed sixteen to twenty animals of both sexes.

Alexander also ran a parallel experiment with control animals in standard laboratory cages. Both groups of rats had access to two water bottles, one filled with plain water and the other with morphine-laced water. It became obvious that the residents of Rat Park overwhelmingly preferred plain water to morphine (the test produced statistical confidence levels of over 99.9 percent). Alexander tried to seduce his rats with sugared morphine water but, Rat Parkers drank far less than the caged rats. The only thing that made the Rat Parkers drink morphine was when Alexander added naloxone, which eliminates morphine's narcotic effects. The Rat Parkers wanted the sweet water, but not if it made them high.

In his "Kicking the Habit" experiment, Alexander allowed both groups of rats only morphine-laced water for fifty-seven days, until they were physically dependent on the drug. But as soon as they had a choice between plain water and morphine, the Rat Parkers "switched to plain water more often than the caged rats did, voluntarily putting themselves through the discomfort of withdrawal to do so."

Alexander's "Rat Park showed that a rat's environment, not the availability of drugs, leads to dependence. In a normal setting, a narcotic is an impediment to what rats typically do: fight, play, forage, and mate. But a caged rat can't do those things. It's no surprise that a distressed animal with access to narcotics would use them to seek relief."

Unfortunately, both Science and Nature rejected Alexander's work. As I mentioned earlier, this type of research goes against the prevailing grain and one reviewer said "I can't put my finger on what's wrong, but I know it's got to be wrong." The Rat Park papers were published in reputable psychopharmacology journals but not the ones that most people read.

In the ensuing years Alexander has proven by reading every paper on addiction that humans become addicted for the same reasons as rats. He's written books and papers, delivered speeches, and testified before the 2001-2002 Senate Special Committee on Illegal Drugs.

"His message—that the core values of Western life have created an environment of rootlessness and spiritual poverty that leads more and more of us to addiction—is Rat Park writ large. And by addiction, Alexander means a great deal more than illegal drugs. There are the legal drugs, alcohol and tobacco, of course. Then there's gambling, work, shopping, the Internet, and anorexia ("addiction to starvation," as Alexander puts it). Research is showing that as far as the brain is concerned, these activities are drugs, too, raising levels of the neurotransmitter dopamine, just like alcohol, heroin, and almost every other addictive substance we know. In this broad—but not loose—sense of the word, addiction is not the preserve of a coterie of social outcasts, but rather the general condition of Western society."

"Naturally, these indictments have not for the most part been warmly received, but Alexander is used to that. For years, he's worked outside the mainstream, without funding, in the face of professional ridicule. The resistance, he says, is based on a pervasive "temperance mentality" that has made drugs—first alcohol, then opium, morphine, cocaine, heroin, and marijuana—the scapegoat for society's ills for centuries. 'We're bathed in this propaganda from childhood, and it's totally persuasive," he says. "It's so much easier to believe that the drug takes people away than that the very civilization we live in is making life miserable for everybody.'"

Carolyn Dean, MD, ND, *Death by Modern Medicine*

Carolyn Dean, MD ND has been on the forefront of the natural medicine revolution for over 30 years. She graduated from Dalhousie Medical School in 1978, holds a medical license in California, and is a graduate of the Ontario Naturopathic College, now the Canadian College of Naturopathic Medicine in Toronto.

Dr. Dean is the author/co-author of 20 health books (print and eBooks) including *The Magnesium Miracle, IBS for Dummies, IBS Cookbook for Dummies, The Yeast Connection and Women's Health, Future Health Now Encyclopaedia, Death by Modern Medicine, Everything Alzheimer's and Hormone Balance.*

Dr. Dean's current work is a unique online wellness program called Future Health *Now*! This program helps members choose a lifestyle and environment that supports health, leaving no room for negative addictions. She presently lives in Maui where she is happily addicted to nature!

ACKNOWLEDGMENTS

I would like to express my heartfelt gratitude to several people. Without their help, this book would not have been possible.

I am most grateful to my entire family for their love and support. I would also like to thank Liane Casten (alias Mama Castini), Garry Van Dijk and my editor, Dr. Kendra Pearsall.

Many thanks to my dear friend and researcher "extraordinaire," Professor Joe Cummins. Scientists like you have shown me that scientific integrity can exist.

I am also very appreciative of the individuals I interviewed for this book: Abram Hoffer, MD, PhD, Jurriaan Plesman, Sally Fallon-Morell, Joan Mathews-Larson, PhD, Charles Gant, PhD, MD, ND, Julia Ross, MA, Carolyn Reuben, LAc, David Miller, PhD, Stan Stokes, MS, CCDC, Natasha Campbell-McBride, MD, Scott Shannon, MD, Peter Whybrow, MD, David Greenfield, PhD and John Abramson, MD. Their commitment to wellness will undoubtedly change the world for the better.

My list would not be complete without acknowledging Sean Denniston and David Thomas. Thanks to both of you for hanging in there.

I would like to take this opportunity to thank our local farmers for their hard work and dedication in supplying us with the nutrient-dense foods we need to maintain or regain our health.

The inspiration for this book comes from all the precious and adorable children in the world, especially my nieces and nephews. Their health and happiness matter more to the "dragon lady" than anything else does. As adults, we are obligated to leave the world a better place than when we found it. For the sake of our children, I can only hope that this book will motivate others to work together to achieve this goal.

INTRODUCTION

All right, every day ain't going to be the best day of your
life, don't worry about that. If you stick to it, you hold the
possibility open that you will have better days.

—Wendell Berry, farmer, poet, philosopher

Unlike other books about addiction, this book exposes one of the greatest mysteries behind the real cause of addictive cravings. For years now, the common theory has been that emotional stress or trauma can lead to addictive behaviors. This approach is clearly too simplistic and has done nothing to reduce the burden of addiction on society. Fortunately, some innovative new addiction recovery centers have discovered that addictive cravings are caused by physical (biochemical) imbalances that can be resolved using sound nutritional protocols. Since addiction is one of the greatest threats to society, finding the real cause of addictive cravings could be one of the greatest discoveries of humankind.

The purpose of this book is to explore the reasons why addictions are so prevalent and how we can easily treat them with amazingly *effective* nutritional approaches. I emphasize "effective" because conventional recovery treatment centers have about an *80% relapse rate*. In essence, they are a miserable failure. While they try to justify their failure rate by saying that "relapse is part of recovery," newer, more progressive treatment centers that use nutrition to balance brain chemistry have about an *80% success rate*! These innovative strategies offer a ray of hope to those struggling with addiction, and we all desperately need to know about them.

The health practitioners who work at these centers are redefining what the term *recovery* really means. Not only is their goal to help individuals abstain from their addictions, they also help them recover from some of the debilitating mental disorders—like depression and anxiety—commonly associated with addiction.

What Is Addiction?

In simple terms, addiction is a compulsive behavior with negative consequences. It is "inescapable irrationality."[2] Individuals struggling with addiction cannot stop their behavior, even when they are making damaging—or even fatal—choices.

Before we can even begin to help those struggling with addiction, we must remove the stereotypes that prevent society from properly addressing the problem. Contrary to popular belief, addiction is not a moral defect; it is a disease just like cancer, heart disease or diabetes. And people struggling with addiction deserve to have effective treatment, just as they would if they had any chronic disease. Another common stereotype is that addicts are jobless street bums who contribute nothing to society. It may surprise you to learn that about 75% of addicts are employed.[3]

Addiction is a form of self-medication. Two of the main reasons why people become addicted are that they are feeling anxious or depressed.* These negative feelings are usually due to an imbalance in our biochemistry caused by nutritional deficiencies, hormonal imbalances and heavy metal toxicities. Once an individual's biochemistry is restored, feelings of anxiety and depression can be alleviated, eliminating the need to use a drug to feel good.

Addictive Environment

Our addictive environment provides us with countless pleasurable things tempting us to develop addictions. In today's fast-paced, chaotic world, addiction has become the norm. It seems as though everyone nowadays is addicted to something—whether it is drugs, food, caffeine, TV, the Internet, video games, shopping, hoarding, work, relationships, negativity/complaining, stress, gambling and so on.

One reason why our addictive environment is so out of control is that we have switched our priorities from "needs" to "wants." Our ancestors focused on their needs (such as nutritious foods, clean water, shelter, spending quality time with friends and family). Today, we tend to focus on our wants (such as money, status, fame, fortune, television, Hollywood, the Internet, video games, texting, face-lifts, Botox treatments, implants, designer clothes and the accumulation of consumer goods).

---

*   Keep in mind that depression and anxiety can go hand in hand. Today, individuals commonly complain of feeling both "wired and tired."

Psychologists have been warning us that in societies that prioritize money, possessions, fame, physical and social appearances (keeping up with the Joneses), people are more likely to suffer from such common mental disorders as depression, anxiety, substance abuse and personality disorders.[4] If we expect to survive in our addictive environment, we must re-evaluate our priorities, focusing more on our needs than on our wants.

Substance Abuse Is Our Number One Health Problem

Of all the different types of addiction, substance abuse is perhaps the most pervasive. In fact, substance abuse has become our number one public health problem. Not cancer. Not heart disease. Not diabetes. Every year, there are more deaths and disabilities from substance abuse than from any other cause.[5]

The Burden Of Addiction

- Drug related deaths have almost doubled since 1990—approximately one in four deaths each year is attributable to substance abuse.[6]
- It is estimated that every man, woman and child in the U.S. pays nearly $1,000 a year for health care, extra law enforcement, auto crashes, crime and lost productivity that results from untreated substance abuse.[7]
- One-quarter of all emergency room admissions, one-third of all suicides and more than half of all homicides and incidents of domestic violence are alcohol-related.[8]

Contrary to what many people may believe, it is not the typical illegal street drugs that are contributing to this public health crisis, but legal drugs, such as alcohol, tobacco and certain prescription medications.[9] Today, on top of the enormous number of drugs available on the streets, there are over 17,000 legal drugs being sold in pharmacies or via the Internet. In 1990, there were only 3,000 medications on the market.[10] The increase in the availability in legal medications has increased our potential for abusing them.

Substance abuse impacts one out of every four families.[11] The yearly costs associated with substance abuse amount to over $500 billion annually.[12] In 2007, an estimated 23.2 million Americans aged 12 and older suffered from dependence on or abuse of drugs and/or alcohol. And 20.8 million of them did *not* receive the help they needed.[13]

It Is A Mad, Mad, Mad World!

In recent history, rates of mental disorders have skyrocketed. The very broad category of mental disorders includes depression, anxiety, post-traumatic stress disorder (PTSD), bipolar disorder, schizophrenia, panic disorders, obsessive-compulsive disorder, phobias, eating disorders, attention deficit hyperactivity disorder (ADHD), autism, Alzheimer's disease and many more.

Alarming Increase In Mental Disorders

- We are one hundred times more likely to suffer from depression today than we were 100 years ago.[14]
- The number of Americans struggling with three or more mental disorders—nearly 1/5 of the population—has more than tripled for the post-WWII generation.[15]
- Since 1987, the number of people struggling with a mental disorder has increased at a rate of 150,000 per year, or 410 people per day.[16]
- Mental disorders—especially depression—are the leading causes of disability in North America.[17]
- About one in four persons aged 18 and older, or 57.7 million Americans, suffer from a diagnosable mental disorder in any given year.[18]
- While growing up, as many as 20% of children may have a diagnosable mental health disorder.[19]

In boom times, history tells us that rates of mental disorders, such as anxiety and depression, will more than likely increase.[20] The economic crash of 2008 has, indeed, challenged us mentally and emotionally.

Families are struggling to make ends meet. Currently, bankruptcies, foreclosures and job losses are occurring at alarming rates. According to a recent survey conducted by the American Psychological Association, *8 out of every 10 Americans are stressed out.* Among those surveyed, 49% said they felt nervous or anxious; 48% reported feeling depressed or sad.[21] The future is looking worse. By 2020, depression is expected to be the second leading cause of disease worldwide.[22]

It has become popular to blame many of the health problems we see today on "stress." However, blaming "stress" has done nothing to improve our health whatsoever! Stress is a vague term, as it can come from a variety of sources. One commonly overlooked source of stress is malnutrition or nutritional stress. Before we can see improvements in our physical and mental health, conventional health practitioners need to acknowledge the very real and damaging side effects of nutritional stress.

Nutritional Stress

For decades now, researchers have known that depriving our brain of certain nutrients can result in psychological disorders, including depression, anxiety, sleep disorders or some form of neurosis. Researchers also know that eating the wrong kinds of foods can contribute to depression. Since the turn of the last century, thousands of highly processed foods began lining our grocery store shelves. In subsequent chapters, I will explain why these foods have compromised our mental well-being by depriving our brains of the nutrients they need to work properly. In order to regain our mental stability, therefore, we must return to the foods that we know kept our ancestors physically and mentally robust for generations.

Progressive Views on Addiction and Mental Health

This book contains interviews with people from a variety of backgrounds who offer their own unique views on diet, lifestyle, mental health and addiction. You will read about several different aspects of addiction, including how returning to three square meals a day can help stabilize our moods and how simplifying our lives could help reduce our stress. You will also read about some exciting new treatments that are being used successfully to treat mental and substance use disorders.

In section 2, you will read interviews from Abram Hoffer, MD, PhD (1917-2009) and Weston A. Price, DDS (1870-1948). Dr. Hoffer was an orthomolecular (nutritional) psychiatrist who, for several decades, used nutritional approaches to treat addiction and mental illnesses, such as schizophrenia. You will also read about Jurriaan Plesman, clinical nutritionist and author of *Getting Off the Hook*, who talks about his struggle with addiction and how he has been able to help others overcome addiction and mental disorders using nutritional protocols.

Dr. Price is the author of one of the most important books ever written about nutrition, *Nutrition and Physical Degeneration*. I have included the foreword that Dr. Hoffer wrote in the fifth edition of Dr. Price's book, published in 1989. As you will discover, Drs. Price and Hoffer shared very similar views in the area of nutritional medicine. Sally Fallon-Morell, president of the Weston A. Price Foundation, speaks about the work of Dr. Price and the importance of nutrient-dense foods.

I also interviewed six of the world's leading experts on addiction: Charles Gant, MD, PhD, ND; David Miller, PhD; Joan Mathews-Larson, PhD; Julia Ross, MA; Stan Stokes, MS, CCDC and Carolyn Reuben, LAc. The interviews with these experts will give you insights into the ways in which they are able to treat addiction successfully using cutting-edge nutritional protocols.

Peter Whybrow, MD, author of *American Mania*, emphasizes the importance of simplifying our lives in our Fast New World. David Greenfield, PhD, author of *Virtual Addiction*, speaks about the problems associated with our obsession with new technologies, including the Internet and video games. John Abramson, MD, author of *Overdosed America*, warns us about the overuse of prescription medications.

Finally, this book would not be complete without offering some solutions to protect our children from developing mental disorders and addictions. Scott Shannon, MD, author of *Please Don't Label My Child*, discusses his views on using alternative approaches when treating children with mental disorders. Natasha Campbell-McBride, MD, author of *Gut and Psychology Syndrome*, explains how she reverses mental disorders in children—including autism—using nutritional protocols.

It is my hope that the messages of these experts will provide the answers we need to effectively prevent and treat both mental and substance use disorders, once and for all.

CHAPTER 1

OUR PERVASIVE DRUG CULTURE

All drugs can alter the natural flow of your own feel-good peptides and so, biochemically, there is no difference between legal and illegal ones: They are all potentially harmful, they can all be abused and they can all contribute to suboptimal health in one form or another, including chronic depression.[23]

—Candace Pert, PhD, *Molecules of Emotion*

There will be within the next generation or so, a pharmacological method of making people love their servitude and producing dictatorship without tears, so to speak, producing a kind of painless concentration camp for entire societies, so that people will in fact have their liberties taken away from them but will rather enjoy it, because they will be distracted from any desire to rebel by propaganda or brainwashing, or brainwashing enhanced by pharmacological methods.

—Aldous Huxley, Tavistock Group,
California Medical School

In 1971, President Nixon declared the "war on drugs."* For well over three decades now, the government has spent hundreds of billions of dollars, the police have made millions of arrests and the justice system has incarcerated millions of prisoners, yet we are still seeing record high rates of drug-related deaths, hospital emergencies, crime, broken families, lost careers and other social and physical consequences. One of the most tragic ironies is that since the launch of President Nixon's anti-drug campaign, we are an even more drugged nation. Unless

---

* At the time, President Nixon was referring to street drugs, such as heroin or marijuana.

we take more proactive measures to solve the epidemic of substance abuse, future generations will continue to carry this very crippling social burden.

Contrary to popular belief, it is the *legal* drugs (i.e., nicotine, alcohol and certain prescription medications) rather than the illegal drugs (i.e., cocaine, heroin, methamphetamines) that are causing most of the substance abuse problems today. According to the Substance Abuse and Mental Health Service Administration (SAMHSA), "legal substances (such as alcohol, tobacco and some medications) are the largest contributors to the Nation's substance-related problems."[24]

The World Health Organization (WHO) considers mood-altering (psychoactive) substance use as a "significant threat to the health, social and economic fabric of families, communities and nations." The number of people using psychoactive substances is estimated to be 2 billion alcohol users, 1.3 billion smokers and 185 million illicit drug users worldwide.[25] According to the WHO, on a worldwide basis, tobacco, alcohol and illicit drugs contribute to 12.4% of all deaths—tobacco accounting for 8.8%, alcohol 3.2% and illicit drugs 0.4%.

World Extent of Psychoactive Substance Use

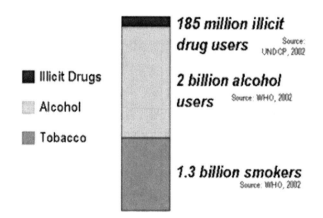

185 million illicit drug users Source: UNDCP, 2002

2 billion alcohol users Source: WHO, 2002

1.3 billion smokers Source: WHO, 2002

■ Illicit Drugs

▨ Alcohol

▨ Tobacco

The Global Burden

Psychoactive substance abuse poses a significant threat to the health, social and economic fabric of families, communities and nations. The extent of worldwide psychoactive substance use is estimated at 2 billion alcohol users, 1.3 billion smokers and 185 million drug users.

Used with permission from the World Health Organization[26]

In the United States, alcohol is a $100 billion business. At a cost of $185 billion, we spend more to repair the damages of alcohol abuse than on the alcohol itself.[27]

—

The average American spends more than 5% of their annual budget on alcohol, consuming 2.6 gallons of spirits, 2.2 gallons of wine and 26.6 gallons of beer every year.[28]

—Michael Gossop, *Living with Drugs*

In the United States, alcohol and tobacco are among the top causes of preventable deaths.[29] Research conducted in Britain concluded that based on the actual risks posed to society, alcohol and tobacco are *more dangerous* than certain illegal drugs like marijuana or ecstasy.[30] According to the study, alcohol is involved in over half of all visits to accident and emergency departments and orthopedic admissions, and tobacco is estimated to cause up to 40% of all hospital illness. One of the studies' authors, Dr. David Nutt, a professor of psychopharmacology at Britain's Bristol University, says, "All drugs are dangerous. Even the ones people know and love and use every day." [31]

All existing drugs are treacherous and harmful. The heaven into which they usher their victims soon turns into a hell of sickness and moral degradation. They kill, first the soul, then, in a few years, the body.[32]

—Aldous Huxley, *A Treatise on Drugs*, October 10, 1931

Medication Overload

In terms of addiction, what makes our society stand out more than any other in the history of mankind is our epidemic abuse of prescription drugs.[33] In 2005, approximately 15.1 million Americans abused controlled prescription substances, far exceeding the amount of people abusing cocaine (5.9 million), marijuana (4 million), hallucinogens (4 million), inhalants, such as glue, solvents and aerosols (2.1 million) and heroin (.3 million).[34]

According to Steve Pasierb, president of the Partnership for a Drug-Free America, "when prescription drugs are abused in the same way as illegal street drugs, they're every bit as addictive and they're every bit as deadly."[35] In addition, there has been an increase in the abuse of legal, over-the-counter (OTC) medications. History has shown that greater availability of mood-altering drugs—legal or illegal—will lead to an increase in recreational use, misuse and abuse.[36]

In emergency departments in the United States, prescription and OTC drugs were the primary substances of abuse for 4% of the 1.9 million patients admitted for drug treatment in 2002. Prescription medications were primarily opioids, stimulants, tranquilizers and sedatives. OTC drugs included aspirin, cough syrup, diphenhydramine and other antihistamines, sleep aids and other legally obtained medications. In 2002, 55% of the total drug-related emergency department admissions were for prescription narcotics.[37]

—James E. Lessenger, MD and Steven D. Feinburg, MD, MPH,
Abuse of Prescription and Over-the-Counter Medications,
Journal of the American Board of Family Medicine

Since 1990, prescription drug sales have soared nearly 500%.[38] More than 128 million people, or about 46% of the American population, take at least one prescription drug daily.[39] On top of purchasing several over-the-counter medications, in 1999 Americans purchased 2,587,575,000 prescriptions—that amounts to nine prescription drugs for every person in the United States.[40]

The United States accounts for approximately half of the global pharmaceutical market, with over $250 billion in annual sales. In 2007, the global market for pharmaceuticals was worth over $693 billion. In 2008, this figure is expected to rise to over $737 billion and, by 2013, will surpass $1 trillion. In 2007, the market for over-the-counter drugs was worth over $90 billion. It is expected to rise to over $95 billion in 2008 and to exceed $135 billion in 2013.[41]

GLOBAL MARKET FOR PHARMACEUTICALS WORTH OVER $1 TRILLION BY 2013

SUMMARY FIGURE
WORLDWIDE MARKET PHARMACEUTICAL PRODUCTS, 2006-2013
($ BILLIONS)

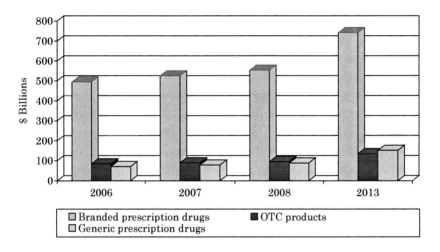

Source: BCC Research

Used by permission of BCC Research

WORLDWIDE MARKET PHARMACEUTICAL PRODUCTS THROUGH 2013($ Billions)

	2006	2007	2008	2013	Compound Annual Growth Rate% 2008-2013
Branded prescription drugs	494.2	525.1	553.2	741.5	6.0
OTC products	84.9	90.0	95.7	135.1	7.1
Generic prescription drugs	70.9	78.5	88.7	151.4	11.3

Used by permission of BCC Research

Non-Medical Use of Prescription Drugs

The misuse of prescription drugs is even a problem among professional and academic circles. According to the 2006 National Survey on Drug Use and Health, almost 50 million Americans (20%

of the population) over the age of 12 reported using prescription psychotherapeutic drugs non-medically during their lifetime.[42] In an online survey of 1,400 readers published by the journal *Nature*, 20% of the respondents admitted to taking prescription pharmaceutical medications such as Ritalin, Provigil and beta-blockers (which are used to treat cardiac conditions but can also reduce anxiety) for the non-medical purpose of improving their concentration, focus and memory. Most of the people who participated in the survey work in professional fields such as science, engineering or education. According to *Nature*, "the numbers suggest a significant amount of drug taking among academics." Wilson M. Compton, MD, MPE, director of the Division of Epidemiology, Services and Prevention Research at the National Institute on Drug Abuse says that "scientists are not immune to substance abuse. This is an example where you think people who are highly educated and knowledgeable might know better and that's not necessarily the case."[43]

In addition to the scientists and other professionals, over 13% of students surveyed at one university admitted to using prescription stimulants such as Ritalin or Adderall for non-medical reasons.[44] Findings like these trouble some scientists. Concerned about the high percentage of people who admitted they were taking Ritalin, Dr. Compton said, "The attitude toward these drugs . . . is that people see them as being safe and not a concern. That's a problem when these are potentially addictive and can be associated with complications."[45]

Mood-Altering Drugs Can Be Addictive

Any drug that has the ability to alter our mood also carries the potential of becoming addictive. According to Peter Breggin, MD, psychiatrist and author of *Medication Madness*, all psychiatric drugs have the potential to be addictive, including antidepressants, stimulants, tranquilizers, antipsychotic drugs and "mood stabilizers" such as lithium.[46]

The psychiatric drugs we see today began to appear in the fifties.* In 1966, there were already 44 psychiatric drugs on the market; by 2008, the number had skyrocketed to 174.[47] Between 1988 and 2000,

---

*   Patented mood-altering drugs have been used since the 1800s.

adult use of antidepressants almost tripled. According to the Centers for Disease Control, 10% of women 18 and older and 4% of men now take antidepressants.[48] Regardless of the widespread use of these drugs, they do not work on the majority of people who take them. In addition, their side effects can be extremely debilitating. In a study published by the *Journal of Clinical Psychiatry*, of the patients taking antidepressants,

- 86% had significant side effects: weight gain, fatigue, sexual dysfunction, insomnia;
- 50% quit taking them after four months;
- success is considered just a 50% reduction in 50% of depressive symptoms for 50% of the patients.[49]

Another widely prescribed class of drugs on the market are the benzodiazepines, which are prescribed to treat anxiety, insomnia, agitation, seizures, muscle spasms and alcohol withdrawal. Currently, there are over 50 benzodiazepines available worldwide. It is estimated that 3-15% of any adult population is using and may be addicted to benzodiazepines, the majority of them women.[50] Because of the highly addictive nature of these drugs and their damaging side effects (benzodiazepines can impair cognitive functioning, memory and balance), the suggested course of treatment is two to four weeks. Unfortunately, people are taking "benzos," whether legally or illegally acquired, on a long-term basis (even for several years). At Health Recovery Center in Minneapolis, Joan Mathews-Larson, PhD, commonly treats "benzo" addiction and contends that it is one of the most difficult addictions to overcome.

While most people think of psychiatric drugs as being the most common mood-altering drugs, other prescription medications also have the ability to alter our mood, including opioids like OxyContin, Vicodin, hydrocodone, methadone, morphine and fentanyl. The number of emergency room visits related to painkillers (narcotic analgesics) has increased by 153% since 1995.[51] In 2004, the number of opioid painkiller deaths (7,500) was more than the total of deaths involving heroin and cocaine.[52] Methadone is a legal drug used to treat heroin withdrawal and cancer pain. Unfortunately, it can come with fatal side effects. A 2007 Justice Department National Intelligence Drug Center report found that methadone-related deaths increased from 786 to 3,849 between 1999 and 2004—an increase of 390%.[53]

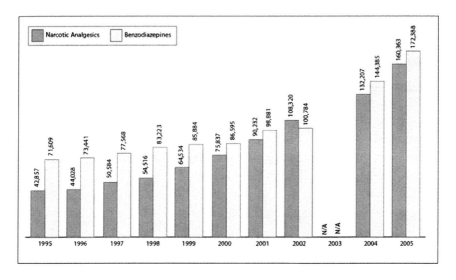

Used by permission of www.painphysicianjournal.com[54]

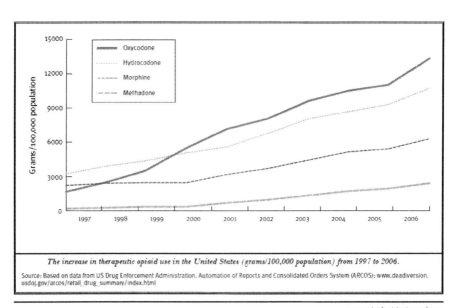

The increase in therapeutic opioid use in the United States (grams/100,000 population) from 1997 to 2006.

Source: Based on data from US Drug Enforcement Administration. Automation of Reports and Consolidated Orders System (ARCOS); www.deadiversion. usdoj.gov/arcos/retail_drug_summary/index.html

Used by permission of www.painphysicianjournal.com[55]

In Ontario, Canada, 84% of physicians feel that their patients may be addicted to commonly prescribed painkillers (i.e., opioids like oxycodone, hydrocodone, morphine, fentanyl, meperidine and acetaminophen-codeine).[56] It has been estimated that approximately 30,000 people in Ontario regularly use illegal opioids.

> Prescription opioid dependence is a growing health concern in Ontario. I have seen firsthand how this type of dependency can affect many aspects of a person's life, including marriage, friendships, employment, financial standing and judgment, whereby personal safety becomes secondary to the need to obtain opioid-based drugs.[57]
>
> —Donnie Edwards, Pharmacist and
> Certified Drugs of Addiction Expert

Legal mood-altering drugs are clearly not the answer to our mental health woes. In fact, because these drugs work by causing brain dysfunction, they are causing even more mental instability.[58] We simply cannot continue to hold on to the fantasy that a miracle drug will be able to stabilize our moods. Instead, we must regain our mental health by returning to the common sense diet and lifestyle habits that kept us mentally and physically healthy for generations.

Legal Drugs Can Be Deadly

> The rate of deaths caused by prescription drugs was three times
> the rate of deaths caused by all illicit drugs combined.[59]
>
> —Florida Medical Examiners Commission

The complications associated with any kind of drug, legal or illegal, can be fatal. The more we abuse drugs, the higher our overdose death rates. Since 1999, overdose fatalities have risen dramatically, largely because of the increase in availability and numbers of prescription drugs. According to the Centers for Disease Control, drug overdose is the second leading cause of non-natural deaths after traffic crashes—a record 33,541 Americans died as a direct result of abusing illicit drugs in 2005, a 61% increase over the previous five years.[60] The category excludes unintentional injuries, homicides, newborn deaths due to maternal drug use and other causes indirectly related to drug use. The figure represents 2,795 deaths per month, 645 deaths per week, 92 per day, or almost four per hour. More lives are lost from drug overdose than from AIDS and gun homicides put together.

Since the increased use of prescription medications corresponds to an increase in adverse events, the projected increase in drug sales will undoubtedly result in more deaths. According to an article published in the *Archives of Internal Medicine*, over the seven-year period from 1998 to 2005, the number of reported seriously adverse drug events for outpatient prescription medications increased two and a half times from 34,966 to 89,842 and fatal drug events among outpatients nearly tripled, from 5,519 to 15,107.[61] Since less than 10% of adverse drug effects are ever reported, these figures in all likelihood drastically underestimate the true incidence of adverse drug reactions (ADRs).

The situation appears to be even worse when we take into account the number of inpatient deaths caused by prescription drugs. Approximately 106,000 people die every year from adverse reactions to properly prescribed and administered medications in hospitalized settings.[62] Even under what would be considered appropriate medical care, prescription drugs are ranked as the fourth leading cause of death in the United States. Only heart disease, cancer and stroke kill more people than drugs prescribed by medical doctors.[63]

According to medical epidemiologist Leonard J. Paulozzi, MD, MPH, the prescription-drug problem is a crisis that is steadily worsening:

> The mortality rates from unintentional drug overdose (not including alcohol) have risen steadily since the early 1970s and over the past ten years, they have reached historic highs. Rates are currently 4 to 5 times higher than the rates during the "black tar" heroin epidemic in the mid-1970s and more than twice what they were during the peak years of crack cocaine in the early 1990s. The rate . . . for 2005 translates into 22,400 unintentional and intentional drug overdose

deaths . . . . We found that street drugs were not behind the increase. The increase from 1999 to 2004 was driven largely by opioid analgesics, with a smaller contribution from cocaine and essentially no contribution from heroin.[64]

According to Jack Kalin, PhD, head toxicologist at the Alabama Department of Forensic Sciences (an agency that analyzes blood from drug deaths):

> We're such a drugged society. I thought we were drugged back in the 60s, but that was illegal drugs. That doesn't hold a candle to what we're dealing with today. There are serious problems with illegal drugs such as methamphetamine and cocaine, but the sleeper problem is multiple legal drugs. You go on television and there's a pill for every ailment we have and some ailments you never even knew you had. Medication has become sustenance. We're sending bad messages, that medicine is the cure for everything.[65]

Adults Are Playing with Fire

Generally, when it comes to using illicit drugs, society labels our youth as "risk takers." However, today, the table has turned and middle-aged Americans have now inherited that reputation. As middle-aged Americans age, more baby boomers are expected to participate in illicit drug use. From 1999 to 2020, illicit drug use in persons age 50 and older is expected to increase from 2.2% (1.6 million) to 3.1% (3.5 million) and non-medical use of psychotherapeutic drugs will increase from 1.2% (911,000) to 2.4% (almost 2.7 million).[66]

In two op-ed pieces (January 3, 2007 and September 17, 2007) published in the *New York Times*, Mike Males, PhD, a senior researcher at the Center on Juvenile and Criminal Justice, wrote about the consequences of the increased rates of drug use, including the skyrocketing deaths from drug overdoses, increased crime rates and arrests in the adult population. What many people may not realize is that drug addiction, overdose fatalities, hospitalizations and criminal activity are far more common among middle-aged adults than among our youth. The stereotype of the young addict is outdated. Today, the stereotypical addict is a middle-aged white American. In the area of addiction, researchers—and, for that matter society as a whole—tend to focus on feared or rejected social groups (urban minorities, immigrants and youth); however, the fastest-growing group of drug abusers is middle-aged white Americans. The consequences of this increase in drug addiction among middle-aged Americans are dire:

- Among Americans in their 40s and 50s, deaths from illicit-drug overdoses have risen by 800% since 1980, by 300% in the last decade.[67]
- The Drug Addiction Help Line reported that the typical overdose victim in 2005 was 43 years old, compared to 32 in 1985 and 22 in 1970.[68]
- In 2004, American hospital emergency rooms treated 400,000 patients between the ages 35 and 64 for abusing heroin, cocaine, methamphetamine, marijuana, hallucinogens and "club drugs" like ecstasy.[69]
- There were 46,925 drug-related fatal accidents and suicides in 2004, leaving today's middle-agers 30% more at risk for such deaths than people aged 15 to 19.[70]

In April 2006, the *Psychiatric Times* reported that the typical addict is likely to be in his or her mid-thirties to mid-fifties, but research, prevention programs and the media often overlook this age group.[71] They would have a difficult time warning people that "mainstream America" has turned into a group of drug addicts. Can you imagine how well that news would go over?

Aging baby boomers have also become America's fastest-growing crime scourge:

- The FBI reports that the number of Americans over the age of 40 arrested for violent and property felonies rose from 170,000 in 1980 to 420,000 in 2008.[72]
- Arrests for drug offenses among those over 40 rose to from 22,000 in 1980 to 360,000 up in 2008.[73]

- The Bureau of Justice Statistics found that 440,000 Americans ages 40 and older were incarcerated in 2005, triple the number incarcerated in 1990.[74]

One of society's greatest concerns today is that over the next decade or so, today's youth may follow in their parents' footsteps by becoming the next drug-addicted generation. Joseph C. Gfroerer, director of the division of population surveys for Substance Abuse and Mental Health Services Administration (SAMHSA), says that it is wrong to focus too heavily on the baby boomer generation alone.[75] He believes that the problem is not going to end with the baby boomers because the next generation already has a high rates of use.[76] According to Gfroerer, "this generation of drug abusers, after causing tremendous damage, is going to die off. We have to ask ourselves, 'Have we set the stage for the next generation of users?'"[77]

The Silent Epidemic—Senior Substance Abuse

Known as the "silent epidemic," substance abuse—in particular, addiction to prescription drugs—is also a very serious problem among our senior citizens. According to the Addiction Prevention and Recovery Administration (APRA), "seniors 60 and older consume more prescription and over-the-counter drugs than any other age group. This number is expected to increase significantly as the population grows, increasing the vulnerability of this age group to prescription drug abuse."[78]

Claire Lakewood, director of Partnership for a Drug-Free America, says, "Older Americans tend to give in to peer pressure. They just do what their doctor tells them because they want to 'be cool' or 'live' and win their doctor's approval. They also want to fit in with all their other elderly friends, who, no doubt, are doing these prescription drugs, too."[79] SAMHSA's Center for Substance Abuse Treatment estimates that up to 17% of adults over the age of 60 (approximately eight million people) abuse substances—primarily alcohol, prescription drugs and over-the-counter medications.[80] By 2030, it is expected that one-third of adults 55 years of age and older will have a substance abuse problem.[81]

When our role models are using and abusing drugs in such epidemic proportions, it is not surprising that our youth also struggle with addiction. As a society, we must set better examples for our children. Otherwise, our addiction epidemic will continue to spread.

Generation Rx

It is disturbing to think we may be creating an entire generation of children who are prone to addiction.[82]

—Stanton Peele, PhD, JD

Teenagers and young adults of today are now joining older generations in increased drug use.[83] In 1972, only 22% of high school seniors reported having used drugs, compared to 48% of the class of 2005.[84] Not only are young people learning from their parents and grandparents that it is acceptable to alter their mood using prescription medications, but millions of children are now being prescribed mood-altering drugs at unprecedented rates.

It is common to find children labeled as suffering from attention deficit disorder (ADD), attention deficit hyperactivity disorder (ADHD), obsessive-compulsive disorder (OCD), oppositional defiant disorder (ODD) and so on. In order to treat these "conditions," prescription drugs are being handed out to our children like candy. Approximately, five million kids take prescription drugs every day for behavior disorders.[85] About 3% of children are treated with a prescription stimulant (such as Adderall or Ritalin), up from less than 1% in 1987.[86] Between 1994 and 2003, the number of American children and adolescents treated for bipolar disorder increased forty-fold.[87] About 800,000 children in the United States, some as young as two, have been treated for bipolar disorder. Despite their serious side effects and the fact that they have not been approved for use by children, antipsychotic drugs, such as Zyprexa and Risperdal, are more and more frequently prescribed to children to treat bipolar disorder. Sales of these drugs have increased more than five-fold in the last 15 years.[88]

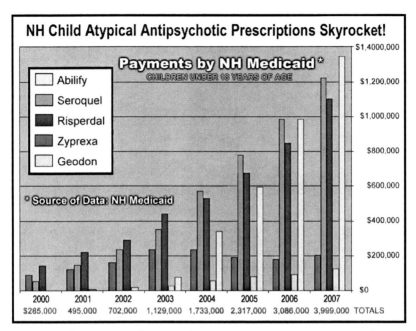

Used with permission from *Northcountry News*, Warren, New Hampshire.

Based upon documentation from the New Hampshire Office of Medicaid Business and Policy, Northcountry News exposed the growing expenditures on atypical antipsychotics in children under the age of eighteen.[89] Note: This chart only illustrates the data from New Hampshire; several other states are experiencing similar patterns.

Teens perceive the use of prescription drugs as being safe and socially acceptable. They do not view them as being as dangerous as street drugs like heroin or cocaine. Because of their widespread use, prescription and OTC medications are the most commonly abused drugs by high school students after marijuana. They represent 6 of the top 10 illicit drugs that twelfth graders reported using.[90] According to an analysis of national surveys prepared by John Walters, director of the White House's Office of National Drug Control Policy, 2.1 million teenagers abused prescription drugs in 2005.[91] Marijuana use has been on the decrease and replaced with OxyContin, Vicodin (both painkillers), Adderall (stimulant) and Xanax (sedative). Joseph A. Califano Jr., chairman of the National Center on Addiction and Substance Abuse at Columbia University (CASA), confirms that "our country is in the throes of an epidemic of controlled prescription drug abuse and addiction. While America has been congratulating itself in recent years on curbing raises in alcohol and illegal drug abuse and in the decline in teen smoking, abuse of prescription drugs has been stealthily, but sharply, rising."[92]

The drug dealer is us.[93]

—John P. Walters
Director of the White House's
Office of National Drug Control Policy

Because prescription and OTC drugs are so readily available through relatives, friends or the Internet, it has become easy for teens to choose them over illicit drugs. "Pharm parties," or pharmaceutical parties, are becoming increasingly popular among our youth. Teens are raiding their parents' medicine cabinets in order to find the drugs they need for these sometimes-fatal pill-popping parties. The trend has its own language: bowls and baggies of random pills often are called "trail mix," and collecting pills from the family medicine chest is called "pharming."[94]

Whether they are self-medicating undiagnosed depression or anxiety, using stimulants to try to get an edge on tests and studying, or abusing prescription drugs at "pharm parties," over the last several years, there has been an increase in the abuse of legal drugs by teens.

- In 2004, nearly half of all emergency room visits resulting from abuse of cough or cold remedies were patients between the ages of 12 and 20.
- Emergency room visits involving prescription and over-the-counter drug abuse grew 21% from 2004 to 2005.
- Between 1995 and 2005, the number of treatment admissions for prescription painkillers increased by more than 300%.
- Every day, 2,500 young people ages 12 to 17 abuse a pain reliever for the very first time.
- Teens abuse prescription drugs more than any illicit drug except marijuana.[95]

Our youth are exposed to more drugs than previous generations and are therefore extremely vulnerable to developing addictions as they get older. Because so many people are taking drugs, including parents and grandparents, few people seem to be acknowledging the fact that we are setting our children up to develop addictions. Unless we do more to stop this addiction epidemic, society will have an enormous problem to clean up over the next several decades.

Trillion-Dollar Trouble

Ironically, even when taken properly, taking all of these prescription and OTC medications has not made Americans any healthier. The United States pays more than $2 trillion a year for health care (more than any other country in the world) and yet ranks only 48th in the world in life expectancy.[96] By 2017, health care spending is projected to exceed $4 trillion.[97] According to John Abramson, MD, author of *Overdosed America: The Broken Promise of American Medicine*, "although Americans spend twice as much per person on health care as the other 21 wealthiest countries, data from the World Health Organization show that we have a shorter life expectancy than the other countries (69.3 years versus 71.8 years)."[98] One of the best indicators of a country's health is the healthy life expectancy (HLE) of its citizens, a measurement developed by the World Health Organization of the number of years that a child born today can expect to live in good health. The chart shows that Americans rank 22nd out of the 22 wealthiest countries.

Healthy Life Expectancy and Per Person Medical Expenses in 22 OECD Countries

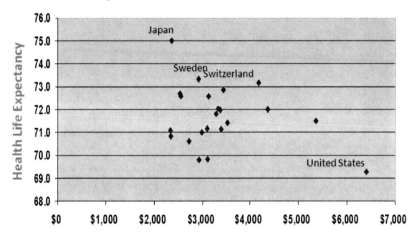

Per Person Annual Medical Expenses (OECD, 2005)

(OECD stands for Organization for Economic Co-operation and Development) Reproduced, with permission, from John Abramson, MD, *Overdosed America: The Broken Promise of American Medicine*, page 47

Brave New World

> Two thousand pharmacologists and bio-chemists were subsidized . . . . Six years later it was being produced commercially. The perfect drug . . . Euphoric, narcotic, pleasantly hallucinant . . . All the advantages of Christianity and alcohol; none of their defects . . . Take a holiday from reality whenever you like and come back without so much as a headache or a mythology . . . . Stability was practically assured. [99]

—Aldous Huxley, *Brave New World*

Our widespread reliance upon mood-altering drugs sounds vaguely familiar. In Aldous Huxley's novel *Brave New World*, the drug *soma* provided people with the illusion of happiness. *Soma* contributed to the creation of a shallow, unempathetic, uncreative, intellectually uninteresting and emotionally stunted society. Rather than heightening one's senses, *soma* numbed its users, purging them of spirituality, intellectual excitement, discovery, emotions and creativity and making them predictable and easy to control.

Published in 1932, Huxley's novel foreshadowed a frightening social phenomenon, which is occurring today. In North America, the sheer number of available drugs has desensitized us to the severity of the drug problem we are facing today—especially when it comes to legal drugs.

Some legal drugs may be necessary to help relieve certain health conditions temporarily. But keep in mind that even legal drugs can come with damaging or even fatal side effects. The number of people unable to function without mood-altering drugs is draining us of our ability to be a vital, freethinking nation. Ideally, we should be enjoying life in a fully conscious state. If society continues to choose the drugged path, we may lose our ability to handle life's everyday experiences—both good and bad. Society must restore its mental vigor by standing up and saying "no" to any unnecessary drugs, including the legal ones.

CHAPTER 2

RISE OF THE PRO-ADDICTION DIET

> In eating disorders and addictions, the quality of the food
> consumed is invariably abysmal. Compulsive overeaters
> tend to choose foods high in refined carbohydrates such as
> sugar, which are known to have dramatic emotional and
> psychological effects.[100]
>
> —Joseph D. Beasley, MD, *Food for Recovery*

People who are most likely to develop addictions are those who are
struggling with mental disorders such as depression or anxiety. Since
malnutrition can lead to mental instability, one thing we can do to
reduce our chances of developing addictions would be to eat the most
nutrient-dense foods possible. Unfortunately, over the last several
decades, we have switched from eating a nutrient-dense diet to a diet
seriously deficient in many nutrients that are crucial for supporting our
nervous system.

Unwarranted fear-mongering over eating animal fats has caused us
to increase our consumption of nutrient-deficient foods—including
grains, margarine, liquid oils, juice (and other sweetened beverages),
soy foods and so on. These plant-based foods have replaced more
nutrient-dense animal foods such as meat, butter, lard and whole milk. To
add insult to injury, increasing our consumption of breads, pasta, juices
and other sweetened beverages has destabilized our blood sugar levels,
compromising our mental state. As you will see in several interviews
later in the book, one of the most prevalent underlying symptoms that
predisposes individuals to developing addictions is hypoglycemia (low
blood sugar).

After hundreds of thousands of years of evolution, one would think
we would know better than to eat foods that compromise our mental and
physical states. This chapter will explain how we got fooled into buying
nutrient-deficient foods and how these foods have made us vulnerable
to developing addictions.

The Great Feeding Experiment

The following is a list of the top nine foods eaten by Americans, as reported by the United States Department of Agriculture.

- Whole cow's milk (pasteurized)
- 2% milk (pasteurized)
- Processed American cheese
- White bread
- White flour
- White rolls
- Refined sugar, which accounts for 15-21% of all calories consumed
- Soft drinks, fruit juices
- Ground beef[101]

Humans have been manipulated into following the biggest feeding experiment in the history of mankind. Over a relatively short period of time, we switched from a wholesome, nutrient-dense diet that sustained us mentally and physically for millennia, to an unhealthy, nutrient-poor diet that has contributed to extraordinarily high rates of chronic disease and mental disorders.*

Throughout the many millions of years of human development, humans lived in small, constantly moving groups, hunting, fishing and foraging for wild plants, such as greens, tubers and berries). Over 99% of our human dietary history occurred during this period. Only 10,000 years young, agriculture is a relatively new phenomenon. The introduction of agriculture meant that we began cultivating the land to grow crops such as wheat, oats and barley. These new foods replaced the traditional nutrient-dense foods of a hunter-gatherer diet (muscle and organ meats,**

---

* To give you an idea of just how quickly our diets have changed, consider that for about 100,000 generations, we were hunter-gatherers. Since the invention of agriculture 10,000 years ago, we have lived for only 500 generations.

** In fact, organ meats such as liver, kidney, heart, brain etc. are the most nutrient-dense parts of the animals. Organ meats such as the adrenal glands and brains of certain animals were consumed for medicinal purposes by our ancestors. For example, here is a recipe dating back hundreds of fish and fowl) with cereal grains—none of which can provide the same nutrient density of a meat-based diet. Rather than consuming muscle and organ meats from a wide variety of wild animals, we have restricted our diet to relatively few domestically raised meats. We also restrict our plant-based foods to about thirty vegetables and/or fruits, rather than choosing liberally from hundreds of species of edible plants.

S. Boyd Eaton, MD, a radiologist and medical anthropologist at Emory University in Atlanta, has spent over two decades investigating how and what our Stone Age ancestors consumed. According to Dr. Eaton, "99.99% of our genes were formed before the development of agriculture."[102] As such, he believes that our bodies have not been able to adapt to the dramatic dietary changes that have taken place over the last 10,000 years. He summarizes his findings as follows:

> We are the heirs of inherited characteristics accrued over millions of years; the vast majority of our biochemistry and physiology are tuned to life conditions that existed prior to the advent of agriculture some 10,000 years ago . . . . The appearance of agriculture and domestication of animals some 10,000 years ago and the Industrial Revolution some 200 years ago introduced new dietary pressures for which no adaptation has been possible in such a short time span. Thus an inevitable discordance exists between our dietary intake and that which our genes are suited to.[103]

According to George Armelagos, PhD, author of *Paleopathology at the Origins of Agriculture*, "when they switched to farming they traded quality for quantity." In other words, when we switched from a hunter-gatherer diet to agriculture, we mistakenly chose cheap calories and poor nutrition over a healthy nutrient-dense diet.

---

years that was used to treat depression, or what was known as dotage or head melancholy: "Take a ram's head . . . take out the brains and put these spices to it, cinnamon, ginger, nutmeg, mace, cloves . . . Heat them in a platter . . . stirring them well . . . and for three days give it to the patient . . . For fourteen days." *The Anatomy of Melancholy* by Robert Burton, 1652, London, page 455.

Jared Diamond, professor of geography and physiology at the UCLA School of Medicine, calls the invention of agriculture "the worst mistake in the history of the human race."[104] Obtained from fossils over the last 30,000 years, there is evidence that shows that eating too many carbohydrates has contributed to a decline in our health. When people switched to an agricultural lifestyle and a grain-based diet, the general result was as follows:

- A reduction in stature. Anthropologist Lawrence Angel found that prior to the invention of agriculture approximately 10,000 years ago, adult males averaged 5 feet, 11 inches in height while adult females stood about 5 feet, 6 inches tall. After agriculture, we experienced a dramatic reduction in height. Males averaged 5 feet, 6 inches and females 5 feet.[105]
- An increase in bone abnormalities and diseases, dental caries and enamel defects. In 30,000 BC, adults died with 2.2 teeth missing; in 6,500 BC, they averaged 3.5 missing; during Roman times, there were 6.6 teeth missing.[106]
- A shorter life span. Studies by George Armelagos, PhD, and his colleagues at the University of Massachusetts revealed that the life expectancy of members of pre-agricultural communities was about 26 years, but when they switched to farming, their lifespan dropped to 19 years.[107]
- A decrease in human brain size of 11% (judging by head circumference).[108]
- A nearly 50% increase in malnutrition; a four-fold increase in iron-deficiency anemia and a three-fold rise in infectious disease.[109]

James Braly, MD, author of *Dangerous Grains*, believes that people eat diets high in grains because grains are cheap and abundant. However, about 90 million Americans may be suffering with symptoms associated with gluten* sensitivity, including psychological depression, neurotransmitter** deficiencies and autism and hyperactivity disorders.[110]

---

*   Gluten is a protein found in grains such as wheat, rye and barley.
**   In Chapter 6, the role neurotransmitters will be discussed. In addition, there
      is a glossary in the back of the book that explains complicated terms.

Thousands of years after the invention of agriculture, the Industrial Revolution and the increase in world trade introduced even more damaging foods into our diet:

- International trade replaced locally grown foods with foods from other countries thousands of miles away.
- With the rise of factories, towns and cities became more crowded, resulting in the need for large quantities of cheap food to sustain the population.
- New food technologies, such as canning and freezing, along with the invention of the steam engine, made it more efficient and cheaper to transport grains and other foods over long distances.
- In the early 1800s, the invention of the steel roller mill, along with lower wheat prices, allowed for the introduction of mass-produced, flour-based foods such as breads and biscuits.
- Today, the results of a cereal-based diet reveal the following:

  o Men over the age of twenty consume about 350 grams of grain products every day.
  o Women over the age of twenty consume about 250 grams of grain products every day.
  o Men and women consume about 80 grams of cereals and pasta per day.
  o Men and women consume about 70 grams of breads and rolls per day.
  o Men and women consume between 100-150 grams of snack foods per day.[111]

The "Big Food" Con

After the invention of agriculture, the next biggest assault on our food system occurred 200 years ago during the Industrial Revolution. During this era, food companies introduced radical changes in our diet by introducing new technologies in food production, processing, storage and distribution. Perhaps the most damaging device invented during the Industrial Revolution was the steel mill—an invention which enabled the flour industry to expand substantially.

Even more radical changes in our diet occurred after WWII. Sugared breakfast cereals, frozen concentrated orange juice and other processed foods were unheard-of before WWII. Approximately 60% of the items on supermarket shelves in 1960 came into existence in the 15 years following WWII.[112] During the war, food technologies were developed to produce packed meals, or what are now known as Meals Ready to Eat (MREs), for our soldiers during times of combat when organized food facilities were not available. In other words, the original goal of the processed food industry was to feed young, healthy men for very short periods of time. The many processed foods that we still see on our shelves today were not designed to be consumed on a daily basis by the masses for years on end.

There are now approximately 320,000 different packaged food and drink products in the marketplace, and the average supermarket carries approximately 25,000 different products on its shelves (fresh food comprising a very small percentage).[113] Worth about *$4.8 trillion*, the packaged food industry is considered to be the world's biggest industry—this includes everything from pasta and cooking oil to canned and frozen foods.[114]

Deceitful Marketing Ploys

Over the last five decades, Big Food has done a tremendous job convincing consumers to spend their hard-earned money on nutrient-poor, processed foods. So much so that today unsuspecting consumers spend about 90% of their food dollars on processed foods.[115] Through the media, the producers of Big Food have fooled consumers into believing that they are a "third arm" or extension of the family, there for us, willing to help us in our time of need. If we buy their products, somehow we will be liberated from the supposedly painful and tedious task of making food from scratch.

In the early part of the 1950s, 95% of women surveyed expressed positive feelings about preparing food from scratch,[116] and nearly 75% said they had enough time to prepare homemade meals.[117] [Remember, back then, women did most of the shopping and cooking.] In her book *Something from the Oven*, Laura Shapiro explains that after WWII, women were very suspicious of the many newfangled packaged foods that began appearing in the supermarkets, including canned foods, boxed cereals and frozen TV dinners. Some women admitted feeling shame and guilt after purchasing these foods.

It took a great deal of money and ingenious marketing to con women into buying foods they would not otherwise have purchased. Food producers were able to convince women to buy their substandard foods by getting women's magazines, newspapers and food writers to publish material persuading women that they were too busy to prepare homemade meals and that cooking food from scratch was a menial task.

1950s Food Ad

Over the last several decades, eating in restaurants has also become more popular. Unfortunately, you have very little control over the ingredients used in restaurants. You may be eating foods prepared with damaging oils and fats or the wrong kind of salt.* One way you can gain more control over the quality of food you are eating is to start preparing your meals from scratch.

> In the U.S., 50% of all food expenditure is on food prepared outside the home—up from 30% in 1965. Fast food sales in the U.S. rose from $6 billion in 1970 to $148.6 billion in 2003 and are still rising.[118]

Consumers need to realize that Big Food is more interested in creating healthy profits than healthy foods. Remember, our ancestors took great pleasure in food preparation, and they had fewer tools available in the kitchen than we do. If they could do it, so can we!

Dubious Health Claims and Endorsements

Those fancy health claims and endorsements on packages from professional nutrition organizations are yet another way that Big Food has manipulated consumers into buying processed foods. Food companies know that the more health claims and endorsements there are on a product, the likelier it is that a consumer will purchase it. These claims or endorsements can come from a variety of organizations, including the American Dietetic Association or the Heart and Stroke Foundation—groups that are funded by Big Food itself. For example, an organization that one would think would endorse the consumption of wholesome foods, the American Dietetic Association (ADA), accepts money from companies such as Coca-Cola.[119] The ADA even distributes nutritional fact sheets that are directly sponsored by specific industry groups.

If you are curious about who is funding which organization or foundation, the Center for Media and Democracy keeps tabs on this issue. You can visit their Web site, www.prwatch.org and click on SourceWatch to find out the names behind the many front groups we see today.

---

* I will have more to say about salt later.

The bottom line: avoid foods with labels. Usually, these are the foods you would find in the middle aisles of the grocery store. If the food has a label, then there is a good chance it is highly processed. Eat more whole foods like healthy meats, vegetables, fruit, nuts and seeds.

Cheap Food = Expensive Health Care

Over the last hundred years or so, as we have been crowded together in cities, there has been a push for consumers to buy more plant-based foods—grains, juices and other sweetened beverages, margarine, spreads, oils and so on. These are foods that happen to be highly processed and nutrient-deficient. It should really come as no surprise as to why we have seen an increase in these foods. Compared to animal foods, plant-based foods are easy to produce and ship; they have longer shelf life, and they are less expensive. Unfortunately, the rise of cheap food has contributed to the decline in our physical and mental health, substantially increasing the cost of our health care.

In 2003, the World Health Organization published an important report, *Diet Nutrition and the Prevention of Chronic Disease,* blaming processed foods for their role in contributing to many of the chronic health problems we see today, including diabetes, heart disease, cancer and obesity.[120] The facts are right there in the report, yet the media and our governments have ignored the WHO's warnings. Why? Well, the processed food companies not only have powerful lobbies in Washington, they also pay a great deal of money to the media. If the media report any news that could hurt their sponsors, they could bite off the hand that is feeding them. Newspapers, radio and television cannot afford to lose advertising money from their major sponsors. Therefore, as a rule of thumb, they will not publish negative stories that could hurt the sale of their sponsors' products.

Our growing reliance on highly processed, plant-based foods is contributing to malnutrition in the Western world. In the United Kingdom, the government-run health care system spends more than £7.3 billion per year to treat malnutrition.[121] One reason for the increase in malnutrition is that plant-based foods are nowhere near as nutritious as animal foods.

Clearly, the more sustainable approach to treating individuals struggling with malnutrition would be to nourish them to wellness, rather than poisoning them with drugs that have potentially dangerous side effects.

Malnutrition and Brain Starvation

It is quite possible to improve disposition, increase efficiency and change personality for the better . . . . The way to do it is to leave the highly refined, rapidly absorbable carbohydrates alone and I mean cane and beet sugar in all forms and guises, all cereal flours which means breads, pies, cakes, spaghetti, macaroni, etc., all refined cereal products such as cold and hot breakfast cereals (except oatmeal), the quickly absorbable carbohydrate vegetables, potatoes, corn and rice, all sweet "soft" drinks and all alcoholic beverages.[122]

—John Tintera, MD, Endocrinologist

Millions of North Americans are overfed and undernourished. They may be eating a lot of food and as a result may be obese, but they may also be starved for critical nutrients, especially nutrients for the brain. There is a host of psychological and physical symptoms associated with malnutrition—hair loss, muscle wastage, food cravings, fatigue, lethargy, depression, anxiety, memory problems, irritability, apathy, poor sleep and loss of concentration.[123] How many people do you know who are struggling with these symptoms (including yourself)?

In order to determine how to recover from the physical and psychological effects of a semi-starvation diet, in the 1940s, Ancel Keys, PhD, conducted a study called "The Minnesota Starvation Experiment" with his colleagues at the University of Minnesota. Fit young men participated in the study and had no history of depression, anxiety, food-or body-image issues prior to their enrollment. The study lasted one year and included a three-month standardization period, during which the men consumed approximately 3,200 calories per day, a six-month semi-starvation phase, during which they consumed approximately 1,800 calories and a three-month nutritional rehabilitation phase. During the six-month semi-starvation phase, meals were very similar to those found in war-torn Europe: the men were given potatoes, turnips, rutabagas, dark bread and macaroni—a diet high in carbohydrates and low in animal fats.

On February 12, 1945, the men sat down for their first semi-starvation meal, comprised of a small bowl of farina, two slices of toast, a dish of fried potatoes, a dish of Jell-O, a small portion of jam and a small glass of milk.

During this phase of the study, the men began demonstrating adverse psychological and physical problems, including inability to concentrate, extreme fatigue, apathy, lethargy, severe depression, irritability, impatience, reduced coordination, dizziness, anemia, decreased libido, neurological deficits, decreased tolerance for cold temperatures, sunken cheeks and bellies, protruding ribs, edema (swollen legs, ankles and faces), hair loss, muscle soreness, ringing in the ears and skin changes. Several of the men had to withdraw from their university classes because they did not have the energy or motivation to attend or concentrate on the material being taught. Two men were briefly admitted to the psychiatric ward of the university hospital after suffering severe psychological distress.

The *St. Paul Dispatch* reported that "the men on the starvation diet have lost so much physically and mentally that their ambition is gone, their will to go forward is gone and they cannot do heavy work such as farming, mining, forestry, lifting and many other types of work necessary to rebuild war-torn Europe." After the semi-starvation phase ended, the men reported that it took them between two months and two years to recover fully.[124]

Your brain is connected to the rest of your body. Since your brain is made up of about 60% fat, it stands to reason that if you are deficient in the raw materials necessary for your brain to function properly, you will feel out of sorts. The trouble is, most people have no idea which fats actually support brain function. Furthermore, because we are eating too many carbohydrates, we are constantly compromising our blood sugar levels (which can cause all sorts of health problems, including mood disorders such as anxiety and depression).

Consequences of Excess Carbohydrate Consumption

> By eating carbohydrates in quantities that humans, as hunters and gatherers, did not evolve to eat, people simply have overwhelmed their bodies' natural ability to process these sugars.[125]
>
> —Christian B. Allan, PhD, Wolfgang Lutz, MD,
> *Life without Bread*

Contrary to popular belief, animal fats do not make us fat. Over the last 50 years, although we have reduced our intake of animal fats, we are fatter than ever. The real culprit behind our obesity epidemic is the overconsumption of carbohydrates. According to Harvard endocrinologist George Cahill, MD, "carbohydrate is driving insulin is driving fat."[126]

For most of human history, humankind ate a diet that never contained more than 40% carbohydrates.[127] Our Paleolithic ancestors ate foods that keep blood sugar levels normal (meat, vegetables, fruit, nuts and seeds) and had no chronic diseases and a very low body fat percentage. Compare that level of perfect health to ours today where our high (65-80%) carbohydrate diet is largely responsible for the epidemic of obesity, diabetes, heart disease and cancer worldwide. According to Loren Cordain, PhD, "there is increasing evidence to indicate that the type of diet recommended in the USDA's food pyramid [with 6-12 servings of grains a day] is discordant with the type of diet humans evolved with over eons of evolutionary experience."[128]

The grains, sugars, fruits and vegetables we consume increase our blood glucose levels and stimulate the release of insulin from the pancreas. Insulin regulates how much glucose stays in the blood and how much goes into the cells. If we overeat carbohydrates, blood sugar levels can skyrocket (hyperglycemia), causing the pancreas to secrete abnormally high levels of insulin to deal with the surplus glucose. This can cause blood glucose levels to plummet (hypoglycemia). In other words, blood sugar levels can spike quickly and then drop even more quickly, causing mood swings, irritability, muscle weakness, headaches, sweating, tremors, lack of focus, inability to concentrate, mental confusion and more. All carbohydrates affect insulin levels. Refined carbohydrates (such as sugar, flour and juices) tend to raise insulin levels quickly, resulting in a "crash," while complex carbohydrates, such as whole grains, fruit or vegetables raise insulin levels more slowly. Regardless of the form of the carbohydrate, it will still raise blood glucose levels, which, if eaten in excess, can compromise our body's biochemistry.

Rather than blaming genetics or traumatic experiences for causing addiction, Joseph Beasley, MD, author of *Food for Recovery*, believes that the root cause of addiction lies in poor blood sugar control: "Research has shown that alcoholism, eating disorders and many drug addictions are associated with abnormal glucose metabolisms."[129] As we will see, poor blood sugar metabolism can cause mental disorders. Remember, two of the main reasons individuals turn toward substance abuse are that they are feeling either anxious or depressed.

According to the Hypoglycemic Health Association of Australia, the symptoms of low blood sugar (hypoglycemia) may mimic and even cause many psychological and physical disorders, including:

Nervousness	Itching and Crawling Sensation on Skin	Exhaustion/Nervous Breakdown
Faintness/dizziness	Fears and Neurodermatitis	Tremors
Cold Sweats	Depression	Migraine Headaches
Insomnia	Digestive disturbances	Forgetfulness
Mood Swings	Anxiety	Aggression/Violence
Phobias	Anti-social Behavior	Sugar Addiction
Drug Addiction and Alcoholism	Bedwetting and Hyperactivity in Children	Limited Attention Span/ Lack of Concentration
Learning Disability	Lack of Libido	Mental Confusion
Irritability	Blurred vision	Nightmares[130]

In his book *The Hypoglycemic Connection II*, George Samra, MB, talks about how hypoglycemia causes stress hormones like adrenaline to be released in an attempt to raise blood sugar levels. This constant strain on the adrenal glands can lead to adrenal fatigue or to what he calls "the hypoglycemic syndrome"—a combination of (1) depression or moodiness, (2) fatigue, (3) memory impairment or poor concentration and (4) history of sugar addiction.[131]

If you want to protect your adrenal glands, it is important to make sure you maintain a healthy blood sugar level. The adrenal glands can either overproduce or underproduce hormones, causing a variety of symptoms that include fatigue, depression or anxiety. Improperly functioning adrenal glands will also adversely affect the thyroid gland.*

---

*   I will have more to say about the thyroid gland later.

Unfortunately, many of the medical tests done today are not accurate enough to spot blood sugar, thyroid or adrenal problems, and so millions of people go undiagnosed. For more information about how to protect or heal your adrenal glands, be sure to read the book *Adrenal Fatigue: The 21st Century Stress Syndrome* by James Wilson, ND, DC, PhD.

Sugar Addiction

I consider sugar to be a drug, a highly purified plant product that can become addictive . . . . Relying on an artificial form of glucose—sugar—to give us a quick pick-me-up is analogous to, if not as dangerous as, shooting heroin. The artificial substance is utilized by the body in the same way as the natural form, but, like a drug, it floods and desensitizes receptors, thereby interfering in the feedback loops that regulate the availability of instant energy, such as glycogen release from the liver. Over eons of time, our bodymind has evolved a system for supplying the brain with the fuel it needs and we would be wise to respect it.[132]

—Candace Pert, PhD, *Molecules of Emotion*

People who are lost in sugar addiction tend to be self-absorbed. I surely was. I was all caught up in my own drama, my own issues and I assumed I had well-adjusted kids. I didn't really spend a whole lot of time thinking about what their days were like after school.[133]

—Kathleen DesMaisons, PhD, *Little Sugar Addicts*

Make no mistake—white refined sugar is not a food and does not provide you with the nutrients your body needs to run on. Millions of us have fallen victim to the addictive nature of sugar. In the 1700s, we only ate about four pounds of sugar per year; today, we are consuming about 150 pounds of sugar per year. Where sugar is concerned, it is clear that we have yet to learn what moderation means.

In 2005, the *British Medical Journal* warned us about sugar's damaging effects:

- Sugar is as dangerous as tobacco and, in terms of world health, far more important.
- Sugar is an enormous burden throughout life: it destroys children's teeth, it leads to obesity and it exacerbates diabetes, a disease that eventually destroys every organ.
- Sugar should be classified as a hard drug, for it is addictive and harmful.
- There will be a considerable cost attached to the cessation of sugar consumption, but this will be negligible in comparison with the cost of the disease burden attributable to sugar.[134]

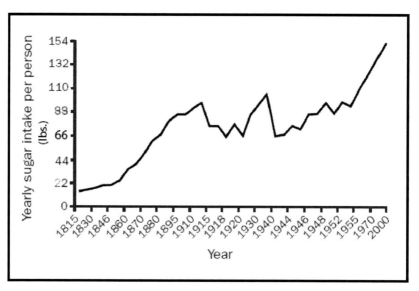

Average Per Capita Consumption of Sugar in England
(1815-1970 and in the United States (1970-2000).

Graph adapted from: James H. O'Keefe Jr, MD and Loren Cordain, PhD. "Cardiovascular Disease Resulting from a Diet and Lifestyle at Odds with Our Paleolithic Genome: How to Become a 21st Century Hunter-Gatherer." *Mayo Clinic Proceedings,* 2004;79:101-108.

Princeton neuroscientist Bart Hoebel, PhD, has spent the last four decades studying how the brain controls appetite and addictive behavior. After conducting some sugar-dependency studies that involved feeding lab rats sugar solutions, he discovered that they developed an addiction to the substance. According to Hoebel, "sugar triggered production of the brain's natural opioids or morphine-like compounds. But they didn't have opiates [drugs]; they just had sugar. The rats were getting addicted to their own opioids like they would to morphine or heroin. Drugs give a bigger effect, but it's essentially the same process."[135]

Not only is sugar an addictive substance, there are many detrimental side effects of this fine white powder. In 1975, Sir Richard Doll, Oxford epidemiologist, and Bruce Armstrong published a seminal analysis of diet and cancer, in which they noted that the higher the sugar intake in different nations, the higher both the incidence of a mortality from cancer of the colon, rectum, breast, ovary, uterus, prostate, kidney, nervous system and testicles.[136]

On her Web site, Nancy Appleton, PhD, author of *Lick the Sugar Habit*, lists 146 reasons why sugar is ruining your health.[137] There are several studies showing why people should eliminate or dramatically cut back on the amount of their sugar consumption:

- The increase in refined carbohydrates, such as sugar, has contributed to the increased incidence of diabetes. Diabetics have twice the incidence of depression.[138]
- Sugar can cause hyperactivity, anxiety, concentration difficulties and crankiness in children.[139]
- Decreasing your sugar consumption improves your emotional stability.[140]
- Sugar can cause fatigue, moodiness, nervousness and depression.[141]
- Sugar can slow down the ability of the adrenal glands to function.[142]
- Sugar can give you a temporary "high," but when that energy boost wears off, you may notice that you are sleepier and slower to react than you were before your "high."[143]

If the above reasons still do not motivate you to at least reduce your consumption of sugar, you may be a "sugar addict." Just like cocaine, alcohol, nicotine and other addictive drugs, sugar appears to cause an exaggerated response in the area of the brain known as the nucleus accumbens—the reward center. People who have powerful cravings for sugar—a sweet tooth—may experience an excessive release of dopamine in that area of the brain when they eat sugar. Just as happens with any other drug, as people go through sugar withdrawal, dopamine levels decrease, causing the individual to feel depressed. Then, as a way to self-medicate, they return to the very substance that led to depression in the first place. This is sugar's vicious cycle of addiction—basically the same as any other drug.

When it comes to being addictive, sugar is not the only culprit in your kitchen. In fact, other refined carbohydrates could potentially become addictive—including another fine white substance, flour.* As Kay Sheppard writes in her book *Food Addiction*:

> Refined carbohydrates stimulate increased transmission of dopamine, serotonin and norepinephrine. As the synapses become flooded with these neurotransmitters, a feeling of euphoria results and craving for more refined carbohydrates is stimulated. One actually becomes intoxicated by the sugar, white flour and other refined carbohydrates as they act as alcohol in the blood system and hypothalamus.[144]

Barry Groves, PhD, author of *Trick and Treat*, cautions about the overconsumption of *all* carbohydrates, not just sugar and flour. Under normal conditions, when we consume carbohydrates, insulin alerts the brain to release our feel-good neurotransmitter, serotonin, after each meal. However, if an individual eats too many carbohydrates—sugar, grain, fruits, vegetables—this will cause excessively high levels of insulin, preventing serotonin levels from rising.[145]

Do Not Drink Your Fruit

Many people believe that juice is a healthy drink, but what they do not realize is that fruit juice is a highly concentrated source of carbohydrates. Drs. Lutz and Allan believe that people mistakenly underestimate the carbohydrate content of both fruit and fruit

---

*   Note that white flour and white sugar are fine white powders, just like cocaine and heroin.

juice. As opposed to whole milk, which has about 11 grams of carbohydrates, an 8-ounce glass of orange juice contains about 20-30 grams of sugar.[146]

- Between 1994 and 1996, the average American consumed about 165 grams of fruit per day, with 65 grams coming from juice.[147]
- Children consumed more than 250 grams of fruit and fruit juice per day.[148]

Frozen concentrated orange juice (FCOJ) is one of our most popular drinks and yet it has only been a part of our diet for the last six decades. Alissa Hamilton, PhD, author of the book *Squeezed: What You Don't Know About Orange Juice*, reveals that

> Frozen Concentrated Orange Juice ("FCOJ") was born in 1948 . . . . According to the USDA Economic Research Service, in 1940, before the invention of FCOJ, per capita consumption of orange juice was 0.08 gallons. By 1950, it had grown exponentially to 0.93 gallons. Today per capita consumption hovers around five gallons. We may say we drink orange juice because it's a good source of vitamin C. It is for soldiers on the battlefront without access to fresh fruits and vegetables. For the rest of us there are many fresh fruits and vegetables, a whole medium orange for one, which boast more vitamin C than a glass of processed orange juice.[149]

Dr. Hamilton also explains that "not from concentrate" orange juice is not as fresh as people may think since it can sit in storage tanks for up to a year. After all the processing, she thinks it a stretch to call such orange juice "natural."[150]

> It's a heavily processed product. It's heavily engineered as well. In the process of pasteurizing, juice is heated and stripped of oxygen, a process called deaeration, so it doesn't oxidize . . . . It gets stripped of flavor-providing chemicals, which are volatile. When it's ready for packaging, companies such as Tropicana hire flavor companies such as Firmenich to engineer flavor packs to make it taste fresh.[151]

Like milk, several brands of orange juice are available in wax cartons—this is to give consumers the illusion that they are buying a product that is nutritionally similar to milk. Juice is nowhere near as nutritious as whole milk, which is what children should be drinking! Do not let the marketing or fancy packaging fool you—juice is loaded with carbohydrates. Rather than drinking juice, you would be better off eating the actual fruit itself.

Caffeine: Adding Insult to Injury

There is no doubt that the excitation of the central nervous system produced by large amounts of caffeine is followed by depression.[152]

—J. Murdoch Ritchie, Professor Emeritus,
Department of Pharmacology,
Yale University School of Medicine

Thousands are in mental institutions today because of no greater matter than that of the use of caffeine. Psychiatrists are now publishing articles indicating that there are numerous cases of depression and anxiety in mental institutions who need no other treatment than to be taken off caffeine. It would seem that with such a simple remedy available, many thousands of people could be returned to their full usefulness promptly.

—Calvin Thrash, MD, *Food Allergies Made Simple*

We are already destabilizing our blood sugar levels by eating too many carbohydrates. Increasing our consumption of caffeinated beverages has only added insult to injury. Caffeine increases our stress hormones—cortisol, epinephrine (also known as adrenaline) and norepinephrine (also known as noradrenaline).[153] This elevates the heart rate and increases the stress response of your body. Increasing your stress response can contribute to blood sugar problems, which in turn can lead to other health consequences, ranging from weight gain and moodiness to heart disease and diabetes. Like amphetamines or cocaine, caffeine affects the neurotransmitter dopamine and can therefore be addictive. This can initially make you feel good, but after its effects wear off, you can feel tired and depressed.[154]

Caffeine is the world's most widely used mood-altering drug. More than 85% of Americans use caffeine on a daily basis.[155] Worldwide, individuals consume about 76 mg of caffeine on a daily basis. Americans consume a whopping 219 mg of caffeine on a daily basis, about three quarters of it coming from coffee.[156] You can also find caffeine in tea, caffeinated soft drinks, energy drinks, chocolate, soap, lip balm, chewing gum, sunflower seeds, potato chips, candies, over-the-counter (OTC) products such as alertness-promoting medications (NoDoz, Vivarin), menstrual aids (Midol), analgesics (Excedrin, Anacin, BC Powder) and diet aids (Dexatrim), various prescription medications (e.g., Fioricet and Cafergot) and many herbal preparations.[157]

Caffeine content of various foods, beverages, medications and supplements.

(Caffeine content is approximate for brewed beverages and chocolate.)

	Amount	Caffeine (mg)
Milk chocolate	8 oz	5
Dark semi-sweet chocolate	1 oz	20
Brewed green tea	8 oz	20
Anacin	one tablet	32
Pepsi cola	12 oz can	38
Espresso	1 oz shot	40
Fiorinal/Fioricet	one tablet	40
Coca-cola	12 oz can	46
Brewed black tea	8 oz	50
Mountain Dew	12 oz can	54
Midol	1 gelcap	60
Excedrin pain reliever	1 tablet	65
Dexatrim Natural	one tablet	80
Jolt cola	12 oz can	80
Red Bull energy drink	8.3 oz can	80
Monster energy drink	16 oz can	80
Jolt caffeine energy gum	2 pieces	100
Penguin caffeinated mints	6 pieces	100
Cafergot	one tablet	100
No Doz	one tablet	100
Brewed coffee	12 oz cup	200
Vivarin	one tablet	200
Ripped Fuel Extreme Ephedra Free	2 capsules	220

Table reprinted by permission of eMedicine.com[160]

Insomnia, depression and anxiety are correlated with caffeine intake.[158] In his book *What Your Doctor May Not Tell You about Depression,*

Michael B. Schachter, MD, explains the link between caffeine and depression:

> [Caffeine] inhibits the brain's levels of serotonin and the hormone into which it converts, melatonin, which aids in sleep. In addition, caffeine depletes the body of nutrients that are essential to maintaining good mood, including vitamin C, magnesium, calcium, zinc, potassium and the B vitamins. Caffeine also hinders the normal metabolism of GABA, which is manufactured in the intestines and, like serotonin, calms stress and anxiety.[159]

Children who consume caffeine can be misdiagnosed as having ADHD.[161] Even children who consume only *28 milligrams* a day (less than an average soda) can feel symptoms from caffeine.[162] Some researchers believe that caffeinated beverages may serve as "gateway" products, putting children at risk for abusing stronger stimulants, such as the prescription drugs amphetamine and methylphenidate (Ritalin).[163]

The floodgates are open; now that children have been socially and physically accustomed to consuming so many caffeinated beverages, it will be difficult to convince them to stop. In order to protect our children from the harmful effects of caffeine, we should be doing our utmost to restrict their consumption of caffeine and to better regulate the beverage industry.

If you think that caffeine is contributing to your symptoms—anxiety, depression, insomnia—it would be best for you to eliminate it from your life rather than continue to let it sabotage your health.

Examples of the Pro-Addiction Diet

> Chronic drug addiction produces in the victims severe subclinical scurvy along with multi-vitamin and mineral dysfunction and protein deficiencies.
>
> —Archie Kalokerinos, PhD and Glen Dettman, PhD
> *The Orthomolecular Treatment of Drug Addiction:*
> *A First Australian Report*

Most people are following diets that are high in carbohydrates and low in the fats necessary to support our nervous system. Addicts are notorious for skipping meals, consuming a lot of sugar (carbohydrates, in general) and caffeinated beverages. These extremely unhealthy eating habits destabilize blood sugar levels and starve the brain. With the help of Pieter Herbst, PhD, counselor at Teen Challenge Farm, Lambeth, Ontario, Canada, I collected the dietary patterns of a few individuals enrolled in their addiction recovery program.*

1. Corey, Age 24, Addicted to Crack/Cocaine

    •   Skipped breakfast and lunch. Only drank coffee in the morning. For lunch, he drank water, beer, pop or juice.
    •   Mid-afternoon, he ate frozen foods that he could put in the microwave (pizza pops, pasta).
    •   At 3:00-5:00 a.m., he ate ice cream, chips, fruit, junk foods.
    •   Overall, he drank a lot of pop and ate a lot of takeout.
    •   Prior to his addiction, he felt depressed, moody, angry and tired. He went to bed between 3:00-5:00 a.m. and slept until 1:00 p.m. He wouldn't feel awake until about 7:00 p.m. Also, spent a lot of time surfing pornography on the Internet.

2. Adam, Age 26, Addicted to "Weed," "E," "K," Crack/Cocaine, Alcohol, LSD, Mushrooms, Nicotine

    •   For breakfast, he ate all high-carbohydrate foods: pancakes, pears, milk, tea, toast with peanut butter and jam.
    •   As a mid-morning snack, he ate peanut butter and jam with milk and pudding.
    •   As a mid-afternoon snack, he ate chips, pop and sunflower seeds.
    •   For dinner, he ate chicken, salad, potatoes, more pop and ice cream.
    •   Prior to his addiction, he was moody and angry, always ready to take on the world. He also had depression and anxiety.

---

*   The examples provided illustrate their diets prior to entering Teen Challenge Farm.

3. Jeff, Age 56, Addicted to Sex, Drugs

- For breakfast he ate a high-carbohydrate breakfast of oatmeal, a banana and coffee.
- For lunch, he ate salad and a bagel.
- As a mid-afternoon snack, he ate an apple.
- For dinner, he ate chicken, potatoes, salad and drank green tea.
- Before bed, he ate popcorn.
- Normally, he ate on the run or in front of the TV
- Prior to his addiction, he had insomnia, was very anxious, tired, depressed, irritable and moody.

It is very probable that had these people eaten a healthy whole foods diet with ample protein and fat and a moderate amount of carbohydrates, they would never have turned to drugs to deal with their negative moods.

In 1980, a clinical study appeared in the *American Journal of Clinical Nutrition* reporting that people who ate too many refined carbohydrates exhibited neurotic tendencies. Personality changes seen in this population, particularly among adolescents, included: sensitivity to criticism, poor impulse control, frequent irritability, hostile behavior and a tendency to anger easily. Other features were: sleep disturbances, including restlessness, night terrors, insomnia and walking or talking in one's sleep; chronic debilitating fatigue; depression; recurrent fevers of unknown origin; abdominal and/or chest pains; and headaches.[164]

—Alexander Schauss, PhD, FACN, *Nutrition and Behavior*

Our ancestors would be rolling over in their graves if they could see what we were eating today! Since switching to a diet that is diametrically opposed to previous generations, we now see unprecedented rates of chronic disease and mental disorders. History, science and common sense show us that animal foods are crucial for optimal health. Not only do they help stabilize blood sugar levels, they also provide our nervous system with key nutrients it needs to function properly.

CHAPTER 3

ANIMAL FOODS ARE KEY
TO OPTIMAL HEALTH

You can change the way you feel by changing what you eat.[165]

—Joseph D. Beasley, MD, *Food for Recovery*

For years, mainstream doctors have told us to eat a low-fat diet* in order to avoid obesity, heart disease and high cholesterol. This recommendation has caused us to reduce our consumption of animal foods, including nutrient-dense animal fats like butter and lard. Historically, humans ate a diet relatively high in animal fats (rich in saturated fat and cholesterol) and lived healthy lives without disease. This is because animal fats do not just stabilize your blood sugar levels, they also provide key nutrients that directly support your nervous system. In this chapter, we will take a closer look at just how animal foods have made us who we are.

- Children on low-fat diets suffer from growth problems and failure to thrive.[166]
- A low-fat diet is associated with greater feelings of depression, dejection and anger. In contrast, a high-fat diet is associated with improvements in mood.[167]
- A low-fat diet is associated with a significant increase in deaths from accidents, suicide and violence.[168]
- A low-fat diet may impair cognitive function.[169]
- Depressed individuals tend to consume more carbohydrates in their diets than non-depressed individuals.[170]
- Research shows that eating adequate amounts of complete protein can increase alertness.[171]

---

* A low-fat diet implies a diet that is low in *animal* fats.

Our ancestors ate three square meals—meaning three meals comprised of adequate amounts of animal fat, animal protein and complex carbohydrates, such as whole vegetables or fruit. Most of us are used to hearing the mantra, "Eat your fruits and veggies." We know that fruits and vegetables are good for us. However, it can be difficult to convince people to overcome their fear of fat. In order to help you overcome your fat phobia, it is important to understand that prior to the 1950s, our ancestors were not at all afraid of animal fats and thrived very nicely on animal foods.

Fat is the most valuable food known to Man.[172]

—Professor John Yudkin (1910-1995)

Anthropologist Dr. H. Leon Abrams says that man has been almost exclusively a meat eater for 99% of the time he has been on earth.[173] John Yudkin, MD, PhD, was an author and researcher in the area of nutrition and a professor of medicine at University College, London, England. He stated that "many human cultures survive on a purely animal product diet, but only if it is high in fat."[174]

In his book *Good Calories, Bad Calories*, Gary Taubes emphasizes the historical importance of animal foods in our diets. According to Taubes:

- One French account from 1793 estimated that Americans ate eight times as much meat as bread.[175]
- By one USDA estimate, the typical American was eating 178 pounds of meat annually in the 1830s, 40 to 60 pounds more than was reportedly being eaten a century later.[176]
- Hunter-gatherers consumed the entire carcass of an animal, not just the muscle meat and preferentially consumed the fattest parts of the carcass—including organs, tongue and marrow—and the fattest animals.[177]

Dr. Weston A. Price, Dr. Vilhjalmur Stefansson and Sir Robert McCarrison have noted the absence of chronic disease in cultures where the people ate adequate amounts of animal fats. While conducting their research, they also took note of their robust mental stability. It stands to reason, then, that if we were to eat the same foods as our ancestors, we too could enjoy optimal physical and mental health.

Weston A. Price, DDS (1870-1948)

Since we know that nutrient deficiencies can lead to disease, it is crucial to consume the most nutrient-dense foods possible. This is why it is so important to understand the work of Weston A. Price, author of the book, *Nutrition and Physical Degeneration*. It was Dr. Price's firm belief that nutritional deficiencies led to chronic disease, mental disorders and delinquency.

While studying the diet of primitive cultures, he noted that the healthiest people consumed ten times the fat-soluble vitamins, such as vitamins A and D—nutrients abundant in pastured or wild animals—and four times the calcium and other minerals as the Western diet. Dr. Price consistently found that healthy "primitives," whose diets contained an adequate amount of nutrients from animal protein and fat, had a cheerful, positive attitude to life.[178] Not only did these cultures enjoy excellent mental health, they were physically healthy as well.

In 1931 and 1932, Dr. Weston A. Price studied the diets of villagers in Switzerland. Approximately 2,000 people lived in the Loetschental Valley located in a mountainous region of the country. When Dr. Price visited their village, he noticed that "they have neither physician nor dentist because they have so little need for them; they have neither policeman nor jail."[179] The diet of these Swiss villagers consisted mainly of high-fat dairy products (raw milk, raw cream, raw cheese and raw butter) and sourdough bread, with meat being served once per week. During athletic contests, athletes were fed bowls of pure cream. These high-fat dairy products, loaded with minerals and the fat-soluble vitamins A and D, protected the village from dental decay, chronic and infectious diseases and contributed to their overall sense of well-being.

Amazed by the overall quality of health of the villagers in the Loetchental Valley, Dr. Price remarked, "One immediately wonders if there is not something in the life-giving vitamins and minerals of the food that builds not only great physical structures within which their souls reside, but builds minds and hearts capable of a higher type of manhood in which the material values of life are made secondary to individual character."[180]

While visiting the Outer Hebrides Islands off the coast of Scotland, Dr. Price observed that residents of these islands ate a diet high in animal fat derived from fish. They also consumed oats and limited amounts of vegetables. He noted that

> it would be hard to visualize a more complete isolation for child life than many of these homes provide and one marvels at the refinement, intelligence and strength of character of these rugged people . . . . On Saturday evening the sidewalks were crowded with happy carefree people, but no boisterousness and no drinking were to be seen . . . . In few places in the world are moral standards so high.[181]

Vilhjalmur Stefansson, PhD (1879-1962)

If yours is a meat diet then you simply must have fat with your lean; otherwise you would sicken and die.

—Dr. Vilhjalmur Stefansson (1879-1962)

Dr. Price's findings were consistent with the work of the Canadian explorer and anthropologist, Dr. Vilhjalmur Stefansson. After spending extensive time among the Inuit in the Arctic, Dr. Stefansson remarked that "the uncivilized Eskimos are the happiest people in the world."[182] One would think, perhaps, that given the harshness of their environment, the Inuit would be miserable. This was not the case. Regardless of their living conditions, they were very happy.

Stefansson went on several Arctic expeditions between 1906 and 1918. He wrote many books, including *My Life with the Eskimos* (1913), *The Friendly Arctic* (1921) and *Discovery* (Stefansson's autobiography, published after his death in 1964). Part of his research included the study of the various northern native cultures, whose diet consisted of high amounts of fat and protein. Stefansson and fellow explorer Karsen Anderson lived on a diet consisting of meat and fat, including seal, polar bear, caribou and fish and enjoyed excellent health. Even though doctors and nutritionists insisted that it would be impossible for humans to subsist on this type of diet, they had no dental caries, no heart disease, no cancer and had excellent bone health.

The natives had warned him that eating lean meats would make him sick. Sure enough, when Stefansson experimented by eating lean meats, he became ill—even after following a low-fat diet for only two weeks. While conducting a nutritional experiment in the United States,

Stefansson and his colleagues discovered that the optimal diet consisted of about 80% animal fat. In order to mimic the Inuit diet, they included foods such as steaks, chops, brains fried in bacon fat, boiled short ribs, chicken, fish, liver and bacon in their experiment.

> Up north, the Eskimos and I had been cured immediately when we got some fat. Dr. DuBois now cured me the same way by giving me fat sirloin steaks, brains fried in bacon fat and things of that sort.[183]
>
> —Dr. Vilhjalmur Stefansson (1879-1962)

Stefansson acknowledged the importance of eating a diet high in animal fats, regardless of whether one lived in a cold or warm climate. He said that even people who live in tropical climates love eating greasy foods.[184]

Even during his lifetime, Stefansson noted that fats were being "crowded out by commerce, fashion and expense." He noted the enormous disparity in cost between fats and sugar, even though fat is more nourishing than sugar. In 1935, he pointed out the following prices: "50 cents per pound (bacon) or 35 cents a pound (butter) while sugar is only 5 ½ [cents per pound]."[185]

Sir Robert McCarrison (1878-1960)

In the early 1900s, General Sir Robert McCarrison, a colonial medical officer, studied the diets of people throughout India. "He noticed that the southern Indians, who ate very little in the way of dairy produce, were of 'stunted growth' and prone to disease. He compared them with their neighbors to the north, the Sikhs. The Sikhs drank a great deal of milk and were fit and healthy."[186]

For seven years (1904-1911), Dr. McCarrison lived with the Hunza.* The Hunza and Sikh ate organically grown, locally produced, wholemeal grains, vegetables, fruit, plenty of whole milk, butter and not much meat or alcohol. They consumed large quantities of lacto-fermented goat milk products. Their diet consisted of adequate amounts of animal protein and animal fat, thus providing them with sufficient amounts of the fat-soluble

---

* The Hunza live in the extreme northernmost point of India.

vitamins A and D. For both the Hunza and the Sikh, meat was consumed about once every ten days.[187] Dr. McCarrison referred to their diet as consisting of "the unsophisticated foods of Nature," or non-industrialized foods. He considered the Hunza "an example of a race unsurpassed in perfection of physique and in freedom from disease in general . . . . They are long-lived, vigorous in youth and age, capable of great endurance and enjoy a remarkable freedom from disease in general."[188]

Dr. McCarrison noted their outstanding health but also their constant cheerfulness. At no time did he see them drink alcoholic beverages to excess. The Hunza were good-tempered and highly energetic—exhaustion was unknown among them. They were always willing to help others, and when work was to be done, they cheerfully embraced the task without complaint.

The Importance of Animal Fats

For decades now, we have been following a stressful diet—a diet that compromises our blood sugar levels, which adversely affects our moods. It is not as if doctors were unaware of the damaging effects of a diet high in carbohydrates. While we have been following this stressful diet, there have been researchers who have recognized the health benefits of a diet high in animal fats. They knew that eating a diet high in animal fats could have helped regulate our blood sugar, improving our mental state. Unfortunately, because of the "push" to increase our consumption of grains, their research was not recognized by the scientific community.

As far back as 100 years ago, physicians knew about the stabilizing effects of a diet high in animal fats and low in carbohydrates. In order to help treat diabetes and stabilize blood sugar levels, Elliott Proctor Joslin, MD, a Harvard-and Yale-educated physician, recommended a high-fat/low-carbohydrate diet. "According to carefully documented patient logs he kept from 1893 to 1916, Dr. Joslin successfully treated dozens of diabetic patients—including his own mother—using a diet made up of 70% fat and just 10% carbohydrates."[189]

Using historical data dating back to the 1800s, Gary Taubes, author of *Good Calories, Bad Calories*, describes the weight loss benefits of a diet high in animal fats and low in carbohydrates. However, one other benefit among the subjects in the studies he cites is improvement in mood and energy. For example, beginning in the 1920s and during the next four decades, Blake Donaldson, MD, treated 17,000 patients for their weight problems. Subjects had three meals a day, in the course of which they consumed half a pound of meat and one small portion of raw fruit or a potato. For exercise, they walked half an hour before breakfast. As far as weight loss was concerned, subjects lost about two to three pounds per week without experiencing hunger. But what was most remarkable was that subjects also experienced an increase in energy and an improved sense of well-being.[190]

In 1944, medical doctors recognized the importance of stabilizing our blood sugar by encouraging the consumption of animal foods. At the University of Rochester School of Medicine and Dentistry, Strong Memorial and Rochester Municipal Hospitals in Rochester, New York, Seale Harris used a high-fat, low-carbohydrate diet to control blood sugar in patients:

> For a 2,250-calorie diet, for example, there should be 90 to 120 grams of carbohydrate and 60 to 75 grams of protein, with the balance of the calories from fat, or a caloric distribution of approximately 10 to 15% protein, 15 to 20% carbohydrate and 65 to 75% fat. An even higher protein diet may be of value because of the slower, steadier formation and absorption of available glucose.[191]

It is important to keep in mind that this was written in 1944; at that time most families were still eating a typical "meat and potato" diet. At the time, he would not have been referring to foods such as low-fat dairy products, boxed cereals, energy bars, soy or margarine. Rather, he would have been recommending traditional foods such as eggs, sausage, meat, fish, pork, cheese, butter, whole milk and so on.

Dr. Wolfgang Lutz, chancellor, professor, Dr. Med. Hebil, doctor of philosophy and doctor of science at Dublin Metropolitan University, worked clinically with patients for over four decades. In 1957, he began persuading his patients to regenerate their health using a high-fat/low-carbohydrate diet and witnessed its benefits in thousands of patients. He claimed that by stabilizing blood sugar, the diet helped support the endocrine system and was a beneficial treatment of diseases such as ulcerative colitis, heart failure, Crohn's disease, weight loss and more.

In his book *Life Without Bread*, which he co-authored with Christian Allan, PhD, Dr. Lutz describes a very simple approach to eating, which can stabilize blood sugar. He noted that stabilizing blood sugar not only helps to prevent or treat chronic diseases, it also helps improve our moods. In order to regulate insulin levels, Dr. Lutz recommends a diet high in animal fats and low in carbohydrates where the total amount of carbohydrates comes to about 72 grams per day. The focus of the diet includes the following:

- Fish
- Any type of animal meat (beef, pork, chicken, lamb), sausage, cold cuts
- Eggs
- Cheese, sour cream, plain yogurt, cream, milk (ideally from local, fresh, raw dairy and high in fat)
- All kinds of animal fats (butter, lard, tallow, duck or goose fat)
- Salads, leaves and stems of vegetables (asparagus, brussels sprouts, cauliflower, lettuce, cabbage, broccoli), cucumbers, avocados, tomatoes
- Nuts (in moderate amounts)[192]

Below is a list of carbohydrates based upon their serving size. Drs. Lutz and Allan suggest eating six servings of carbohydrates per day, with each of these servings representing approximately 12 grams (for a total of 72 grams):

- 1 slice of bread (preferably sourdough)
- 2/3 cups of peas
- 2 tbsp dried beans (soaked and cooked, of course)
- ½ a medium potato
- 1 medium apple
- 1 cup broccoli[193]

In a recent one-year study, sponsored by Health Canada and the University of British Columbia, Jay Wortman, MD, Department of Health Care and Epidemiology, Faculty of Medicine, University of British Columbia, tested the health effects of a diet high in animal fat and low in carbohydrates on approximately 100 people in Alert Bay, British Columbia. The diet consisted of foods as follows:

- Wild salmon
- Oolichan grease (the fat of a native, wild fish)
- Bacon
- Eggs

- Cauliflower, broccoli and salad greens
- Beef, pork, chicken, fish or seafood
- Cream (but not milk, because it contains lactose—sugar)

Subjects in the study reported successful weight loss and improved physical health, but also remarked that they were much happier than they were prior to changing their diets. One gentleman, who was known as the town grouch, had a complete "about face," dramatically improving his mood. In March 2008, the Canadian Broadcasting Corporation (CBC) aired a documentary, *My Big Fat Diet* (http://www.cbc.ca/thelens/bigfatdiet/), highlighting the results of the study.

If you have been eating a diet high in carbohydrates your whole life, it could take some time to increase your intake of animal fats and decrease your intake of carbohydrates. There are Web sites available that can help you keep track of your daily intake of carbohydrates, but if you focus on eating adequate amounts of animal protein and animal fat, you should notice that your intake of carbohydrates will go down naturally. Some people may find that they feel better if they consume more than the 72 grams of carbohydrates recommended by Drs. Lutz and Allan. If necessary, you may need to work with a qualified health practitioner who is familiar with the importance of including adequate amounts of animal fats in your diet. Otherwise, you will have to listen to your body and decide for yourself what ratios of fat/protein and carbohydrates work best for you.

We Are "Fat Heads"

Approximately 60% of our brain is made up of fat. About 25% of that fat is the omega-3 fatty acid DHA, while 14% is the omega-6 fatty acid arachidonic acid (AA).[194]

It is crucial that we provide our brains with the appropriate raw materials it needs to function properly. According to Barry Groves, PhD, the development of our brains could not have happened without having eaten large quantities of the right kinds of fatty acids, which would have come from animal meats.[195] Our ancestors would have consumed *most* of their fats from animal sources and only *some* of their fats from plant-based sources such as greens, nuts and seeds. The bulk of their fats came from eating animal foods, such as fish, shellfish, meat, lamb, goat, poultry and eggs. These foods provided them with the long-chain fatty acids, such as DHA and AA that play an important role in the functioning of our nervous system.

Dr. Joseph Hibbeln is a psychiatrist who believes that the dramatic increase in our consumption of omega-6 fats has contributed to the societal burden of depression.[196] A study published by the journal *Psychosomatic Medicine* found that the imbalance of fatty acids in the typical first world diet is likely associated with the sharp increase in depression and inflammatory diseases seen over the past century.[197]

This fatty acid imbalance has been caused by increasing our consumption of plant-based oils and fats. At the end of the nineteenth century, our average consumption of liquid plant-based oils was only about one pound per year; today, we consume *over 75 pounds* per year.[198] Our grocery store shelves are lined with soy, corn, cottonseed, canola and sunflower oils, which are high in the pro-inflammatory omega-6 fatty acids. Omega-6 fatty acids are not inherently bad for us—they play an essential role in nerve function, brain development, bone health and regulating metabolism. The problem is that because we are eating far too many omega-6 fatty acids, they are contributing to chronic health problems, including cancer, heart disease, diabetes and mental decline.[199]

Our consumption of plant-based partially hydrogenated fats has also increased dramatically over the last 100 years. These industrialized fats are found in margarines, spreads and thousands of other processed foods such as cookies, crackers and pastries. The reason why trans fats are so destructive to health is because they interfere with our body's ability to use natural fats, such as DHA and disrupt the health of our cell membranes.

Cell Membrane Health

The health of our cell membranes is essential to our overall health. The proper communication of the chemicals in our brains (neurotransmitters) depends upon having healthy cell membranes. For neurotransmitters such as serotonin and dopamine to be able to latch on to their receptors, the cell membranes must be structurally sound. Our cell membranes are like the concrete that forms the foundation of a house. The concrete is only as strong as the materials used to make it. If the foundation is faulty or weak, the house might very well collapse. On the other hand, using the right materials makes for a strong foundation. Healthy cell membranes are built from healthy materials—fatty acids such as DHA and AA, cholesterol, phospholipids and protein. Unfortunately, because fish and other seafood can be extremely expensive or inaccessible and because animal fats and cholesterol have been demonized, we are not consuming enough animal foods to supply these key nutrients.

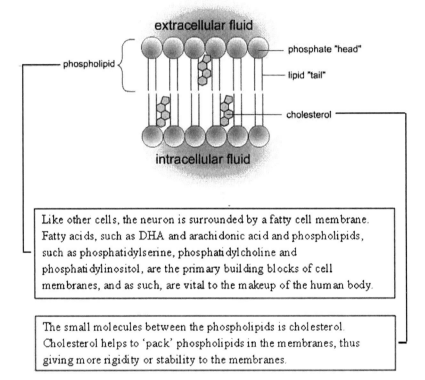

Like other cells, the neuron is surrounded by a fatty cell membrane. Fatty acids, such as DHA and arachidonic acid and phospholipids, such as phosphatidylserine, phosphatidylcholine and phosphatidylinositol, are the primary building blocks of cell membranes, and as such, are vital to the makeup of the human body.

The small molecules between the phospholipids is cholesterol. Cholesterol helps to 'pack' phospholipids in the membranes, thus giving more rigidity or stability to the membranes.

The Phospholipid Membrane
Image used by permission of Roger McFadden, Birmingham City University[200]

DHA (Docosahexaenoic Acid)

Adequate levels of DHA ensure the fluidity of the cell membrane, which is necessary for the proper functioning of our neurons and synapses. Neurons are also known as nerve cells. They are excitable cells in the nervous system that process and transmit information by electrochemical signalling. Synapses are the connections between neurons.* Neurons do not actually touch. They depend on chemicals (neurotransmitters) to move their signals across the synapses before landing on their receptor.

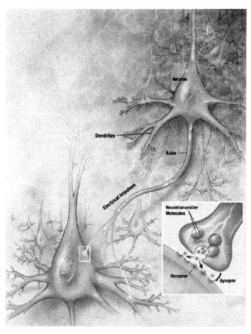

Neurotransmission
1. Electrical signal travels down axon.
2. Chemical neurotransmitter is released
3. Neurotransmitter binds to receptor sites

Process of Synaptic Transmission in Neurons
Source: U.S. National Institutes of Health, National Institute on Aging[201] (Public Domain)

A deficiency of DHA can cause a dysfunction in the transmission of the neurotransmitters serotonin, dopamine and norepinephrine, leading to depression and other mood disorders.[202] One recent study discovered that a cocktail made of three ingredients (the omega-3 fatty acid DHA, the phospholipid, choline and uridine—all components of mother's

---

*   Researchers have discovered that Alzheimer's disease is characterized by the loss of synapses.

milk) boosts the formation of new synapses, thereby improving cognitive skills in rodents.[203] An additional very exciting new study showed that a combination of EPA (another omega-3 fatty acid found in fish and pastured meats, eggs and dairy products), DHA, AA and folic acid could be of significant benefit in dementia, depression and Alzheimer's disease and improve cognitive function.[204] These studies could have tremendous implications for any type of brain injury, including brain starvation or in cases where the brain has been damaged due to drug abuse.

---

1. Over the last century, decreased omega-3 fatty acid consumption correlates with increasing rates of depression.[205]
2. People with a high consumption of fish appear to have a lower prevalence of major depressive disorders.[206]
3. One very encouraging area of research involves the potential benefits of omega-3 fatty acids for people suffering from such mood problems as depression, bipolar disorder, or schizophrenia.[207]

Fatty fish, such as sardines, mackerel, kippers, salmon and tuna are the best food sources of the omega-3 fatty acid DHA. Unfortunately, only 40% of Americans consume an adequate supply of omega-3 fatty acids, and approximately 20% of the population has blood levels so low that they cannot be detected. [208]

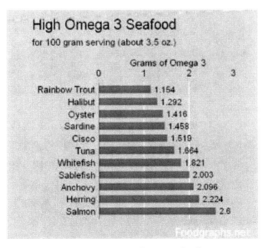

Omega-3 Levels in Seafood

Given all of the research studies showing the potential health benefits of omega-3 fatty acids, fish oil supplements have been understandably increasing in popularity. Health Canada recommends up to 3,000 mg of fish oil per day,[209] which is consistent with recommendations from the World Health Organization and the National Institutes of Health.[210]

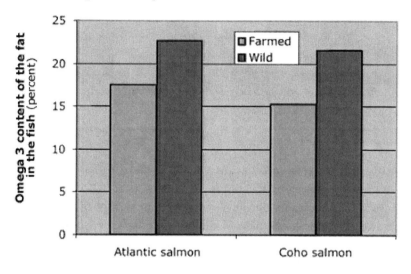

The fat in wild salmon is richer in healthy omega-3 fatty acids than farmed salmon fat

Source: EWG analysis of data from USDA (2002).

Wild fish have higher levels of omega-3 fatty acids than farmed fish.
Used with permission from Environmental Working Group (http://www.ewg.org/node/8518)

If you are not eating adequate amounts of wild fatty fish, grass-fed meats, dairy or eggs, it is likely that you are not consuming optimal amounts of omega-3 fatty acids. However, depending upon your symptoms, if you suspect that you do require omega-3 fish oil supplements, it would be a good idea to get your fatty acid blood levels tested and monitored by a qualified health practitioner. Eventually, as you improve your diet, you should notice that your fatty acid profile will balance out and you may be able to stop taking your omega-3 fish oil supplements.

Benefits of Pasture-Based Farming

It is well-known that fish are a source of omega-3 fatty acids, but you may not be aware that these fats are also available from other animal sources, such as pastured meat, dairy and eggs, or in the form of minimally processed rendered animal fats such as butter, lard, tallow, duck fat, goose fat and so on.

Switching to meat and dairy products of pastured animals is yet another very healthy way to obtain omega-3 fats in your diet.[211] When chickens are housed indoors and deprived of the foods they would normally eat in nature, like greens, worms and insects, their meat and eggs also become artificially low in omega-3. Eggs from pastured hens can contain as much as 10 times more omega-3 than eggs from factory hens.[212]

In an ideal world, we would be hunting for our meats and fish, but today, since most of us do not hunt or fish, the next best source is a vendor of wild fish or from farms where the animals are allowed to graze in open pastures. As the charts illustrate, when animals are fed too much grain in factory-farmed settings, this causes a reduction in omega-3 fatty acids.

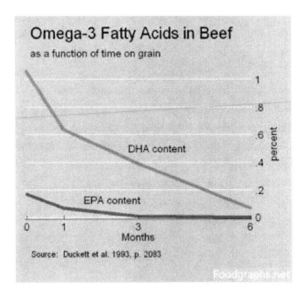

Prior to WWII, more than 90% of American cattle were grass-fed.[213] Over the last five decades, our major sources of animal products (beef and dairy cattle, poultry and pork) have been clustered together in factory farms, depriving them of the pasture and sunshine they need for proper health. Providing pasture and sunshine also helps to optimize the nutritional value of the foods rendered from the animals.* Pasturing animals is not only a more humane way to raise them, it also helps increase levels of omega-3 fatty acids, vitamin A and vitamin D.

Arachidonic Acid (AA)

Animal foods provide us with other brain-healthy nutrients such as cholesterol and arachidonic acid (AA). AA, along with vitamins A and D, are converted as needed to the endocannabinoids, which are molecules within the central nervous system that support the production of adequate dopamine (to help you feel motivated) and curb the excess production of the stress hormone cortisol. In doing so, they help prevent anxiety and depression while supporting the motivation to achieve your goals.[214]

A tremendous amount of the research surrounding our brain health is focused on DHA. Because AA is found in animal fats—and animal fats have been vilified over the last five decades—scientists have largely overlooked this very important fatty acid.

> AA is one of the most abundant fatty acids in the brain. It serves many important purposes. Deficiencies of AA can lead to several health complications.
>
> - Patients with autism, schizophrenia, bipolar disorder and depression show low levels of AA in their bodies and could be worsened by eating a diet low in animal fat.[216]
> - Individuals with ADHD have significantly lower levels of both AA and DHA.[217]
> - Alcoholics are deficient in DHA and AA.[218]
> - AA increases sleep quality during the night and increases energy during the day.[219]

---

*   As cows graze upon grass, they convert the carotenoids into vitamin A and the sunshine will help make their vitamin D. To compensate for the reduction of vitamins A and D in milk, the dairy industry has to add vitamin A and D in their products.

FOOD	Arachidonic acid content in mg/100mg of food
Duck egg yolks	891
Chicken egg yolks	390
Duck paté	311
Ox Liver	294
Lamb kidney	153
Emu	130
Turkey (skinless)	100
Atlantic salmon (skinless)	100
Pork leg steak (lean)	56
Lamb filet (lean)	49
Beef sirloin (lean)	30
Chicken legs (skinless)	56
Chicken breast	31

AA Content in Food[215]
(Unfortunately, the figures were done by "fat phobic" researchers.
Be sure to keep the skin on and eat the fattiest meats.)

Cholesterol

Our bodies make cholesterol, but it is also naturally occurring in animal foods, including eggs, meat and dairy products. It is a vital component of your body's biochemistry. One of the most important functions of cholesterol is to support the nervous system. In fact, low cholesterol levels have been linked to aggressive and violent behavior, depression and suicidal tendencies.[220] Cholesterol is essential for the machinery that triggers the release of neurotransmitters. According to a recent study, cholesterol increased neurotransmitter function five-fold.[221] Cholesterol also acts as a precursor to our sex hormones—testosterone, estrogen and progesterone—and to vitamin D, which helps support our nervous system and insulin production. In addition, cholesterol is needed for the proper functioning of serotonin receptors in the brain.[222]

Cholesterol is abundant in the tissue of the brain and nervous system. Myelin, which covers nerve axons to help conduct the electrical impulses that make movement, sensation, thinking, learning and remembering possible, is over 1/5 cholesterol by weight. The brain only makes up 2% of the body's weight and contains 25% of its cholesterol.[223] Vitamins D and B12 are also essential to maintaining optimal myelin and nervous system health.

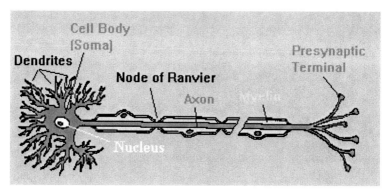

Long nerve cell extensions, the axons, are covered by myelin, a fatty electrical insulator. Myelin is over one-fifth cholesterol by weight.
Used by permission of Dr. Eric H. Chudler, Neuroscience for Kids, University of Washington[224]

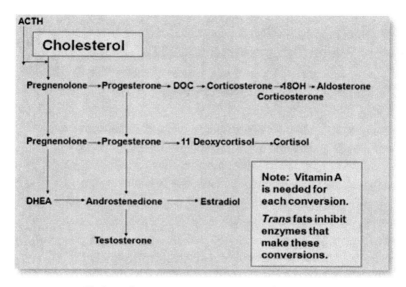

Cholesterol acts as a precursor to our sex hormones— testosterone, estrogen and progesterone.
Used by permission of the Weston A. Price Foundation

Cholesterol plays an important role in the following ways:

- Aids athletic performance
- Controls blood pressure
- Regulates mineral balance
- Keeps your cell membranes intact
- Boosts mental performance
- Aids digestion
- Builds muscle and strong bones
- Maintains your energy, vitality, libido and fertility
- Regulates your blood sugar
- Repairs damaged tissue
- Protects against infectious diseases[225]

Protein

As mentioned above, our cell membranes are made up of fatty acids, phospholipids, cholesterol and protein. Protein is also an important building block for all of our communication signals in our body, including our receptors and neurotransmitters.* As we will see in chapter 7, amino acids—which are the building blocks of protein—act as precursors to our neurotransmitters. For example, the amino acid tryptophan is the precursor for the neurotransmitter serotonin and the amino acid tyrosine is the precursor for the neurotransmitter dopamine.

One way to ensure that we are eating adequate amounts of amino acids is through the consumption of high-quality animal protein. As you can see in the following charts, wild game contains some of the highest amounts of amino acids, including tyrosine and tryptophan.

---

*   I will discuss more about neurotransmitters in chapter 6.

TYROSINE LEVELS IN FOOD[226]		
FOOD	AMOUNT	CONTENT (GRAMS)
Wild game	1 pound	3.00
Pork	1 pound	2.50
Cottage cheese	1 cup	1.70
Turkey	1 pound	1.30
Duck	1 pound	1.10
Wheat germ	1 cup	1.00
Chicken	1 pound	0.80
Granola	1 cup	0.40
Whole milk	1 cup	0.40
Oatmeal	1 cup	0.35
Cheese	1 ounce	0.30
Egg	1	0.25
Avocado	1	0.10
Sausage meat	1 pound	0.05

- Tyrosine can increase dopamine production in the brain.[227]
- Tyrosine may be an effective natural treatment for depression.[228]
- Tyrosine may provide some temporary benefit for attention deficit disorder (ADD).[229]

TRYPTOPHAN LEVELS IN FOOD[230]		
FOOD	AMOUNT	CONTENT (GRAMS)
Wild game	1 pound	1.15
Pork	1 pound	1.00
Cottage cheese	1 cup	0.40
Avocado	1	0.40
Wheat germ	1 cup	0.40
Duck	1 pound	0.40
Turkey	1 pound	0.37
Sausage meat	1 pound	0.30
Chicken	1 pound	0.28
Oatmeal	1 cup	0.20
Granola	1 cup	0.20
Whole milk	1 cup	0.11
Egg	1	0.10
Cheese	1 ounce	0.09

- Acute tryptophan depletion produces depressive symptoms and results in worsening of mood.[231]
- Tryptophan is an effective antidepressant in mild-to-moderate depression.[232]
- In healthy people who tend to be irritable, tryptophan increases agreeableness, decreases quarrelsomeness and improves mood.[233]
- A minor constituent of milk, α-Lactalbumin, is one protein that contains relatively more tryptophan than most proteins. Heavy doses of α-lactalbumin by humans can improve mood and cognition in some circumstances, presumably owing to increased serotonin.[234]

Since most of us do not hunt or fish, the next best source of animal protein would be to buy from farms where the animals are out on pasture. These foods will not only provide more optimal levels of amino acids, but healthier levels of the fat-soluble vitamins (A and D) and omega-3 fatty acids.

As we will see in chapter 7, if you have been starving your brain by following fad diets, skipping meals or damaging your brain with drugs, you may need to supplement your diet with certain amino acids for a while until you notice your mood and memory improve. Depending upon your circumstances, you may only need to supplement for a few weeks, months or longer.

Phospholipids

The integrity of a cell membrane not only depends on protein, fats and cholesterol but on phospholipids as well. In fact, phospholipids are the main structural components of all cell membranes. Technically, they are not fats, but are distantly related to fats. Phospholipids play a crucial role in the complex communication going on between our neurons—in essence, they are the "ears" listening to the messages coming from the neurotransmitters. A few of the important phospholipids that make up cell membranes are phosphatidylcholine, phosphatidylserine and phosphatidylinositol.* Dietary sources rich in phospholipids include egg yolks, organ meats (including liver, kidney or brain), meats, fish and shellfish.[235]

Because phospholipids play an important role in the health of cell membranes, they help support your mental health. One phospholipid, phosphatidylserine, has been thoroughly studied by Parris Kidd, PhD. In his book *PhosphatidylSerine: Nature's Brain Booster*, Dr. Kidd lists the following clinical benefits of taking phosphatidylserine as a supplement:

- Phosphatidylserine improves memory, learning and other cognitive functions in people who are substantially impaired compared to others in their age group.
- Phosphatidylserine can improve activities of daily living (ADL) and other components of the quality of life, for people who suffer from more severe memory loss.
- Phosphatidylserine can improve negative mood (depression) and ease anxiety in both young people and the elderly.

---

*   While there is a fair amount of data showing the various health benefits of dietary phosphatidylcholine and phosphatidylserine, there is not much research on the physiological function of dietary phosphatidylinositol (Shirouchi 2008).

- Phosphatidylserine can help individuals cope with stress, both physical and emotional.
- Phosphatidylserine has the potential to help children with attention and behavior problems.[236]

The following chart shows the phosphatidyleserine content of different foods:

FOOD	Phosphatidylserine (PS) content in mg/100g of food
Bovine brain	713
Atlantic mackerel	480
Chicken heart	414
Atlantic herring	360
Eel	335
Offal (average value)	305
Pig's spleen	239
Pig's kidney	218
Tuna	194
Chicken leg, with skin, without bone	134
Chicken liver	123
White beans	107
Soft-shelled clam	87
Chicken breast, with skin	85
Mullet	76
Veal	72
Beef	69
Pork	57
Pig's liver	50
Turkey leg, without skin or bone	50
Turkey breast, without skin	45
Crayfish	40
Cuttlefish	31
Atlantic cod	28
Anchovy	25
Whole grain barley	20

Phosphatidylserine Content in Food [237]

Another important phospholipid is phosphatidylcholine. Phosphatidylcholine depends upon the B vitamin choline.* Choline is also a precursor to acetylcholine, an essential neurotransmitter that plays a crucial role in learning and memory. Choline, along with B12, is necessary for myelin formation.[238]

FOOD	Choline content in mg/100g of food
Egg yolk (raw, fresh)	682
Eggs (whole, cooked)	273
Chicken liver (all kinds, simmered)	290
Turkey liver (cooked, simmered)	220
Pork (cured, bacon, cooked, pan-fried)	131
Spices (mustard seed, yellow)	123
Almonds	52
Cauliflower (cooked, boiled, drained)	39
Artichokes (cooked, boiled, drained)	34
Green peas (frozen, cooked)	28
Spinach (whole leaf, frozen)	28
Red cabbage (cooked, boiled drained)	22

Source: USDA Database for the Choline Content of Common Foods March, 2004

For decades, millions of us have been scared to eat a typical traditional "meat and potatoes diet"—a diet that usually consists of adequate amounts of animal foods. While we have reduced our consumption of nutrient-dense animal foods, we have increased our consumption of plant-based foods like grains, margarine, juice and so on. Since making

---

* The messages our brain sends back and forth between our nerves depend on B vitamins, such as folic acid, vitamin B6 and choline. Vitamin B5 promotes the conversion of choline to acetylcholine.

this dietary shift, we have deprived ourselves of some very key nutrients that are key to optimal health. So go ahead and enjoy your meat and potatoes—and do not be afraid to load your potatoes with lots of butter and high-fat sour cream.

CHAPTER 4

NUTRITIONAL DEFICIENCIES AND YOUR NERVOUS SYSTEM

At this very moment, fifteen trillion nerve cells in your brain are hungry for specific nutrients that they need to function. Deprive your brain of these nutrients—even one—and the result can be devastating. Nutrients are necessary for neurotransmitter production, hormone secretion, nerve transmission and cell metabolism. When nutritional imbalances occur, . . . each of these areas can suffer and the result can be depression, confusion, fatigue, insomnia, loss of sex drive, anxiety and other symptoms that often accompany mood disorders. When you correct nutrient deficiencies, however, symptoms can be alleviated and mind-body harmony can be restored.[239]

—Michael B. Schachter, MD,
What Your Doctor May Not Tell You about Depression

Over the last several decades, we have ignored the wisdom of our ancestors, replacing nutrient-dense foods with nutrient-poor, industrially processed foods. We have also received a great deal of incorrect nutritional advice from the media and so-called experts. Since the 1950s, nutritionists have been telling us to reduce our consumption of animal fats. However, a diet low in animal fats is associated with lower levels of calcium, zinc, magnesium, iron, phosphorus, vitamin E, vitamin D, vitamin A, vitamin B12, vitamin B6, folic acid (vitamin B9) and niacin (vitamin B3).[240] Such poor dietary advice has caused some very serious widespread nutritional deficiencies and, as such, contributed to a decline in our physical and mental health.

As we have already seen, changes in mood and cognition are among the first signs of malnutrition. What many people may not realize is that specific nutritional deficiencies can negatively affect our nervous system[*] and contribute to mental disorders. For example, deficiencies of magnesium, vitamin B12 and folic acid are associated with psychiatric symptoms, such as dementia and depression.[241] The purpose of this chapter is to point out the importance of some of the common nutritional deficiencies we are facing today and how these deficiencies can negatively influence our mental stability.

Balance Zinc and Copper Levels

The body has its own very sophisticated system to keep minerals in balance. A deficiency in one mineral will cause an excess in another mineral. For example, a deficiency in zinc will cause the body to accumulate copper contributing to a host of conditions, including schizophrenia, bipolar disorder, autism, fatigue, depression, anxiety, hyperactivity, obsessiveness, compulsiveness, phobias and so on.

Our fear over eating animal fats has led to the reduction of several important nutrients including zinc, which is crucial for a healthy nervous system. The best sources of zinc are animal foods—red meat, organ meats and seafood, especially oysters. Inadequate levels of zinc are associated with depression, changes in behavior, including a reduction in learning and mental function, such as ADHD and autism, impaired memory, white spots on the nails and schizophrenia.[242] In his book *The UltraMind Solution*, Mark Hyman, MD, describes the story of a schizophrenic male who woke up from his madness by taking high doses of zinc, vitamin B6 and vitamin B3 (niacin).[243]

Zinc is involved in the synthesis of neurotransmitters such as serotonin, norepinephrine and GABA. It is also necessary for healthy thyroid function and maintaining the optimal balance of estrogen, progesterone and testosterone.

You need some copper in your diet; however, it is important to make sure you do allow copper levels to get to high. Copper is a highly

---

*   In simple terms, the nervous system is a network that relays messages back and forth from the brain to different parts of the body. The nervous system and endocrine system (which includes the adrenals, thyroid and sex glands) are separate systems and often work together to help the body function properly.

conductive metal. Excessive copper can over-stimulate neurotransmitters such as serotonin, norepinephrine, epinephrine and dopamine. The Pfeiffer Research Center has reported that 80% of hyperactive patients and 68% of behavior-disordered patients have elevated blood copper levels.[244]

Adrenal fatigue, copper imbalance and addiction are strongly related. The adrenal glands must be working properly in order to excrete metals such as copper. In other words, when your adrenal glands are overly stressed, they cannot produce adequate amounts of hormones to stimulate the liver to remove excess copper from the body.

Excess copper can also interfere with your thyroid gland, a gland found in the neck region that influences metabolism and mood, as well as methylation, an important process in the brain, which will be explained later. Therefore, protecting your adrenal glands will support other important metabolic processes in the body.

As we have seen, one way to protect the adrenal glands is by regulating blood sugar levels through a proper diet. On a daily basis, we should be eating three square meals—meals that include an appropriate amount of animal protein, fat and complex carbohydrates. People who follow diets too high in carbohydrates not only risk throwing off their blood sugar levels, they may also cause an imbalance in their levels of zinc and copper. The reason why this can happen is that plant-based foods contain high levels of copper and low levels of zinc. In order to prevent the accumulation of copper, individuals should consume foods high in zinc, such as eggs, poultry and beef, which has a four-fold greater bioavailability of zinc than do high-fiber cereals.[245]

Part of the draw toward stimulating substances such as cocaine, caffeine, nicotine, amphetamines and sugar or stimulating behaviors such as exercise, anger, fear, overactivity or thrill-seeking, may have something to do with their ability to help lower copper temporarily by stimulating the adrenals. Stimulating the adrenals would cause the body to dump copper. Without this stimulation, copper builds up quickly in the body, making one feel fatigued, moody or depressed. Hence, the vicious cycle of addiction.

Aside from integrating adequate amounts of high-quality animal foods in your diet, supplementation can help balance copper levels and support adrenal function. In her book *Why Am I Always So Tired?* Ann Louise Gittleman, PhD, CNS, recommends the following daily regimen for copper overload: 25-50 mg zinc, 15-30 mg manganese, 100-300 mg vitamin B6, 1,000-3,000 mg vitamin C and 30-60 mg lipoic acid. In addition, she suggests a complete multi-vitamin/mineral complex without copper.[246]

Before supplementing with minerals, it is best to test levels through a Hair Tissue Mineral Analysis. The lab I use to test for both minerals and heavy metals is Analytical Research Labs Inc. at www.arltma.com/HairAnalysis.htm.

Iodine and Thyroid Health

Since depression is the strongest single risk factor for developing addictions, it is important to make sure your thyroid gland is working properly. Profound fatigue, depression, cold hands and feet and inability to lose weight are just a few of the most prominent symptoms of hypothyroidism or low thyroid. Several nutrients are necessary for the proper function of your thyroid. One nutrient in particular, iodine, plays a crucial role in the functioning of your thyroid gland.* It has been estimated that up to 80% of the population may have low thyroid function (hypothyroid).[247] That means that millions of people are being misdiagnosed as having a "normal" thyroid when, in fact, they are suffering from hypothyroidism. While several variables could be causing this hypothyroid epidemic, one contributing factor could be a widespread iodine deficiency. In his book *What Your Doctor May Not Tell You about Depression*, Michael Schachter, MD, writes that he considers iodine deficiency in *all* of his patients struggling with depression.[248]

In his clinical practice, Dr. David Brownstein has discovered that over 80% of his patients are iodine deficient. Vegetarians and vegans are especially at risk for developing iodine deficiencies.[249] In addition to recommending iodine supplementation, Dr. Brownstein also recommends taking adequate amounts of a very high quality, unrefined sea salt. As you will see, unrefined sea salt provides the body with over 80 important minerals that help support your metabolism. For information about his protocols, refer to Dr. Brownstein's Web site for his books, www.drbrownstein.com. Other informative Web sites include www.iodine4health.com (which also has a very helpful chat room, the Iodine Group) and www.breastcancerchoices.org.

The Broda O. Barnes, MD, Research Foundation has found that many of the hyperactive children who have been prescribed medications,

---

* Other nutrients, such as selenium, zinc, vitamin C, magnesium, B vitamins and vitamin A, which work in conjunction with iodine, also help support the thyroid.

such as Ritalin, are actually suffering from low thyroid function. They contend that blood tests only identify 2-5% of the people struggling with low thyroid! Fortunately, there is a simple test that you can do yourself to check basic thyroid functioning. Before the use of the current blood tests, the basal body temperature test was widely used to check thyroid function. Body temperature reflects metabolic rate, which is largely determined by the hormones of the thyroid gland. Today, many practitioners are reverting to this simple and cost-effective method.

Testing Basal Metabolic Rate:

- Place a mercury or titanium thermometer by the bedside before going to sleep. Make sure it is ready to use.
- Immediately after waking, place the thermometer under the armpit for a full five minutes. Take your temperature three times, every three hours. Record the temperatures.
- Do this for seven consecutive days, preferably at the same time of day.
- Menstruating women must perform the test on the week of menstruation.
- Take an average of the temperatures for the week.

Interpreting the Test

- Normal body temperature is 36.5 °C + or - 0.2 °C (97.6 °F-98.2 °F).
- Low basal body temperatures may reflect subclinical or fully developed hypothyroidism.
- High body temperatures may point to hyperthyroidism (an overactive thyroid gland).*

---

* An overactive thyroid gland, hyperthyroidism, is less common than an underactive thyroid gland. Signs and symptoms from each condition can be similar; however, hyperthyroidism is also associated with weight loss, sweating, tremors, Hashimoto's Disease and Grave's Disease.

If you think you can obtain adequate amounts of iodine from iodized salt or seaweed, think again. Iodine can vaporize from salt, and you may not be able to find out the iodine content of seaweed. Therefore, iodized salt and seaweed may not necessarily be good sources of iodine and supplementation may be required. Aside from standardized seaweed supplements, there are different iodine supplements available in pharmacies, health food stores or through the Internet—Lugol's, Iodoral, Atomidine, Iosol, among others. Individuals may need to experiment with different types of iodine before finding the one that works best for them. In addition, the dosage of iodine is different for everyone. Generally, clinicians recommend starting with one drop of iodine in a glass of water and working your way up slowly to about four drops per day. When you are feeling better, you may be able to reduce your dosage to one drop per day.

If you have hypothyroid symptoms, it is imperative to find an *iodine literate* physician to work with in order to help determine the type and dosage of iodine that you may require. These physicians should also have access to labs that can adequately test you to see whether you have an iodine deficiency. Follow-up testing can be done to ensure that your iodine levels are normalizing.

Some people take prescription medications to treat low thyroid, such as Synthroid or Armour. These medications may help some individuals. However, they do not help everyone who takes them. It is for this reason that individuals should also consider nutritional solutions if they are experiencing hypothyroid symptoms.

Keep in mind that the thyroid gland and adrenal glands work as a gas and brake pedal. For example, if your adrenal glands are working too hard (stressed), this will put the brakes on your thyroid gland, causing hypothyroid symptoms. One way to keep your stress levels down is by making sure your blood sugar levels are balanced. And that means eating three square meals per day that include adequate amounts of animal foods.

Cod Liver Oil

The wrongful demonization of foods containing saturated fat and cholesterol (butter, egg yolks, liver,* meats) has deterred people from

---

* Contrary to popular belief, the liver does not store toxins; it neutralizes them. Liver can, however, contain parasites. If you are worried that there consuming foods that would normally provide them with the fat-soluble vitamins A and D. Cod liver oil is an excellent way to ensure you are obtaining adequate amounts of these two very critical vitamins. Vitamin A is known for its role in supporting eye health and vitamin D for its role in supporting bone health, but what many people may not realize is that these two vitamins also play a critical role in supporting our nervous system and can, therefore, play an essential role in affecting our moods. A recent study in Norway found that the longer a person had been supplementing with cod liver oil, the less likely they were to be depressed.[250]

Vitamin A

> Weston Price considered the fat-soluble vitamins, especially vitamin A, to be the catalysts on which all other biological processes depend. Efficient mineral uptake and utilization of water-soluble vitamins require sufficient vitamin A in the diet.[251]

—Sally Fallon and Mary Enig, PhD, *Vitamin A Saga*

Almost one-third (27%) of Americans have vitamin A intakes below 50% of the RDA.[252] Vitamin A (retinol) is found in animal products, such as liver and eggs and should not be confused with beta-carotene, which is found in fruits and vegetables. Vitamin A is vital for the growth and repair of body tissues.

may be parasites in liver, be sure to freeze the organ meat for two weeks. Your best bet is to buy organ meats from pastured animals.

Vitamin A:
- supports healthy vision
- promotes healthy fertility in males and females
- contributes to the health of the immune system
- allows for proper embryonic development
- plays an important role in the detoxification process
- assists with the proper assimilation of protein and calcium
- helps to build strong bones and teeth and rich blood
- helps with the production of stress and sex hormones
- helps protect mucous membranes of the mouth, nose, throat and lungs
- is involved with the proper functioning of the thyroid gland.

The thyroid gland does not only depend upon iodine in order to function properly; sufficient vitamin A, from foods such as liver, eggs and cod liver oil, must be present for the thyroid gland to absorb enough iodine. The thyroid gland requires more vitamin A than any of the other glands. Animals that do not consume adequate amounts of vitamin A are limited in their ability to produce thyroid-stimulating hormone (TSH).[253] In their article "Vitamin A Saga," Sally Fallon and Mary Enig, PhD, write, "Foods high in vitamin A are especially important for diabetics and those suffering from thyroid conditions."[254]

As our stress levels increase, we require more vitamin A. Stress can come in many forms including heavy exercise, fever and illness, cold weather or exposure to toxins. Several substances or physical states have been identified as antivitamin A (i.e., they can prevent a vitamin from exerting its typical biologic effects), including alcohol, coffee, cold weather, cortisone, diabetes, excessive iron, infections, laxatives, liver disease, mineral oil, nitrates, sugar, tobacco, vitamin D deficiency and zinc deficiency.[255]

Vitamin D

Vitamin D is often referred to as the sunshine vitamin because the body produces it from cholesterol by the action of sunlight on the skin. It is also found in liver, eggs, dairy and cod liver oil. Not only does exposure to sunlight build our vitamin D levels, it also plays a role in the conversion of the amino acids into our "feel good" neurotransmitters—tryptophan to serotonin and tyrosine to dopamine and norepinephrine. Vitamin D helps with the proper development and functioning of our brain and preventing mood problems, such as depression.[256] It also plays a role in the prevention or treatment of many of the chronic illnesses we see today—cancer, autoimmune diseases, infectious diseases and cardiovascular disease.

A reduction of animal fats, along with our fear of going out in the sun, has contributed to an epidemic of vitamin D deficiency. Up to half of all adults and 30% of all children and teenagers are vitamin D-deficient, although this can be as high as 97% in populations who have little sun exposure such as those who live in the north during the cold snowy winters.[257]

Vitamin D
- is necessary for healthy bones and teeth
- supports the body's ability to detoxify
- is one of the most potent inhibitors of cancer cell growth
- stimulates the pancreas to make insulin
- regulates the immune system
- affects proteins in the brain known to be directly involved in learning and memory, motor control and possibly even maternal and social behavior[258]
- increases nerve growth factor in the brain[259]
- helps regulate the production of dopamine, epinephrine and norepinephrine[260]

Evidence exists that major depression is associated with low vitamin D levels and that depression has increased in the last century as vitamin D levels have surely fallen . . . . Vitamin D has profound effects on the brain, including the neurotransmitters involved in major depression. If you suffer from depression, get your 25(OH)D level checked and, if it is lower than 35 ng/mL (87 nM/L), you are vitamin D deficient and should begin treatment. If you are not depressed, get your 25(OH)D level checked anyway. If it is lower than 35 ng/mL (87 nM/L), you are vitamin D deficient and should begin treatment.[261]

—John Cannell, MD,
author of the Web site www.vitamindcouncil.com

Supplementing with vitamin D may help alleviate depression in "Seasonal Affective Disorder" (SAD) or what is now being called "low-light winter blahs," a type of depression that occurs during the winter months when exposure to sunlight is minimal.[262] Studies have found that even short-term, low-dose treatments of vitamin D (400 IUs) can help symptoms of depression related to Seasonal Affective Disorder (SAD).[263] In a study comparing vitamin D and two-hour daily use of "light boxes," depression completely resolved in the group taking vitamin D, but not the group using the light box.[264]

When it comes to sun exposure, we must return to common sense. After all, our ancestors survived for millennia enjoying fresh air and sunshine—and they did not use suntan lotion! If you do use suntan lotion, not only are you blocking the beneficial rays of the sun, which help build vitamin D in the body, you are slathering on a cream filled with potentially cancer-causing agents. In the spring, start going out in the sun slowly. Do not overdo it. When you notice that the skin is turning pink, go in the shade. Gradually, build up to a tan.

The Miracle of Vitamin D by Krispin Sullivan, CN

Used with permission from the Weston A. Price Foundation.

According to vitamin D researcher, Dr. Reinhold Vieth, the minimal daily requirement of vitamin D should be in the range of 4,000 IU from all sources.

Food Sources of Vitamin D

USDA databases compiled in the 1980s list the following foods as rich in vitamin D. The amounts given are for 100 grams or about 3 1/2 ounces. These figures demonstrate the difficulty in obtaining 4,000 IU vitamin D per day from ordinary foods in the American diet. Three servings of herring, oysters, catfish, mackerel or sardines, plus generous amounts of butter, egg yolk, lard or bacon fat and 2 teaspoons of cod liver oil (500 IU per teaspoon) yield about 4,000 IU vitamin D—a very rich diet indeed!

Cod Liver Oil	10,000
Lard (Pork Fat)	2,800
Atlantic Herring (Pickled)	680
Eastern Oysters (Steamed)	642
Catfish (Steamed/Poached)	500
Skinless Sardines (Water Packed)	480
Mackerel (Canned/Drained)	450
Smoked Chinook Salmon	320
Sturgeon Roe	232
Shrimp (Canned/Drained)	172
Egg Yolk (Fresh)	148
(One yolk contains about 24 IU)	
Butter	56
Lamb Liver (Braised)	20
Beef Tallow	19
Pork Liver (Braised)	12
Beef Liver (Fried)	12
Beef Tripe (Raw)	12
Beef Kidney (Simmered)	12
Chicken Livers (Simmered)	12
Small Clams (Steamed/Cooked Moist)	8
Blue Crab (Steamed)	4
Crayfish/Crawdads (Steamed)	4
Northern Lobster (Steamed)	4

For more information about vitamin A, D and cod liver oil, visit www.westonaprice.org.

Homocysteine, Methylation and B Vitamins

Homocysteine is an amino acid formed in the body through a process in the brain called methylation. Since 1990, thousands of scientific studies have been published showing that homocysteine is a significant risk factor for several diseases, including depression, cognitive decline, dementia, Alzheimer's, schizophrenia, bipolar disorder, birth defects, diabetes, osteoporosis, macular degeneration, heart disease and cancer.

Amino acids act as the building blocks for our neurotransmitters, but methylation will affect how efficiently you turn the amino acids into neurotransmitters. In their book *How to Quit without Feeling S**t*,

Patrick Holford, David Miller, PhD and James Braly, MD, explain that methylation "helps make, break down and balance neurotransmitters, build nerve cells and protect your brain from damage."[265] Under healthy conditions, homocysteine is converted into the amino acid S-adenosylmethionine (SAM-e), which does all the methylation. However, high levels of homocysteine can interfere with the methylation process. Therefore, in order to protect your mental well-being, it is crucial that you maintain a low level of homocysteine.

Since individuals struggling with addictions develop neurotransmitter deficiencies, it is essential that you do what we can to prevent those deficiencies by making sure you have normal levels of homocysteine and B vitamins in the body.

A simple blood lab test can help you determine your homocysteine score. The ideal homocysteine level should be below seven. If you have a high homocysteine level, there are some supplements that can help improve methylation and decrease homocysteine: vitamin B2, vitamin B6, vitamin B12, folic acid (also known as vitamin B9), zinc, choline and either trimethylglycine (TMG) or SAM-e. TMG is more stable and less expensive than SAM-e. Since the body can make SAM-e directly from TMG, it is a reasonable substitute.

The specific nutrients that help lower homocysteine are vitamin B6, vitamin B12 and folic acid, all of which are best found in animal foods such as liver, kidney, meat, fish, shellfish, raw dairy products* and eggs.

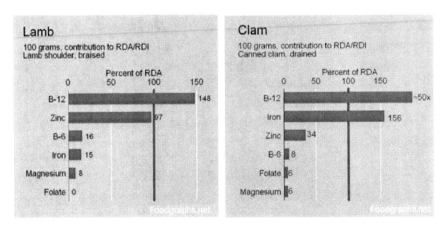

_____

* For information about how to find raw dairy products, visit www.realmilk. com or www.westonaprice.org.

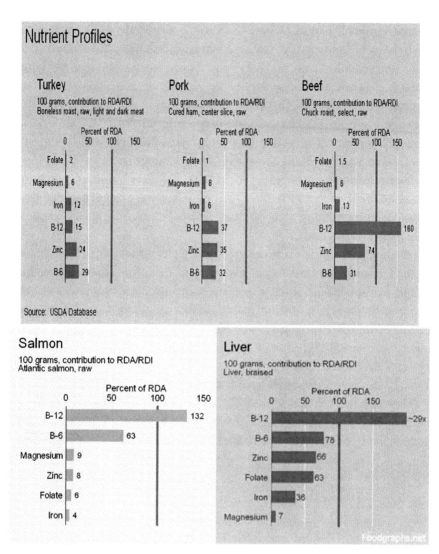

Amanda Rose, *Rebuild from Depression* (www.rebuild-from-depression.com and www.foodgraphs.net)

Folic acid is found in the form of folate in several foods, including leafy greens, whole grains, dried beans, peas, citrus and nuts. One reason why we can easily become deficient in folic acid is that 50-95% of the folate content of food can be easily destroyed by sunlight, overcooking, processing or the storing of foods at room temperature for an extended period of time.[266] Some of the best sources of folate are, therefore, animal foods—especially organ meats, such as liver and kidneys.

FOOD	Folate content
Liver, chicken, 3.5 oz, cooked	770
Liver, beef, 3.5 oz, cooked	220
Blackeyed peas, 1 cup, boiled	210
Lentils, ½ cup, cooked	179
Beans, white, ½ cup, boiled	144
Broccoli, ½ cup, cooked	104
Spinach, ½ cup, cooked	103
White pasta, ½ cup, cooked	98
Romaine lettuce, 1 cup	76
Papaya cubes, 1 cup	51

Folate Content of Food[267]

Supplements That May Help Treat Depression

Vitamin B12 plays a crucial role in supporting our nervous system. Recent studies reveal that one in four adults in the United States is deficient in vitamin B12 and nearly half of the population has suboptimal blood levels.[268] Vitamin B12, which can only be found in animal foods such as liver, kidney, meat, fish, shellfish, milk products and eggs, has been shown to help depression.[269] If supplementing with vitamin B12, it is recommended that B12 and folic acid be taken together.[270]

- A deficiency of vitamin B12 has profound effects on several neurotransmitter systems and results in significantly reduced norepinephrine, serotonin and dopamine levels in the brain, which may lead to depression.[271]
- Vitamin B12 supplementation can help with sleep disorders as the nutrient is involved in the production of melatonin.[272]
- Researchers have found that those of us who are depressed also tend to be high in homocysteine and deficient in B6,* B12 or folic acid and that supplementing with these vitamins may improve depression.[273]

---

* Some people find they respond better to the biologically active form of vitamin B6 called P-5-P.

- Another safe and effective treatment for depression is S-adenosylmethionine (SAM-e).[274] SAM-e is made from the amino acid methionine, but vitamin B12 and folic acid also play a crucial role in its creation.[275] A 2002 research review concluded that compared to placebo, three weeks of treatment with SAM-e was associated with a significant improvement in depression.[276] TMG is a supplement that is cheaper substitute for SAM-e.

According to Wolfgang Lutz, MD and Christian Allan, PhD, authors of the book *Life Without Bread*, diets high in carbohydrates (grains, fruits and vegetables) can cause elevated homocysteine levels.[277] Vegetarian or vegans have higher levels of homocysteine compared to people who consume high amounts of fat and meat.[278] [Vegetarians and vegans are also at risk for developing deficiencies in certain amino acids—tryptophan, methionine and lysine—which are important building blocks for our neurotransmitters.] If meat eaters are eating too many carbohydrates and not enough animal foods, their homocysteine level may be elevated as well.

Drs. Lutz and Allan recommend a diet high in animal fat and low in carbohydrates in order to maintain a low homocysteine level in the blood. For a healthy homocysteine level, be sure to eat sufficient amounts of animal foods such as beef, liver, oysters, eggs, raw dairy products, along with some whole grains (soaked and fermented) and green vegetables.

Pyroluria

Pyroluria is also known as HPU (hemopyrrollactamuria). It is a genetic blood disorder that creates by-products during hemoglobin synthesis, which bind to zinc and B vitamins—especially vitamins B6, B5 and B3—and cause deficiency symptoms of these nutrients. Pyrolurics also tend to have low levels of manganese, taurine and the omega-6 fatty acid arachidonic acid. A by-product of pyroluria is the gradual exhaustion of the adrenal glands. This can result in hard-to-treat depression and other mental health conditions. The following questionnaire may help to determine if you or someone you care about has pyroluria. There are several labs that test for pyroluria, including the Bio Center Laboratory (800-494-7785) or Vitamin Diagnostics (732-583-7773).

If you answer "yes" to several of the following questions, you may have pyroluria:

- Do you have little or no dream recall or nightmares?
- Do you struggle with cluster headaches or migraines?
- Do you have or have you ever had bouts of persistent constipation?
- Do you have a tendency to skip breakfast or have morning nausea?
- Do you have white spots on fingernails?
- Do you have pale skin, poor tanning, or burn easily in the sun?
- Are you sensitive to bright light?
- Are you sensitive to loud noises?
- Are you experiencing reading difficulties (e.g., dyslexia)?
- Are you overly dramatic?
- Are you argumentative?
- Do you experience mood swings or temper outbursts?
- Are you more alert and active in the evening compared to mornings?
- Do you have abnormal body fat distribution?
- Do you have a tendency toward iron-deficiency anemia or test borderline?
- Do you have stretch marks even without a large weight gain or weight loss?
- Do you tend to be apathetic or pessimistic?
- Do you feel fatigued or depressed?
- Do you struggle with anxiety?
- Have you ever struggled with addiction?
- Do you have a low tolerance for alcohol or drugs, including caffeine?
- Do you have members in your immediate or extended family with mental health problems?
- Do you have unusual smelling breath and body odor?
- Is it difficult to recall past events or people in your life?
- Do you tend to be a loner or prefer the company of one or two close friends rather than a gathering of friends?
- Have you ever been a vegetarian?
- Do you dislike eating protein?
- Are you prone to developing acne, eczema, or psoriasis?
- Do you have a poor appetite?
- Do you have a pain or creaking in your knees?
- Do you have tingling sensations in your arms or legs?

Not all the symptoms are present for everyone struggling with pyroluria, but any number of them should make you suspicious.

If you believe that you may be lacking important nutrients, you can work with a qualified health practitioner who has access to labs that can test for imbalances or deficiencies through blood, urine or hair analysis. Interestingly, when it comes to our mental health, the nutrients we appear to be most deficient in seem to be most abundant in animal foods. Taking unrefined sea salt and/or specific supplements will help restore the nutrients we need for our nervous system to function properly, but another very practical solution would be to return to a traditional diet, comprised of adequate amounts of animal foods.

CHAPTER 5

SECRETS OF "HAPPY" CHEMISTRY

Increasing the standard of living does not necessarily bring about an increase in happiness. It's a fundamental fact in happiness research. The standard of living has increased dramatically and happiness has increased not at all. And, in some cases, has diminished slightly . . . . Getting rich isn't making us happier. We clearly need something else.[279]

—Daniel Kahneman, PhD,
Professor of Psychology, Princeton University

Our ancestors had the wisdom to know what to do in order to stay physically and mentally healthy. They had no choice but to focus on their needs over wants; consequently, their lives were much less stressful than ours. One of their main priorities was to maximize nutrients—they ate locally produced, organically grown foods, used unrefined sea salt and understood the health benefits of lacto-fermented dairy products and soaking and fermenting grains. They also understood the importance of getting appropriate amounts of sleep, exercise and sunshine. In addition, they did not stress their nervous systems with the thousands of toxic man-made chemicals we are exposed to today. The more we can learn about the healthy dietary and lifestyle habits of our ancestors, the greater the chances that we can build and maintain a healthy and "happy" chemistry.

Buy Local

In a 2003 agricultural census conducted by the USDA, large-scale and corporate farms, representing just 9% of all farms in the nation produced an astounding 73% of total food supply.[280]

The longer the distance food travels, the fewer the nutrients it will contain. Today, on average, our food travels about 1,500 miles. In order to increase your chances of consuming the most nutritious food possible, you could grow your own food or buy your food from small local farms. One of today's popular food trends is to buy food that has been produced within one hundred miles from your home.* Buying local foods means that you will help reduce your carbon footprint and support the local economy. In addition, locally produced foods taste better and they retain more nutrients.[281] If you can find a local farmer who does not use chemical fertilizers or pesticides, organically grown foods tend to contain higher amounts of nutrients. According to the Organic Center for Education and Promotion (OCEP), we can increase our antioxidant intake by 30% by choosing organically grown foods.[282]

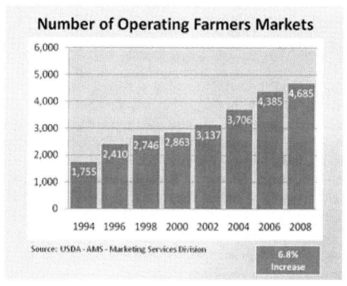

Agricultural Marketing Service/USDA (Public Domain)

An increasing number of savvy consumers are seeking out local foods through CSAs (Community Supported Agriculture), direct sales from local farmers or farmers markets. As you can see by the chart, the number of farmers markets in the United States has been steadily

---

*   Be sure to read the book *The 100-Mile Diet* by Alisa Smith and J. B. MacKinnon—a book about their attempts to eat only food grown within 100 miles of their home. More information about sourcing local foods can be found in the appendix found toward the end of this book.

increasing over the last 15 years or so. Even though farmers markets are supposed to be selling local foods, this is not always the case. If you do buy your food from a farmers market, be sure to verify with vendors about where the food has been grown or produced. Occasionally, you may discover that vendors are brokering foods that have been shipped in from miles away.

Salt Your Way to Health

Water and salt are necessary for metabolism, detoxification and transportation of nutrients as well as optimal functioning of the hormonal, nervous and immune systems.[283]

—David Brownstein, MD, *Salt Your Way to Health*

Our ancestors consumed significantly more minerals than we do today. They followed sustainable agricultural practices and respected soil fertility. They knew that fertile soils produced nutrient-dense foods. Our new industrialized agricultural practices do not respect soil quality and as such, produce foods that are deficient in many important nutrients. According to Donald R. Davis, PhD, FACN, a former research associate with the Biochemical Institute at the University of Texas, Austin, food not only tastes worse than it did in your grandparents' days, it also contains fewer nutrients.[284] Dr. Davis claims the average vegetable found in today's supermarket is anywhere from five to 40% lower in minerals (including magnesium, iron, calcium and zinc) than those harvested 50 years ago.

Because our foods are nowhere near as nutritious as the foods our ancestors consumed, we risk becoming deficient in several important nutrients, including minerals. In an ideal world, unrefined sea salt could help compensate for the loss of minerals in our food. However, nutritionists and dieticians have been giving us extremely unwise dietary advice by telling us to avoid salt.

It is true that we should avoid common table salt that is highly refined and only contains two elements, sodium and chloride. Because the majority of minerals are removed from most of the commercial salt, we are being deprived of some very essential nutrients. In addition, refined salt causes an imbalance in your mineral levels by supplying it with too much sodium. It is the excessive amount of sodium that is contributing to many of the health problems we see today. Unlike refined salt, unrefined sea salt brings your minerals into balance. It does this because unrefined sea salt contains over 80 minerals, providing a proper balance of nutrients your body needs.

Avoiding the kind of salt we should be consuming, unrefined sea salt, can lead to mineral deficiencies and contribute to the development of chronic disease. For several years now, David Brownstein, MD, author of the book *Salt Your Way to Health*, has successfully treated his chronically ill patients using unrefined sea salt along with a complete holistic program. He believes that unrefined sea salt is vital in the treatment of several health conditions, including debilitating fatigue, depression, allergies, high blood pressure, hypertension, headaches, anxiety, brain fog, seizures, thyroid disorders, fibromyalgia, muscle aches and pains, joint pain, eczema, low libido and blood sugar problems. Over the course of a day, he recommends that his patients take ½ teaspoon of unrefined sea salt in water twice a day—once first thing in the morning and the other shortly before the point in the day when fatigue typically starts setting in.

According to Dr. F. Batmanghelidj, author of *Your Body's Many Cries for Water* and *Water: Rx for a Healthier Pain-Free Life*, consuming a sufficient amount of unrefined salt helps to reduce stress—both physical and psychological. He has found that unrefined salt helps prevent several health conditions, including heartburn, asthma, varicose veins, spider veins and osteoporosis. Furthermore, unrefined sea salt is

- a vitally needed element in the treatment of diabetics and plays an important role in balancing blood sugar levels,
- a natural hypnotic and helps with sleep regulation,
- essential for preserving the serotonin and melatonin levels in the brain,
- important in helping nerve cells in your brain and body to transfer information and
- vital for the absorption of food particles through the intestinal tract.

Rather than scaring us from eating salt, nutritionists and dieticians should have simply told us to avoid processed foods and highly refined table salt and switch to unrefined sea salt. Most unrefined sea salt on the market is pink or grey in color. You will probably spend more for unrefined sea salt, but it is worth every penny.

Be Aware of Common Food Sensitivities

The food industry is in business for one reason—to make a profit. They are not interested in making healthy foods. The thousands of industrially processed foods that line our grocery store shelves not only lack necessary nutrients, they can also interfere with our digestive and immune systems. Since 70% of our immune system is on the lining of the gut, the two systems are closely connected. As such, protecting our digestive system will also help support our immune system.

Two highly processed foods that are difficult to digest are pasteurized dairy products and grain-based products such as breads and pasta. When foods are not properly digested, individuals can develop what are known as "food sensitivities," a somewhat "hidden" condition that causes adverse symptoms, including interfering with neurotransmitter function. It is estimated that up to 75% of the population suffers from food sensitivities. Food sensitivities can contribute to behavioral effects including perceptual and cognitive problems, changes in behavior, mood and emotional response, autism, schizophrenia, ADHD, psychosis, epilepsy and depression.[285]

Two of the most common food sensitivities are to gluten, a protein found in such grains as wheat, barley, spelt, oats, rye and casein, a protein found in dairy products. If grains and dairy products are not properly digested, "feel good" opioid-like chemicals, or morphine-like compounds, can be formed in the brain, creating strong food cravings. Individuals with food sensitivities begin the vicious cycle of addiction, self-medicating with foods rather than drugs.

In order to be properly digested, grains need to be properly soaked and fermented. This is why our ancestors ate sourdough breads. As for dairy products, many people complain that they cannot digest pasteurized dairy products. Generally, when these people switch to raw dairy products*—especially fermented dairy products such as yogurt and kefir—they tend to find that this problem goes away.

People who are the most sensitive to gluten have been found to have low levels of three key neurotransmitters, serotonin, dopamine and norepinephrine.[286] Eliminating certain grains and dairy from the diet can raise the levels of these neurotransmitters back to normal.

---

*   Raw dairy products contain important enzymes that help aid in the digestive process.

Several doctors around the world are now successfully treating their patients by removing commercially processed gluten-containing grains and dairy products from their patients' diets. In his book *Dangerous Grains*, James Braly, MD, outlines dozens of different conditions that could be successfully treated by removing grains from one's diet: autism, schizophrenia, depression, anxiety, ADHD, ADD, cancer, heart disease, MS, lupus, AIDS, sleep disorders, headaches, chronic fatigue, thyroiditis, chronic liver disease, diabetes and so on.

Raw dairy products and grains that have been soaked and fermented (traditionally prepared) may be better tolerated. People with gluten intolerance or celiac disease can tolerate sourdough wheat bread if traditional fermentation techniques are used.[287] Depending upon one's symptoms, therefore, foods such as raw dairy products and traditionally prepared grains may be fine. On the other hand, in certain individuals—especially those with very weak digestive tracts—even these foods could exacerbate symptoms. If this is the case, then it may be necessary to remove even raw dairy products and/or traditionally prepared grains, including sourdough bread, from one's diet until the digestive system is working more efficiently and symptoms have been alleviated.*

If you are interested in learning more about how to prepare grains properly, be sure to read the cookbook *Nourishing Traditions* by Sally Fallon. According to Ms. Fallon,

> soaking allows enzymes, lactobacilli and other helpful organisms to break down and neutralize phytic acid. As little as seven hours of soaking in warm acidulated water will neutralize a large portion of phytic acid in grains. The simple practice of soaking cracked or rolled cereal grains overnight will vastly improve their nutritional benefits. Soaking in warm water also neutralizes enzyme inhibitors, present in all seeds and encourages the production of numerous beneficial enzymes. The action of these enzymes also increases the amounts of many vitamins, especially B vitamins.[288]

---

*   Tip: Another traditional food that has long been recognized for its gut-healing properties is homemade bone broth. Homemade bone broth contains many important healing compounds, including gelatin, that are able to aid in the digestion of food (including grains) and soothe the intestinal tract.

Also, refer to the article "Be Kind to Your Grains . . . and Your Grains Will Be Kind to You" at http://www.westonaprice.org/foodfeatures/be_kind.html.

Keep Gut Flora in Check

All diseases begin in the gut.

—Hippocrates (460-370 BC)

If you have ever felt butterflies in your stomach, you would have realized that your digestive system is closely connected to your emotions and state of mind. Researchers now acknowledge that there is a link between the nervous system and the digestive system. This is why the digestive system (or "gut") is known as our second brain. Food sensitivities can adversely affect our behavior but so, too, can an imbalance in our internal ecosystem or gut flora. As such, it is crucial to make sure your digestive system is working properly.

As Natasha Campbell-McBride, MD, explains in her book *Gut and Psychology Syndrome*, we have an epidemic of compromised gut flora that began in the 1970s and 1980s when doctors began prescribing antibiotics for everything and anything.* Since the gut lining is home to about 70% of the body's immune system, it is essential to keep the gut flora in balance. Antibiotics weaken the immune system by destroying friendly bacteria in the gut, encouraging the overgrowth of yeast and other pathogenic organisms.

The average adult has about 4 to 6 pounds (or 2 to 3 kilograms) of bacteria in the gut. When the flora in our gut are in balance, healthy bacteria can activate neurons in the brain that make serotonin.[289] According to Dr. Campbell-McBride, our gut bacteria, among many other functions,

- have a protective and barrier role against invasive pathogenic microorganisms;
- play a major role in the digestion and absorption of all nutrients;

---

* Antibiotics may be necessary to treat serious infections. They can even save one's life. However, if you or your children take antibiotics, it is important to support your immune system by replenishing your gut with friendly bacteria.

- provide a major source of nourishment and energy for the gut lining;
- synthesize various amino acids, vitamin K, pantothenic acid, folic acid, thiamin (vitamin B1), riboflavin (vitamin B2), niacin (vitamin B3), pyridoxine (vitamin B6) and cyanocobalamin (vitamin B12);
- help recycle bile acids and assist normal cholesterol metabolism and
- have a major immunomodulating role by stimulating antibody production, interferon synthesis and inhibition of IgA degradation (IgA is secreted into the lumen of the digestive tract in response to approaching food and is essential for the proper digestion of that food).[290]

Our Standard American Diet (SAD), which includes lots of denatured processed foods, altered fats and proteins, has set people up for chronic health problems. Breads, crackers, cakes, sweets, potato chips, breakfast cereals, pasta and sweet yogurts are the perfect foods for compromising our gut flora, producing "a river of toxicity flowing from the gut to the brain."[291] An overgrowth of yeast and other pathogenic organisms in the bowel can cause depression and anxiety by degrading tyrosine and tryptophan—important precursors for serotonin and norepinephrine. It can also increase toxic chemical by-products such as ammonia and acetaldehyde, which reduces the production of GABA and dopamine. Renowned Japanese professor Kazudzo Nishi estimated that at least 10% of psychiatric conditions are due to self-intoxication coming from the bowel.[292] Dr. Campbell-McBride believes that "every so-called psychological and mental disorder is a digestive disorder at its core—whether it is substance abuse, schizophrenia, bipolar, obsessive-compulsive behavior, depression or just a cranky teenager—look first at their digestive system."[293]

In order to encourage the growth of healthy organisms in your gut, it is important to consume raw milk and lacto-fermented foods, such as kefir, yogurt and sauerkraut. Consuming raw milk derived from trustworthy local farmers who raise healthy, grass-fed cows is an excellent way to take in the beneficial bacteria that help encourage the growth of healthy bacteria (flora) in your gut. Fermented foods, including kefir, yogurt and sauerkraut, also help support our gut flora. Beneficial lactic acid bacteria are produced during the fermentation process. Initially, fermentation was used as a way to preserve foods. However, our ancestors also learned that fermented foods had powerful healing properties.[294] Ideally, you should make kefir, yogurt and sauerkraut at home, as store-bought versions of these foods will more than likely be pasteurized and/or contain unwanted additives. If it is not possible for you to obtain these foods, then it may be necessary to supplement with probiotics.

> I believe that all lactic acid products, buttermilk, sour milk, clabber milk, koumiss, Leben, kefir and yogurt, are invaluable in the treatment of the sick and their use is deservedly increasing . . . . In certain medical circles . . . there is no particular profit in prescribing these simple foods as there is in dispensing medicines.[295]
>
> —Charles Stanford Porter, MD,
> *Milk Diet as a Remedy for Chronic Disease*, 1905

Fermented foods have the following benefits:

- Fermentation increases the vitamin and amino acid content of the food.[296]
- The health-promoting microorganisms that are formed during lacto-fermentation produce beneficial enzymes that help digest the food.
- Substances in fermented foods have been found to increase resistance to intestinal infections, stimulate the immune system and possibly protect against cancer.[297]
- The lactic acid bacteria found in fermented dairy products are also known to release compounds that may help prevent infections and tumors.[298]

To help heal and seal the gut, Dr. Campbell-McBride recommends the removal of commercially processed foods and the addition of a traditional, whole foods diet including foods such as meat, fowl, eggs, fish, lamb, animal fats (butter and lard), kefir, yogurt, bone broth, sauerkraut and nuts.*

---

* Since 90% of a successful treatment protocol relies on the diet, Dr. Campbell-McBride only recommends a few supplements, including

Hydrochloric Acid (HCL)

In order to keep gut flora in check, it is also important to make sure your stomach is producing enough hydrochloric acid (HCL). HCL is an acid produced in our stomachs that helps break down protein into amino acids.* An adequate level of acid in your stomach helps to discourage the growth of unwanted bacteria, yeast and parasites in the intestines.

Poor diet, stress and the aging process can reduce our levels of hydrochloric acid. It is common to find deficient levels of hydrochloric acid in individuals who follow diets high in carbohydrates—including vegetarians and vegans.[299] If you are not producing enough HCL in your stomach, you may not be properly absorbing certain minerals or vitamin B12, nutrients which support your mood.

If you are suffering with digestive difficulties (burping, gas, heartburn, a heavy feeling after eating a meal, constipation, diarrhea), you may be deficient in stomach acid and should consider taking a supplement called hydrochloric acid (normally, this supplement contains another digestive enzyme called pepsin). It is believed that the regular use of supplemental HCL can "re-train" the stomach to produce higher concentrations of acid on its own.

Absence of hydrochloric acid in the gastric juice is a common symptom in depressive neuroses. It is frequently associated with mental fatigue, persistent worry and strain especially in persons with a congenital unstable psyche. The symptoms are very vague, lack of appetite, fullness after eating, gaseous eructations and diarrhea is more common than constipation. Pain is absent.[300]

—Thomas McPherson Brown, MD
(1906-1989)

---

therapeutic-strength probiotics, gamma-linolenic acid (GLA) and cod liver oil. (Campbell-McBride, p. 179)

*   Protein needs to break down into amino acids which then fuel the rest of our body, including our neurotransmitters.

An excellent book about the many benefits of hydrochloric acid is called, *Why Stomach Acid is Good for You* by Jonathan V. Wright, M.D. and Lane Lenard, Ph.D. Dr. Wright recommends starting with one capsule of betaine HCL containing about 650 mg, with pepsin, at the early part of each meal.

In order to determine how much HCL you may need, start by taking one capsule per meal. Monitor how your stomach feels after eating. If any burning you have been experiencing has been worsened by the use of HCL, then do not continue using this supplement. If the first dose of HCL produced no noticeable stomach discomfort, try taking two capsules with your next meal. Again, monitor for a burning sensation after eating. If taking two capsules produces some discomfort, but one capsule does not, restrict yourself to one capsule with each meal. If the two capsule dose produced no discomfort, try three capsules with your next meal. When you reach a dose where you feel a burning sensation, return to the previous dosage and stick with that. Some individuals may need up to seven capsules per meal. If this is the case, then Dr. Wright recommends taking half the dose after the first few bites, then the rest halfway through the meal. Taking a digestive enzyme supplement with your meals, containing pancreatin, amylase, protease, lipase and ox bile, may also help support your digestion.

For individuals who cannot tolerate HCL, lemon or vinegar diluted with water may be helpful. Start off with one teaspoon of freshly squeezed lemon juice or vinegar mixed with anywhere from four to eight ounces of water and gradually increase to one tablespoon. Drink this mixture about 20 minutes prior to each meal.

Avoid Infections—Keep Your Immune System Strong

Not only can environmental toxins, digestive disorders, food sensitivities, malnutrition and caffeine interfere with your nervous system, so can infections. How many people do you know who say that they never felt quite right again after having a serious case of the flu?

Infectious agents could play a role in causing various neuropsychiatric disorders including schizophrenia, autism, depression and obsessive-compulsive disorder.[301] According to E. Fuller Torrey, MD, of the Stanley Medical Research Institute, Bethesda, Maryland, "many infectious agents have been shown to act directly on neurotransmitters, including dopamine, serotonin and GABA. In addition, infectious agents in the developing brain, both in utero and in childhood, could well account for neurodevelopmental abnormalities."[302] Author of the book *The Edge Effect*, Eric Braverman, MD, writes that "in order to maintain optimal health, it's important to keep your body free of infections. Even the smallest infections can affect our brain in many ways. Infections can trigger an abnormal immune response, resulting in drastic illnesses, including mental disorders and some cancers . . . . When you are infected with the flu, your dopamine level is diminished."[303]

To help ward off infections, it is important to keep your immune system strong. This means eating the right foods and getting the appropriate amounts of sleep and exercise. Another extremely important thing we can do to support our immune system is to make sure we are getting enough vitamin D. Vitamin D is one of the most powerful antimicrobials we know of.* The best way to get vitamin D is from exposure to the sun, but you can also find vitamin D in foods such as butter, liver or cod liver oil. According to John Cannell, MD, vitamin D has profound effects on human immunity.[304] Research shows that vitamin D may also act as a potent antibiotic by increasing the body's production of naturally occurring antimicrobial peptides.[305] For more information about vitamin D (including dosage and testing), be sure to visit Dr. Cannell's Web site, www.vitamindcouncil.com.

Avoid Neurotoxins

As we have seen, supporting our inner ecology helps to support our nervous system. We can also protect our nervous system by avoiding external environmental toxins. Unlike our ancestors, we are exposed to over 75,000 improperly regulated man-made chemicals in our environment.[306]

Exposure to neurotoxins can compromise our neurotransmitters and have large and long-lasting effects upon behavior and cognition.[307] According to a 2005 report by the General Accountability Office, the U.S. Environmental Protection Agency is failing to protect the public from tens of thousands of toxic compounds because it has not gathered data on the health risks of most industrial chemicals.[308] Many environmental toxins can act as trigger neurological problems in certain individuals. Author of *Multiple Chemical Sensitivity: A Survival Guide*,

---

*   There is a very good reason why, for generations, mothers made sure that their children got plenty of fresh air and sunshine!

Pamela Reed Gibson, PhD, says that there are many symptoms that people can experience from chemical exposure including tiredness/lethargy, difficulty concentrating, muscle aches, memory difficulties, long-term fatigue and depression.[309]

Do your best to protect your family by avoiding environmental toxins including molds and pollen and synthetic, man-made chemicals. Dozens of commercial household products can contain extremely toxic ingredients that could be interfering with your nervous system. Some of the most obvious offenders are scented products such as soaps, shampoos, conditioners, hairspray, body lotions, candles, air fresheners, laundry detergents, incense, cosmetics and perfumes. Other potential offenders include the following:

- Tap water—fluoride
- Traffic exhaust or gasoline fumes
- Phthalates/plasticizers (in everything from children's toys to shower curtains)
- Secondhand smoke
- Nail polish remover
- Newspaper ink
- Paint or paint thinner
- Pesticides (On average, we consume a gallon of neurotoxic pesticides and herbicides annually by eating conventionally grown fruits and vegetables.[310])
- Artificial colors, sweeteners, flavor enhancers and preservatives in food
- Alcohol
- Formaldehyde
- Cleaning products
- Adhesive tape
- New carpet
- Flame retardants on clothing and furniture (such as mattresses)
- Felt tip pens
- Chlorinated swimming pools
- Outdoor pollutants
- Printing and office products

As consumers, it is important for us to apply the scientific mantra, the "precautionary principle" in our lives. That is, "if in doubt, leave it out." Be sure to get rid of any questionable household items and replace them with safer alternatives. Several Web sites and books can educate you about how to minimize your exposure to everyday toxic chemicals. To help get you started, be sure to visit www.safecosmetics.org or Debra Lynn Dadd's Web site, www.dld123.com.

Sunshine

Sunshine on my shoulders makes me happy, sunshine in my eyes can make me cry. Sunshine on the water looks so lovely, sunshine almost always makes me high.

—John Denver

Vitamin D researcher Dr. Reinhold Vieth says that the minimal daily requirement of vitamin D should be in the range of 4,000 IU from all sources, including sunshine. Depending upon where you live in the world, it may be difficult to get enough sunshine to make the vitamin D your body needs, especially during the fall, winter and spring. Ideally, full exposure to sunshine for 20-30 minutes per day when the sun is reasonably high should make about 10,000 IUs of vitamin D.

Aside from producing vitamin D in the body, sunshine is also known for its ability to increase our "feel good" neurotransmitter, serotonin. If you cannot find the time to get outside during the day, you could invest in special lamps that have been designed to help simulate the sun. Research shows that they may help treat seasonal affective disorder and depression.[311] Bright light not just improves mood but also helps at being more sociable, happier and more pleasant to be with.[312] "Light cafes" pioneered in Scandinavia are now being used in the United Kingdom to help people alleviate their "winter blues."[313]

Exercise

We now have evidence to support the claim that exercise is related to positive mental health as indicated by relief in symptoms of depression and anxiety.[314]

—Daniel M. Landers, PhD, Arizona State University

By enhancing neurotransmitters, including our feel-good neurotransmitters such as serotonin and the endorphins and reducing levels of stress hormones, appropriate amounts of exercise can have a positive impact on our psychological well-being (decreased depression, improved mood, reduced anxiety, fatigue, sadness, irritability, anger, self-doubt, hopelessness, stress and so on).[315]

Even for healthy adults, excessive exercise can be counterproductive. So be careful. If you are experiencing some health challenges, then you may want to start with something as simple as deep breathing or stretching. You may need to experiment until you find what form of exercise works best for you. Also, be sure that you *enjoy* the type or types of exercise you choose so that you will be motivated to keep doing it.

Sleep

The amount of sleep one needs varies from person to person. But generally, adults need anywhere from 7 to 8 hours of deep, restorative sleep per night.

As many as 70 million Americans may be affected by chronic sleep loss or sleep disorders, at an annual cost of $16 billion in health care expenses and $50 billion in lost productivity.[316] Research shows that sleep deprivation can lead to poor mood, and insomnia is a common symptom of depression.[317] The majority of people suffering from addictions, or in recovery, do not get enough sleep, that, in turn, makes them less likely to quit their addiction and more likely to relapse.[318] In their book, *How to Quit Without Feeling S**t*, Patrick Holford, David Miller, PhD and James Braly, MD, write that "sleep-deprived individuals are twice as likely to develop an addiction, twice as likely to feel anxious and four times more likely to feel depressed."[319]

In 2008, consumers spent a whopping $19 billion dollars on prescription sleep medications.[320] Not only are sleeping pills potentially addictive, taking them will more than likely make matters worse for you. There is plenty of evidence that sleeping pills cause major harm and little evidence of clinically meaningful benefit.[321] Ironically, sleeping pills are not very effective. In a study conducted by the American National Institutes of Health, drugs like Ambien (zolpidem) only made volunteers fall asleep 12.8 minutes faster than when they had taken a placebo and slept for a mere 11 minutes longer.[322]

To help get a good night's sleep, it is important to learn good sleep hygiene—and that includes avoiding caffeine and alcohol, especially in the evening. To help set the tone for a restful sleep, other healthy habits include the following:

- Use the bed only for sleep and sex.
- Remove electronic devices, such as TV and computer, from the bedroom.
- Ensure that the bedroom is dark and cool—open a window for fresh air.
- Take a hot bath before bed.
- Listen to soothing music.
- Read positive or inspiring books.
- Avoid eating a big meal before bed.
- Avoid exercising after 7 pm.
- If you have cold feet, wear a nice warm pair of socks to bed.

If these healthy sleep habits are not enough to help you get a good night's sleep, then you may need to turn to the aid of supplements. Certain supplements, such as vitamin B12, magnesium, melatonin, tryptophan, inositol, GABA, phosphatidylserine, may help you feel more relaxed so that you can fall asleep. Make sure that you work with a qualified health care practitioner to help you decide that supplements are best for you.

Relaxation

If sleep, sunshine and exercise are not helping you to balance out your biochemistry, then you may benefit from various forms of therapeutic relaxation techniques, including massage, reflexology, acupuncture, meditation and so on.

- Massage therapy supports our nervous system by decreasing the stress hormone cortisol and increases serotonin and dopamine in patients with depression.[323]
- Research shows that acupuncture has significant benefits for depressed adults.[324]
- Meditation can increase the release of dopamine.[325]

In their book *Stress Solution*, Penny Kendall-Reed, ND and Stephen Reed, MD describe the destructive effects of stress and emphasize the importance of relaxation. Our ancestors had to deal with stress, but nowhere near to the same levels we are facing today. Therefore, it is important to counter the effects of our modern day stressors by integrating relaxation techniques in your life as often as you can. Drs. Kendall-Reed and Reed point out that proper relaxation techniques also support the hypothalamus—pituitary—adrenal axis, or HPA axis, a major part of the neuroendocrine system* that controls reactions to stress.

Hypothalamus—Pituitary—Adrenal Axis (HPA Axis)

The HPA axis refers to the hypothalamus, pituitary and adrenal glands. Researchers and clinicians have discovered a link between the dysregulation of the HPA axis and chronic mood disorders including anxiety disorders, depression, bipolar disorder, insomnia, post-traumatic stress disorder, borderline personality disorder, ADHD, burnout, chronic fatigue syndrome, fibromyalgia, irritable bowel syndrome and alcoholism.[326]

Many stressors can dysregulate the HPA axis, including infection, malnutrition, blood sugar irregularities due to a diet high in carbohydrates (especially refined carbohydrates such as juice, sugar and other commercial sweeteners including high fructose corn syrup, aspartame etc.) and skipping meals, chronic and acute psychological stress, sleep deprivation, excessive physical stress such as over exercising, head injuries and drugs, including caffeine, alcohol and cocaine.

The HPA axis controls reactions to stress and regulates many body processes, including digestion, body temperature, hunger, thirst, heart rate, sleep, the immune system, mood and emotions, sexuality, and energy storage and expenditure. The hypothalamus gland is located in

---

* The neuroendocrine system pertains to the nervous system plus the endocrine system and the interactions between them. The endocrine system is a system of glands, each of which secretes a type of hormone to regulate the body. The nervous system is the system of cells, tissues and organs that regulates the body's responses to internal and external stimuli.

the base of the brain and is the main regulatory center in the body. Its role is so crucial, if the endocrinal glands were a football team, then the hypothalamus would be the quarterback. The hypothalamus secretes hormones that control the pituitary gland. The pituitary gland, located in the base of the brain in close proximity to the hypothalamus, is considered the "master gland" of the endocrine system because it secretes hormones that control other glands, including the ovaries, testes, adrenals and thyroid glands.

In order to support your HPA axis, it is important to minimize stress in your life. As mentioned, this can be accomplished through relaxing therapies such as acupuncture, massage and reflexology. Avoid over exercising. Instead, choose activities such as light walking, yoga, stretching, deep breathing, weight lifting, meditation, prayer, tai chi or qigong. Get adequate amounts of high quality, restorative sleep. It is also important to regulate your blood sugar levels. To do this, be sure to eat three square meals—including adequate amounts of animal fats—in each meal. These meals should be timed appropriately throughout the day (i.e., immediately upon arising for breakfast, five hours later for lunch and five hours later for dinner). If you wish to snack in between meals, choose foods such as nuts, meat, high fat cheese or plain high fat yogurt with a little fruit. Keep your immune system strong by getting proper amounts of sunshine, exercise, vitamin D, and eating foods which support the gut lining such as bone broth, sauerkraut, yogurt and kefir.* Additionally, it goes without saying that you should avoid, or at least limit your exposure to drugs, including caffeine, nicotine, sugar and alcohol.

Finding natural approaches that could help to regulate the HPA axis may be promising treatments for mood disorders and addiction. Further research needs to be conducted in this area, however. Glandular supplements such as hypothalamus, pituitary and adrenal are available through health food stores and may be viable options. Herbal supplements, known as adaptogens, are commonly used to help our bodies 'adapt' to stress. Adaptogenic herbal remedies can include ingredients such as

---

* In order to make sure you are getting the highest quality broth, sauerkraut, yogurt or kefir possible, prepare these foods on your own. Also, the kefir and yogurt should be high in fat.

licorice, ginseng, ashwagandha root, schisandra chinensis and rhodiola rosea.

In Memory of Three Square Meals

Our ancestors understood the importance of eating three square meals. If you wait too long in between meals or skip meals, your blood sugar levels drop (hypoglycemia), making you feel irritable or tired. The more you skip meals, the more stress you put on your body. To make matters worse, many individuals start their day off with a cup of coffee and/or high carbohydrate foods such as cereals, breads and juice—terrible habits which destabilize our biochemistry.

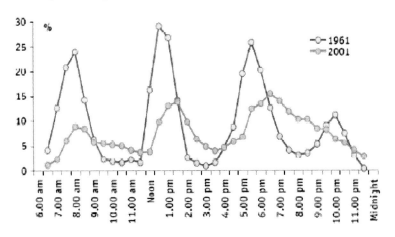

Food: an analysis of the issues, The Strategy Unit, Cabinet Office, UK, January 2008 (Updated August 8, 2008).[327] Used by permission.

The practice of skipping meals began about 200 years ago during the Industrial Revolution, when our lives became busier. Of course, over the last 50 years, our lives are busier yet and the problem has only worsened.

Breakfast has always been considered the most important meal of the day, but because of our fast-paced lives, things have changed. According to Mark Pendergrast, author of *Uncommon Grounds*, prior to the Industrial Revolution "people typically ate five times a day, beginning with soup for breakfast . . . . As women and children entered the organized workforce, there was less time to run a household and cook meals . . . . Because coffee was stimulating and warm, it provided an illusion of nutrition."[328]

- Scientists at the Cancer Research UK Health Behavior Unit, University College London, discovered that teenagers who were stressed were less likely to have eaten breakfast and more likely to have other unhealthy eating patterns.[329]
- In a survey conducted by *ABC News*, nearly 4 in 10 adults usually skip breakfast entirely.[330]
- Based on surveys, more than 90% of the students at eight Ivy League schools said they do not consume anything except coffee before 11:30 a.m.[331]

Studies show that a breakfast consisting solely of coffee will cause a drop in blood sugar levels, causing an increase in hunger, fatigue, lassitude, irritability, nervousness, exhaustion and headaches.[332] A high-carbohydrate breakfast, consisting of juice, toast and jam, boxed cereal, low-fat milk and sugar will also quickly raise blood glucose levels, resulting in similar symptoms. Walter Futterweit, MD, FACP, FACE, a specialist in diabetes and other endocrine disorders at the Mount Sinai School of Medicine in New York City explains that when you start the day with refined carbohydrates, "you're getting a sudden burst of pure sugar, which causes an immediate release of insulin. An hour or two later, you may start feeling edgy, irritable, have difficulty concentrating and you're driven to eat again."[333]

In her clinical practice, psychotherapist Julia Ross notices that clients who consume plenty of protein and fresh vegetables three times a day and avoid caffeine and processed foods feel much better physically and emotionally than clients who consume caffeine and a high-carbohydrate, processed foods diet. To summarize her dietary recommendations, she offers the following nutritionally sound advice in her books, *The Diet Cure* and *The Mood Cure*:

- Do not skip meals.
- Eat at least 25% of the day's calories at breakfast.

- Do not undereat.
- Start your meals with plenty of protein—20 grams or more of protein per meal.
- Eat 4-5 cups per day of low-carbohydrate vegetables, such as zucchini, asparagus, broccoli, green beans and cabbage with your protein. Eat some red and yellow vegetables too.[334]
- For snacking, eat fruit or vegetables with proteins.
- Be sure to include some good fats in each meal.
- Stop counting calories and fat grams.[335]

On top of the fats that should be naturally occurring in meats, eggs and fish, she also recommends extra virgin olive oil for salads, coconut oil, butter, ghee (clarified butter), avocados and coconut milk.

Examples of healthy protein servings at a meal:

- 3 eggs (24 grams of protein)
- 3 ounces tuna (22 grams of protein)
- 2/3 cup or 5.3 ounces cottage cheese (20 grams of protein)
- 3-4 ounces meat, fish or poultry, approximately the size of the palm of your hand (20 grams of protein)[336]

If you want to reduce stress, and stay energized, up-beat and alert, it is important to normalize your blood sugar levels by eating three square meals per day, including a hearty breakfast comprised of adequate amounts of animal protein and fat, including, for example, 2-3 eggs, bacon or sausage, buttered sourdough bread and full-cream milk.[337] [Hopefully, you can obtain most of these foods from a small local farm where the animals are allowed to graze on pasture.] In other words, if you can imagine what your great-great-great grandparents would have eaten, you will be close to understanding this important piece of our food history.

Our ancestors had the wisdom to know what they needed to do in order to achieve optimal health. They did not have well-equipped laboratories, fancy medical equipment or expensive pharmaceutical drugs. Even though we spend trillions of dollars on our health care, chronic diseases account for about 85% of all deaths.[338] In addition, since spending all of this money on our health care, our mental stability has declined dramatically. It is really no mystery as to why we are so sick. Unfortunately, a great deal of "clutter"—marketers, greed, bad science and an overall sense of chaos—prevents us from learning the truth about our health. Fortunately, now that you are armed with the correct information, you will not be a victim of this unhealthy chaos and can take better control of your mental and physical health.

CHAPTER 6
THE ROLE OF NEUROTRANSMITTERS

To a significant degree, compulsive behaviors can be explained neurochemically. Once you come to understand and utilize this knowledge with your clients, it all begins to make sense to them and you.

An alteration in the balance of brain chemistries alters our thought, feelings and behaviors. People with well-balanced brain chemistry not only appear enviably assertive, confident, in control, concerned for others and able to think quickly, but will feel these same capabilities within themselves. Alcohol and other drugs present a destabilizing influence to them. They sense chemicals as "dope."

But people who gain positive feelings from chemicals, in spite of adverse effects, may think of these chemicals as "hope." To wage an effective war on drugs and dysfunctional compulsive behaviors, we need to make "peace" with our biochemistry.[339]

—Terry Neher, DDS, CCDS III,
Chemical Dependency Specialist

Over time, drug abuse, alcoholism and eating disorders cause chronic disturbances in neurotransmitter activity and deplete the brain's reserves so badly that it becomes dependent on the outside drugs (or, in the case of eating disorders, excessive stimulation) in order to maintain even a semblance of balance. Take away the drugs and the brain is left "empty-handed"—its reserves exhausted, its ability to produce neurotransmitters severely impaired. At this point, the addicted person starts feeling the symptoms of withdrawal and often rushes back to the drug or behavior that will make him or her feel normal.[340]

—Joseph Beasley, MD, *Food for Recovery*

In this chapter, you will read about how neurotransmitters influence your mood. Neurotransmitters, or what are sometimes referred to as "brain hormones," are tiny chemical messengers that allow various parts of the brain to communicate with each other and with the rest of the body.

As we age, our ability to make neurotransmitters declines. After the age of 20, you could lose 6% of the neurotransmitter dopamine per decade; after the age of 40, 60% of all adults are dealing with some degree of neurotransmitter deficiency.[341] People who are most at risk for developing deficiencies in their neurotransmitters are those who follow fad diets—diets deficient in adequate amounts of animal foods such as high-carbohydrate/low-fat diets, calorie-restricted diets, veganism, meal skipping etc. For example, within two weeks of following a low-calorie diet, your supply of neurotransmitters known as catecholamines can drop by half.[342]

A deficiency in neurotransmitters can cause individuals to feel persistent negative emotions. The reason why people can turn to drugs is that drugs stimulate the neurotransmitters that are deficient, temporarily making them feel better. The problem is that after a person has been using a given drug over an extended period of time, his or her brain can no longer make the neurotransmitter on its own, and he or she must depend upon that substance in order to feel good.

Low beta-endorphin produces low self-esteem. It causes you to seek things that raise your beta-endorphin so you feel better about yourself. The substances and experiences that do this tend to be addictive. They include drugs like alcohol, heroin, morphine and codeine and behaviors like gambling and debting. You remember the rush and go back for more. But after a while you no longer get a rush and you feel terrible when withdrawal hits. Life becomes a search for ways to stave off the withdrawal. This is the cycle of addiction.[343]

—Kathleen DesMaisons, PhD, *Little Sugar Addicts*

Ronald Ruden, MD, PhD, believes that the root of addictive behavior occurs when the neurotransmitters dopamine and serotonin go out of balance: "Addictive cravings are caused by an excess of the neurotransmitter dopamine relative to serotonin. Dopamine drives towards activity ("Gotta have it!"), while serotonin causes the feeling of satisfaction ("Got it!")."[344] Dopamine raises energy, whereas serotonin is calming. When working properly, they create balance in our moods, desires and sense of well-being.

Until recently, scientists knew very little about neurotransmitters. To date, they have identified more than 200 of these brain chemicals. The catecholamines (dopamine, norepinephrine and epinephrine), endorphins and enkephalins, serotonin, GABA and acetylcholine are considered to be among the most important.

The Catecholamines—Dopamine, Norepinephrine and Epinephrine

If your brain is producing adequate amounts of the catecholamine neurotransmitters (dopamine, norepinephrine—or, noradrenaline and epinephrine—or, adrenaline), then you should feel energized, upbeat and alert. If you are not producing enough of these neurotransmitters, then you may feel down, easily distracted, have poor focus and concentration and could possibly be drawn to stimulants such as caffeine, chocolate, or even cocaine to pick you up.

According to Julia Ross, depletion of the catecholamines "accounts for the long-term withdrawal depression that stimulant addicts experience after they quit taking drugs and it's what drives 90% of them back to their drug use."[345]

Generally, addicts turn to drugs in order to stimulate their catecholamines. However, addiction is not just limited to drugs. Activities can stimulate these neurotransmitters as well. Gamblers and compulsive shoppers get a norepinephrine and dopamine rush from their gambling and shopping that temporarily lifts depression and may substitute for feelings of inadequacy. When they purge, bulimics cause a rush of norepinephrine and dopamine, gaining a sense of energetic and pleasurable "control "through this behavior. "Workaholics" get a "rush" from taking on more tasks and from being in control—they are seeking to fill a void of inadequacy with the feelings they get from stimulating their norepinephrine and dopamine.[346]

Dopamine

Dopamine is the most abundant catecholamine in your brain. It can be made from the amino acids tyrosine or phenylalanine.* It is also a building block for the creation of norepinephrine, which, in turn, is further converted into epinephrine. In response to fear, dopamine, norepinephrine and epinephrine are involved in what is known as the "fight or flight" reactions of the brain and body, increasing cardiovascular, respiratory and muscle activity. Dopamine is associated with the integration of our thoughts and feelings. In order to have healthy perceptions of reality, it is important to have balanced levels of dopamine.[347]

Optimal levels of dopamine contribute to arousal, awareness, alertness, assertiveness, respiration, cardiovascular and muscle activity, feelings of pleasure, feelings of attachment/love, sense of altruism—and they make you feel sexy. Some people can experience moderately elevated levels of dopamine, which can cause such symptoms as aggression, impulsivity, irrational behavior, anxiety, fear, feelings of detachment, sleep disturbances and a tendency to take pleasurable activities such as gambling, sex, or eating to an addictive level.[348]

Dopamine deficiencies can cause the following symptoms:

- Anhedonia (the inability to experience pleasure from normally pleasurable life events, such as eating, exercise and social or sexual interaction)
- Depression
- Irritability
- Low energy
- Trouble waking up in the morning
- Have to push self to exercise
- Tendency to gain weight easily and difficulty taking it off
- Need for excess sleep or other sleep disturbances
- Social withdrawal
- Lack of remorse about actions
- Distractibility, inattention
- Lack of ability to feel love, sense of attachment to another

---

* There will be more information on the link between amino acids and neurotransmitters in chapter 7.

- Suicide or preoccupation with thoughts of suicide
- Muscular disturbances and Parkinson's disease
- Tendency to seek out and use stimulating substances including alcohol, amphetamines, caffeine, cocaine, heroin, marijuana, nicotine and sugar (some drugs can raise dopamine levels by up to 1,400%)[349]

Norepinephrine

The neurotransmitter, norepinephrine is essential in all functions of alertness including muscle activity, the constriction and dilation of blood vessels, elevated heart rate and breathing. When adequate norepinephrine is available, a person feels energetic, motivated and full of "drive." If norepinephrine is lacking, a person has no energy, lacks motivation and drive and feels depressed.

Optimal norepinephrine levels are important for the following:

- Attentiveness
- Emotions
- Sleeping
- Dreaming
- Learning
- Fight-or-flight response

Norepinephrine deficiencies are associated with the following:

- Lack of energy
- Depression
- Weight gain
- Lack of motivation
- Changes in menstruation
- Decreased sex drive
- Foggy or sluggish thinking
- Apathy
- Anorexia and/or bulimia
- Attention deficit disorder
- Insomnia
- Disorientation

- Short-term memory loss
- Male impotence[350]

High levels of norepinephrine can lead to the following:

- Anxiety
- Excess energy
- Racing and pounding heart
- Increased blood pressure
- Decreased insulin release
- Increased breathing
- Weight loss
- Increased sex drive[351]

Endorphins and Enkephalins

The endorphins and the enkephalins are the opioid neurotransmitters. When there are adequate levels of the endorphins and enkephalins, you feel focused, calm and have a sense of completeness. When you feel that "runner's high" after completing a long run, that is because of the release of your endorphins. The endorphins work by moderating physical pain and the enkephalins appear to have a profound effect on emotional memory. If your enkephalin levels are low, you could feel incomplete, inadequate and unworthy. Children with low enkephalin levels may be extremely shy or never quite feel as though they are as good as his/her peers. DL-phenylalanine is an amino acid that increases endorphins and enkephalins.*

Adequate levels of the endorphins and enkephalins play a role in the following:

- Feelings of internal peace
- Sense of well-being
- Feelings of euphoria
- Self-concept
- Pain management

---

* If you are taking an antidepressant medication, you should consult your doctor before taking phenylalanine.

- Psychological pain relief

Deficiencies of the endorphins or enkephalins may contribute to the following:

- Anxiety, internal turmoil
- Fearful, insecure feelings
- Phobias
- Lack of completeness
- Sense of inadequacy
- Feelings of inferiority
- Never feeling equal
- Poor pain control
- Difficulty feeling pleasure
- Tendency toward addictive behaviors (such as alcoholism or smoking) and obsessive—compulsive disorder
- Inability to give or receive affection or love[352]

Starvation, as in anorexia, can increase the opioid neurotransmitters. This is the body's attempt to keep individuals calm while a food source is found. Since these people are not taking in the foods necessary to support the brain, they must emaciate their own muscle tissue for protein. Overeaters also cause an increase of the opioids by overindulging in food, especially pleasant-tasting foods. When they are stressed, they may eat excessively in order to return to calm via enkephalin release.[353]

Serotonin

You don't have to be a drug addict to upset the balance of your brain chemistry. Millions of people do themselves harm through legal and socially accepted means. You might drink gallons of coffee and eat lots of sugar to increase your energy—a dopamine high. Perhaps you get an acetylcholine boost in the form of a regular nicotine fix to help yourself think clearly, or you binge on carbohydrates, a GABA tranquilizer, to feel better. Maybe you consume alcohol, a serotonin enhancer, a little too often so that you can shut down and get to sleep. While self-medicating through diet might seem to work in the short term, it only provides the illusion of solving the problem and over time it can negatively affect your health. The damage from these everyday habits can be as serious as that from drug addiction—it will just take a little longer to show up.[354]

—Eric Braverman, MD, *The Edge Effect*

Our emotional stability relies upon optimal serotonin levels. At her Recovery Systems Clinic near San Francisco, psychotherapist Julia Ross says that serotonin deficiency is the most common mood problem she sees. She believes that serotonin starvation is an epidemic in the United States, contributing to several mood problems. People with low serotonin levels may lack rational emotions, feel depressed, irritable, be bothered by noise, or experience sleep disturbances. Serotonin deficiency could be affecting over 80% of adults in the United States.[355] Eric Braverman, MD, believes that only 17% of the population produces enough of the "feel good" neurotransmitter, serotonin. He describes these people are the ones who are upbeat and know how to enjoy themselves.

Serotonin is responsible for our feelings of well-being, personal security, relaxation, self-esteem, confidence, appetite control, concentration and the ability to have a deep night's sleep.

Low levels of serotonin are associated with the following:

- Irrational emotions, impatience, quickness to anger
- Anxiety, tendency to have panic attacks
- Obsessive thoughts that can't be stopped
- Inflexible behavior patterns that are difficult to stop
- Phobias of all kinds, including fear of heights, of snakes, of leaving the house, etc.
- Fluctuations in appetite, cravings for carbohydrates and sweets
- Eating disorders
- Decline in mood
- Irritability
- Depression
- Premenstrual Syndrome (PMS) in women
- Tendency to be negative and pessimistic
- Dislike of cloudy days, tendency to be depressed during the winter

- Sleep disturbances
- Low energy and fatigue
- Low self-esteem, lack of confidence, tendency to be shy or fearful
- Poor concentration
- Difficulty making decisions
- Decrease in sex drive
- Excessive feelings of guilt and unworthiness
- Violence, antisocial behavior, suicide[356]

In order to build serotonin levels in the brain, the amino acid tryptophan is required. Of the 22 amino acids found in protein, tryptophan is the least abundant; therefore, it can be difficult to obtain adequate amounts of this amino acid. Because tryptophan is crowded out by other important neurotransmitters such as tyrosine and phenylalanine, it has difficulty crossing the blood-brain barrier.

Some researchers believe that small amounts of carbohydrates are necessary to help deliver tryptophan to the brain. When we eat carbohydrates, the body secretes large amounts of the hormone insulin to lower the ensuing high blood sugar. The insulin clears most of the competing muscle-building amino acids from the blood, moving them into muscle cells. With most of the amino acids now out of circulation, tryptophan can now easily enter the brain to produce serotonin. When serotonin is synthesized, you may feel sleepy and content. However, it can also result in feeling restless, irritable or inattentive. This is the reason why people with low serotonin often crave carbohydrates. When they feel depressed, stressed or anxious, they eat large amounts of carbohydrates like bread, cakes, pies, ice cream, chips, pizza, candy and so on, which further taxes their nervous system.

Gamma-Aminobutyric Acid (GABA)

The neurotransmitter, GABA, can be made from the amino acid glutamine. It is known as our own natural tranquilizer. GABA is our brain's brake pedal and plays a role in the modulation and lessening of anxiety. Extremely low levels of GABA may be associated with anxiety, panic attacks and eventually convulsions. GABA depletion is associated with delayed stress syndrome and may result in various phobias. GABA accounts for up to 40% of the brain's neurotransmitters.[357]

Low GABA levels are associated with the following:

- Increased anxiety or nervousness
- Feelings of exhaustion associated with stress
- Feeling tense, trouble relaxing, sleeplessness
- Overreacting in stressful situations
- Feelings of being overworked, pressured or overwhelmed
- Seizures[358]

High GABA levels are associated with the following:

- Muscle relaxation
- Quieting effects
- Increased sleep[359]

Acetylcholine

The vitamins choline and B5 help to build acetylcholine, a neurotransmitter which plays an essential role in smooth, coordinated muscle movements and in memory. Low levels of acetylcholine are associated with memory loss, Alzheimer's disease, tardive dyskinesia (uncontrollable jerking movements of the face, tongue and upper body) and decreased sex drive.

Acetylcholine deficiencies are associated with the following:

- Impairment of vision
- Decreased sweating
- Urine retention
- Increased heart rate
- Loss of taste
- Nervousness
- Weakness
- Drowsiness
- Mental confusion
- Impotence
- Insomnia
- Constipation[360]

Nourish Your Neurotransmitters

As we age, we all want to stay happy, mentally alert and energized. This is one of the main reasons why we need to eat the foods that best support our nervous system. Three meals per day, be sure to include adequate amounts of complete protein from animal sources so that you know you are obtaining the amino acids you need to feed your neurotransmitters and support your mental and emotional well-being. While this dietary principle would help anyone—even healthy individuals who are not struggling with addiction—addicts require much more nutritional support. Unlike healthy people, addicts are severely deficient in neurotransmitters. Therefore, in the next chapter, you will read about how targeted amino acid therapy can help repair neurotransmitter deficits in recovering addicts so that they can go on to lead productive happy lives.

CHAPTER 7
NEW ADDICTION RECOVERY TREATMENTS

> If we demand behavioral change from our patients without allowing them to bring their brain chemistry into more positive balance, we simply set them up for failure.[361]

> —Terry Neher, DDS, CCDC III

Ignaz Semmelweis, MD (1818-1865) is known as the Father of Infection Control. He received a tremendous amount of criticism by his medical peers over his view that puerperal sepsis (childbed fever) was a contagious disease spread by contaminated hands of physicians. At the time, childbed fever was a common cause of mortality of young mothers. Semmelweis was fired from his position as the director of a maternity hospital for suggesting that physicians should wash their hands in between patient examinations. Despite the fact that mortality rates declined dramatically after medical students began disinfecting their hands with chlorinated lime water, his views were not widely accepted among the medical community until long after his death.

Like Semmelweis, recovery therapists who have been using nutritional approaches to treat addiction are having a difficult time convincing mainstream treatment facilities of their efficacy. It can take a long time for new ideas to be accepted by society. Imagine how difficult it would have been convincing people that the earth was round after generations of believing it was flat!

Need for Change

For decades now, mainstream medicine and addiction treatment centers have ignored the possibility that nutrition can help in the recovery process. Given their embarrassingly high relapse rates, detoxification centers and drug addiction practitioners truly need to consider new options.

According to Dr. Karen Miotto, director of UCLA's Alcoholism and Addiction Medicine Service, there is a 75-80% relapse rate in most conventional treatment programs.[362] Approximately 80% of addicts who do relapse believe that addiction is virtually incurable.[363] In his book *End Your Addiction Now*, Charles Gant, MD, PhD, explains,

> There's no doubt that traditional drug and alcohol treatment strategies used by most physicians and in most drug and alcohol rehabilitation facilities have enjoyed some success. On average, around 25% of the people who use these traditional methods do recover. But there's a catch: Approximately 20% of all substance abusers recover with no treatment at all. In any case, if you have a substance problem, your chance of recovery through traditional methods is about one in four and I think those are lousy odds.[364]

There are differing views on rates of success using traditional 12-Step programs. A study conducted by Alcoholics Anonymous (AA) following 65,000 patients after completing treatment using their 12-Step program found that "AA attendance proved to be the most powerful predictor of sustained sobriety. Of patients who attended AA at least weekly for one year, 73% stayed sober. Of those who attended AA only occasionally, 53% stayed sober and of those who never went to AA or who quit going, 44% stayed sober."[365] These numbers may sound good, but they do not include information about how well—or unwell—the alcoholics are feeling. Generally, even though they may not be drinking, alcoholics feel lousy and develop unusual behavior patterns. Research shows that 75-95% of recovering alcoholics experience long-term withdrawal symptoms, including depression, anxiety, irritability, nervousness, moodiness, lethargy, fatigue, "brain fog," inability to concentrate, problems with abstract reasoning, irrational thought patterns, obsessive thoughts, poor memory, emotional hypersensitivity (cry easily or temper tantrums), emotional exhaustion, insomnia, dizziness, poor coordination, clumsiness and so on. Unaware that there is a physiological (biochemical) reason for their peculiar behavior, relatives, friends, coworkers and health care professionals may *label* recovering alcoholics as "neurotic," "anxiety-prone," "chronically depressed" or "immature."[366]

> Research does not demonstrate the effectiveness of AA or other 12-Step approaches in reducing the alcohol use and achieving abstinence compared with other treatments . . . . In fact, other treatments that are more effective than the 12 steps . . . are rarely utilized.[369]
>
> —Stanton Peele, PhD, JD, *Addiction-Proof Your Child*

Many recovering alcoholics substitute other addictions such as caffeine, nicotine and junk food for alcohol. Therefore, one has to ask if they have truly recovered. After months of sobriety when, despite what they were promised, not everything has fallen into place, recovering alcoholics may find themselves thinking, "Something must be wrong with me because I'm sober, but I'm definitely not enjoying myself."[367]

The process of identifying and treating neurotransmitter deficits is a crucial part of the recovery process. Chemical dependency specialist, Terry Neher, CCDC III, says that therapy is only helpful when a patient's brain is capable of rational thought.[368] This state is not possible until their neurotransmitters are in balance.

Learning from Success

As we will see in an upcoming interview with Dr. Abram Hoffer, nutritional approaches have been used to successfully treat addictions for several decades now. In the 1970s, Archie Kalokerinos, PhD and Glen Dettman, PhD, published an article *The Orthomolecular Treatment of Drug Addiction: A First Australian Report*, where they described their addiction protocol in detail.[370] On drugs, addicts lose their appetite for food and develop severe protein and vitamin malnutrition. Drs. Kalokerinos and Dettman discovered that chronic addicts suffer from a Hypoascorbemia-Kwashiorkor type of syndrome, a vitamin C and protein deficiency. In order to help heroin addicts recover, they recommended a diet of food rich in protein during the withdrawal phase—foods such as boiled eggs, dairy products, white meats and any fresh fruit or vegetables. They also suggested that addicts avoid junk food, starchy foods and any refined carbohydrates and take vitamin C (in the form of sodium ascorbate), niacin (vitamin B3), a vitamin-mineral complex and a predigested protein supplement.

After the publication of their protocols, Drs. Kalokerinos and Dettman were shocked and frustrated that the media, addiction therapists and health practitioners denied their efficacy.

Another notable pioneer in the addiction field is James Milam, MD, co-founder of Lakeside-Milam Recovery Centers. Originally written in 1981, his book *Under the Influence: A Guide to the Myths and Realities of Alcoholism*, co-authored by Katherine Ketcham, was one of the first books to deal with the role diet played on addiction. In the foreword, Mel

Schulstad, co-founder and past president of the National Association of Alcoholism Counselors, wrote,

> "Under the Influence" will aid and advance by light years the understanding of alcoholism and the recovery process. The labors of Milam and Ketcham in researching, documenting and writing *Under the Influence* have placed us all in their debt. Let us hope that this book will spread light into darkness and bring us closer to a complete understanding of the disease alcoholism and through this new understanding reach millions of our fellow men and women who today are suffering—and dying—because of society's ignorance.[371]

In the 1980s, Julia Ross, psychotherapist and author of *The Mood Cure*, began utilizing nutritional protocols with clients suffering from addictions and mood disorders. She discovered that improving their diets was not enough to get them well. Then she learned about amino acid protocols through the work of Kenneth Blum, PhD, author of *Alcohol and the Addictive Brain* and that of Joan Mathews-Larson, PhD, author of *Seven Weeks to Sobriety* and *Depression-Free, Naturally*. In her book, Ross writes about one compelling study that emphasizes the importance of using amino acid therapy with addicts:

> Raymond Brown, Ph.D., a San Francisco psychologist and addiction specialist, conducted a study in 1989 comparing groups of cocaine addicts who had been given an amino acid formula high in tyrosine and L-phenylalanine with those who got no amino acid supplementation. The results were dramatic: The success rate after ten weeks for those on the amino acid formula was 80%; for those not on aminos, it was 13%! Says Brown, "I would never again try to work with addicts without amino acids."[372]

Joan Mathews-Larson's treatment facility, the Health Recovery Center in Minneapolis, also uses nutritional protocols, including amino acid therapy. She conducted a study to monitor abstinence rates among individuals who had gone through their program. One year after treatment, their success rate was 92%. After 3 1/2 years, 74% of these individuals were still abstinent. Not only do they track abstinence levels, they also take into account the ongoing emotional and physical well-being of clients (mood, sleep patterns, memory and energy levels).

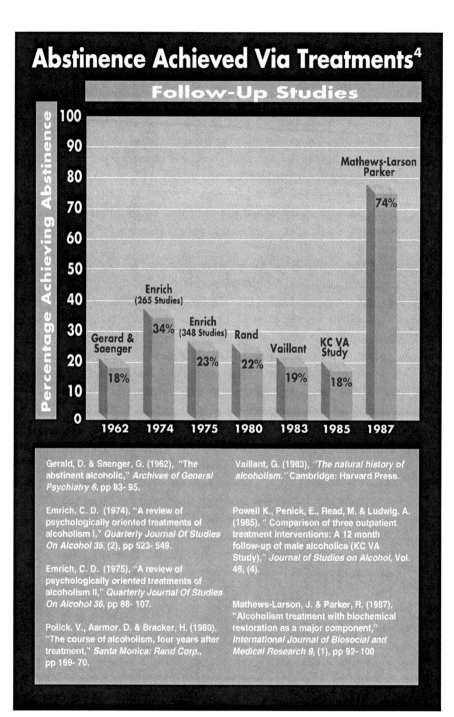

Abstinence Achieved Via Treatments[4]

Follow-Up Studies

Gerald, D. & Saenger, G. (1962), "The abstinent alcoholic," *Archives of General Psychiatry 6*, pp 83- 95.

Emrich. C. D. (1974), "A review of psychologically oriented treatments of alcoholism I," *Quarterly Journal Of Studies On Alcohol 35*, (2), pp 523- 549.

Emrich, C. D. (1975), "A review of psychologically oriented treatments of alcoholism II," *Quarterly Journal Of Studies On Alcohol 36*, pp 88- 107.

Polick, V., Aarmor. D. & Bracker, H. (1980), "The course of alcoholism, four years after treatment," *Santa Monica: Rand Corp.*, pp 169- 70.

Vaillant, G. (1983), *"The natural history of alcoholism."* Cambridge: Harvard Press.

Powell K., Penick, E., Read, M. & Ludwig. A. (1985), " Comparison of three outpatient treatment interventions: A 12 month follow-up of male alcoholics (KC VA Study)," *Journal of Studies on Alcohol*, Vol. 46, (4).

Mathews-Larson, J. & Parker, R. (1987), "Alcoholism treatment with biochemical restoration as a major component," *International Journal of Biosocial and Medical Research 9*, (1), pp 92- 100

Health Recovery Center, Minneapolis, MN
http://www.healthrecovery.com/HRC_2006/AlcoholTreatment.htm

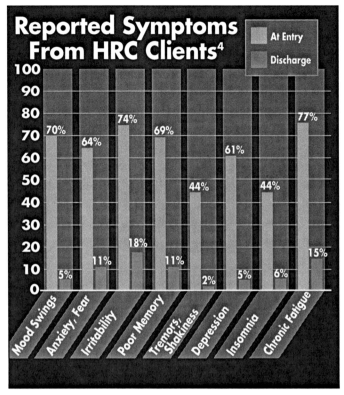

Health Recovery Center, Minneapolis, MN http://www.healthrecovery.com/
HRC_2006/AlcoholTreatment.htm

In 1994, Joseph Beasley, MD, author of the book *Food for Recovery: The Complete Nutritional Companion for Recovering from Alcoholism, Drug Addiction and Eating Disorders*, offered more research to support the role that diet plays on addiction. Led by Dr. Beasley,

> researchers at Brunswick Hospital Center and at Comprehensive Medical Care in New York . . . in conjunction with statistical experts at the State University of New York at Stony Brook, applied a . . . program to 111 patients with severe and chronic alcoholism. All had long and difficult histories of alcohol and drug abuse, with many failed treatment attempts . . . . All had deficient diets, 80% were clinically malnourished, almost two thirds had liver disease and almost half were also addicted to other drugs . . . . The patients spent twenty-eight days in the hospital in a treatment program . . . . In addition to the nutrition education, supplements and a monitored diet,

each patient underwent blood testing to identify potential food allergens . . . . At the end of the twenty-eight days, the patients began a twelve-month program of medical follow-up. In addition to aftercare and AA meetings, patients came in for medical evaluations and workups at least once a month, nutrition counseling and supplements and random urine screens and blood work.

At the end of one year, 91 of the original 111 patients were still in the program. Of these, 74% were sober and stable . . . . After years of reading about failure rates that hovered around 85%, they were finally seeing successful outcomes . . . . Indeed, it should be possible to turn those 85% failure rates to 85% success.[373]

For some time now, therapists have been considering biochemical restoration as the key to successfully treating addiction and mood disorders. As you will learn from the upcoming interviews with therapists from the Alliance for Addiction Solutions (in part 2, section 2), they offer a very comprehensive program that includes eating three wholesome meals per day and identifying and treating problems with blood sugar, thyroid, adrenals, nutritional deficiencies and so on. Regardless of the multi-dimensional nature of their approach, however, they admit that amino acid therapy is truly the secret to their success.

Amino Acid Therapy

As we have seen, brain cells (neurons) communicate through highly specialized chemicals known as neurotransmitters. They play a crucial role in your emotional well-being. However, when neurotransmitters malfunction, you can feel depressed, anxious, fatigued, etc. Blood sugar irregularities, nutritional deficiencies and drug and alcohol abuse can cause neurotransmitters to malfunction.

Most people associate protein with the building of muscle, but it also plays a key role in the development of your neurotransmitters. As you digest protein, it breaks down into small units, known as amino acids. There are two basic categories of amino acids: essential and nonessential. Researchers believe that there are anywhere between eight and eleven essential amino acids. In his book, *The Healing Nutrients Within*, Eric Braverman, MD, writes that the following nine amino acids are now considered to be essential: lysine, leucine, isoleucine, methionine, phenylalanine, valine, threonine, tryptophan and tyrosine.[374] The reason why they are considered "essential" is because your body does not make these amino acids on its own and must come from your diet. Dr. Braverman has done a tremendous amount of research in order to learn how to manipulate the amount of amino acids necessary to maintain health and treat illness. After treating thousands of patients with a variety of health issues, Dr. Braverman believes that "virtually all stress states require more amino acids, some more than others."[375]

Addictive cravings are a sign that the body is under stress and neurotransmitters are malfunctioning. Specific amino acids can work rapidly to help repair weakened neurotransmitters, thus eliminating addictive cravings and improve mood. Therapists with the Alliance for Addiction Solutions believe that for addiction recovery to be effective, individuals must take targeted amino acid supplements—through pills or IV. In many cases the improvement can be dramatic. If, after years of feeling lousy, addicts finally feel better, that might catch their attention and they may actually stay for the recovery process.

Individuals who abuse drugs and alcohol can damage their neurotransmitters. Some of the neurotransmitters that are disrupted by drugs are dopamine, endorphins, serotonin and GABA. While all drugs directly or indirectly affect dopamine, some specific drugs can act on other neurotransmitters. For example, LSD and ecstasy affect serotonin, heroin and morphine alter opiate receptors and alcohol acts on almost every neurotransmitter, but especially GABA and glutamate.[376]

In her book, *The Mood Cure*, Julia Ross has questionnaires that can help determine your neurotransmitter deficits. She summarizes her findings on the Web site for the Alliance for Addiction Solutions as follows:

1) The supplements L-tryptophan and 5-HTP (5-hydroxy tryptophan) are used to manufacture the neurotransmitter serotonin, your brain's natural antidepressant. These supplements may help individuals who crave sweets and starches, use nicotine, marijuana and alcohol for relaxing and comfort when stressed. Individuals struggling with depression may take drugs such as Lexapro, Zoloft, Paxil, Prozac, Effexor or Cymbalta.

2) The supplement GABA (gamma-amino butyric acid) may help individuals who crave carbohydrates, nicotine, marijuana or alcohol. GABA can help alleviate anxiety. Individuals

struggling with anxiety may take prescription tranquilizers such as Valium, Neurontin, Xanax and Ativan.

3) The amino acid D-phenylalanine helps support your endorphins, the pain-relieving "feel good" chemicals. (L-phenylalanine is a form that stimulates the nervous system). D-phenylalanine is a powerful pain reliever without being a stimulant. It is available online. Most health food stores sell a mixed form called DL-phenylalanine. Ross advises against taking D—or DL-phenylalanine if you have melanoma, Grave's disease or phenylketonuria (PKU). Be cautious about taking phenylalanine if you have migraines, Hashimoto's thyroiditis, high blood pressure or manic depression (bipolar disorder). Endorphin-deficiency symptoms include crying easily even over commercials on television, chronic pain, emotional fragility, particularly sensitive to pain. Individuals with endorphin deficiency can crave numbing foods like sweets and starches or use substances like nicotine, marijuana, heroin or alcohol to numb their feelings. These people may take prescription pain relievers like Vicodin or OxyContin.

4) The amino acid L-tyrosine is used to manufacture catecholamines such as dopamine, norepinephrine and epinephrine. These neurotransmitters cause you to wake up in the morning alert and refreshed with a clear mind, able to concentrate and focus on your goals. Catecholamine-deficiency symptoms include fatigue, lack of focus, lack of motivation, depression, apathy, feeling of boredom but no energy to do anything more interesting, possibly diagnosed as having attention deficit disorder (ADD). Individuals who are deficient in catecholamines tend to crave things that will stimulate the nervous system such as sweets and starches, caffeine, aspartame or drugs like methamphetamine and cocaine. These individuals may also use tobacco, marijuana, opiates or alcohol as stimulants; choose risky sports and activities such as gambling or unsafe sex to raise catecholamine levels to feel more alive. Catecholamine-deficient people may take prescription drugs such as Ritalin, Wellbutrin or Adderall. Ross advises against taking L-tyrosine if you have had melanoma, Grave's Disease or phenylketonuria (PKU). Be cautious about taking L-tyrosine

if you have migraines, Hashimoto's thyroiditis, high blood pressure or manic depression (bipolar disorder).

5) The amino acid L-glutamine is a perfect fuel for the whole brain, balancing blood sugar levels to maintain energy and clear thinking. It helps fuel GABA, the relaxing neurotransmitter. L-glutamine may be helpful if you have blood sugar deficiency symptoms such as irritability, shakiness, weakness, dizziness—especially if too many hours have passed since the previous meal. Individuals who crave sweets, starches and alcohol may benefit from taking L-glutamine. Ross advises against taking L-glutamine if you have manic depression (bipolar disorder). While low doses of L-glutamine may relieve bipolar depression, in approximately 50% of bipolar cases normal doses of L-glutamine can trigger mania.[377]

The Drug-Neurotransmitter Connection

Drug	Brain Needs	Useful Amino/ Dosage	Results
Cocaine/ meth	Catecholamines	Tyrosine 1,500-2,000, mg 3x/day	clears thinking, lifts mood/energy
Heroin/ marijuana	Endorphins	DL-Phenylalanine (DLPA) 1,000-2,000 3x/day	relieves pain/sadness, adds pleasure
Prozac	Serotonin	5-HTP 100-200 mg 2-3x/day Or Tryptophan (late afternoon) 500-1,000 mg	stops depression and compulsions, enables sleep
Valium	GABA	GABA (250-1,000 mg 2-4x/day)	calms anxiety, reduces tension
Alcohol and marijuana can affect all the neurotransmitters.			

Adapted and abbreviated from an expanded version found in "Nutritional Rehab." In *The Mood Cure* by Julia Ross. New York: Viking Penguin, 2002, p. 250.[378]

Deficiencies in certain neurotransmitters will determine which drugs an individual will be drawn to. The amino acids listed in the chart help repair the affected neurotransmitters.

Remember, aside from amino acids, in order to make our neurotransmitters, certain vitamins and minerals are also required—for example, to make the "feel good" neurotransmitter, serotonin, the brain requires the amino acid tryptophan along with vitamins B6, B12 and folic acid (vitamin B9). Vitamin B6 is essential in the conversion of tryptophan to serotonin, but this vitamin is also dependent on the presence of the mineral zinc. Some of the best sources for these nutrients are liver, shellfish or meat. Individuals may also supplement by taking a B-complex vitamin or nutritional yeast.

Depression is not a Prozac deficiency. Similarly, ADHD is not a Ritalin deficiency. Mental disorders are a sign that our bodies are deficient in the nutrients that build the neurotransmitters. According to Pfeiffer's law (from the work of Carl C. Pfeiffer, MD, PhD), "For every drug that benefits a patient, there is a naturally occurring substance that can achieve the same effect." By ingesting amino acids like DL-phenylalanine, GABA, L-tyrosine and L-tryptophan, we can rebuild these four missing neurotransmitters and create a safe, non-addictive natural "high." Using a natural substance over a toxic pharmacological agent also eliminates the possibility of adverse side effects.

Low Dose Naltrexone

One very safe drug that is showing promising results in addiction recovery is called low dose naltrexone (LDN). In the 1970s, the prescription drug, naltrexone, was prescribed to treat heroin addicts. The dose used to treat heroin addiction has typically been 50 mg. At this high dose, addicts complained that they felt much worse; consequently, the drug was not very successful.

In 1985, Bernard Bihari, MD, a neurologist and immunologist in New York, pioneered the use of low dose naltrexone (LDN). He discovered that at a much lower dose, LDN could successfully treat many conditions, including HIV/AIDS, pancreatic cancer, prostate cancer, carcinoid cancer, Hodgkin's disease, multiple sclerosis (MS), non-Hodgkin's lymphomas, rheumatoid arthritis, lupus (SLE), lymphocytic leukemia, psoriasis, neuroblastoma, Behcet's disease, colorectal cancer and chronic fatigue syndrome. Research conducted by Dr. Jill Smith, Professor of Gastroenterology at Pennsylvania State University, also shows that LDN could help treat Crohn's disease.[379] Mood disorders, such as depression, are yet other common symptoms that seem to be alleviated using LDN.

Naltrexone works by blocking opiate receptors, thus increasing the supply of endorphins. Endorphins are your "feel good" neurotransmitters which create a feeling of euphoria. Not only can increasing endorphin levels make you feel better emotionally, it can also improve your immune system. By resolving an endorphin deficiency using a non-addictive, inexpensive, safer drug like LDN, individuals may be less likely to turn to addictive substances or activities. Moreover, LDN could also help other immune-related conditions they could be experiencing.

If you spend some time searching for information about LDN online, you will discover many blogs and chat rooms written by people who have been helped by LDN. Some individuals who have been helped by LDN refer to their condition as being caused by endorphin deficiency syndrome (EDS).

At low doses (anywhere from 1.5-4 mg), LDN has little to no side effects and is not addictive. Because it is recommended that individuals take LDN at bedtime, some complain that it can inhibit sleep. If this happens, it may be necessary to take LDN in the morning.

There are several Internet resources (sites, blogs, chat rooms and videos) dedicated to sharing news about the benefits of LDN. One popular site is www.lowdosenaltrexone.org.

Hope for the Future

A century ago, people suffering from epilepsy were regarded as being possessed by "spirits." We now know that epilepsy is a very real neurological disorder. It will take time to educate people that, like epileptics, individuals suffering from addiction are dealing with a very real biochemical disorder. New testing procedures can identify nutritional and neurotransmitter deficiencies, hormonal imbalances (thyroid, adrenal, blood sugar) or heavy metal toxicities, which can then be corrected using sound nutritional protocols along with psycho-spiritual approaches.

The next section includes interviews from a wide variety of people sharing their views about addiction but in part 2, section 2, you will meet several clinicians who belong to an organization called the Alliance for Addiction Solutions. They are having remarkable success in helping people who are struggling with mental and substance use disorders. Their goal is to teach nutritional protocols to other therapists working in the field of addiction recovery.

PART II

I am deeply honored to have interviewed some extremely insightful and progressive individuals for this book. Each interview offers a unique and refreshing perspective on diet, lifestyle, mental health and addiction. The messages offer hope where there would otherwise be none.

Section I
Tribute to Two Pioneers in the Field of Nutritional Medicine, Abram Hoffer, MD, PhD (1917-2009) and Weston A. Price, DDS (1870-1948).

- Interviews with Jurriaan Plesman, clinical nutritionist and Sally Fallon-Morell, MA, President of the Weston A. Price Foundation

Section II
Alliance for Addiction Solutions

- Interviews with Charles Gant, MD, PhD, ND; David Miller, PhD; Joan Mathews-Larson, PhD; Julia Ross, MA; Stan Stokes, MS, CCDC and Carolyn Reuben, LAc

Section III
Our Fast New World Meets Cyberspace

- Interviews with Peter Whybrow, MD and David Greenfield, PhD

Section IV
America's Other Drug Problem

- Interview with John Abramson, MD

Section V
Preventing Future Addicts

- Interviews with Scott Shannon, MD and Natasha Campbell-McBride, MD

SECTION I

A TRIBUTE TO TWO PIONEERS IN THE FIELD OF NUTRITIONAL MEDICINE: WESTON A. PRICE, DDS AND ABRAM HOFFER, MD, PHD, INCLUDING INTERVIEWS WITH SALLY FALLON-MORELL AND JURRIAAN PLESMAN

Men can know more than their ancestors did if they start with a knowledge of what their ancestors had already learned . . . . That is why a society can be progressive only if it conserves its traditions.

—Walter Lippmann
American author and journalist (1889-1974)

MEDICAL PIONEER USES NUTRITION
TO TREAT MENTAL ILLNESS AND ADDICTION
ABRAM HOFFER, MD, PhD (1917-2009)

Dr. Hoffer's Foreword to the Fifth Edition
of
Nutrition and Physical Degeneration

Dr. Weston A. Price published this remarkable book—now a classic work—in which he discussed the anthropology, clinical ecology and nutritional aspects of health, in 1939. The 1970 Heritage Edition contains a foreword by Dr. Granville F. Knight, which is a prescient account of the fruits of modern, high-technology malnutrition. Dr. Knight also provides an outline of corrective measures one can take to overcome some of the defects in our present system. It is 50 years since this great book first appeared. Perhaps now is the time for modern medicine and dentistry to at last take a serious look at what Dr. Price found.

Dr. Price became interested in determining why high-tech societies (and in 1938-1939 high-tech would be considered primitive compared to today) contained so many people whose physical health was so poor, especially their mouths, gums and teeth. He found that people living in areas where the types of food they had been eating had not changed for centuries generally suffered few dental problems; dentists would not have been very affluent then. But as diets changed and approached our high-tech diet, their teeth and the structure of their jaws became more and more like ours. The mass of evidence presented in his clinical descriptions and the many photographs are indeed very persuasive.

Why, then, has the message not been accepted? Mainly, I believe, because very few of the professions either knew about or bothered to read this book. Before World War II, interest in some aspects of nutrition was high and rising, as one vitamin after another was identified and made available. The war and, following that, the introduction of the "wonder drugs" like the corticosteroids and antibiotics turned medical schools away from nutrition, leaving it in the hands of a new profession of dieticians or nutritionists and professors of biochemistry. These professional people could not study the effects of malnutrition firsthand, as they were not able to treat patients. Their interest remained academic and, according to Prof. Ross H. Hall, nutrition became fossilized around 1950. Had clinical nutrition remained alive as a subject in medical schools, physicians reading Dr. Price's book would have been much more sympathetic and moved by it.

There appears to be a 40-year rule in medicine. Major discoveries have required over 40 years before becoming generally accepted. Thus, the English navy added citrus fruits to the navy diet 40 years after Dr. James Lind proved they were curative for scurvy. During those 50 years, an estimated 100,000 English seamen died from scurvy—the high price of delay. I expect the cost of ignoring Dr. Price's conclusions is incalculable.

Dr. Price found that people eating fresh, whole foods, uncontaminated by additives such as sugar and salt, grown on soils still rich in essential minerals, grew and maintained healthy jaws and teeth. In modern terms, people should consume foods they have adapted to over 100,000 years because these foods are essential for health.

He describes the onset of degeneration of people in many societies. Were he to repeat his studies today, he would find that the situation is no better and probably is much worse. The food is even worse: more high-tech, polluted, corrupted and even farther removed from the food to which we have been adapted. The exceptions are people who knowingly avoid all junk food as much as they can.

Dr. Price believed in the innate wisdom of primitive people. I believe in this he was wrong. I do not think there is any inborn wisdom when it comes to nutrition. The best evidence for this is that . . . primitive people who come in contact with high-tech foods soon give up their own diets and adopt the high-tech foods. They appear to be even more susceptible to the sugar, alcohol, white flour and other junk foods present. Perhaps this is because there has been too little time to allow nature to eliminate the worse examples of people damaged by high-tech food.

There is no innate wisdom because, until chemistry was discovered and applied to food technology, there was no need for it. Early peoples had little choice but to eat foods that they had adapted to, for no other food was available. The local animals, fish, whole grains, vegetables, some fruits and nuts provided a limited choice. They could not browse in supermarkets containing 15,000 items of which 90%, or perhaps more, are junk. If primitive peoples had obtained their food from a supermarket, they would have consumed as much junk as do high-tech peoples.

Since there is no inherent wisdom, we must use our intelligence and reason. If we do not, we are all heading for the most serious problem of all time, rivaling the damage to our atmosphere by pollution, which is causing world climatic changes and massive deterioration of our general health.

Recent intergenerational research in animals and people has shown that, on a uniformly poor diet, the offspring of each generation deteriorates more and more, and in rats this continues up to eight generations. We do not know what the final stage will be in human deterioration. I suspect that many of the people with psychiatric disorders today, the addicts, the high degree of violence, the tremendous number of depressions and tension states and the great number of physical degenerations such as diabetes, arthritis, etc., are the modern manifestations of this continuing degeneration. I have seen no experiments, however, which show what happens when the diet continues to get worse with time. I shudder to think of the final outcome.

Even if we eventually become much more intelligent and our society begins to provide the kind of food we have adapted to, it will take many generations before we can regain the earlier health that our genes have programmed us to have, provided we had given them the right tools to work with. I wish we did have some innate intelligence when it comes to nutrition, but I am afraid this is a myth.

In my own practice, I am now seeing children who are the second generation of junk-consuming peoples. The results are obvious and depressing.

I cannot emphasize too much the importance of this book. It should be made compulsory reading for every person who has anything to do with the people's health, especially when it involves their nutrition. Unless we begin to take the message seriously, which was so well described by Dr. Price, I think we are in for some major health catastrophes.

Abram Hoffer, MD, PhD

Victoria, BC, Canada
March 1989

Used with permission from Price-Pottenger Nutrition Foundation (www.ppnf.org)

Abram Hoffer was a pioneer in the field of alternative health. He authored over 500 scientific publications and 15 clinical nutrition books, including *Dr. Hoffer's A.B.C. of Natural Nutrition for Children, Healing Schizophrenia: Complementary Vitamin & Drug Treatments, Healing Children's Attention & Behavior Disorders: Complementary Nutritional & Psychological Treatments* and *Adventures in Psychiatry: The Scientific Memoirs of Dr. Abram Hoffer.* In 1940, he received a master's degree in agriculture (MSA) from the University of Saskatchewan. In 1944, he received a PhD in biochemistry from the University of Minnesota. In 1949, he graduated with an MD from the University of Toronto and completed his psychiatric training in 1954.

Dr. Hoffer was a member of the faculty of the college of medicine at the University of Saskatchewan from 1955 to 1967. He served as the director of psychiatric research for the Saskatchewan Department of Public Health in Regina from 1950 to 1967.

Appalled by the way schizophrenics were treated at hospitals and discouraged by the lack of effective treatments, Dr. Hoffer began using nutritional therapy in 1952. He published his first megavitamin treatment paper in 1957. Unfortunately, the psychiatric establishment refused to support his nutritional research. They were more interested in promoting the use of treatments such as tranquilizing drugs or psychoanalysis. In 1967, he went into private practice, where he was able to help thousands of patients suffering from mental illness by using nutritional protocols.

> Sugar is an addiction far stronger than what we see with heroin. It is the basic addictive substance from which all other addictions flow. Refined sugar and all refined foods such as polished rice, white flour and the like, are nothing less than legalized poisons.[380]
>
> —Dr. Abram Hoffer

Using high-dose vitamin therapy and addressing the problems with hypoglycemia, he was able to help Bill Wilson (known as Bill W.), co-founder of Alcoholics Anonymous. Bill W. understood the link between hypoglycemia and alcoholism better than most. In 1968, in a memo to AA's physicians, Bill W. wrote that "we alcoholics try to cure these conditions [of hypoglycemia], first by sweets and then by coffee . . . . In exactly the wrong way, we are trying to treat ourselves for hypoglycemia."[381]

Sadly, Dr. Hoffer passed away several months after being interviewed for this book. Trained directly by Dr. Hoffer, Frances Fuller continues to run their nutritional clinic, the Orthomolecular Vitamin Information Centre, in Victoria, British Columbia. Her Web site is www.orthomolecularvitamincentre.com. The Web site for the International Society for Orthomolecular Medicine (ISOM) is www.orthomed.org.

* * *

PAM: You are a pioneer in the area of using nutritional approaches in order to help treat psychiatric conditions. In the 1950s, most medical doctors turned toward patented pharmaceutical drugs, but you took a different path.

HOFFER: The medical profession has forgotten its main purpose, which is to give the body what it needs in order to be healthy. Before the 1950s, the medical schools had some interest in nutrition, and afterward, there was a major shift from nutrients to "wonder drugs" such as corticosteroids and antibiotics. Suddenly, the medical schools shifted their focus from food and vitamins to these new drugs. The teaching of nutrition vanished from the medical schools. In Canada, for example, in four years of medicine, you're lucky if you get one hour of nutrition. Doctors have become the handmaidens of the drug industry, or drug pushers. I am convinced that if we were to banish all of the drugs on the market, perhaps except vitamins and the bio-identical hormones, we would all be better off.

PAM: Why did you decide to switch your focus to nutrition?

HOFFER: I was trained as a regular medical doctor. I prescribed drugs. And then we began to work with niacin as a treatment for schizophrenia and became aware that nutrition was essential to health. I've seen some fantastic effects by recommending niacin to my patients. Not only can niacin help normalize lipid levels in the blood, it can also help treat psychiatric conditions, such as schizophrenia. It's non-toxic and has anti-inflammatory effects. It's a fantastic vitamin.

PAM: When did you start using niacin?

HOFFER: In the 1950s, I began using vitamin and mineral therapy with schizophrenics. One of the main nutrients we used was niacin.

PAM: How long have you been practicing medicine and how many schizophrenic patients have you seen?

HOFFER: I've been practicing since 1950 and have seen over 5,000 schizophrenic patients.

PAM: How many schizophrenic patients have you been able to help?

HOFFER: The word *schizophrenia* has a terrible social meaning. It doesn't help determine the cause of schizophrenia, nor does using this label help treat people. I think we should use the word *pellagra*. Many schizophrenics suffer from a skin condition called pellagra, which is caused by a deficiency of niacin (B3) and protein. If a schizophrenic comes to me and they've been sick for two years or less and if they stay on the program for two years, then 90% of them will be well. And by "well," I don't mean that they're sitting at home watching TV and drooling. I mean that they're free from symptoms, getting along with their family and paying income tax. Some of my patients have been able to get well and have gone on to become professors, medical doctors, etc.

PAM: What did you do when you treated people suffering from serious mental illness, including psychosis? You speak about being very conservative when it comes to prescribing psychiatric medications.

HOFFER: As long as the medication doesn't prevent the patient from getting well, I'm not completely against medication. What I learned, though, was that the more we used vitamins, the less often we used medication. Sometime around 1954-56, I was one of the first doctors in North America to start prescribing tranquilizing drugs. At that time, I was one of the five directors of psychiatric research in the province of Saskatchewan. If you have a psychotic patient that could kill himself or someone else on the ward, you have to use something.

One approach we used was to lock them in an isolation room until they calmed down. Otherwise, we used drugs like the tranquilizer Haldol, a derivative of morphine, to help calm these patients down. These types of psychiatric drugs are very toxic and have terrible side effects. They put people in a catatonic stupor. I thought there must be something else we could do to help these patients. So very early on in my career, I also began to use vitamins. We discovered that if we used vitamins such as niacin and vitamin C, we could decrease the dosage of drugs we prescribed. We also noticed that if we did have to prescribe small doses of Haldol and used vitamins, that the side effects were minimized.

PAM: At the time, vitamins were still relatively new. How were you able to get supplements?

HOFFER: In 1960, I was the only doctor in Canada who had access to 500 mg of vitamin C or 500 mg of niacin. You simply couldn't get these vitamins in drug stores. But I made arrangements with companies to make them for me.

PAM: Can you tell us about Bill Wilson, founder of Alcoholics Anonymous?

HOFFER: I met Bill Wilson in 1958 while we were at a meeting in New York City with Dr. Humphry Osmond. This was the meeting that led me to meet Aldous Huxley. Bill Wilson called himself the worst drunk that ever lived. Bill didn't have his first drink until he was 21 or 22, and he became an alcoholic that same night. He couldn't stop. When I met him, he was a "dry drunk" (he had stopped drinking, but was still not feeling well), which is a very common thing with members of AA. He remained thoroughly depressed, anxious, tired and unhappy. He was also insomniac.

Even though he had all of these problems, he was fantastically productive and brilliant. He was one of the most productive men I've ever met. He was a charismatic and marvelous human being. We already had a lot of experience using niacin, so I recommended it to Bill. He was so desperately tense and unhappy and trusted us as physicians, so he started taking niacin. And within two weeks on niacin, he became totally normal. After he recovered (with the help of niacin), he and I became very close friends. We'd often go out together to a pub, eat their good food and not touch their liquor.

PAM: When he recovered on niacin, he wanted to share his experience with other alcoholics, but I understand he ran into some resistance.

HOFFER: He had started doing his own research and had several friends from AA who were congressmen, senators, actors, wealthy businessmen, etc. He ran in a very high society. Members of AA were very devoted to him. After giving niacin to thirty of his friends from AA, he told me that "ten of them were normal in ten days, ten were normal within the second month and the other ten had not yet responded." He was getting the same results as we were in Saskatchewan. He decided that this information was too important to be hidden, but he ran into a problem from the international headquarters of AA. They didn't like what he was doing. They told him that he didn't have any right to be practicing medicine.

PAM: Even though he was consulting with medical doctors?

HOFFER: That's right. He decided that he would work with nutritional therapies outside of AA and needed some money for more research. At the time, I was the president of the Huxley Institute of Biosocial Research in New York City, and I provided him with a grant. He had a document called "Communications to AA Doctors (I, II, III)." In these communications, he described his research, including the work of another orthomolecular psychiatrist, Dr. David Hawkins, who was getting fantastic results helping people with schizophrenia and alcoholism. He also included research from Russell Smith, who was in charge of a hospital treating people for alcoholism. Bill W. compiled some of the most important findings involving the use of niacin.

PAM: Like drug addicts, alcoholics are stereotyped to be the derelicts of society, but in fact, they're physically unwell.

HOFFER: We are dealing with sick people. If you have diabetes and you take insulin, you don't say you have a disease called "insulinic," do you? The same thing applies to alcohol. Why do we call them alcoholics? If someone takes penicillin, do we call them "penicillinics"? The name is all wrong. We shouldn't call them alcoholics. They're sick people, and we have to get them well. Going to AA helps alcoholics stop drinking, but it doesn't help them get well, it just gets them sober. That's why so many of them relapse. You have to get them well by using the right nutrition, including B vitamins.

PAM: Alcoholics are also suffering from hypoglycemia, correct?

HOFFER: I've tested over 300 alcoholics, and they're all hypoglycemic. It's very important for them to eat wholesome foods, including animal protein and complex carbohydrates (rather than refined carbohydrates) throughout the day, in order to help balance their blood sugar. Chromium can also help regulate their blood sugar.

PAM: What are the limitations of psycho-spiritual approaches such as AA?

HOFFER: The 12-Step program can be very helpful. People in AA may not be drinking, but unfortunately, they are not well. That's what Bill Wilson realized. He knew that they weren't well and knew that they needed good nutrition in order to fully recover.

PAM: So, you've seen that nutrition can play a role in reversing addiction. When the body has a deficiency, you can fill that void with a nutrient and you feel better. That's remarkable. What's causing the deficiencies in the first place?

HOFFER: Sugar is one of the most basic addictive compounds there is. Millions of people are addicted to sugar. In fact, alcohol is a liquid sugar. One of the major contributors to this addiction is baby's formula, which is full of sugar. Parents are programmed to feed their children sugar. From birth, they give them sugar. Then, as the child gets older, parents believe that if they love their child, they should feed their child what he or she wants. So, if they want sugar, they feed them sugar.

PAM: Unfortunately, rather than loving their child, parents are actually hurting their child by feeding them sugar.

HOFFER: Exactly and if the entire family is addicted to sugar, it can be difficult to get them to stop eating sugar. If a child refused to avoid sugar, I would give them permission to eat as much sugar as they wanted on Saturday, as long as they agreed to avoid it during the week. On Sunday, of course, they would have headaches, nausea, or vomiting from their Saturday sugar binge. That's usually enough to convince them to stop eating sugar.

PAM: Addictions are incredibly destructive. Why are people drawn to such self-destructive habits?

HOFFER: Primarily it's because addictive compounds make people feel good. You don't need fancy psychological theories. Why does a man drink? Because he feels better when he's drinking than when he's not drinking. After he's an alcoholic, why does he continue to drink? Because if he stops drinking, he feels even worse. The same thing can apply to other drugs. Why does a man take heroin? Because he feels better when he's taking it than when he's not taking it. It's that simple.

PAM: Why do they feel better? What are they trying to accomplish?

HOFFER: It's very complicated, but I believe that they are deficient in B vitamins. Several years ago, a study was done on lab rats. They put these rats in a revolving cage and measured the number of times the rats turned the cage, in order to monitor their behavior. On a healthy diet, the rats went about two to three miles per day. If you starve the rat by not giving them enough calories, then they went about five to six miles per day. Now, that makes sense, because in the wild, if a fish is hungry, it's more apt to move faster because it knows that the more it moves, the more likely it is that it will run into food. The same thing with humans. The one thing that motivates them is hunger. Then they fed the rats ample calories, but didn't give them any of the B vitamins and they ran as if they were starving. The rats knew that they were missing vitamins, and therefore they would run faster hoping to find more food. I think that's what's happening with addiction. With food addiction, people are missing important nutrients and end up eating too much in order to compensate for the missing nutrients. When you give people enough nutritious food and remove the sugar, people can get well.

PAM: That leads us to the work of Weston A. Price and his warnings about the problems surrounding processed foods.

HOFFER: He was right on.

PAM: Dr. Price showed us that healthy cultures consumed adequate amounts of animal fats, which are critical for our overall health, including the proper functioning of our endocrine system and brain function. Unfortunately, over the last few decades, animal fats and cholesterol have been wrongly demonized and, as a result, we're much sicker.

HOFFER: Your diet must include adequate amounts of fat. Gary Taubes wrote a great book about the importance of animal fats and cholesterol (*Good Calories, Bad Calories*, 2007). As he points out, since increasing the consumption of carbohydrates and decreasing the consumption of animal fats, our health has deteriorated. Dr. Price's pictures, showing the physical deterioration after traditional cultures started eating Western foods, are so convincing.

PAM: Ninety-two percent of doctors, including many holistic health practitioners, are still recommending a low-fat diet.

HOFFER: That's crazy! Totally ridiculous! I recommend a sugar-free diet and tell my patients to reduce carbohydrates and eat a lot of fat. I tell them to eat animal protein and plenty of fatty fish. Salmon, sardines, kippers. As a rule, as much of these foods as possible, I'd encourage people to eat their ancestral diet. They need to eat animal protein at least three times per day.

PAM: What do you recommend for people who aren't producing enough stomach acid and aren't able to break down and absorb protein?

HOFFER: In order to improve the acidity of my stomach and improve the absorption of protein, I take apple cider vinegar every day. If you want to see whether you're properly absorbing protein, a urine analysis will be able to measure your amino acids.

PAM: Are we living in an addictive society?

HOFFER: Yes. More and more we are living in an addictive society. Today, in the U.S., there are one million children diagnosed as being bipolar. Can you imagine diagnosing a three-year-old child as being bipolar? It's totally crazy. It's no longer considered normal to cry, laugh, or to race around acting silly. These behaviors are no longer considered a normal part of growing up. Rather, you're bipolar. Then, the child is put on some very toxic drugs. When you start a child on these very toxic drugs, you are setting them up for a lifetime of using drugs. I'm very frightened to see what will happen to our society over the next 20 years, when our society is so dependent upon drugs that we can't live without them.

PAM: Other than a heavy marketing campaign, what is setting children up for this?

HOFFER: Sugar, bad diets, processed foods, allergies, pasteurized milk. When you remove highly processed foods like pasteurized dairy and wheat from their diets, a child who is suffering from hyperactivity can return to normal. I've even seen schizophrenics return to normal after removing the highly processed dairy and wheat products from their diets.

PAM: What are the implications of being an addictive society?

HOFFER: We really are a drug culture, and if we continue to be a drug culture, we could be taken over by other nations who are more alert than we are.

PAM: In other words, we will be so dumbed down, turned into zombies, it will be easy to conquer us.

HOFFER: Yes. That's right.

PAM: Today, more and more teenagers are going to get their caffeine fix at local cafes. By letting kids drink coffee, we are telling

them that it's okay to take something to change their mood.
What are the dangers of sending children this message?

HOFFER: Coffee disturbs your blood sugar levels, especially when you
drink it on an empty stomach. Coffee is a stimulant and
can create depression and anxiety. A stimulant is a substance
that can take away your inhibitions, so that you temporarily
forget your anxiety. But they don't really sedate or calm you
down—they fool the brain into thinking that it's feeling
better. The same thing applies for giving children Ritalin,
which is a stimulant. As long as they're under the influence,
they're better. Some time ago, caffeine was recommended for
hyperactive kids.

PAM: Rather than encouraging habits like drinking coffee, adults
should really be encouraging children to gravitate to healthy
food habits. Right?

HOFFER: If you were to give these kids good food and make sure
they were getting all of the necessary nutrients, they
wouldn't turn to drugs. I have a rule: you have to be sick
to begin with before you become addicted. Normal people
will never become addicted. When you take an addict and
get them well, they don't have any trouble with the drugs
anymore.

PAM: Even though the side effects of street drugs are very well
known, people still take them. Why is that?

HOFFER: If we look at cocaine, for example, it is a hallucinogen and can
make you psychotic. They are buying cocaine to help them feel
better, and they have discovered that cocaine works better for
them than anything else, including prescription drugs. Drug
addicts use the streets for their drug store. Very often, a coke
addict is a schizophrenic who finds that coke works better for
him than prescribed drugs. I think an addict is doing what we
all do—millions of people go to a doctor to get a prescription
to help them feel better. An addict can't get a prescription for
street drugs, so he has to buy them on the street.

PAM: Prescription drugs are an even bigger problem than street
drugs are.

HOFFER: Many patients have come to me complaining about the side
effects from psychiatric drugs and they want me to help
them come off the drugs. When we turn on our TV, there's a

commercial pushing another drug. These ads are developed by very intelligent people, who work in "public relations" (also known as propagandists). They're beautifully designed, and they entice people into going to their doctors and asking for the drug. The whole drug industry is built upon fraud. We need more doctors who are willing to practice orthomolecular (nutritional) psychiatry. Doctors need to have an epiphany. They need to reach a point where they realize that what they're doing (by prescribing very toxic psychiatric drugs) isn't helping people and that they're actually hurting people. I think things are moving in that direction.

PAM: People who work in recovery say that recovery is not the cure. In other words, conventional therapists know that their approaches are not curing people. People give up one addiction, but still have symptoms or cravings for cigarettes, caffeine, or sugar. Clinicians who are using nutritional approaches have incredibly high success rates. Not only can people stop doing damaging drugs, they can also stop their cravings for cigarettes, caffeine and sugar.

HOFFER: When you get people well, they can go off the drugs, whether they're street drugs or prescription drugs. If you want to get most psychiatrists angry, ask them how many of their patients on the antipsychotic Zyprexa pay income tax. They're zombies and can't function.

PAM: Psychiatric medications, such as Prozac, Paxil, Effexor, etc., have devastating side effects. Yet nutritional psychiatrists have natural solutions for people suffering from mood disorders.

HOFFER: For mild to moderate depression, studies have shown that antidepressants don't work any better than a placebo. They also have several dangerous side effects. Drugs are poisons that don't quite kill you. If I were the president of a drug company, I would sell a drug that would give people the illusion that they're feeling better but won't make them well, and it will make them addicted. Then I could make lots of money because I'd have a customer for life. I couldn't sell a drug that could make someone well because then I couldn't make any money on them. That's why drug companies don't like selling antibiotics—because they're short-term.

PAM: For several decades now, you've been a critic of mainstream medicine.

HOFFER: Sewage, sanitation, clean water, hand washing—these things have helped more people than anything medicine has offered.

PAM: It is really thanks to your research in the area of supplements such as niacin that we now have nutritional psychiatry. Unfortunately, very few doctors even know about this supplement, or how to use it.

HOFFER: Right dosage for the right effect. Doctors have an unreasonable fear of niacin because of the flushing effect. Some doctors will sell hundreds of dollars worth of supplements, but not sell niacin and the patient won't get well. For many patients, niacin is the missing link—they absolutely need niacin in their protocol, and they need the right dosage.

PAM: Given how successful orthomolecular psychiatry has been, why don't more psychiatrists use nutritional approaches in their practices?

HOFFER: We were making great progress, but in 1971 the American Psychiatric Association (APA) wrote a document attacking orthomolecular psychiatrists. There has been a very clear agenda to push for patented pharmaceutical drugs over natural remedies for several decades now.

PAM: What is in store for the future of medicine?

HOFFER: I think the future looks pretty good. Give us 50 years and I think we'll make some progress.

PAM: As long as we move toward nutrition, correct?

HOFFER: That's right. We have to move toward nutrition. We have no other choice. As a matter of self-defense, nutrition will be forced upon society.

PAM: How very true! It's been an honor and privilege speaking with you. You've had a tremendous career. Thank you for having the courage to go beyond mainstream medicine and help so many people get well.

Treatment Protocol for Alcoholism by Abram Hoffer, MD, PhD
Orthomolecular Medicine News Service, July 1, 2005
http://www.orthomolecular.org/resources/omns/v01n06.shtml

A message from Dr. HOFFER:

What should the alcoholic do to help stop drinking and return his or her body to normal functioning? In addition to taking niacin:

1. Vitamin C to saturation (approximately 10,000 to 20,000 mg per day and more). High doses of vitamin C chemically neutralize the toxic breakdown products of alcohol metabolism. Vitamin C also increases the liver's ability to reverse the fatty buildup so common in alcoholics.

    To titrate to saturation, take 1,000 mg of vitamin C every hour. When saturation is reached, there will be a single episode of diarrhea; then reduce the dosage to 1,000 mg every four hours.

2. A B50-complex tablet (comprising 50 mg of each of the major B vitamins, six times daily).

3. L-Glutamine (2,000 or 3,000 mg). L-Glutamine is an amino acid that decreases physiological cravings for alcohol. It is one of the two primary energy providers that burn glycogen to provide fuel to the brain, and it stimulates many neurofunctions. L-Glutamine is naturally produced in the liver and kidneys. Alcohol harms the kidneys and liver; thus supplementation is vital (concurrently reducing cravings for sugar and alcohol).

4. Lecithin (two to four tablespoons daily) provides inositol and choline related to the B complex. Lecithin also helps mobilize fats out of the liver.

5. Chromium (at least 200 to perhaps 400 mcg chromium polynicotinate daily). Chromium greatly reduces carbohydrate mis-metabolism and greatly helps control blood sugar levels. Many, if not most, alcoholics are hypoglycemic.

6. A good high-potency multi-vitamin, multi-mineral supplement as well, containing magnesium (400 mg) and the antioxidants carotene and d-alpha tocopherol.

HYPOGLYCEMIA AND ADDICTION
JURRIAAN PLESMAN, CLINICAL NUTRITIONIST

Jurriaan Plesman is a clinical nutritionist and an expert in drug addiction and hypoglycemia. He is the author of *Getting off the Hook: Treatment of Drug Addiction and Social Disorders through Body and Mind.* Because of his own personal struggle with depression and addiction, Jurriaan began studying the work of orthomolecular (nutritional) psychiatrists, including Dr. Chris M. Reading and Dr. Abram Hoffer.

Jurriaan is in his 83rd year and is now retired from private practice. He is still very committed to his field and works diligently on his Web site, teaching thousands of people around the world about proper nutrition and the role that hypoglycemia plays on mood and addiction.

His Web site, www.hypoglycemia.asn.au, offers current information about addiction, hypoglycemia and nutrition.

*   *   *

PAM: Jurriaan, could you please start by telling us about your background as a clinical nutritionist?

PLESMAN: I have degrees in psychology and clinical nutrition and began my career in the field of addiction in 1967, when I worked for a drug rehabilitation center. At the time, I was very interested in the biochemical aspect of drug addiction. When I did a post-graduate course in clinical nutrition, I was very fortunate to get to know one of my teachers. He happened to be a nutritional biochemist, but he was also an alcoholic. Not only did he come to me for treatment, he was also very interested in learning about my findings on the metabolic aspects of alcoholism. He helped me to understand the biochemistry of human behavior.

PAM: What did he mean by the nutritional or metabolic aspect of alcoholism? How does this relate to our biochemistry?

PLESMAN: I had a sense that there was a connection between alcohol/drug addiction and diet. At the time, I was working in a drug rehabilitation center, so I was concentrating on drug addiction. Because the drug addicts were very interested in learning about nutritional psychology, I began teaching classes about hypoglycemia and combined it with psychotherapy. Unfortunately, drug rehabilitation therapists were not interested in learning about the nutritional aspects of addiction.

PAM: How does hypoglycemia tie into addiction?

PLESMAN: Hypoglycemia causes emotional disorders. The reason why someone is feeling emotionally lousy about himself could be that he's feeling physically lousy. The biological self is controlling the emotional self and that could have a tremendous effect on one's self-image.

A car needs fuel to run. In a similar fashion, our brains need biological energy to convert one set of molecules into another set of molecules. In order to produce serotonin, you need energy. The energy comes from food, in particular, your carbohydrates. It is crucial to have proper blood sugar control. If you have poor blood sugar control, then you won't be able to absorb or metabolize your carbohydrates into energy. The carbohydrates will accumulate in your body as fat cells. You will find that many people who are suffering from depression also have a problem with obesity.

PAM: So protein and appropriate amounts of carbohydrates are necessary in the production of neurotransmitters.

PLESMAN: Yes. Neurotransmitters originate from the protein (amino acids) in our food. But you need carbohydrates to transform these amino acids into neurotransmitters. However, eating too many carbs can interfere with the conversion of amino acids into neurotransmitters (for example, tryptophan to serotonin).

PAM: How widespread is hypoglycemia?

PLESMAN: Most people suffering from chronic degenerative diseases are likely to be hypoglycemic. Because hypoglycemia can't be treated with drugs, doctors tend to ignore the condition and the patient is often misdiagnosed.

PAM: How did you find out about the link between blood sugar problems and mood?

PLESMAN: I had to study how nutrition affects blood sugar in order to get myself well. For years, I suffered from depression and addiction and didn't realize that I was hypoglycemic. As a hypoglycemic, my attention span was very short (maybe about 30-45 minutes). I was always amazed how well other people could concentrate, yet I couldn't.

PAM: Can you tell us about your experiences working with prisoners and how you were able to help them?

PLESMAN: Through my work, I discovered that about 95% of alcoholics and drug addicts are hypoglycemic. This has been confirmed by a special glucose tolerance test for hypoglycemia as designed by Dr. George Samra, Kogarah, Australia. (However, we must also realize that there are many other "silent diseases," in addition to and apart from hypoglycemia that can be responsible for mood disorders.*) Prisons are full of people suffering from hypoglycemia. The jails are full of mentally ill people—they are either drug addicts, have depression, have obsessive-compulsive disorder (OCD) or some other mental disorder. About 75% of prisoners have comorbid drug addiction. It may be alcoholism, it may be marijuana or any other kind of substance. If they didn't have these addictions, many of them wouldn't commit these crimes. Another 10% of the prisoners are likely schizophrenic. I have seen alcoholics come in and out of jail for 25 years who tell me that they're hearing voices through the radio. Alcoholism can actually be a symptom of schizophrenia.

Back in the 1960s, I began reading the work of Dr. Abram Hoffer. Eventually, I met Dr. Hoffer and was able to tell him about my experiences working with prisoners. Upon discussion, Dr. Hoffer agreed with my findings.

PAM: What is the usual progression of events? Does hypoglycemia precede substance abuse and substance abuse precede criminal behavior?

PLESMAN: Correct. Hypoglycemia is first. Followed by the rest.

PAM: What about attention deficit hyperactivity disorder (ADHD)? Millions of children are now being diagnosed with this condition.

---

* See article by Jurriaan Plesman, "Silent Diseases and Mood Disorders" at: http://www.hypoglycemia.asn.au/articles/silentdiseases.html

PLESMAN: The reason people are hyperactive has to do with the underproduction of noradrenaline in the brain. Noradrenaline is a form of adrenaline. Apart from being a fight-or-flight hormone, adrenaline is also a focusing hormone. It forces you to focus on your enemy. People who can't produce noradrenaline become hyperactive because they can't focus their attention on whatever they're doing. Noradrenaline is made from the amino acid phenylalanine. Magnesium is a coenzyme in the production of noradrenaline and is therefore also required.

PAM: When you mention adrenaline, what is the connection between adrenaline and hypoglycemia?

PLESMAN: When sugar levels drop from high to low, threatening the energy supply to the brain, stress hormones are released—among these, adrenaline—that converts stored sugar (glycogen) back into glucose. Initially, the overproduction of adrenaline can make people feel anxious, but over time this may lead to adrenal insufficiency (fatigue, depression).

PAM: What about mood-altering drugs, including the opiates? How do they influence our biochemistry?

PLESMAN: All of the psychotropic drugs are anti-adrenaline. Alcohol, opiates, marijuana, amphetamines. The interesting thing that happens with amphetamines is that they stimulate the production of adrenaline and the adrenaline stimulates the production of glucose (the reward). Caffeine produces similar results—it stimulates the production of adrenaline, which in turn increases your blood sugar. So for a short period you might feel good. But then you have hyperinsulinism and your blood sugar will eventually crash. Then, you need another cup of coffee.

PAM: The majority of people suffering from anxiety or depression don't go for help. Why is that?

PLESMAN: Usually, people are not aware that they feel low or are even mildly depressed. Some people are depressed their whole lives and don't realize it.

PAM: It has been said that two of the main reasons people turn to addiction is that they're feeling anxious or depressed.

PLESMAN: That's true. Depression is definitely the forerunner to addiction. By helping people get off their addiction and onto good foods, which will normalize their biochemistry, they finally announce that they feel good. At this point, they can acknowledge that they had been depressed for years. Now, they have to go for psychotherapy because their metabolism has damaged their personality.

PAM: According to what you are saying, the reason why people become addicted has more to do with biochemistry than with emotional trauma or the dysfunctional family.

PLESMAN: A dysfunctional family is a group of people who have metabolic disorders and pass the problem on from one generation to the next. For example, I had a client who was a young man. He was addicted to marijuana. His father was an alcoholic and diabetic. His mother is a perfectionist. Now, perfectionism is a sign that someone has high adrenaline. Perfectionism can be partly genetic and partly learned. If you want to treat a dysfunctional family, you first have to treat them metabolically before you can help them with anything else. You can't reform a dysfunctional family if they all suffer from hypoglycemia.

PAM: Can you explain why so many drug addicts also suffer from hyperreligiosity?

PLESMAN: When an individual is anxious and is pumped up with adrenaline, they can turn to a higher power to help them calm down. Religion is an anti-stress treatment—if you believe in God and God is good, then that could be a good antidote to your high adrenaline. Remember: adrenaline is a focusing hormone, so it can also make you become very rigid in thought. If you're full of adrenaline and you are antidoting yourself with religion or God, then you have to believe in God for every second of the day. If you don't believe in God, then you can't calm your adrenaline levels. It's the same with perfectionism. Perfectionism means, I have to be better than what I am. They also tend to have a low self-image.

PAM: So you're saying that most addicts are looking for a way to self-medicate.

PLESMAN: Gamblers, bank robbers, thrill seekers are hypoglycemic and are probably depressed. They do what they do because they're looking for a dopamine rush.

PAM: I've seen very addictive-like behaviors in people suffering from workaholism. Clearly, workaholism can be a very

serious problem, especially when it interferes with healthy
relationships or even destroy marriages.

PLESMAN: With these people, I use a method called "values clarification."
A workaholic will devote 2/3 of his life to work and 1/3 to
sleep. They have different priorities. There's no sense doing
psychotherapy with someone who isn't motivated. Some
people are unaware—they have different values. They may
not be aware of what is valuable in their lives. If you don't
value your wife or your children, then they can't be your
motivators. Couples who fill out the values clarification
discover more about their marriage—they may share similar
values and have a happy marriage. If they have different
values, then that could split up the marriage.

PAM: What about rageaholics?

PLESMAN: Rageaholics have high adrenaline and low self-image and have
explosive personalities. It can lead to murder, or even mass
murder. I have met murderers who have a real problem with
anger, and they don't know where the anger comes from. They
don't know how or why they lost their temper. Hypoglycemia
is a silent disease, so they don't understand that they are flooded
with adrenaline, and when they are flooded with adrenaline,
they will flood their reasons on to the world. If I were to inject
an individual with adrenaline, he may become angry. They
blame the outside world for how they feel.

PAM: Can you describe some other common traits of people
suffering from addiction?

PLESMAN: They have a very difficult time expressing their feelings.
They tend to blame others for their problems. They're very
manipulative, and they tend to be pathological liars. When
you are addicted, you aren't in control of your emotions. You
can't understand why you need a drug. Nor can you explain
it. There's no rational reason.

PAM: Birds of a feather flock together. Why is it that addicts tend
to gravitate toward other addicts?

PLESMAN: Negative attracts negative. A person with a negative self-image
is usually attracted to another person with a negative
self-image. Addicts hang out with other addicts or people
who have a low self-image. They don't have to be addicts.
The people they choose to be with can also be enablers.

PAM: What has been your experience working within the prison system? Were officials open to your nutritional approaches?

PLESMAN: I tried to introduce nutritional therapies to probation parole services in New South Wales, Australia, and they stopped me from treating drug addicts. I believe probation parole services and correctional services around the world do not seem to be interested in rehabilitating prisoners. They appear more interested in promoting crime, so they get more lawyers, more psychologists, more psychiatrists, more welfare officers, more prisons and prison staff . . . this is an industry that you can't get rid of. They're interdependent. Today, it seems as though they're promoting mental illness, rather than looking for practical solutions.

PAM: There's a lot of money to be made in the field of addiction or mental illness.

PLESMAN: I believe that mental illness and addiction are big business. Mental illness, mood disorders and addiction will only get worse. Depression is a very profitable business. You can't beat the processed food industry or the pharmaceutical industry. They're too powerful. You can't beat the World Trade Organization (WTO), because the leaders have a vested interest in promoting drug oriented medicine. The only way to win is to educate people.

PAM: Ultimately, if hypoglycemia is the result of eating too many carbohydrates, then in order to balance blood sugar, is it important to eat adequate amounts of protein?

PLESMAN: Yes. If you notice that your moods go up and down, or that you feel good one day and bad the next, you're probably hypoglycemic. You would improve your moods and energy levels by following the hypoglycemic diet—a diet which provides adequate amounts of complete protein so that it stabilizes blood sugar levels. Even people who suffer from bipolar disorder do very well on the hypoglycemic diet. It can take about three months. If you've been using either legal or illegal drugs, you've damaged your receptors for neurotransmitters, and they need to be rebuilt by taking amino acid supplements and eating adequate amounts of complete protein. It could take up to a year before a drug addict fully recovers.

PAM: Aside from recommending high-quality animal protein and amino acid supplements, what other supplements do you recommend for people suffering from hypoglycemia?

PLESMAN: Our diets are so depleted that we definitely need supplements. You'd be hard-pressed to find someone who isn't zinc-deficient. As I mentioned, magnesium is also very important. I also recommend other vitamins, including vitamins B1, B2, B3, B6. I've been in this field for about 50 years, so I can assess someone in about 15 minutes. Normally, I can diagnose someone by using a questionnaire, but physical tests may be in order (hair analysis, amino acids, pyroluria, glucose tolerance test, etc.).

PAM: As a clinical nutritionist, you are challenging the beliefs of the majority of mainstream psychologists.

PLESMAN: Conventional psychologists believe that mental illness is all in the mind. They believe that people suffer from illnesses of the mind and they don't realize that the mind is a reflection of your biochemistry. If you can't produce serotonin, you can't produce a happy, healthy mind. You can't think. You can become irrational. After years of education, psychologists are brainwashed into believing that mental illness is an illness of the mind. They need to be re-educated. They don't realize that mental illness is far more simple than they realize. They only really need to study some very basic biochemistry.

PAM: As a clinical nutritionist, what is your main goal?

PLESMAN: My goal is to bypass what mainstream psychologists are doing by educating people suffering from mood disorders or addiction about how they can get well by using nutrition and balancing their biochemistry. After 25 years of suffering from depression, anxiety or addiction, clients came to me ready to get well, fed up with mainstream therapies. My hope is that people can prevent themselves from becoming mentally ill or developing mood disorders by using nutrition. Biochemistry is not as complicated as it sounds. Anybody can do this work.

PAM: Thanks, Jurriaan, for speaking with me today. I'm sure that your work has and will continue to inspire others.

EXPLAINING THE WORK OF DR. WESTON A. PRICE
Sally Fallon-Morell, MA

> During the sixty-year period from 1910 to 1970, the proportion
> of traditional animal fat in the American diet declined from
> 83% to 62%, and butter consumption plummeted from
> eighteen pounds per person per year to four. During the past
> eighty years . . . the percentage of dietary vegetable oils in
> the form of margarine, shortening and refined oils increased
> about 400% while the consumption of sugar and processed
> foods increased about 60%.[382]
> —Sally Fallon and Mary Enig, PhD,
> *The Skinny on Fats*

Sally Fallon-Morell is the president and founder of the Weston A. Price
Foundation in Washington DC and author of the cookbook *Nourishing
Traditions*. Through the work of Dr. Weston A. Price, her goal is to
teach people about the importance of returning to our nutrient-dense
traditional foods. Over the last hundred years, we have dramatically
changed our diets, introducing high amounts of foods our ancestors
would not have recognized. Since incorporating all of these newfangled
foods into our diet, we have become physically, mentally and emotionally
sicker.

The Weston A. Price Foundation (www.westonaprice.org) has over
10,000 members worldwide. It has become the leading consumer-based
advocacy group promoting and supporting sustainable agriculture.
They hold a conference every year, hosting some of the most influential
speakers in the area of health and nutrition and publish a quarterly
newsletter with the most current dietary news. Local chapters organize
regular meetings as a support for families who are interested in learning
how to obtain and prepare the most nutritious food possible.

Sally Fallon-Morell's extremely informative Web site is www.
westonaprice.org.

*   *   *

PAM: Dr. Weston A. Price is known for his research into discovering
              the fundamental characteristics of a healthy diet and how diet

influences chronic disease. I don't think that people realize that, while he studied the diets of primitive cultures around the world, he also observed their moods and behavior.

FALLON-MORELL: He was really impressed by both their physical health and mental health. He often wrote about their cheerfulness, optimism, balance and reverence for life.

PAM: What was the critical component of their diets that caused these cultures to be so physically and mentally fit?

FALLON-MORELL: He studied several different cultures that ate varying amounts of fat, protein and carbohydrates. The most important feature of the diets he studied was the emphasis of the fat-soluble activators (vitamins A and D), which come from animal foods. He also noted the importance of saturated fats. There are two ways to get saturated fat. One way is to eat saturated fats and the other way is to eat carbohydrates, which convert into saturated fat. Either way you get the saturated fat, you must also get the critical fat-soluble vitamins (A and D). For example, in the South Seas, where people eat a lot of fish, shellfish and yams, the yams would be their source of saturated fat, but they would get the fat-soluble vitamins from the fish and shellfish.

PAM: And it's the fat-soluble vitamins that are critical for the proper functioning of our nervous system, including our brain and hormones (adrenals, thyroid).

FALLON-MORELL: You need vitamin A to make all of the sex and stress hormones as well. The thyroid gland needs the fat-soluble vitamin A in order to make thyroid hormones. The thyroid gland needs more vitamin A than almost any other part of the body except the eyes. If you're on a low-fat diet and not getting the right amounts of vitamin A, then your thyroid won't function very well.

PAM: Many people are mistaken into believing that beta-carotene, from, say, a carrot or tomato, is the same thing as vitamin A.

FALLON-MORELL: Beta-carotene is not the same as vitamin A—it is the precursor to vitamin A, and people should not confuse the two.

PAM: Aside from fish and shellfish, which you mentioned, what are some other good sources of the fat-soluble vitamins A and D?

FALLON-MORELL: Liver (cod, beef liver, pork, duck) and fish eggs are great
sources of the fat-soluble vitamins A and D. Hopefully, your
food sources are from animals that are grass-fed (pastured)
or wild. If you're not eating these foods every day, you may
want to supplement with cod liver oil. The cod liver oil will
provide the fat-soluble vitamins along with small amounts of
EPA and DHA. The cod liver oil should be about 10:1 ratio
of vitamin A to D.

PAM: The foods we're eating today are so far removed from the
foods that kept our ancestors healthy for millennia . . .

FALLON-MORELL: It's bad enough that we've cut back dramatically on
animal fats that provide important nutrients like vitamin A.
In their place, we're eating a lot of trans fats, which interfere
with the production of the hormones.

PAM: And the trans fats interfere with the uptake of good fats into
the brain as well.

FALLON-MORELL: Right. The trans fats mess up the receptor sites and
enzymes. So communication between, say, the hormones
and neurotransmitters won't work properly. The bottom line
is that the liquid vegetable oils cause *uncontrolled* reactions
in the body. And the trans fats *inhibit* reactions in the body.
Biochemically, things are just a mess!

PAM: Research shows that many of us have way too many omega-6
fats in comparison to the omega-3 fats. I understand that
about one hundred years ago, we ate less than one pound
of vegetable-based oils per year—only a trace, because they
really didn't exist—and now we're eating about 75 pounds.
Today the ratio of omega-6 to omega-3 can average anywhere
from 20:1 to 50:1.

FALLON-MORELL: People are eating too many vegetable-based oils and
fats. The omega-3 and omega-6 fats are the liquid oils that
we see in the stores. The trans fats are found in the hardened
fats, such as margarines or spreads and can be made out of
omega-3s or omega-6s. Many of the processed foods we see
in the grocery store contain these industrialized vegetable
oils and fats, which have high amounts of omega-6.

PAM: We're being told that we should be eating more fish in order
to increase our omega-3 fats. For many of us, it's impractical
to get our omega-3 fats from fish.

FALLON-MORELL: You should be able to get all the omega-6 and omega-3 fats you need from butter and meat fats. Again, hopefully, your sources are from a local farm that has the animals out on pasture.

PAM: Over the last one hundred years, just how much have we reduced our consumption of animal fats such as lard or butter?

FALLON-MORELL: Our consumption of butter has plummeted. We've seen a five-fold increase in the consumption of shortening and a 16-fold increase in the consumption of liquid vegetable oils. In 1900, we used to eat about 18 pounds of butter per person per year (which doesn't seem like much to me!), and now we eat about five pounds per person per year.

PAM: In her book *The Mood Cure*, Julia Ross explains that the rates of mood disorders, such as depression, have risen dramatically over the last five decades or so. As we've reduced our consumption of animal fats, increased our consumption of vegetable fats, the rates of mood disorders have increased.

FALLON-MORELL: That's right. It may not be proof, but it's definitely a correlation. We can also point to the science. We also have to consider our frenzied lifestyle, eating on the run. It's rare for families to sit down and eat three square meals a day the way we used to.

PAM: What do you suggest for people who are dealing with mood disorders?

FALLON-MORELL: They absolutely need animal fats because they need the saturated fats that come from meats, for example, along with the vitamins that are contained in the animal fat. We've had people whose lifelong depression has cleared up just by getting on cod liver oil and butter. We've seen people overcome sugar addiction, aspartame addiction, and one woman who was bulimic overcame her eating disorder after switching to a traditional food diet. The brain is very high in saturated fats, and it's very high in arachidonic acid (AA). Arachindonic acid is an omega-6 fat that has been wrongly demonized. People have been misled into believing that arachindonic acid is bad because it causes inflammation, which is not true. You absolutely need AA for your brain. It's in butter, meat fat, lamb fat, beef fat—all the good animal fats.

PAM: So how do these animal fats help support the neurotransmitters in the brain?

FALLON-MORELL: They influence how the receptors work in the brain—the receptors for the feel-good chemicals such as serotonin.

PAM: In Barry Groves's book *Natural Health and Weight Loss*, he makes it clear that our brains would not have developed from our ape ancestors were it not for animal fats.

FALLON-MORELL: That's true.

PAM: Our ancestors thrived on diets rich in animal fats and cholesterol. Because of some very misleading information, most people still believe that animal fats and cholesterol are bad for us. Many people don't realize that cholesterol is critical for brain function.

FALLON-MORELL: Cholesterol-lowering protocols are bad for the brain. We know that depression and violent behavior are associated with low cholesterol. If a low-fat, low-cholesterol diet can cause anxiety and depression, then it would be wise to avoid that way of eating.

PAM: When it comes to educating people to overcome their fear of saturated fat and cholesterol, what do you tell them?

FALLON-MORELL: The biggest stumbling block for most people is this fear that saturated fat and cholesterol are bad for us. If you're afraid of cholesterol and saturated fat, you're going to go down the wrong road, nutritionally speaking. Until you get over these fear of eating cholesterol and saturated fat, you can't get on to a healthy diet.

PAM: Dr. Price saw people living in harsh conditions, yet he was amazed at how happy they were. What else can we learn from his work that could help us prevent mood problems, such as depression or anxiety?

FALLON-MORELL: It is critical to keeping blood sugar stable. That means, eating three regular meals per day comprised of real food with animal protein and plenty of fat. I really can't stress enough the importance of that. When your blood sugar drops, that's when you feel depressed, anxious and angry.

PAM: Thanks so much for taking the time to share your thoughts with me. Keep up the great work!

SECTION II

ALLIANCE FOR ADDICTION SOLUTIONS

Interviews with Charles Gant, MD, PhD, ND; David Miller, PhD; Joan Mathews-Larson, PhD; Julia Ross, MA; Stan Stokes, MS, CCDC and Carolyn Reuben, LAc

> There is a principle which is a bar against all information, which is proof against all arguments and which cannot fail to keep man in everlasting ignorance—that principle is contempt prior to investigation.
>
> —Herbert Spencer (1820-1903)
> British philosopher, evolutionist and sociologist

CHARLES GANT, MD, PhD

Charles Gant has practiced integrative medicine, psychology and psychiatry for over 35 years. Dr. Gant received his BS in chemistry from Hampden-Sydney College and his MD from the University of Virginia. He has enjoyed postgraduate training in Family Practice and Psychiatry. His 1984 PhD psychology thesis, "A Neurophysiological Model of the Transformational Psychologies," proposed that potentially measurable and progressive neurophysiological changes should necessarily accompany the process of psycho-spiritual self-actualization. Recent neuroimagery studies have proven this model to be true. While serving as a psychiatric consultant at mental health clinics, Dr. Gant's research proved that massive cuts in medication were possible if mental health clinicians move from a pharmaceutically based, disease model of treatment to a self-actualization, wellness model, by combining various types of psychotherapy (such as family systems therapy, Gestalt therapy, rational emotive therapy), various spiritual practices and nutrition.

His ADHD research suggests that ADHD is caused by easily correctible brain toxicity and/or nutritional deficiencies and that pharmaceutical treatments for ADHD are now obsolete. Dr. Gant's book, *ADD and ADHD: Complementary Medicine Solutions*, summarizes his work into the orthomolecular medicine approach to ADHD and provides practical guidelines for treatment. His books, *End Your Addiction Now* and *End Nicotine Addiction Now*, empower recovering laypersons and clinicians with practical ways of identifying probable and specific neurotransmitter deficiencies through self-administered questionnaires, and based on those results, then guides consumers in the selection of nutritional protocols to mitigate symptoms of addiction and to improve outcomes (studies available).

In his lectures and writings, Dr. Gant proposes that orthomolecular medicine—a term coined by the Nobel prize-winning scientist, Linus Pauling, PhD—will force a complete rethinking of the premises upon which modern medicine and psychiatry is based. Through a national lecture tour, professional meetings, webinar trainings/certifications and publications, Dr. Gant provides health care professionals with information about natural, safer, more efficacious and cost-effective treatments that will ultimately guide medicine back to its ethical and healing traditions. For more information, visit his Web site, www.charlesgantmd.com.

* * *

PAM: Dr. Gant, in your experience can you please explain what is
            going on in the brain of an addict?

GANT: Addicts are trying to alleviate the pain of not being able to be
            in the *now*. Recent neuroimagery studies of the brain strongly
            suggest that the frontal lobes and associated structures are
            designed to assist us to stay in the *now* and let go of the fear
            of the future and the past. You can see this neuroimagery
            phenomenon in the frontal lobes when people practice
            meditation, for example. Humans generally don't know how
            to live in the *now* and this brain activity is relative dormant
            in most people and needs to be part of our educational
            curriculums just as training the intellect or the motor parts
            of the brain are done in sports. Meditation, prayer, spiritual
            paths, psychotherapy are all various modalities that try
            to help bring us back to the *now* and to train and utilize
            this dormant faculty. But in order to accomplish this for
            many individuals, the brain chemistry must be in balance,
            detoxified and working properly.

PAM: I think many people will be surprised to learn that there's
            more to lifting mood than simply using psycho-spiritual
            methods.

GANT: I have compassion for people who are trying to get well by
            using yoga, psychotherapy, meditation, prayer, etc. They
            know that they're up against something tough and often don't
            realize that the reason they're struggling is that they're not
            producing enough critical neurotransmitters such as serotonin,
            an important brain neurotransmitter that does exactly what
            its name suggests—brings serenity. Without serotonin, you
            can't activate dopamine or your frontal lobes optimally, so it
            becomes much more difficult to be mindful of what it is that
            you need to observe or take responsibility for.

PAM: When you mention brain chemistry, exactly what do you
            mean?

GANT: When it comes to balancing the brain, I primarily look at the
            four main neurotransmitters, although there are at least eight
            others that assist us in letting go of past resentments or future
            fears. GABA is the neurotransmitter that helps relieve us of

anxiety and fear. Serotonin relieves us of past resentments and self-loathing. Endorphins relieve post-traumatic stress. The only excitatory neurotransmitter, dopamine, relieves us of boredom, to make mundane experiences more exciting, like sitting for hours practicing mindfulness. So if these four neurotransmitters are fully activated, which are often deficient in many people, then the stage is set for us to practice living in the *now*.

PAM: So when these neurotransmitters are working in a proper balance, one can feel peace. On the other hand, when they're not working properly, one can feel stress, anxiety or depression.

GANT: Exactly. When we're compromising our neurotransmitters through improper diet, toxin exposures and lifestyle factors like using psychotropic chemicals, then any psycho-spiritual path becomes much steeper—and people are overlooking the importance of the amino acid-neurotransmitter connection.

PAM: How then do you repair this brain chemistry imbalance?

GANT: In short, we deal with three key elements: nutritional deficiencies, toxicities and neurotransmitter imbalances. We do a form of diagnostic testing called functional medicine testing to see which neurotransmitters are out of balance, define the toxicities like heavy metals that interfere with optimal functioning, and look at deficiencies in critical brain nutrients like essential fatty acids. Then, using nutrition and detoxification strategies, we help repair that imbalance.

PAM: If addiction can be defined as an imbalance in the chemistry of the brain, what then puts us at risk for addictive tendencies?

GANT: The more damaged the brain is, the more risk for addiction, because we will reach out for something out there to modify our pain and not correct what is internal. Therefore, we're all at risk for developing addictions in a junk food-laden world where environmental degradation is poison to all of life. It's human nature for us to do things to avoid suffering, to self-medicate. People turn to addictions in order to relieve themselves from how badly they feel. It could be an addiction like an activity (for example, gambling) or a street drug or pharmaceutical drug like Ritalin or Prozac; regardless, they're trying to relieve themselves of their suffering which is, in part, usually driven by severe brain chemistry imbalances. Addiction is merely a coping mechanism to get a person through their own personal suffering by resorting to artificial chemicals that mimic the natural "feel good" neurotransmitters that are supposed to do the job.

PAM: If you're saying that the natural state of the human being is not to suffer, then is it also fair to say that it is natural for us to turn toward addictive substances to escape suffering?

GANT: We all have addictions. It can be power, sex, control, gambling, drugs, etc. It's just up to each of us to work out what our addictions are and how we deal with them. The more we replace our natural neurotransmitters with artificial chemicals, the more the brain stops making the natural neurotransmitters to compensate for the toxic stuff. Understanding this general self-defeating principle—that most attempts to escape suffering lands people in deeper suffering—can move us to have compassion for those who do this, as well as ourselves.

PAM: Addicts can go to the streets to help make themselves feel better, but many people who have mood problems are now going to the medical profession to get prescriptions to help themselves feel better.

GANT: It's called "America's Other Drug Problem." By receiving that doctor's prescription, legitimacy of the condition is created. It then becomes socially acceptable to medicate your way out of a problem. Ultimately, though, they are destroying the person's brain physically and preventing them from a spiritual transformation. But they call it therapy. At least it has the veneer of therapy. History is replete with examples like this, where it becomes profitable to injure people, while glibly scamming them that something of benefit is happening.

PAM: But these people are being turned into zombies.

GANT: That's right. If the pharmaceutical companies offer the illusion of false therapeutic effects, then they can advertise. They're just capturing a market share. The Colombian drug cartel can't advertise. The cigarette companies can't advertise. Alcohol has very limited advertisements. Pharmaceutical companies are taking advantage of some very wide gaps in the advertising world. It's a marketing bonanza for them. They can capture market share from the other purveyors of psychotropic chemicals. Twenty percent of humanity is going to be addicted at any time anyway so why not capture a larger and larger market share from the alcohol and tobacco industry?

PAM: What's the connection between addiction and mental illness? Why is it so common to find addicts who are also suffering from a mental illness such as psychosis or schizophrenia?

GANT: Like addiction, mental illness is a reflection of the inability to stay here in the *now*, largely due to relatively more severe biochemical imbalances that they suffer from. People suffering from mental illness are physically unwell. When they learn that their problems are physical and they apply the nutritional protocols, they can then begin the road to recovery.

PAM: What's your view about the millions of teenagers who are now drinking caffeinated beverages or coffee?

GANT: Caffeine is a stimulant. It's marketed as something to take when you're trying to make a mundane task more exciting. This is what stimulants do. People who take stimulants are trying to enhance their experience of the *now*. This is just another thing we do to improve the attraction of living in the present, which of course induces more brain imbalances that we have to dig ourselves out of later.

PAM: But doesn't caffeine lower GABA and serotonin levels in the brain?

GANT: Yes. There is no way out with chemicals and no way home.

PAM: What then will happen to children who feel a buzz from caffeine now, when they reach their 20s or 30s?

GANT: They could gravitate to something stronger. If they're a catecholamine-deficient person—that is, deficient in the natural Ritalin or amphetamine called dopamine—then they will likely gravitate to the stimulants. If they have driven their serotonin and GABA over the edge, then they'll have anxiety, and they could gravitate toward antidepressants like SSRIs or to GABA-like drugs such as a benzodiazepine. If they have been traumatized, then they could gravitate toward the opioids such as heroin and OxyContin. People are attracted to the drug that can temporarily bring them back to the peace of *now* based on the kind of neurotransmitter that they can't make in the first place. All drugs will destroy the neurotransmitter that it's intending to replace. If you take an SSRI (antidepressant), you'll eliminate your serotonin. If you take benzodiazepine, you'll eliminate GABA. If you use amphetamines, you'll eliminate dopamine. And if you use heroin or OxyContin, you'll eliminate your natural opioids. The reason for that is that the brain will only compensate for the presence of the drug by making less of the natural substance. The person then gets hooked because they have to keep using the artificial stuff just to be able to cope or to enjoy any kind of joy or pleasure in their lives. Otherwise, they can't function.

PAM: How long have you been working in the field of psychiatry and addiction?

GANT: I've been doing this work for about 32 years. I'm really a psychotherapist, plus I teach meditation. While practicing as a psychiatric consultant early in my career, I was medical director at a large outpatient clinic where I did my PhD on a study that looked at the power of stress reduction, psychotherapy and family therapy to get people off the psychiatric medications. Interestingly, we could only get them off about 2/3 of their medications using these modalities. The last third of their meds was something biochemical. So I had to go back and look at a biochemical factor that could be repaired to get to that other part of it. That's when I started studying the amino acid-neurotransmitter connection, brain metabolism, toxicity-induced disorders, genetic vulnerabilities and other biochemical problems that limit the full potential we should be capable of.

PAM: In 1980, while you were a resident psychiatrist, you discovered neurochemistry accidentally when you yourself took tyrosine and your mood lifted. How new is this science?

GANT: We've only known about the molecules in the brain for about 20 or 30 years. So it's a new idea for our civilization. Understanding the neurochemistry of the brain is so new, in fact, that it hasn't yet reached mainstream consciousness. Imagine what it would be like finding out that the earth is actually round, when for many years everybody believed it was flat.

PAM: And you've had a lot of trouble convincing modern medicine and conventional therapists of the importance of nutrition to mental health and well-being.

GANT: Psychotherapists and psycho-spiritual teachers are marginalized and shoved aside throughout their entire careers. Despite the fact that we have the studies that show the importance of our neurotransmitters, modern medicine doesn't believe in the human's potential based upon our neurological equipment. Modern medicine just doesn't recognize that humans can extricate themselves from their suffering. Therefore, they "pathologize" everything and believe that they need to anesthetize the past and future with chemicals or to stimulate the present with amphetamines. These are the only options they consider, the quick fix, not the bigger picture of life's purpose and meaning.

PAM: They're not trained to think that the body can heal.

GANT: That's right. It's a denial of life. It's a denial of the beauty and potential of what it means to be human. It's a denial of spirituality, of every source of hope.

PAM: What's the difference between the nutritional protocols you are using and the methods used by conventional medical?

GANT: We're balancing brain chemistry with nutrition, meditation, psychotherapy, etc. according to inviolable laws of biochemistry that took eons to evolve, or if you prefer the theological approach, the chemistry we were created to fully utilize. Conventional medicine is simply sealing over symptoms with medications, which creates increased imbalance in the brain chemistry. They actually injure the brain chemistry even more by taking drugs. The hole gets deeper and deeper.

PAM: Can you talk about the results you're getting?

GANT: We see tremendous results. We test our patients with functional medicine at certified labs all around the country to find out what exactly the imbalances are. Then by correcting those biochemical imbalances with nutrition and detoxification, they will eventually be able to stop taking drugs because patients simply feel better and the need to cover up suffering with chemicals just falls away. Once they make the proper dietary changes, we can see in the neuroimagery, the amazing transformation that the brain makes. Their brain chemistry improves, their moods improve, their coping skills improve and neurotic tendencies subside. The possibility opens up to ask the questions: Why am I here? And, what should I be doing to make a contribution that matters?

PAM: Mainstream therapists treat patients as though their head is detached from the body. Since our brain is comprised of molecules and those molecules come from food, then it only makes sense that what we eat affects our brain.

GANT: They don't understand that there's a quantum molecular field underneath, which explains so much of what we are. Our brain is roughly 2% of our body's weight, and it metabolizes 20% of the body's calories. It's an energizer bunny. It's our powerhouse. It's made of good fats like omega-3 and omega-6 fatty acids and phospholipids from lecithin foods, not trans fats and petrochemical-derived pharmaceuticals.

PAM: Your protocol emphasizes the importance of amino acids, which come from eating protein. If someone has been dieting or following a high-carb, low-fat diet, it would go without saying that they may not be getting enough protein to supply the neurotransmitters.

GANT: Proteins and fats are essential to life. Carbs are nowhere near as essential as protein and fat. Our ancestors may have thrived on about 70% fat in their diets, but it was the good fats that repair the brain and decrease inflammation. I get people to reduce their intake of carbohydrates in general. Before man developed agriculture about 10,000 years ago, as hunter-gatherers, we used to eat our carbohydrates for a few months of the year (growing season) so we'd fatten up for the winter. For about nine months out of the year, we had little to no carbohydrates. We ate fish, which provided us with the omega-3 fats (EPA and DHA) we needed in order for our brains to develop.

PAM: And fish, of course, is known to be a brain food.

GANT: Many studies reveal that fish oil is one of the most powerful antidepressants there is. When the British imposed poaching laws that prevented the Irish from catching salmon in the early 1800s, they became very, very depressed and resorted to alcohol to medicate their depression. It was biochemical genocide. That's how the Irish developed their reputation as being heavy drinkers.

PAM: It sounds like we have to go back in time in order to learn how we've been making ourselves so sick.

GANT: We need to relearn the fundamental principles about how life has evolved. So much of it is considered "passé." Doctors prefer looking at the next exotic drug. What they don't get is that almost all technologies we use in present day have been designed and created by humans, except for health care. But realistically, health care technology is reverse engineering. They are attempting to reinvent what has taken four billion years to happen by trial and error, but with artificial chemicals. We need to work our way back to see what four billion years did. It's akin to a bunch of cavemen finding a Boeing 707 and trying to figure out what it does. We still have so much to learn about the complexities of even one cell.

PAM: Dr. Weston A. Price studied the diets of healthy societies, and he discovered that most of them ate moderate to high amounts of animal fats. Since the 1950s, we have become a fat-phobic society, and we are sicker, fatter and more mentally unstable than ever before. The beauty of Dr. Price's work is that it is so easy to understand.

GANT: Yes, and it's so profound. He discovered what happened before we lost our common sense in the area of nutrition. He looked at what was basic to survival and health. When you study his work, you can see how far we've deviated from what sustained humanity for eons.

PAM: What you're doing is not only challenging conventional addiction therapies, you're also threatening the sales of pharmaceutical drugs.

GANT: In a military sense, conventional medicine has tried to take out those who are at the forefront of the transformation. The health care system has deliberately destroyed the lives of those who are the most thoughtful healers. Doctors are blindly following the establishment. When they find out what authentic healing is and gravitate toward natural healing, they don't realize what they're up against. They're up against some very diabolical people. Fortunately, I've survived beautifully.

I live by the Nietzsche quote, that whatever doesn't kill me will make me stronger.

PAM: The health care system is clearly not working. Despite spending trillions of dollars on our health, over 80% of us are dying from chronic disease, and millions more are suffering from depression, anxiety, mental illnesses, personality disorders, etc. Many people are quick to blame doctors for this very dysfunctional, unsustainable health care system. Who's really at fault?

GANT: Doctors go into medical school for all the right reasons. They are just the sergeants carrying out the orders. They typically have nothing to do with what's going on behind the scenes. Doctors are being targeted because they're at the forefront, the ones people see. They're not making any of the decisions. If your plane was going down would you blame the stewardesses?

PAM: What about the insurance companies? Insurance (public or private) doesn't seem to be solving our health care crisis.

GANT: I think that there's a revolution going on. Doctors and patients are fed up with the insurance companies because they realize that insurance is not the solution. Insurance companies are just part of the MIOPIC. The Medical Insurance Overregulated Pharmaceutical Industrial Complex.

PAM: In Aldous Huxley's novel *Brave New World*, the drug *soma* was used to control the people. Do you see any similarities between the society described in *Brave New World* and our society today?

GANT: Huxley saw what was coming. Historically, drugs have been used as weapons of social control so that people will stop questioning the system. The more complacent we are, the more we will lose our democratic freedoms. Addictions can make us very complacent. Today, we have more things to be addicted to-street drugs, legal drugs and even the media. All of these things can make us complacent. In fact, TV is a drug-the way it acts on our brain. Furthermore, if people are watching TV and popping beers or Prozac, then they won't be out picketing in the streets. When life stops mattering, when a purpose for being alive ceases to be important on a wide-scale basis, civilization is finished.

PAM: Is the problem going to get worse before it gets better?

GANT: Unless people wake up to what's really going on, things will
         get worse. We'll continue to get sicker, and pharmaceutical
         companies will continue to profit from our illnesses. But
         pharmaceutical stocks, especially antidepressants, are really
         crashing right now because they do not work. In exposing
         the problem with drugs, others suggest that the solution
         is psychotherapy, and that's bunk. Drugs are physical
         substances that have a physical effect on a physical organ,
         and to say that the problem is psychological is absurd. You've
         got to deal with the physical aspects of addiction and brain
         disorders first. In order to bring ourselves back into a balance
         of love, kindness and compassion, a stewardship philosophy
         has to be directed toward our internal/external ecology.

PAM: Several health practitioners are using nutritional protocols
         to help people suffering from addiction and mood disorders.
         You're forming an Alliance for Addiction Solutions with
         other clinicians using nutritional protocols to help addicts.
         What do you hope to accomplish?

GANT: We want to be able to share our knowledge and give other
         therapists our "Good Housekeeping Stamp of Approval."
         Because it's a new field, we want to develop a standard of
         ethics and science and hold the health care industry's feet to
         the fire.

PAM: I've seen you speak before an audience, and it's clear that you
         are committed to helping addicts and the mentally ill get
         well.

GANT: I love what I'm doing. I love my patients. How could you
         not be happy telling the truth and helping people truly get
         well?

PAM: That's very true. Thanks for your time and all of your hard
         work and dedication.

DAVID MILLER, PhD

For the last 30 years, David Miller has worked in the addiction field both as a professor and as a counselor. Since 1974, Dr. Miller has been in recovery from alcoholism himself. For several years, he struggled with hypersensitivity, mood swings, irritability and anger outbursts, even while he was working as an addiction professional. He finally found relief from his symptoms after taking amino acid supplements. Invigorated by the improvements he felt on these supplements, he set out to search for more effective ways to help relieve what he calls "abstinence symptoms" in several different types of addiction.

His research has led him to the conclusion physical problems interfere with an addict's ability to recover. He has developed a variety of holistic strategies (nutritional, alternative therapies such as acupuncture and massage, psychosocial and even exercise) that help addicts stay clean and sober.

He is the author of several books, including *Staying Clean and Sober* (co-authored with his wife, Merlene Miller, MA), *Overload: Attention Deficit Disorder and the Addictive Brain*, (co-authored with neuroscientist, Kenneth Blum, PhD) and his newest book (2008) *How to Quit without Feeling S**t* (co-authored with Patrick Holford and James Braly, MD). He has also acted as consultant to numerous treatment centers, including Bridging the Gaps (www.bridgingthegaps.com) and Lifestream (www.lifestream-solutions.com).

Dr. Miller's Web site is www.miller-associates.org.

* * *

PAM: Many people working in the field of alternative medicine focus on chronic disease but neglect to look at natural remedies for reversing addiction and mood problems.

MILLER: And just look at how many health problems we have because of addiction. Not only are we addicted to alcohol and drugs, we're also addicted to carbohydrates. Our addiction to refined foods such as sugar and flour is contributing to many of the chronic illnesses we see today.

PAM: Addiction is crippling society. When and how did you learn about the "addiction as disease" model?

MILLER: My wife, Merlene, and I have given our whole lives to the field of addiction. My experience goes back to the 1970s, when the focus was on alcoholism. Rather than blaming the patient, I began exploring the underlying reasons why alcoholics relapse.

PAM: When you talk about the underlying reasons for addiction, what do you mean?

MILLER: We determined through our observations that focusing solely on the psycho-spiritual aspects of alcoholism wasn't cutting it. Sure, it would often get the alcoholic to stop drinking, but it didn't seem to clear up the cravings or withdrawal symptoms. We seemed to be missing the mark somewhere. That's when we decided to go looking deeper. We were no longer just looking for psychological reasons for addiction but physiological reasons.

PAM: You talk about continued cravings and post-withdrawal symptoms after the person has quit drinking. It seems as though people in recovery simply settle for feeling lousy.

MILLER: The term most people are familiar with is *dry drunk*. Most alcoholics abstain from drinking but still feel an array of symptoms. We started using the term *chronic abstinence symptoms*. They had a very uncomfortable recovery.

PAM: What types of symptoms are you referring to?

MILLER: They experience both cognitive and behavioral symptoms (confusion, fuzzy thinking, memory problems, anxiety, being overly sensitive to the environment—noises can be louder, colors can be brighter, touch can be very uncomfortable—a hug may be aggravating). Addicts suffer from these symptoms before and after using drugs or alcohol. It is because of these symptoms that some addicts turn to drugs or alcohol. In other words, they are drawn to drugs or alcohol to calm their symptoms down.

PAM: How did you first learn about the role that amino acids play in the recovery process?

MILLER: I knew that oral amino acids worked because I had studied the work of Kenneth Blum, PhD, who had developed an oral formula with amino acids and vitamins. In fact, I began taking the formula in 1980, in response to my own addiction problems. This was 10 years after my own recovery, so I had to struggle with those symptoms for 10 years before I found relief with oral supplements. From the first day I took the supplement, it helped me.

PAM: Addiction centers that are using amino acid protocols may also inject the amino acids using intravenous therapy.

MILLER: The first time I observed IV therapy, I was surprised at how well it worked. In fact, I noticed that the infusion therapy was working better than anything I had ever seen before. I couldn't believe it. I had taken part in detoxification programs many times and had never seen this type of success. The IVs work very quickly by helping to build neurotransmitters that aren't working properly and by creating healthier receptors.

PAM: As Julia Ross explains, she gave a crack addict the appropriate dose of the supplement, tyrosine and he felt better within minutes.

MILLER: The same thing can happen with kids with ADD. Tyrosine can help get them out of that fuzzy state of thinking and start feeling better.

PAM: Can you test their neurotransmitters and amino acids?

MILLER: Blood tests and urine tests will show you deficit amounts. We're now training treatment centers about how to do their own testing and the IV protocol.

PAM: The idea that addicts come from bad families is really very flawed.

MILLER: It really is. They really have done a disservice to society by thinking this way. I think it is fairly obvious that there is a much deeper issue than one that is psychological. This can be shown by the amazing transformation of an addict using the IV protocol. Don't get me wrong, psycho-spiritual approaches can be very helpful, but they're not dealing with the underlying physical deficiencies that can cause the chronic cognitive and behavioral problems that can lead to addiction.

PAM: In your book *Staying Clean and Sober*, you describe several other treatment approaches one can turn to during the recovery process, including acupuncture, chiropractic, exercise, humor and so on.

MILLER: IV therapy should be offered as part of a complete program. We don't just give them the IVs and send them home. Ours is a

PAM:

MILLER:

program based not only on the physiologic aspects of addiction, but we also incorporate psycho-spiritual approaches.

PAM: I understand that the amino acids can work quickly enough to gain the attention of the addict.

MILLER: The IVs can work very fast. Although they are more expensive than oral supplements, they capture the attention of the client right away. Instantaneously, the IVs can reduce cravings and improve emotional and cognitive symptoms. This allows them to get a good foothold in recovery by having repaired brain function.

PAM: You also write about the importance of eating adequate amounts of protein.

MILLER: Protein is key to brain chemistry. Clients need to eat at least three wholesome meals a day. Each meal needs to include sufficient quantities of high-quality proteins.

PAM: So even for people struggling with attention deficit disorder (ADD), you're recommending high-quality animal protein and supplements to help build the neurotransmitters?

MILLER: Right. When I worked with kids with ADD, I ask them if they liked eggs. The usual response is yes. They like eggs because they know intrinsically that eggs will make them feel better. Eggs are such a complete food. Just switching to a complete protein like eggs (instead of carbohydrates) can cause improvements in a child's behavior and even their grades. People think complicated problems need complicated solutions, but it's not true. A small change in the diet can bring about a wealth of wonderful change in a child.

PAM: What do you see with regard to the diets of addicts?

MILLER: Their diets are awful. If people are addicted to uppers, they may not eat for days on end. When they do eat, they eat junk. Their diets are full of simple carbohydrates (sugar) and processed foods. The nutritional deficiencies further aggravate the problems they already have. They further compromise their neurotransmitters.

PAM: So addiction begins with damaged neurotransmitters brought about by malnourishment. The addict then self-medicates with a given substance that further destroys their neurotransmitters, which in turn calls for more self-medicating.

MILLER: Right. Rather than producing its own supply of neurotransmitters, the brain relies on drugs. Basically, the brain shuts down production of certain neurotransmitters. That's why addicts experience symptoms of withdrawal—because the brain begins to depend upon the alcohol or other drugs to try and create homeostasis.

PAM: In your book *Overload: Attention Deficit Disorder and the Addictive Brain*, you describe how you and Dr. Blum discovered the connection between ADD and addiction.

MILLER: It's a natural connection. Neurotransmitters need to work together in a reward cascade. When this doesn't happen, then there's a deficiency. And when there's a deficiency, an individual may begin to self-medicate. ADD and addiction are signs that brain chemistry is out of balance.

PAM: In simple terms, children who are diagnosed with ADD are being given drugs to mask the symptoms of malnutrition.

MILLER: Absolutely! And we still don't really know the long-term damage being done by giving children drugs like Ritalin. When I used to see children with ADD, I used to recommend natural solutions and try to prevent them from going on Ritalin.

PAM: Why does a child with hyperactivity get a stimulant like Ritalin?

MILLER: Ritalin normalizes their brain. Their brain is under-reactive. A stimulant will give them something they don't have ordinarily. It brings them to baseline "normal" and is not making them euphoric. The body and brain are always trying to make up for what is lost.

PAM: Can children with ADD also be low in dopamine?

MILLER: They need dopamine and norepinephrine to activate the frontal lobes. And there are much better options available than what the medical community has to offer to stimulate the frontal lobes. For example, if I take tyrosine, B6 and DL-phenylalanine, I can tell you the moment I start feeling better. I have more energy, and I start thinking more clearly. It has a subtle yet reinforcing effect.

PAM: That combination sounds like it would be much better than caffeine as a stimulant.

MILLER: The difference between a cup of coffee and an amino acid, like tyrosine, is that the amino acid actually rebuilds the neurotransmitter and the caffeine actually interferes with the proper functioning of the neurotransmitters.

PAM: Do you believe that we are turning our children into addicts?

MILLER: Well, just look at sugar. Even in processed foods, energy drinks, etc. They're even calling sugar-laden drinks "healthy." Children are very vulnerable.

PAM: But doesn't sugar act like a drug in the body? Doesn't it diminish the brain's ability to produce serotonin?

MILLER: Right. Essentially, in response to an imbalance in their brain chemistry, children are drugging themselves with sugar.

PAM: So if they feel a lull in the day, they grab for more sugar or sometimes even caffeine. If adults are allowing their children to consume caffeinated beverages, including coffee, they're telling them that it's okay to alter their moods with a substance.

MILLER: Right. They see adults eating sugar and drinking coffee, so it stands to reason that they would do the same thing.

PAM: When people are feeling depressed or anxious, they're not able to create those brain waves to make them feel calm, peaceful, joy.

MILLER: Absolutely. One thing leads to another. A domino effect takes place. If they feel anxious or depressed, then they're not going to eat properly and they'll undoubtedly make bad decisions. They may turn to drugs, alcohol or even become violent. There are a lot of people in jail right now who have these problems and could be helped with good nutrition. If fact, some studies have shown remarkable improvements in violent prisoners after improving their nutrition.

PAM: What will it take before governments, health practitioners, hospitals and addiction centers start to acknowledge the importance of nutritional protocols?

MILLER: I don't know. I think it will be up to grassroots programs, which is what is starting to happen now. We need to pool our resources together. The Alliance for Addiction Solutions and CARA (Community Addiction Recovery Association) are groups that are helping to educate people about the importance of nutritional protocols. We need more practitioners learning and implementing our protocols.

PAM: What is the key message you want to get out to those working in conventional addiction centers?

MILLER: Mainstream addiction therapists need to learn that if an addict gives up their addiction, they're still not well, more work needs to be done in order to help that individual. Addiction is a physiological problem. It is a brain/body problem and is not just a behavioral problem.

PAM: Thank you for your sharing your time and wisdom with me.

JOAN MATHEWS-LARSON, PhD

I'm head strong about not calling anything psychological until you can prove to me that there's not an underlying physical reason.

—

For most treatment centers, it's about getting them off street drugs and getting them on prescription drugs for life.

—Joan Mathews-Larson, PhD

Joan Mathews-Larson holds a doctorate in nutrition and is the founder and executive director of a new psycho-biological model for treating addictions and emotional disorders at Health Recovery Center in Minneapolis, Minnesota. Over the last twenty years, she has treated addictions and mood disorders in over five thousand people from all over the world. The unique focus of the Health Recovery Center includes repairing the biochemical damage behind impaired mental functioning and behavior problems. Because of the high recovery rates at Health Recovery Center, her work has received national recognition and been published in scientific journals. Her best-selling books *Seven Weeks to Sobriety* (1992) and *Depression-Free Naturally* (2000) have led to over 500 television and radio appearances including 20/20, CNBC-TV, *The Susan Powter Show*, ABC Network News, Universal Studios American Health Network and CBN-TV's *The 700 Club*.

Dr. Mathews-Larson offers a tremendous amount of information at her Web site, www.healthrecovery.com.

* * *

PAM: At your Health Recovery Center in Minneapolis, you're helping people overcome addiction and emotional problems. What brought you to this field?

MATHEWS-LARSON: I entered this field after experiencing a great deal of tragedy in my life. My husband died of a heart attack when my son was about 13 years old. When he was young, he was a happy-go-lucky child but grief probably played a role, and he stopped caring about school and started gravitating toward kids who were drinking beer or smoking marijuana. He stopped coming home for meals, ate lots of junk food. He was up and down with his moods. So at a very young age, my son developed addictions to alcohol and marijuana. It took me a few years before we admitted him into a hospital-based addiction program that made all sorts of promises to help him. After treatment, sadly, he committed suicide.

PAM: I'm sorry to hear that. What did you do to help deal with his death?

MATHEWS-LARSON: After my son's suicide, I questioned the effectiveness of these 12-Step programs and thought there must be something more to the roots of addiction and emotional problems. I began questioning conventional treatment programs. I knew what they were doing wasn't adequate, and I needed to understand what happened. I had no idea what I was looking for, but I started studying nutrition and discovered that when the body is given what it needs, the brain can function much better. People are misled into believing that toxic pharmacological drugs can balance the brain. In fact, our brain depends on nutrients. In the 1970s, I started learning about the precursor amino acids that build neurotransmitters and essential fatty acids. And in 1980, I started Health Recovery Center dealing with nutritional medicine as it applied to addictions and mood disorders.

PAM: What is the main problem you see with conventional treatment programs?

MATHEWS-LARSON: Many of our clients have gone to several different treatment programs without success. They're still not well. Many conventional drug treatment programs rely on talk therapy, and you simply can't talk someone out of an addiction. In fact, about 98% of treatment still uses the 12-Step approach. During treatment, many of them are also put on five psychiatric drugs, and they're expected to stay on these drugs even though they create terrible side effects. Psychiatry makes them prisoners for life. The people who are peddling drugs are doing such harm.

PAM: By the time they come to see you, they must be at their wit's
                end.

MATHEWS-LARSON: They feel hopeless and helpless. After paying lots
                of money, entrusting their lives into the hands of supposed
                "experts," they're desperate to learn about our nutritional
                program. While in other conventional treatment centers,
                they were promised the world by doctors telling them that
                a magic pill will help them feel good again. These people
                were already magical thinkers before they came to treatment,
                when they were chasing drugs. They're very vulnerable. If
                an "expert" tells them a pill is the answer to their mood
                problems, of course they'll believe him. It's very easy to get
                them hooked again.

PAM: Do you think neurotransmitter testing could revolutionize
                medicine and recovery programs?

MATHEWS-LARSON: Neurotransmitter testing helps us learn things
                about a client that we would otherwise not be able to find
                out. Amino acid testing is helpful, but it doesn't tell us how
                the neurotransmitters are firing. For example, we tested a
                client the other day who was firing lots of dopamine, but the
                dopamine wasn't going on to make norepinephrine, which
                was why he was tired and didn't have a bubbly energy that
                he wanted.

PAM: There are two tests then, one for neurotransmitters and one
                for amino acids.

MATHEWS-LARSON: Yes. There are over 100 amino acids. We only know
                about a few. They hold the secrets of life. We need these
                amino acids to produce our serotonin, norepinephrine,
                dopamine, etc. With the information we have now, we can
                help people get well, but we still have a lot to learn about
                the amino acids and neurotransmitters. For example, there's
                been some recent interest in the amino acid theanine. It's an
                amino acid that can help calm you down, yet at the same
                time leave you alert.

PAM: At Health Recovery Center, do you do a lot of testing?

MATHEWS-LARSON: We do a tremendous amount of testing, including
                adrenals, thyroid, amino acids, neurotransmitters, allergies,
                blood sugar and pyroluria. Testing provides the proof you

need to convince the client that he/she's dealing with a very physical problem.

PAM: Some of the very common problems include hypoglycemia and adrenal problems.

MATHEWS-LARSON: They all have blood sugar problems—they're all hypoglycemic. We do the 5-hour glucose tolerance test and also test their adrenals. Normally, the adrenals are tired, overworked, because when their blood sugar is going up and down on a daily basis, the adrenals rush in to release emergency sugar to save the day. Over time, this can exhaust the adrenals. We test the adrenals in the 24-hour urine hormone test. We look at the levels of cortisone, cortisol, DHEA and variations of different hormones working together. Endocrinologist John Tintera believed that alcoholics suffered with hypoadrenocorticism (the lack of adequate adrenal cortical hormone production or imbalance among these hormones). He wasn't far off base—we see a lot of people who have very stressed adrenal glands. We have an adrenal formula that has phosphatidylserine, DHEA and other ingredients. Plus, we teach our clients how to take care of their adrenal glands.

PAM: So you teach them how to relax?

MATHEWS-LARSON: When you have too much cortisol going through the body, you can't learn how to relax. People who are wrapped up with the idea that psychological approaches will solve people's problems are off target. In order to help these people truly get well, they need to look at the physical (biochemical) imbalances. If someone has a personality or mood disorder, don't judge them or psychoanalyze them. Look at their adrenals, thyroid, blood sugar, etc., to see what is causing their peculiar behavior. Inevitably, their lab tests show that their problems are biochemical and that they don't have a personality disorder at all.

PAM: Julia Ross calls peculiar behavior "false moods." These people could be bitchy, grumpy, irritable, forgetful, judgmental, perfectionists, etc. Thanks to your testing, we can say that these false moods are not natural to man. Not long ago, we only ate a few pounds of sugar a year, now we're eating up to 150 pounds of sugar a year. We have a nation of "wacky" sugar addicts.

MATHEWS-LARSON: Someone who is hypoglycemic and addicted to sugar will not give up their sugar until you convince them with a test. Remember, they're addicted to sugar, so it's very difficult for them to give it up.

PAM: Sugar is a drug.

MATHEWS-LARSON: Absolutely it's a drug. I used to be addicted to sugar, so I know what being addicted to sugar feels like. The symptoms feel psychological, but they're really physical. People feel like they're cracking up.

PAM: Dr. Hoffer emphasizes the importance of B vitamins.

MATHEWS-LARSON: He's always focused on the B vitamins, especially niacin (B3). When I started out, we gave everyone a lot of niacin, two to three grams a day. Some didn't respond. Others, however, regained their sanity after years of suffering from alcoholism. It was miraculous. Bill W., co-founder of Alcoholics Anonymous (AA), cited a story about an alcoholic taking three grams of niacin, but who was still not very functional. But when he took eight grams, which is a very high dose, he was fine.

PAM: Dr. Hoffer explains that niacin is a dose-dependent supplement. If you don't take the right dose, you probably won't feel the benefits. The B vitamins play a role in the production of the neurotransmitters.

MATHEWS-LARSON: The messages our brain sends back and forth between our nerves depend on B complex vitamins. In other words, the B vitamins need to be there in order for the neurotransmitters to be used and distributed properly. Partially hydrogenated fats block the body's ability to bring the essential fatty acids to the brain. Millions of people are missing the essential fatty acids and B vitamins that control all the nerve circuitry. That explains why so many people appear to be crazy.

PAM: I understand that 90% of our hormones are either produced in or controlled by the brain.

MATHEWS-LARSON: And the brain is 2/3 essential fatty acids and cholesterol. If the pharmaceutical companies get their way, they could influence doctors to put millions of children on statin drugs, which would be a disaster. Their brains aren't fully formed, and they're trying to reduce their cholesterol. That's crazy!

PAM: Do you see clients who have developed mood disorders or addictions after being exposed to environmental toxins, or after developing a systemic infection?

MATHEWS-LARSON: Many of our clients have had serious health problems after being exposed to environmental toxins, including mold, industrial chemicals, etc. They may have worked in beauty salons, factories, or been exposed to industrial cleaning solvents. Their immune systems have broken down. They're struggling with candida (imbalance in gut flora). They can't tolerate chemicals or environmental toxins and are very reactive. We had one young man who came to see us who had acne. He'd been on antibiotics for 10 years, which compromised his immune system. He got into drugs and alcohol. He was on all kinds of psychiatric drugs. He had lots of personality problems. The personality is just a reflection of an underlying physiological cause, and if you don't treat the cause, you can never win. You can't use band-aid solutions.

PAM: What about people who have systemic infections? In psychiatry, doctors know that peoples' personalities can change after being exposed to an infection. Their adrenals and neurotransmitters are compromised. Even though they know this, they don't do the proper testing, nor do they help patients by repairing the damage done by the infection.

MATHEWS-LARSON: Of course, you're right. It's unfortunate that in psychiatry, they don't do these tests.

PAM: What are the symptoms of someone who is a "dry drunk"?

MATHEWS-LARSON: They have all the characteristics of someone who has hypoglycemia and hypoadrenocorticism. In my book, I write about a study done by a doctor who had just graduated from medical school. He was too sick to practice medicine and figured out on his own that he had hypoglycemia. He tried to find help in the medical world, including the Mayo Clinic, but couldn't find the help he needed. He studied the symptoms of hypoglycemia: mood swings, anxiety, exhaustion, poor memory, shakiness, dizziness, depression, suicidal intent, etc. When he learned about hypoglycemia and got well, his entire practice focused on hypoglycemia.

PAM: Have you studied hypoglycemia before and after treatment?

MATHEWS-LARSON: In the 1980s, I did a study looking at symptoms of hypoglycemia before and after treatment, and after treatment, their symptoms, including cravings, almost entirely disappeared. Most of the people in the study had chronic fatigue . . .

PAM: Based on the symptoms you described, hypoglycemia appears to be an epidemic, why don't doctors diagnose or treat it?

MATHEWS-LARSON: First of all, getting people to change their diets is too much work. Writing prescriptions is a quick process, and that way, they can see more patients. The more patients they see, the more money they make. Secondly, most doctors don't like to do the 5-hour glucose tolerance test because it takes time and work.

PAM: Ninety percent of addicts don't go for help. Even though they know their addiction could be killing them, they don't seem to want to let it go.

MATHEWS-LARSON: They don't want to give up their addiction because they get some real relief from how they feel. It lessens their depression. It takes away their anxiety. They're emotionally unstable and want relief.

PAM: Drugs and mental illness seem to go hand in hand.

MATHEWS-LARSON: Schizophrenics love marijuana and nicotine. They feel better on these drugs. Aside from other side effects, marijuana lowers zinc in your body, and zinc controls the rise of copper to the brain. People with high copper are very untrusting and are antisocial. Many addicts have pyroluria, which means they are low in vitamin B6 and zinc. Pyrolurics can experience angry outbursts, hyperactivity, paranoia and even experience hallucinations from the high copper.

PAM: People come to see you after they've been promised the world by psychiatrists who prescribed legal drugs.

MATHEWS-LARSON: They've tried to get off prescription drugs and can't. They have horrible side effects: shocks, depression, hopelessness. The side effects make you think you have to go back on the drugs. Instead of pulling the drugs, doctors double the dose. We see people who are on very high doses of drugs such as antipsychotics (Zyprexa, Abilify). Some of these drugs have black box warnings because they can cause people to commit suicide. These drugs can also cause diabetes.

PAM: I understand that benzodiazepines are very difficult to come off.

MATHEWS-LARSON: They're the worst. A lot of women take benzos because they're feeling anxious. If someone has been on benzos for 15 years, we'd have a really tough time getting them off. Structurally, their brains have changed. The side effects from coming off these drugs can be very uncomfortable. If they're young and they come to see us after they've been taking the drugs for a year or two, we can do something. Psychiatrists feed on their patients' weaknesses, then they fill them up with drugs. These people typically test hypoglycemic, or have pyroluria, thyroid, adrenal problems, or are allergy-addicted.

PAM: Can you explain what you mean by "allergy-addicted"?

MATHEWS-LARSON: People who are allergic to certain foods and who keep going to those foods do so because these foods release endorphins, which gives the individual a sense of comfort. Eventually, they're in a funk and have to keep going back to that food in order to make themselves feel good. Alcoholics who are allergy-addicted go back to alcohol because it gives them an energy boost. This type of alcoholic is not really an alcoholic at all—they're allergy-addicted. The real alcoholic can drink you under the table and may show no effects at all for many years. They have an enzyme that is very efficiently processing the alcohol (or any other drug, for that matter) so that they're less affected. This behavior can go on for many years before the body starts breaking down.

PAM: What kinds of results are you getting?

MATHEWS-LARSON: We did a study that showed that we have a 74% success rate after 3½ years. It was a very good study. The 26% who failed had gone back to smoking.

PAM: I think people are catching on to the excessive use of prescription drugs, especially by psychiatry. Overall, about 50% of Americans are taking prescription drugs.

MATHEWS-LARSON: When it comes to psychiatric drugs, psychiatry used to say 1/20 had psychiatric problems, now they're saying ½. That's rubbish!

PAM: By prescribing these drugs, psychiatry is adding insult to injury.

MATHEWS-LARSON: That's right. Medical doctors are good at helping us recover from accidents or other acute health problems. As for chronic conditions or "psychological" disturbances, they really aren't helping by prescribing toxic drugs.

PAM: Chronic disease is really all about carbohydrate addiction. I think if more clinicians would treat people for their carbohydrate addiction first, they would have more success in treating people with chronic disease.

MATHEWS-LARSON: Thank you for saying that. I absolutely believe that. Look around us. Even the diabetic association won't loudly warn people about carbohydrates. They'd rather endorse drugs.

PAM: The carbohydrates are contributing to malnutrition, brain starvation, hypoglycemia, etc.

MATHEWS-LARSON: And they lead to psychiatric disturbances.

PAM: Everyone I've interviewed looks up to you. You are a true pioneer in this field. How have you been received by those working in conventional treatment centers?

MATHEWS-LARSON: When I went into this field in 1976, I was excited to tell the world about our findings. I thought people working in the addiction field would want to learn this information, or at least leave us alone to do our work. In the beginning, it was awful. The majority of people working in this field have a great deal of condemnation for what we're doing (namely, repairing the damage that's been done from drugs and addiction). We have a logical approach, but they still fight what we're doing here. I never understood their opposition. I guess what we're doing challenges all of their psychology degrees. After all these years being here in Minnesota, there's not one treatment center that does what we're doing at Health Recovery Center. We've had a lot of opposition from the treatment field but overwhelming support and recognition from clients worldwide.

PAM: How would you best describe the vicious cycle of addiction?

MATHEWS-LARSON: When people take drugs for the first time, the experience can be like Alice in Wonderland. You can't wait for the second time. But it never holds up. And gradually, it turns on you and sometimes you can't get out. It owns you. People don't have any idea what they're taking on when they get hooked.

PAM: Are we living in an addictive society?

MATHEWS-LARSON: Of course! After a child takes Ritalin, then eventually they, he/she, may turn to a full-blown amphetamine. When kids are introduced to a substance that alters their mood, what does that teach them? By the time they're teenagers, they could be out on the streets looking for something else. Not just what their psychiatrist is prescribing. They may also have an array of drugs in their parents' medicine cabinets. (The street dealer is slowly going out of business, because psychiatry is stocking peoples' medicine cabinets.) It's a candy store.

PAM: Are we turning our children into addicts?

MATHEWS-LARSON: It's unbelievable what psychiatry is willing to do to our children. I don't understand how cruel they can be—after all, they have children too! I see so many horror stories every day. I can't believe what psychiatry is willing to do to people. This isn't any different than what went on in Nazi Germany. Developing brains do very poorly on toxic drugs. I've been treating a steady stream of young people, mostly young men, who've been put on drugs for attention deficit disorder (ADD), like Ritalin, which is slowed-down cocaine. And six-year-old children are taking this drug. I see people much younger damaged now. Legally so.

PAM: Have you had a lot of success getting young people off drugs like Ritalin?

MATHEWS-LARSON: Every person we've seen with ADD who has been on psychiatric drugs like Ritalin—we've been able to get them off these drugs with no bad results. We treat the underlying causes by fixing their biochemistry.

PAM: Low cholesterol will increase your risk for depression or suicidal thoughts. And the precursors to addiction are depression or anxiety.

MATHEWS-LARSON: Absolutely. Putting kids on statin drugs is yet another vicious attack against them. Very few people realize the devastating effects of anti-cholesterol drugs (statins). They will destroy their brain even more. The most common element in the brain is fat and cholesterol. Lowering their cholesterol will cause all sorts of symptoms, including depression and memory loss. And remember, depression is a precursor to addiction.

PAM: What is the main message you'd like to share with people about the work that you're doing?

MATHEWS-LARSON: The reason we do this work is that we want people to realize that their addiction and/or mood problems are not a life sentence and that they can get well using nutritional protocols.

PAM: So you have a message of hope for people dealing with addictions and mood disorders or mental illness?

MATHEWS-LARSON: Yes.

PAM: By the time they've gone through your program, what kinds of changes do you see in your students/clients?

MATHEWS-LARSON: By the time they graduate from here, we want to make sure they leave without cravings and that they feel whole and happy. For some individuals, their cravings are gone within the first week. When they come to our center, we give them hope. They come in feeling shame and guilt, and they leave feeling balance, joy, happiness.

PAM: How does it make you feel knowing that you've been able to help thousands of people recover from addiction?

MATHEWS-LARSON: We have been able to help people from all over the world. It's very rewarding to see people get their lives back. My goal is to be able to share this approach with everyone who is dealing with addiction or a mood disorder—even with therapists who are burned out because their conventional approach is not working. Everyone who is touched by addiction deserves to know that there are effective natural solutions.

PAM: Your big motivation has been your son's suicide.

MATHEWS-LARSON: That made me oblivious to any criticism or turning away from my intent. I've persevered.

PAM: You also wanted to save the next child.

MATHEWS-LARSON: You bet! And we are helping young kids get off alcohol and all kinds of drugs, including prescription drugs.

Our children are our most precious resources, and they deserve to be given the best that life has to offer.

PAM: Thank you for your time. It's been a pleasure speaking with you today. I appreciate your passion and commitment in helping so many people get well.

JULIA ROSS, MA

> My introduction to the fields of addiction and eating disorders
> led me to expect miracles from psychotherapy and instead I
> found dismal failure.

> —

> Most addicts are so depleted that to restore the deep deficiencies
> in the brain neurotransmitters that can pull up their moods
> and eliminate their cravings for alcohol, drugs and junk
> foods, they need neurotransmitter first aid: brain-targeted
> nutritional supplements called amino acids.

> —Julia Ross, Smart Life Forum, December 16, 2004

Julia Ross is a psychotherapist and a pioneer in the field of nutritional psychology. Since 1975, she has been helping individuals suffering from addictions, eating disorders and mood problems. She is the founder and director of Recovery Systems in Mill Valley, California, an outpatient treatment clinic for alcohol, drug and food addictions and mood problems. She says that her clients are suffering from "false emotions," which are generated from a malnourished brain. She does not believe that addictions and mood disorders can be blamed on psychological stress and says that the cause has to do with the highly stressful diets we have adopted over the last 40 years. She attributes a large part of her success to encouraging her clients to return to our age-old custom of eating "three square meals" per day. In addition, she has also seen a tremendous amount of success in recommending nutritional supplements, specifically brain-targeted amino acids.

After using nutritional therapies for more than thirty years, she says, "Several thousand clients later, the amino acids are our most effective weapons for fighting addiction."[383] Furthermore, she adds, "Addicts who took the amino acids were able to stay away from drugs and alcohol. Those who took no aminos had four times higher relapse rates!"[384] She has also had remarkable results with those who suffer from eating disorders: "In two weeks on the aminos . . . they have freed themselves of their obsessions with food and most of their associated mood problems."[385] Using her nutritional protocols, cravings for food and drugs can disappear within 24-48 hours.

For more information about her work, visit her Web site at www.moodcure.com or www.recoverysystemsclinic.com.

* * *

PAM: Prior to integrating nutrition into your counseling programs, what types of psycho-spiritual approaches were you using to help people recover from addictions and/or eating disorders?

ROSS: In order to reduce costs, most treatment programs provide only 12-Step meetings and group therapy and may only offer 30-day programs. Compared to these treatment centers, our facility used a broader base of very intensive therapies. Not only did we offer group therapy, we also instituted family and individual therapy, early childhood weekend workshops, art therapy, drama therapy and more. Furthermore, most residents stayed in the program for up to two years! Everyone attended 12-Step programs. We had an exceptional opportunity to work with people using a rich blend of approaches and still we were not getting the results we were hoping for.

PAM: What happened in the 1980s that made you start looking for more answers?

ROSS: Crack cocaine. We had no idea how to deal with it. In spite of how intensive our counseling and 12-Step treatments were, in the 1980s when crack hit the streets, our success rates dropped dramatically. Relapse rates went from 50% to 100%! That meant 100% relapse 24 hours after leaving treatment. This was standard throughout the U.S. after the crack epidemic hit. And many crack addicts could not even tolerate more than a few days in treatment. The AWOL rate was 40%.

PAM: As a psychotherapist, how did you first start exploring the effect that nutrition has on moods and addiction?

ROSS: I found research indicating that nutrition might be a helpful avenue to pursue. I read the work of James Milam about the central role of pathological, genetic hypoglycemia in alcoholics. In *Under the Influence* he showed how much better people did when they removed sugar, white flour and caffeine from their diets. We then began adding nutritional education to the programs we already had. But, unlike Milam, we had an outpatient program with no control over our clients' diets. Fortunately, in 1986 I began learning about amino acid therapy in relation to addiction treatment. On top of making dietary suggestions, we began adding brain-targeted nutritional supplements. Dr. Kenneth Blum's clinical research was a revelation. He discovered the neurotransmitters that are deficient in alcoholics and drug addicts, including GABA, endorphin, dopamine and serotonin. He also developed and researched amino acid formulas that helped alcoholics and drug addicts recover by raising all of these neurotransmitter levels.

PAM: When did you start recommending supplements to your clients?

ROSS: As soon as we read Blum's early studies in 1986 and had their findings confirmed by Joan Mathews-Larson. Our clients reported that when they started taking the amino acids at home, they started feeling better almost immediately. In 1994 we started giving our clients the amino acids during their first appointment at our office, and we could see that they actually responded within 5-10 minutes.

PAM: That's remarkable! Can you give an example of how the amino acids have worked that quickly?

ROSS: The first person we ever gave the amino acids to was a crack addict. He took some tyrosine and was able to stay clean for the first time in years. Tyrosine typically works wonderfully for people who are addicted to any stimulants.

PAM: When that happens, not only must you get their attention, you probably also give them some hope right away.

ROSS: Yes. And we confirm their own sense of the problem. They don't want to be abusing alcohol or drugs, but they don't "feel normal" within themselves and never have. They feel *sub*normal and so they are forced to self-medicate. When their sense of well-being improves after taking the amino acids, it confirms that something really was wrong with their mood chemistry, not their moral fiber. In taking a different approach to the problem (i.e., using the amino acids to rebuild the neurotransmitters), we can repair the biochemical flaw that created the addictive cravings in the first place.

PAM: So in turning to street drugs, they are actually trying to give themselves a "lift" because they feel low.

ROSS: That's right. Sometimes, they've been battling lifelong depression or anxiety, or both. They don't know where to turn to correct the negative moods, so they turn to drugs. Then they discover that cocaine or meth can lift their spirits. And when they get that lift, they can't stop. Then when they discover the amino acids, a natural substance that doesn't harm them, that helps rebuild the neurotransmitters and helps give them a natural lift, they're thrilled. They no longer feel so ashamed of themselves for having used drugs. And their families see their addiction in a new light, too and their pain and *resentment* ease as well.

PAM: Based upon your initial experiences as a psychotherapist, you've learned that psycho-spiritual approaches are not adequate.

ROSS: The 12-Step programs offer the fellowship of other people struggling to stay clean, but they can't help change genetically entrenched neurotransmitter deficits. Even though I value counseling and 12-Step programs, spiritual and psychological approaches can't reverse the biochemical problems. Recovering addicts go to lots of meetings where they drink coffee and eat cookies. It would be better if they didn't serve anything at all! Bill Wilson, co-founder of AA, knew that psycho-spiritual approaches weren't enough and tried to recommend nutritional treatments to members of AA, but he was told that if he did, he'd have to resign from the board of AA. They told him he could teach nutrition privately, but that they wouldn't support it.

By normalizing their neurotransmitters, we help people develop the capacity to experience spiritual meaning and psychological healing. When they're exploring psycho-spiritual healing, recovering people complain that they can't focus, pray, or meditate because their minds won't turn off. They can't sit still. They're anxious and can't calm down. They can't tolerate the pain of reliving the past in psychotherapy because their pain tolerance is biochemically crippled. Once stabilizing neurotransmitters are restored, then they can effectively focus on psycho-spiritual work.

PAM: What types of clients do you see at your clinic?

ROSS: My clinic treats food addictions and mood problems as well as alcohol and drug addictions. The most motivated people we see are those who suffer from compulsive eating, because they want to lose weight! We see even more of them than we do alcoholics and drug addicts, probably because there are so many more of them now, as our obesity epidemic explodes. My first book, *The Diet Cure*, about recovering from carbohydrate addiction, draws food addicts to our clinic from all over the world. Many of them are in recovery from alcohol or drug addiction and have used substitute brain addicters like sugar to cope. Sugar is four times more addictive than cocaine because of its neurotransmitter effects, but the amino acids turn off the cravings as our clients quickly discover

PAM: I understand that it may be difficult to convince addicts that your treatment is different and that it's more successful than other conventional treatment programs.

ROSS: Alcohol and drug addicts can be very leery about any treatment programs because they have failed in conventional treatment and know so many people who have been through programs and failed. To overcome this understandable resistance, we assess their *neurotransmitter function as soon as they come in and start them on the appropriate amino acids right in the office. Positive results are apparent within 10 minutes.* That motivates them to continue.

PAM: When it comes to following your protocols, are your clients compliant?

ROSS: By the time people come to us, most of them have tried everything else. They're ready to listen and tend to be extremely compliant. Especially after they've felt the effects of the aminos in the office they are very excited and they notice that when they forget to take the aminos that they feel the cravings and negative moods come right back. So they tend to be very committed to their regimens (which last 6-18 months.) Some alcohol and drug addicts are so destabilized by their substance use that they're not very functional by the time they come to us. We are an outpatient program. We need to send these more progressed addicts to inpatient programs. But we send them after we have put them on a full vitamin, mineral and amino acid protocol. And we only send them to inpatient programs that will co-operate with these nutritional protocols and provide healthful food. Once they start the neurotransmitter therapy, they typically start to feel better right away—then they're more willing and able to follow through with our entire treatment process, which involves nutritional education and food preparation as well as monitoring and altering their supplement and dietary intake, as needed (e.g., to remove foods they're intolerant to.

PAM: So often today we hear about people suffering from mood problems or addiction. Road rage, explosive anger, depression, anxiety, obsessive-compulsive behavior, etc. I've also noticed how critical and negative people can be. This can't be normal behavior. What's changed over the last few decades that could be contributing to these problems?

Ross: Since we began eating more refined sweet and starchy carbohydrates and less fresh produce, animal protein and traditional (i.e., saturated) fats in our diets, we have literally been starving our brains. In the 1960s, we were still eating home-cooked food three times a day, and our food was still relatively fresh. Fast food was very rare. There were still few people who were overweight or addicted. In the 1970s, the cholesterol scare really changed our diets for the worse. The whole culture became terrified of fats, of heart disease and of getting fat. We were terrorized into a low-fat diet. And then all these low-fat, high-sugar foods hit the market. Because we were being told to give up fat, we started loading up on carbs. And we equated eating carbs with being athletic. The whole country began eating a low-fat, high-carb diet. The more fanatical and addicted we got about this diet, the less animal protein we ate as well (because animal protein contains fat). Without this protein, our neurotransmitters have become depleted. That's when brain starvation, depression, anxiety and obesity really took hold. More people began to gain weight and as a result, yo-yo dieting started *leading to* even worse brain starvation.

PAM: When people are in a low mood, they tend to eat simple carbohydrates in order to bring their mood up.

ROSS: Yes, they do. We used to hear our parents say, "Don't eat sugar. It ruins your appetite." Now, our appetites have been ruined. Nobody eats real meals anymore. They go back and forth drinking caffeine, skipping meals, eating nutritionally empty high-carb foods and dieting. This is a recipe for brain and body malnutrition on an unprecedented scale.

PAM: The first signs of starvation are anxiety and depression. This way of eating has contributed to many problems, not just obesity and overweight. When clients come to you suffering from mood problems (or what you call "false moods") and/or addictions, does part of their healing include eating three wholesome meals per day?

ROSS: Yes. It can't be done otherwise. Their blood sugar is typically so unstable, that they often actually need to eat more than three times per day. In helping to maintain stable blood sugar, I find that the amino acid glutamine and the mineral chromium, taken between meals, are often critical. This is especially true for alcoholics and carb addicts, whose overpowering cravings are often triggered by hypoglycemia.

PAM: What is the link between addiction and eating disorders?

ROSS: We see many people who are suffering from compulsive overeating and bulimia. When it comes to these types of disorders, any or all of the neurotransmitters can be at issue, just as they can be in alcohol and drug addiction. We have them fill out questionnaires in order to identify which neurotransmitters are deficient. For example, endorphin-deficient bulimics experience an endorphin level rise after they binge, but with some of them, endorphin levels rise higher when they purge. Some people get an endorphin high when they starve. Other overeaters who, like most alcoholics, only binge in the evenings, suffer from serotonin deficiency. Most are hypoglycemic as are all alcoholics. Most addicts and alcoholics switch to sugar and starch in recovery, which keeps them unstable and leads to relapse. It's not unusual for bulimic women to switch from carbs to alcohol addiction and back again.

PAM: So people suffering from eating disorders are experiencing a form of addiction?

ROSS: These people are physiologically addicted (auto-addicted) to endorphins and serotonin. They have to overeat because they're addicted to the endorphin and/or serotonin rush that junk foods elicit. They have to binge and purge for the same reason. That's why we have to use the aminos to repair the endorphin deficit as well as the other neurotransmitters, including serotonin, in order to stop the food cravings. When blood sugar drops too low, it can trigger uncontrollable, addictive cravings for either carbs or alcohol.

PAM: Many people blame eating disorders on skinny models. Based upon what you're saying regarding deficient neurotransmitters, is this an oversimplification?

ROSS: Wanting to emulate skinny models can be the trigger, causing them to begin the cycle by undereating. Once they start starving themselves because of this false beauty image they're trying to mimic, then their neurotransmitters levels drop and they can become obsessive and can't stop starving themselves. Others begin bingeing as an involuntary reaction to too much low calorie dieting. Since the 1970s, when we first began seeing eating disorders, these problems have gotten much worse. Especially for those with a genetic tendency to produce marginal amounts of the key neurotransmitters, any *dieting* can be a disaster. I discuss this at length in *The Diet Cure*.

PAM: When individuals suffer from eating disorders, it must be difficult to get them to eat even healthy foods.

ROSS: No, it isn't. We love working with bulimics and overeaters, whose carb cravings we can stop, typically within a few days. With an anorexic, it's a different story. We don't even talk about eating more food for a few weeks, because we know they can't hear us. If they're dangerously thin, we send them to the hospital, but if they're not, then we put them on nutrient supplements. They're not afraid of supplements which contain little or no calories. Gradually, the nutrients start to rebuild their brain chemistry and they start to feel happier and less obsessive. The brain will then guide their eating in a healthier direction that they can tolerate.

PAM: What type of testing do you do in order to determine their neurotransmitter deficiencies?

ROSS: Normally, we don't have to do testing. We mainly assess
           through symptom questionnaires. Since the 1970s, the
           symptomology of neurotransmitter deficiency has been
           very well established in the scientific literature. If there's a
           complicated situation, then we do blood testing for amino
           acids and neurotransmitters. We have found urine testing to
           be very unreliable.

PAM: It seems as though the human race is deteriorating. Over
           the last century, we've seen an enormous increase in chronic
           diseases, but we've also seen an increase in mood problems,
           including depression and anxiety. During this time, we've
           reduced the amount of protein we consume and increased
           our carbohydrate consumption. It seems as though we're
           stuck in a vicious cycle because carbohydrates (especially
           refined carbohydrates like flour and sugar) can be very
           addictive.

ROSS: Prior to 1950, the mood and weight problems we see today
           were rare, as was addiction. Before 1900, they were almost
           nonexistent. We were mentally and physically very much
           more robust, resilient and healthy until after 1970. Since
           then we've become addicted to toxic foods that literally spoil
           our appetites for the wholesome foods that would otherwise
           be preserving our natural capacity for optimal mood and
           health. The food industry is aware of this. It knows that
           heavily processed foods can be very addictive, including
           breakfast cereals, which are now up to 55% sugar and corn
           syrup.

PAM: Which is what millions of children eat for breakfast in
           the morning! As we've incorporated more commercially
           processed foods into our diets, we've become much sicker.
           Your books offer very simple nutritional solutions. As these
           problems have become worse over the last 20 years or so,
           even people who work in the natural health field don't seem
           to know much about the effects that protein and amino acids
           have on brain chemistry.

ROSS: The crucial connection between the amino acids found in dietary
           protein or in supplements and the brain's neurotransmitter
           function is little understood. Ethical and/or experimental
           diets are confused with healthy diets. For example, veganism

compounds the problem of protein deficiency tremendously. Our only safe course is to return to the pre-1900 diet that provided us with such solid mental and physical health.

PAM: Is there a growing awareness about how amino acids help with addiction and mood problems?

ROSS: The awareness is growing. We recently had a breakthrough. An organization that puts on large national conferences on addiction co-hosted a conference with The Alliance for Addiction Solutions, our international association promoting holistic treatment. Over 600 people attended! This was a shock that is reverberating through the whole treatment community in the U.S. Unfortunately, most addiction treatment programs still tend to undermine recovery by encouraging the use of sweets as a substitute for drugs and alcohol. Conventional doctors and psychiatrists get no nutritional training in medical school and so have no information about any solutions beyond the *pharmaceutical.* The public needs to be educated by books like this so that they can put pressure on treatment professionals.

PAM: Given how effective your treatments are, I'm surprised more therapists are not aware of your work.

ROSS: My books continue to sell very well in the U.S. and are being translated and sold in Europe, Australia, Japan and France as well. But the addiction treatment field is archaic, particularly on the subject of nutrition. Many program directors and other staff members have become so dependent on sugar, caffeine and tobacco in their own "recoveries" that they cannot tolerate the idea of living without them. The addicts are willing, but the staff is not. It's tragic for all concerned. Younger people who work in the addiction field feel as though they have to pretend that their treatment works, but they don't like what they see. They know that what they're doing isn't working. They're more ready than those who have been in the field for a long time to look at new approaches.

PAM: What I found most encouraging about your books, *The Diet Cure* and *The Mood Cure*, is how easy you make it to understand how food and certain supplements can affect our moods.

Ross: Thank you. That was my intent. People suffering from
          addictions feel helpless and hopeless and it's so unnecessary.
          These simple tools can make all the difference.
Pam: I appreciate your time and wisdom. Thank you for the
          incredible work you are doing.

STAN STOKES, MS, CCDC

Stan Stokes is the CEO and president of Bridging the Gaps Inc.—an integrated addiction treatment facility for adults in Winchester, Virginia—who has also worked in the field of addiction for the last 30 years. At Bridging the Gaps, qualified therapists have designed a highly successful approach that provides the nutritional treatments necessary to rebalance brain chemistry (oral and intravenous), along with a 12-Step-based psychosocial program.

With the help of Dr. Charles Gant, Dr. David Miller, Merlene Miller, Dr. James Braly, Dr. Joan Mathews-Larson and Julia Ross, Stokes has been able to develop a very successful treatment protocol using nutrition and amino acids. For more information, visit his Web site at www.bridgingthegaps.com.

* * *

PAM: What types of disorders are you treating at Bridging the Gaps?

STOKES: We see just about every disorder, including depression, anxiety, bipolar and several different types of addiction. Most of our clients have been to other treatment centers but haven't been able to get well.

PAM: How did you end up in the addiction field?

STOKES: I went through treatment over 30 years ago (1973). Back then, I was told that when you stop one drug, you pick up other addictions. For example, before treatment I used to smoke between three quarters of a pack and a pack of cigarettes per day. After treatment, I started smoking two to three packs per day. I used to drink one or two cups of coffee, but after treatment, I started drinking 12-15 cups of coffee per day. We would sneak out of the treatment center to go and get ice cream. We didn't go to get drugs, but as far as I'm concerned, sugar is a drug. After treatment, I would go to a 12-Step meeting and have cookies, ice cream and go home and be so depressed I would want to hurt myself. I couldn't understand what was going on. While I was in "recovery," I was having terrible mood swings. They told me that I would smoke more and drink more coffee, so I was doing what they told me I would do. I didn't see anything wrong with what I was doing. Except that it made me feel "wacky."

PAM: You were replacing one addiction with several other addictions.

STOKES: That's right.

PAM: Can you tell us about your addictions?

STOKES: In the throes of my alcoholism, I would start drinking at lunch because I had convinced myself that alcoholics started drinking in the morning. I'd have a few drinks, then I'd go home and take a nap, then I'd get up and do some serious drinking at night. In recovery, if I were to sit down in the afternoon and watch a movie, I would gorge myself with a large bag of corn chips and salsa, a two-liter bottle of pop and about a half pound of cookies. Then I would take a nap. I didn't realize that I was hypoglycemic and that I was allergic to corn. I found these things out later on. Gorging myself on junk foods wasn't much different from what I had been doing with alcohol. I gained a lot of weight (I gained 15 pounds in treatment and another 15 pounds within 30 days after treatment ended).

PAM: And what about your mood swings and depression?

STOKES: My mood swings and depression also got worse, and I had tremendous headaches almost every day. I had to question whether I truly was in recovery. It certainly didn't feel as though I was recovered. I used to ask myself, "Is *this* recovery?"

PAM: What were your drugs of choice?

STOKES: I was doing alcohol and hashish. I was too scared to do heroin and fortunately never did cocaine. I knew that, because of my personality, if I had turned to cocaine, I would have been in incredible trouble.

PAM: You describe yourself as having been depressed. Were you also very hyperactive? Manic-depressive?

STOKES: If a psychiatrist had diagnosed me, I would have been given the label manic-depressive. I don't believe I'm manic-depressive. I have attention deficit hyperactivity disorder (ADHD) and am learning-disabled. I'm dyslexic and dysgraphic. I didn't know I was any of those things, and I didn't know how they were affecting me. I had no idea that any of these things affected my ability to recover. Nor did I understand how my hypoglycemia and dysbiosis (imbalance in gut flora)—all the physical problems—affected my behavior. Even when I was very young, I can look back and see that my neurotransmitters have been out of balance for a very long time. At about the age of 4-6, for the thrill of it, I was already stealing out of stores. I was looking for the "high" that one can get from thrill-seeking. At a very young age, I was already doing things to elevate my mood.

PAM: How did you end up realizing that your symptoms were caused by poor nutrition and hypoglycemia?

STOKES: Nobody in the treatment field is talking about the role that diet and allergies could play in the area of addiction and mood problems. I sensed that food played a role in my condition, so I did as much research about nutrition as possible. I was inspired by my father, who, because of his colitis and allergies, learned about nutrition. We were raised on a whole-food diet and didn't eat white sugar. My mother even made her own yogurt. As part of my recovery, I remembered what my father had taught me at a young age. I bought several books about nutrition. My first book was called *Mega Nutrients for Your Nerves*. One book led to another book and then, in 1981, I read the book *Under the Influence* by Dr. James Milam and Katherine Ketcham and the book *Eating Right to Live Sober* by Katherine Ketcham and Anne Meuller. That was the first book that I found that referenced the work of Dr. Roger Williams. He had been studying alcoholism since the 1950s, and nobody seemed to be paying attention to his work. So I started reading all of Dr. Williams's work. In 1984, I retired from the air force and took a year off to further my education and to learn about how to get well. I went to Seattle to visit the Milam Institute and met with Dr. Meuller.

PAM: As a youngster, how did you manage to stray so far from a whole-foods diet?

STOKES: I rebelled against this diet when I got my own paper route at the age of 11. I had my own money, so I was able to buy soda pop and drink it for breakfast (away from home).

PAM: What therapeutic approaches do you use at Bridging the Gaps?

STOKES: Along with nutritional protocols, we also use psycho-spiritual approaches. Most conventional addiction treatment centers focus too much on psychological and spiritual approaches, and that's not enough to help addicts recover. They don't do anything to help balance the brain chemistry, except giving them drugs, which end up tricking the brain. Because they don't deal with the physiological aspects of drug and alcohol addiction, they have very high failure rates (it depends upon the facility, but it can be above 50%). The addict is then caught in the vicious circle of treatment, relapse, back to treatment. To me, what is sad is that it becomes a never-ending emotional roller coaster. At Bridging the Gaps, we look at traditional addiction treatments and alternative/integrative therapies that heal at the physical roots of the disease of addiction. We believe that physiology is the basis for addiction and then the psychological spiritual healing can take place. It's also important for the addict to be able to dedicate 90 days toward his/her recovery.

PAM: What patterns precede addiction? Most traditional therapies believe that it's because the addict comes from a dysfunctional family, but I know addicts who come from good families who are addicts and other people who come from very dysfunctional families and aren't addicts.

STOKES: One of the questions in our questionnaire is, "In your family tree, who has had addictions, who has had diabetes?" There's a big correlation between diabetes and addiction. There's also a strong correlation between compulsive overeating and addiction. In our questionnaire, we're looking for clues that would show a pattern toward an imbalance in brain chemistry.

PAM: When you were drinking, did you gravitate toward people who would enable your addiction?

STOKES: Of course. When I was addicted to alcohol and hash, I chose to work for a man who knew that I wouldn't make it to work until noon or at all for that matter. He, too, was an alcoholic, so he let me get away with my behavior. Addicts are very manipulative and search around until they find people they can control. They grow into this pattern as a survival mechanism.

PAM: Can you explain the reason why addicts also tend to be pathological liars?

STOKES: Addicts don't necessarily start off as pathological liars; it's because of their addiction, that they can become liars. The addict doesn't know he/she is lying. Somehow the brain is "damaged" to the point where they can't tell the difference between the truth and the lie. It's the pathological lying that can drive people crazy. Addicts absolutely believe what they are saying. Even when they are intoxicated, you can accuse them of being drunk, and they'll completely deny it. That's scary!

PAM: How can one tell if their brain chemistry is out of balance?

STOKES: Here's a good analogy: If all cars have eight cylinders, everyone's brain would be an 8-cylinder engine if you're "normal." The more cylinders you run off of, the better you feel about yourself, the better able you are at coping, the better able you are at interacting with others, the more you feel comfortable in your skin. So Suzi may have been born with all of her eight cylinders. But with wear and tear, on a bad day, she may run on only five cylinders. On a good day, the best she may do is run on seven cylinders. It's normal to seek out pleasant experiences, but if your biochemistry is compromised, then you may be vulnerable and could get addicted more easily than someone who is running on all cylinders. One could get addicted to sex, work, gambling, anything that would give you a rush (i.e., raise your dopamine). An addict would be running on three, four or five cylinders. Here's an example, when I was eight, a few of my friends and I would climb up a pine tree, bend it over and two of us would jump off of it. Imagine the thrill. Some would consider this behavior normal, which is true. But what if a child is thrill-seeking all the time? A child who is running on three, four or five cylinders and is thrill-seeking is just looking to operate at six, seven or eight. So what happens when I find alcohol, pot, sex, gambling? Then I'm going to want to continue to do that. Unless I balance my brain chemistry, I'll keep seeking out the addiction.

PAM: You're talking about a very powerful force.

STOKES: When someone has an imbalance in their brain chemistry, it's amazing to see the lengths they will go to in order to give themselves a rush. When Nancy Reagan said "just say no" (to drugs) . . . . Are you kidding me? How could you possibly convince an addict to say no to drugs when their brain chemistry is out of whack? It's ludicrous.

PAM: What are you noticing about trends in addiction? Are we more addicted today?

STOKES: Absolutely. And why not—we've got more things to be addicted to. We've got Internet porn, gambling. Our society is also causing us to become more competitive, and that in and of itself is destructive. You can bring competitiveness to work. Many alcoholics and drug addicts, after treatment, become workaholics. I'm seeing increased rates of addiction in so many areas, including workaholism. There's a fine line between enjoying what you do and being addicted to what you do.

PAM: Can you describe the typical diet of an addict?

STOKES: Throughout their whole lives, addicts usually have never eaten consistently. They usually subsist on junk foods.

PAM: Can you tell us about the diet you recommend at Bridging the Gaps?

STOKES: One of the most important things an addict can do is to eat three wholesome meals a day and to eat that meal while sitting at the table. During treatment here at Bridging the Gaps, they eat three wholesome meals with their peers. Some students even participate in the food preparation.

PAM: Are you helping people who are addicted to prescription drugs as well?

STOKES: We try to get people off all drugs, legal or illegal. Prescription drugs trick the neurotransmitters in the brain just like street drugs do. They deal with the symptoms, but not the cause. If you're a recovering addict and you're taking a prescription antidepressant, this can substantially increase the risk of suicide.

PAM: Testing is important so that people know they're dealing with something very physical and that it's not "in their head." Can you describe the testing that you do?

STOKES: The testing is extremely important for the addict. Because their brain chemistry is off, alcoholics and drug addicts aren't very trusting. In order to get them to believe what you're saying, it's important to be able to show them their test results and/or get them to read lots of books. Some of the testing we provide includes thyroid, amino acid analysis (blood), elemental analysis (blood, hair, urine), comprehensive vitamin profile, fatty acid analysis (blood), allergy profile (blood), saliva testing (hormones), comprehensive digestive stool analysis and a 5-hour glucose tolerance test (GTT). Usually, everyone who comes in has a problem with reactive hypoglycemia. After any or all of the tests, they can see for themselves that something is physically wrong with them.

PAM: Addicts and their families must have a sense of relief when they find out that the underlying problem is physical rather than mental.

STOKES: When people realize that their addiction has a physiological basis, it can really help alleviate a great deal of guilt and shame.

PAM: Millions of people suffering from mood problems and addiction don't go for help. Do you think that when these people find out that there's a real physiological basis for their problems, they will be more motivated to seek out nutritional help to balance their brain chemistry?

STOKES: Yes. I think that when the families find out more about the connection between nutrition and brain chemistry and they tell the addict, he or she will be more likely to seek help.

PAM: When you give an addict the correct dosage of an amino acid, their craving can go away and their mood can improve, sometimes instantly. This must be an indication that they are dealing with some sort of deficit.

STOKES: An addict's driving force is that they're trying to compensate for a deficit in the brain. We need to determine where that deficit comes from. By gravitating toward any given addiction, an addict is simply trying to normalize his or her biochemistry. In our treatment center, when they take the amino acids, they can feel better quickly. That can help get their attention so that they are more motivated to follow the program.

PAM: On top of hurting themselves, addicts are hurting their family and friends. What is the last straw before they get the help they need?

STOKES: That's difficult to answer. Let's say you go to a company party and get drunk and act out. You make a fool of yourself. Someone who is not an addict will correct that behavior in some fashion. If someone keeps repeating this behavior, then he/she is an addict. They may convince themselves that their behavior isn't affecting their lives, but there's a disconnect. Someone who is not addicted to alcohol can get a DUI. Then they don't do it again. But an alcoholic can get a DUI and repeat their behavior over and over again.

PAM: Do you think that the rates of addictions and mood problems are going to get worse before they get better?

STOKES: Yes. It's unfortunate, but I think that things will get worse before they get better. This country runs on crisis. I used to work with adolescents, so I've witnessed what our kids are going through. This next generation will experience a great deal of crisis, and I'm very worried about what this will mean for their physical and mental well-being.

PAM: Earlier, you mentioned competitiveness. Many parents push their kids academically or in sports. Have you seen how this type of pressure has affected children?

STOKES: Kids are even going to school after school. They're not coping with the pressure they're getting to perform well at school, sports or working toward their careers.

PAM: You're a recovered addict and have a lot of empathy for people who are going through addiction. I sense that you don't want people who have gone through conventional therapies to "settle" for how they're feeling, and that you want them to recover fully so that they can lead full, healthy and happy lives.

STOKES: Many addicts come here after failing at other conventional treatment programs. They're still symptomatic (they are still hypoglycemic and have mood swings, depression, anxiety, etc.) and may be smoking two packs of cigarettes a day, eating lots of sugar, drinking lots of coffee, etc. They may be on a couple of prescription drugs. At Bridging the Gaps, we offer as many holistic approaches as we can in order to help them fully recover. After three months, when they leave here, our goal is that they're feeling well and their cravings are gone.

PAM: Thank you for all of your hard work and dedication. Keep up the great work, Stan!

CAROLYN REUBEN, LAc

> Perpetrators involved in drug use are also involved in
> - more than 50% of violent crimes,
> - 60-80% of child abuse and neglect cases,
> - 50-70% of thefts and property crimes and
> - 75% of drug dealing.
>
> —Belenko and Peugh, 1998;
> National Institute of Justice, 1999

Carolyn Reuben is the executive director of Community Addiction Recovery Association (CARA), which she formed as a non-profit organization with a group of other acupuncturists and supporters in 1994. CARA is comprised of 13 part-time employees, including Carolyn. She is the author of several books, including *Cleansing the Body, Mind and Spirit* (1998). With the help of a sound nutritional protocol, acupuncture and other alternative health approaches, she hopes to revolutionize addiction treatment, especially in the field of criminal justice.

With over two million people incarcerated, the United States prison system is burdened with heavy costs and overcrowding. As many as 80% of these prisoners are there because of drug—or alcohol-related problems. If we were to treat only 10% of our prisoners using more *effective* treatment strategies, the increased economic benefits after their release from prison would amount to a savings of more than $11.5 billion.[386]

In 1995, Sacramento County had a terrible problem with overcrowding in their jails, and local criminal justice departments were looking for ways to solve this very costly problem. That same year, officials formed a drug court and hired CARA to help rehabilitate probationers using acupuncture. Since that time, clients were offered acupuncture five days a week, one hour a day in addition to psychological counseling, oversight by a judge dedicated to rehabilitation and a coordinated program involving the district attorney, public defender, probation, CARA staff, case managers and counselors. Over time, CARA integrated nutrition education and movement therapies, such as tai chi or yoga into the program.

There are over 2,000 drug courts in the United States. Judges monitor the progress of non-violent offenders, including substance abusers. Their goal is restorative justice, including victim restitution, an end to the probationer's drug addiction and a return to being a productive citizen. Offenders are monitored for drug use through group and individual counseling sessions and drug screening. In Sacramento County, they take part in treatment for a minimum of ten months, reporting on a regular basis to the judge. What makes the drug court in Sacramento County unique is that they have contracted the help of CARA to integrate nutritional and holistic approaches to their program.

Carolyn Reuben's Web site is www.carasac.org.

* * *

PAM: How did you first learn about the link between acupuncture and drug addiction?

REUBEN: While I was still in acupuncture college back in 1980, I heard a stirring presentation by Michael Smith, MD, the psychiatrist who was using auricular therapy to treat heroin-addicted patients in his methadone clinic at Lincoln Hospital in the South Bronx.

Smith had learned about this treatment from a neurologist in Hong Kong who, in the early 1970s, accidentally discovered that he relieved one of his patients from opium withdrawal symptoms after he gave him ear acupuncture to prepare him for brain surgery. When the neurologist learned this, he started experimenting on other opium addicts in Hong Kong. Eventually, he received grants from the World Health Organization to do research using acupuncture on opium addicts. Back in New York, Dr. Smith discovered that the technique was useful for any drug user, not just for heroin addicts, because it relieved stress, anxiety and other common triggers for use. It relaxes a person and helps relieve emotional and physical pain without any need to talk. This is especially important for trauma victims of all kinds, which is why the technique has been used successfully for first responders after 9-11 in New York, after Katrina in New Orleans and during the forest fires of California.

By 1985, Smith and a few colleagues created NADA, the National Acupuncture Detoxification Association, which teaches people all over the world how to do this work.

PAM: I've never heard of acupuncture being used to help treat addiction. How widespread is this treatment in North America?

REUBEN: People are doing this treatment called Acudetox, in more than 1,500 clinical sites across the US, Canada, Europe, Australia, Latin America, Africa and the Caribbean. The Acudetox approach is also being used in eight English prisons. You don't have to be an acupuncturist to do it in 16 American states and three Canadian provinces. You just need to be working in a certified drug and alcohol treatment program. The procedure is quite simple. The same five points in the ears are used for all patients, no matter what drug they used or what their cause of trauma. Then the patient sits quietly for about 30-45 minutes. Then the needles are removed and disposed of in a medical contaminated waste container. The patient or client can notice a feeling of peace and relaxation immediately, or it may take more than one treatment. The response is individual, but it is a collectively positive experience. And it's cumulative so the more treatments, the longer lasting the results.

PAM: How does acupuncture work?

REUBEN: Acupuncture works on multiple levels. On one level it works by influencing the nervous system, through cranial nerve branches, stimulating the release of neurotransmitters such as the endorphins, thereby reducing stress and cravings. On another level it influences the circulating energy of life which the Chinese call qi (pronounced chee).

PAM: Has anyone ever done any research on the positive effects of acupuncture on addiction?

REUBEN: Oh yes. In 1999, Dr. Michael Shwartz from the school of management of Boston University and his colleagues showed that addicts who were treated with acupuncture were less likely to be readmitted to a detoxification program within six months compared to similar clients who didn't receive acupuncture. Back in 1989, a study published in *The Lancet* done by the University of Minnesota showed that severely recidivist alcoholics, even six months after they stopped drinking, were half as likely to start drinking again as those who didn't get the acupuncture. These are very encouraging studies.

PAM: So it sounds like acupuncture is an accepted form of treatment. Why has it been so difficult to add nutrition to treatment programs?

REUBEN: In a nutshell, prejudice. There's no caché, no credibility, no respect, no understanding of the incredible biochemical power of clinical nutrition and the changes it can make—quickly. Stephen Schoenthaler, PhD,* professor of criminal justice and sociology at California State University-Stanislaus, proved that within three days, when the most anti-social prisoners in adult or juvenile facilities are given a cheap multi-vitamin mineral (that costs a few cents each), there was a noticeable improvement in their behavior. They were calmer and had less reactive violent episodes and rule infractions.

PAM: That's incredible. What is the cost-effectiveness of this type of nutritional treatment?

REUBEN: At the end of the month, an investment of $1 returned $1,000 to the correction department's budget. They saw fewer lockdowns, fights and injuries due to fights.

PAM: Surely, this type of information must catch the attention of officials working in the prison system.

REUBEN: I've written letters to officials, but they ignore this type of research. I keep talking to politicians. I will not stop trying to get the message out that if malnutrition is corrected, drug addicts not only reform their lives, they feel healthy and happy instead of suffering through sobriety.

PAM: How did you first learn about the connection between nutrition and addiction?

---

* Stephen J Schoenthaler, PhD, has published several articles in the International Journal of Biosocial Research, including "Diet and Crime: An Empirical Examination of the Value of Nutrition in the Control and Treatment of Incarcerated Juvenile Offenders" and "The Northern Californian Diet-Behavior Programme: An Empirical Examination of 3000 Incarcerated Juveniles in Stanislaus County Juvenile Hall." From his own work, he concluded that reactive hypoglycemia is a leading cause of delinquent and criminal behavior. He contends that a high proportion of prison inmates—up to 90%—are in fact hypoglycemic. See the *Hypoglycemic Association Newsletter*, Vol. 6 (No. 4), Dec. 1990.

REUBEN: My first influence was Kathleen DesMaisons, PhD, author of *Potatoes Not Prozac*. Through her work, I learned about the importance of eating whole foods and including protein at every meal, including snacks. She also emphasizes the importance of eating fruits and vegetables and removing highly processed food from the diet (sugar, pop, etc.). Thanks to her work, we taught our clients about proper blood sugar control. Then in the late 1990s, I learned about the work of Joan Mathews-Larson, PhD and Julia Ross, MFT, who use targeted nutritional supplements in addition to wholesome food.

PAM: So you have about 10 years of experience using nutrition in drug court?

REUBEN: More like 14 years. Unfortunately, our drug court program was cancelled for lack of funds in 2009. However, it remains as a model for other jurisdictions, and the drug court staff has applied for grants to bring us back. Our part of the program grew over time to be one of the most successful aspects of the entire drug court program in Sacramento County. First, we did acupuncture, then we taught clients about healthy food, then we added movement therapies, then we added the supplements. We also added a chef who came in twice a week to make food for the clients. We had a refrigerator available, so that the clients helped themselves to food and took it home to prepare their own wholesome meals.

PAM: How did you help them monitor any improvements?

REUBEN: Kathleen DesMaisons taught me the importance of a food-mood journal. Our clients wrote down everything they ate, and then once a week, they met privately with a nutrition educator and discussed what they had learned from the food-mood connection.

PAM: What is your goal with CARA?

REUBEN: My goal is to get wholesome nutrition into prisons and jails so that by improving the nutritional status of inmates, we will improve their brain function and help them stay clean, sober and out of the criminal justice system. My agency has been approved to be a provider of continuing education for prison guards, sheriffs, police, parole and probation officers. Dr. Schoenthaler and I have a lot to share with them about the power of nutrition within the criminal justice setting. Hopefully, step by step, we will establish a nationwide program.

PAM: Why is it taking so long for you to get into the prison system?

REUBEN: They don't yet understand that people who have addictive disorders have a disease that has to do with a biochemical abnormality. And that this abnormality cannot be cured with pharmaceuticals, though it might be temporarily controlled by them. I met a nurse who worked in an American prison and was shocked to be ordered to give individual prisoners as many as 15 different pharmaceuticals per day, with one to counteract the side effects of another. They don't understand that many of the original symptoms were due to malnourishment, particularly of B vitamins and minerals. They don't understand that that biochemical abnormality could be genetic and that the prisoner hasn't got the biochemical resources to cope with their situation. The only way for them to find relief is drugs. The same broken brain that produces criminal behavior is also frequently diagnosed with mental health problems. Mental illness and addiction can both be solved using nutrition.

PAM: What do you think will have to happen before people realize how healthy eating can positively influence our mood?

REUBEN: In the 1800s, we learned about the importance of hand washing to stop the spread of disease. Now, moms make their children wash their hands before dinner. It's just a matter of time before moms understand that they have the power in their own hands to manipulate their own biochemistry. Eventually, they'll say to their child, "You're being obsessive-compulsive. You need more serotonin in your nervous system, which is why you are nagging me for candy. I know you really need to eat more protein, or you need to take some tryptophan or 5-HTP."

PAM: It sounds like you're up against a system that doesn't want to change. It's a very cut-and-dry system. You commit a crime, and as a consequence you go to prison. There's not a lot of room for compromise.

REUBEN: Politicians need to be taught the importance of biochemical restoration and safety. It's a question of social marketing.

PAM: Not to mention grassroots activism geared toward helping
            remove the stigma attached to mental health and addiction.

REUBEN: The California Legislature has an independent board called
            the Little Hoover Commission, a watchdog group that
            investigates certain subjects and then makes recommendations
            to the legislature for action. Five years ago, they interviewed
            numerous experts and suggested what could be done to help
            addiction. Last spring, they addressed the issue yet again.
            They said that we needed more creative solutions, that
            mental health and addiction shouldn't be separate issues
            and that they should be combined into one funding stream
            so people could be treated for the two simultaneously.
            They also recommended that incentives should be offered
            for successful, innovative programs. If the programs didn't
            meet their self-professed goals, then public funds should be
            withdrawn.

PAM: I've heard of different rates of success with various
            conventional addiction treatment centers.

REUBEN: Johnny Allen, a recovering alcoholic and former director of
            the Johnson Institute, an organization that is committed to
            finding solutions for addiction problems, has said that the
            success rate for long-term sobriety is only 17% (that figure is
            based upon the 12-Step programs, psychotherapy and group
            work). Considering that Alcoholics Anonymous started in
            the 1930s, it's unbelievable that they would settle for such
            a low success rate. On top of that, recovering alcoholics are
            dying from suicide, kidney disease, heart disease, etc.

PAM: In his book *Nutrition and Physical Degeneration*, Dr. Weston
            A. Price shows photos of physical degeneration in prisoners.
            Through his photos, he noted physical abnormalities in their
            facial structure that, according to his research, was indicative
            of malnutrition.

REUBEN: Our clients exhibit many signs and symptoms of
            malnourishment (rotted teeth, poor digestion, sallow and
            marked skin and nerves on edge). Stephen Schoenthaler, PhD,
            has taught about signs in their face, lips and tongue to warn
            criminal justice professionals that certain individuals can't be
            trusted to be reasonable and that they could be violent at any
            time. He has also shown that criminals have a problem with

heavy metals and have poor digestion. Barbara Reed Stitt, PhD, did similar work analyzing things like heavy metals in their hair analysis.* Bill Walsh at the Pfieffer Institute could tell 99 out of 100 times whether a person was imprisoned for a violent crime based upon the ratio of the minerals. The only person that he missed was a guard. Poor gut health equates to poor mental health. Natasha Campbell-McBride, MD, writes about this in her book *Gut and Psychology Syndrome*. The majority of prisoners have attention deficit disorder. Their cognitive skills are low. Many are illiterate.

PAM: In order to help them with their cognitive function, you're also giving them fish oil.

REUBEN: According to studies, subjects taking fish oil increased their dopamine by 40%. One of my acupuncture patients in my private clinic was a young boy with attention deficit disorder. The only thing we did was to give him fish oil, and his behavior improved dramatically. When people enroll in our substance abuse program, everybody is handed several supplements, including fish oil, multi-vitamins and vitamin C.

PAM: However, in prison, where they may or may not have access to street drugs that gave them some relief, they find themselves on prescription drugs.

REUBEN: These drugs don't solve the problem. They still have all sorts of psychological or mental symptoms. They're on antidepressants, psychotropic drugs for schizophrenia, etc.

PAM: Can you describe the environment that you provide for your clients?

REUBEN: The focus of our drug court is rehabilitation. We offer a very nurturing environment. Everyone who works in the building has a positive attitude, encouraging the clients to improve their behavior and stay clean. We do everything we

---

* In her book *Food Teens and Behavior* (1983), parole officer and nutritionist, Barbara Reed Stitt, PhD, documented an 85% reduction in recidivism among 1,000 parolees, including violent offenders, when she put them on a high-protein, low-carbohydrate diet, eliminated sugars, food dyes, additives and focused on nutrition.

can to help them graduate. Compared to other treatment programs, we offer more biochemical support.

PAM: What type of feedback do you get?

REUBEN: It often changes people's lives. One woman with two children told me that when she used to walk into the grocery store, she thought that the fruit and vegetable section was a nuisance because it was in the way between the entrance and the Pepsi. After the nutrition education, she buys fruits and vegetables for her children.

PAM: Do they tell you about any health improvements?

REUBEN: Sometimes within a week, using the supplements and five days a week of acupuncture, people have told me that they're sleeping better and their cravings for drugs or alcohol are gone.

PAM: Do your clients complain about whole foods, thinking that they may be more expensive or too much work? Do you help them to understand the cost-benefit analysis of eating whole foods?

REUBEN: I hear it all the time. It's a knee-jerk reaction for people to think that whole foods are more expensive than processed foods. Our nutritionist teaches them that consumers pay for the packaging. In other words, if you buy applesauce, it's going to be more expensive than buying an apple. If you buy a breakfast cereal, you're paying for the artwork on the package. We explain to them that if you eat processed foods and end up with a headache, stomachache, cancer or children with behavior problems, there are costs associated with these things. Eating processed foods has expensive consequences in terms of our health and well-being. In order to stay in this program, they have to pay restitution to the victims, including the county. They're spending a lot of money that they wouldn't have had to spend if they had just taken care of themselves with proper diet and lifestyle in the first place.

PAM: Have you been able to evaluate the effectiveness of your program?

REUBEN: We've been a part of the drug court since its inception 15 years ago. In order to determine the cost-effectiveness of my part of the program, the California State Administrative Office of the Courts has been collecting data on every interaction between my staff and the clients and then looking at the effect on the client. They found that the drug court is estimated to have saved Sacramento County $20 million in its first ten years. When California State University-Sacramento evaluated drug court's 2006 graduates for one year after graduation, they found that 87% of them stayed out of the criminal justice system.

PAM: That's extremely encouraging news. With such a high success rate, hopefully other drug courts will start using your protocols. Within your drug court, can you tell us just how popular your program is?

REUBEN: The success of the program has been rising. We had 15 people at our last graduation, which is the largest that we've ever had. The importance of that figure is that we have the largest number graduating, even though the overall number of people coming to drug court is lower. One reason why our success rate is improving is that, two years ago, we started providing them with more food. We transformed their entire eating experience by nicely decorating their dining room and bringing in a chef to feed the people with healthy, delicious, gourmet meals. Essentially, we taught them to "eat with their eyes" and treated them with respect. It's a very nurturing environment. When they're in jail, they're not treated with respect at all. One person told me that the guard said, "See you next time." There's such an expectation for our clients to fail. Our environment tells them that they're human beings and that they are capable of making good decisions. They come here because they feel hope. They can tell we think that they're worthy. This environment helps them believe that they can transform their lives.

PAM: How much does it cost to incarcerate someone?

REUBEN: It costs $72 per day per person to put someone in Sacramento county jail.

PAM: Even though your program is proving to be beneficial, have you been experiencing any resistance?

REUBEN: Yes. Four years ago, there was a threat that the probation department was going to be removed from the drug court and that the health and human services department was going to take it over. Our clients wrote letters to the board of supervisors and showed up at their meeting to testify about their experiences in our program. Not only did they like our part of the program (the acupuncture and nutrition, yoga, tai chi), they also liked being accountable to a probation officer. They acknowledged the importance of having a complete system. Many of them said that it was the best program they had ever been in (and some had been through several probation programs). They were so convincing, the board of supervisors found more money for the program and agreed to keep our program intact. However, as I mentioned, at the end of the last fiscal year our county board of supervisors demanded the probation department dramatically cut their expenses and probation handed the entire drug court over to the Department of Health and Human Services, which eliminated CARA's services. A new probation department chief realizes that was a mistake and is searching for funds to bring us back.

PAM: Can you tell us about a few success stories?

REUBEN: One man sent in a testimonial explaining that he had been in and out of jail several times and had already cost the county a lot of money. He would have cost the county even more money. After the program, he was a homeowner, he had his own business, he paid taxes and he was a reputable citizen participating in civic life. He attributed that to the drug court program:

> At drug court, I was also taught how to eat properly. This has helped me greatly, and I still use the skills that I have learned in my eating habits today. Since graduating from the drug court program in February of 2000, I have the same job that I did when I started the program, and I recently celebrated four years of sobriety. I am a homeowner now and have my own vehicle that is paid for, insured and registered in my own name. If it weren't for drug court, I would have been sent to prison for 14 years at the expense of California taxpayers.

ADDICTION: THE HIDDEN EPIDEMIC

Another woman admitted that she had been in a nice home, had a family, a business, nice car, etc., then got into drugs and prostitution. She lost everything, but thanks to the program, she got everything back and is now studying to be a nurse.

I have been a drug addict on Meth- for 21 years. I failed drug diversion, Prop 36, and the stars program.
Since starting drug courts I have lost all cravings for any use. This I give credit to the Amino Acids and all the vitamins introduced to me here in this program.
I passed through Level I in 4 weeks time. The minimum time possible. Since I have been here my life has come together in so many positive ways, this I feel I owe to the drug courts program.

John Lohmann

Community Addiction Recovery Association (CARA) Testimonial

PAM: What is your vision for the future of CARA?

REUBEN: My hope is that we can get nutritional treatments into prisons and jails throughout the U.S. The minute someone with an addiction leaves a prison or jail and starts a drug treatment program, he or she should instantly be given a nourishing meal and supplements—amino acids, fish oil and, if they're alcoholics, B vitamins. Each person also needs to be evaluated for any nutritional deficiencies. If we want to see improvements in the criminal justice system, we need to employ biochemical restoration. Otherwise, we'll continue to see overcrowding and violence and overuse of our emergency rooms for ailments that are simply the result of malnourishment.

Pam: Thank you, Carolyn, for spending the time to speak with me. Best of luck in the future. I can only hope that officials within the criminal justice system acknowledge the importance of your work.

SECTION III

OUR FAST NEW WORLD MEETS CYBERSPACE

Are we going to try and remake people to fit into the light-speed culture we have inadvertently created, or are we going to try and reshape that culture to fit who we are?[387]

—Bill McKibben,
Enough: Staying Human in an Engineered Age

Compulsive drug use has functioned as a metaphor of consumption out of control in a society whose culture is increasingly dominated by consumerism.[388]

—Caroline Jean Acker, *Creating an American Junkie*

If you look at what makes people happy, income is important, but human relationships are much more important. And we've increasingly allowed our human relationships to deteriorate.[389]

—Lord Richard Layard,
Director of the Centre for Economic Performance,
London School of Economics,
Author of *Happiness: Lessons from a New Science*

Close Your Eyes . . . and Go Back
(Adapted from unknown Internet source)

Go back.
Before the Internet or PC or the Mac . . .
Before semi-automatics and crack . . .
Before Playstation, SEGA, Super Nintendo, even before Atari . . .
Before cell phones, CDs, DVDs, voice mail and email . . .

Go way back . . . way, way, way back . . .
I'm talking about playing Hide and Seek at dusk
Kickball and dodgeball until the first . . . no . . . second . . . no . . .
third street light came on
Red Light, Green Light
Red Rover, Red Rover
Ring around the Rosie
London Bridge
Hot Potato
Hopscotch
Jump Rope
YOU'RE IT!

Parents stood on the front porch and yelled or whistled for you to
     come home—no pagers or cell phones
Seeing shapes in the clouds
Endless summer days and hot summer nights with the windows
     open (no air conditioners)
The sound of crickets
Running through the lawn sprinkler
Catchin' lightning bugs in a jar on Christmas morning
Your first day of school
Good night kisses
Climbing trees
Swinging as high as you could in those tall swings to try and reach the
     sky
A million mosquito bites and sticky fingers

Jumpin' down the steps
Jumpin' on the bed
Pillow fights
Laughing so hard that your stomach hurt
Being tired from PLAYING
WORK meant taking out the garbage, cutting the grass, washing
the car, or doing the dishes
Your first crush
Your first kiss
Rainy days at school and the smell of damp concrete and chalk
erasers

Giving your friends a ride on your handlebars of your bike
Attaching pieces of cardboard to your bike frame to smack against
your spokes

Wearing your new shoes on the first day of school
Class field trips with soggy sandwiches
When nearly everyone's mom was at home when the kids returned
from school

When a quarter seemed like a fair allowance and another quarter a
MIRACLE
When ANY parent could discipline ANY kid, or feed him or ask
him to carry groceries . . . and nobody, not even the kids, gave
it a second thought
When your parents took you to the cafeteria and it was a real treat
When being sent to the principal's office was nothing compared to
the fate that awaited you at home
If we lived in fear for our lives, it wasn't because of drive-by shootings,
drugs, gangs . . . We simply didn't want our parents to be mad
at us
Decisions were made by going "Eeny-Meeny-Miney-Mo"
Mistakes were corrected by simply exclaiming "Do over!"
Catching fireflies was enough to occupy an entire evening
It wasn't odd to have two or three "best" friends
Nobody was prettier than Mom

Scrapes and bruises were kissed by Mom and made better
Getting a foot of snow was a dream come true
Abilities were discovered by a "Double-Dog-Dare"
Spinning around, getting dizzy and falling down was cause for
    giggles
The worst embarrassment was being picked last for a team
Water balloons were the ultimate, ULTIMATE weapon

If you can remember most or all of these, then you have lived during
    a simpler and more pleasant time!
If you do not remember, then ask your parents, grandparents, or
    great-grandparents about their youth.
We went from AM radio to the stars. Your era is here; be a part of it.
Make it worthwhile for future generations to build on.

Whatever happened to the days when children walked to school, families enjoyed eating home-cooked meals together and children played outdoors after dinner? Instead of valuing our friends and family, we now worship athletes and movie stars and measure success in terms of financial gains. Today, we find our identity more through brand names than through any meaningful acts of kindness. Rather than enjoying spending real time with friends and family, we detach ourselves from intimacy by turning to inanimate electronic devices.

In his famous spoof *A Place for My Stuff*, comedian George Carlin (1937-2008) mocked society's fixation on material goods. He joked, "That's all your house is. It's a pile of stuff with a cover on it . . . . It's a place to keep your stuff while you go out and get more stuff." The irony is that buying all of this "stuff" has not made us any happier.[390]* In fact, we are less happy today than we were during the Great Depression, a period of time when we had much less.[391]

---

*   A number of surveys conducted during the 1980s and 1990s recorded a declining satisfaction with life in America. (See the following interview with Dr. Whybrow.)

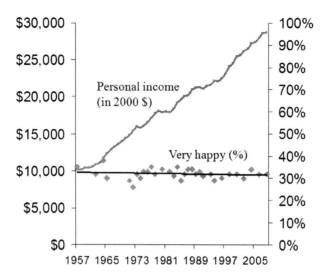

Courtesy of David G. Myers (davidmyers.org), author of *The Pursuit of Happiness.*

More than ever, we have big houses and broken homes, high incomes and low morale, secured rights and diminished civility. We excel at making a living but often fail at making a life. We celebrate our prosperity but yearn for purpose. We cherish our freedoms but long for connection. In an age of plenty, we feel spiritual hunger.[392]

—David Meyers, Psychologist

While there are several reasons for this decline in happiness, one contributing factor involves our obsession with keeping up with the Joneses. This includes our tendency to buy things we do not really need—a compulsive shopping disorder or shopping addiction. The medical term for shopping addiction, or shopaholism, is *oniomania.* It has been estimated that shopping addiction affects 2-8% of the U.S. population.[393] There is also a high cost associated with shopping addiction. As we will see in the following interview with Peter Whybrow, MD, Americans are carrying heavy credit card debts, which could be contributing to increased stress levels. Since stress can increase one's chance of developing addictions, perhaps it would be a good idea to spend your money wisely and avoid going into debt.

Some people shop to help themselves feel better. The feel-good brain chemical, dopamine, can be released when you shop. "Dopamine is all about the hunt and the anticipation. It is released as you conjure up in your mind the thought of this purchase and anticipate how it will look and how you will use it," said Gregory Berns, a neuroscientist at Emory University in Atlanta.[394] Researcher Michael Bardo discovered that rats experience surges of dopamine as they explore a new cage.[395] Exploration and novelty, therefore, can contribute to a dopamine rush. Shopping allows for this search for novelty and exploration and can induce dopamine surges in consumers. In order to measure dopamine levels, neuroscientist David Lewis attached a special device to shoppers' heads and discovered that "as a shopper hunts for an item, finds it and makes a purchase, levels of dopamine flowing between nerve cells in the brain raise appreciably."[396]

After the planes hit the twin towers in New York on September 11, 2001, President Bush urged Americans to go shopping.[397] While nobody seems to know why he did this, some people speculate that either he was looking for a way to stimulate the economy or he was offering a solution to distract Americans, hoping to elevate their mood. After all, shopping can be very therapeutic. "MRI studies of brain activity suggest that surges in dopamine levels are linked much more with anticipation of an experience rather than the actual experience—which may explain why people get so much pleasure out of window-shopping or hunting for bargains."[398]

The downside to spending your money unwisely is that it can make individuals feel worse. When the dopamine rush declines after making the purchase, this may result in a sense of letdown or "buyer's remorse." Since the 1930s, we have been on the greatest shopping sprees in the history of mankind. Perhaps this decline in happiness is simply society's way of demonstrating that they have "buyer's remorse."

Just how obsessed are we with shopping? In their book *Affluenza: The All-Consuming Epidemic*, authors John De Graaf, David Wann and Thomas Naylor explain just how infected we are with the "spending virus":

- Americans spend about $6 trillion a year, more than $21,000 per person, most of it on consumer goods.
- Americans spend more on shoes, jewelry and watches ($80 billion) than on higher education ($65 billion).

- Americans have twice as many shopping centers as high schools.
- 70% of Americans visit malls each week.
- 93% of teenage American girls rate shopping as their favorite activity.
- In 2000, 40 billion mail-order catalogues flooded our homes, about 150 for every American.
- 20% of Americans spend at least five hours a week on the Internet, much of it spent shopping. In 1999, online purchases exceeded $33 billion.[399]

Maybe the economic crash of 2008 will help millions of consumers re-evaluate their priorities, forcing them to be more careful about how they spend their money. As people simplify their lives, maybe we will be able to restore our sense of community and build healthy relationships. After all, healthy relationships are priceless, and they can give us what we need emotionally, mentally and spiritually.

The daily bombardment of advertising images leaves us forever dissatisfied with our own appearances and those of our real-life partners. "Advertising encourages us to meet nonmaterial needs through material ends," says Laurie Mazur. "It tells us to buy their product because we'll be loved, we'll be accepted and it also tells us that we are not loveable and acceptable without buying their product." To be loveable and acceptable is to have the image. Authenticity be damned.[400]

—John De Graaf, David Wann and Thomas Naylor
Affluenza: The All-Consuming Epidemic

Genetically, emotionally, socially, psychologically and physically, our Fast New World has disoriented us and contributed to our high rates of chronic disease and mood disorders. We are both mentally and physically malnourished. While it is apparent that we are having a difficult time adjusting to our new surroundings right now, the good news is that man has always been able to adapt to his surroundings.

PETER WHYBROW, MD

> Roughly half of the average family's food budget is now spent
> on food eaten out and 45% of the dinners eaten at home have
> no home cooking associated with them.[401]

—Peter Whybrow, MD, *American Mania*

Peter Whybrow, author of *American Mania: When More Is Not Enough*, is a psychiatrist trained in neurobiology, endocrinology and neuropsychiatry. He is an authority on the role the thyroid plays in brain and human behavior. Dr. Whybrow is director of the Semel Institute for Neuroscience and Human Behavior at the University of California in Los Angeles and the executive chair of the Department of Psychiatry and Biobehavioral Sciences at the David Geffen School of Medicine. Born in England and now living in the United States, Dr. Whybrow is the author of numerous scientific papers and five books, including *A Mood Apart: The Thinker's Guide to Emotion and Its Disorder*. He lectures widely across the United States and Europe.

Dr. Whybrow is concerned about how poorly we seem to be coping in what he calls our Fast New World, a world where consumers are subject to unprecedented levels of physical, emotional and financial stress. As reward-driven creatures, an ancient adaptation to the world of scarcity in which humans evolved, we have been seduced into wanting more by an environment that promotes excess. He refers to this Fast New World that we have created as an "addictive environment." Dr. Whybrow says, "Too many of us are now addicted to the treadmill we have created and we are making ourselves sick."[402]

According to Dr. Whybrow, "we have become victims of our own success."[403] He is not only pointing out the problems behind this frenzied, manic new world, he is also offering very sound advice to solve our many physical and emotional problems. He believes that one thing we can do in order to counter the insanity of our Fast New World and to improve the quality of our lives is to return to community-oriented activities, such as the simple ritual of sharing a homemade family meal.

Dr. Whybrow appreciates the importance of eating wholesome foods. He is a member of Slow Food, an international organization based in Italy, whose goal is to help "people rediscover the joys of eating and understand the importance of caring where their food comes from, who grows it and how it's made."[404]

For more information, visit his Web site at www.peterwhybrow. com.

* * *

PAM: In your book *American Mania*, you use the word *addiction* quite a bit. What are your views about addiction?

WHYBROW: Most people associate the word *addiction* with an unfortunate individual lying in the street. That's not the case at all. We're all prone to becoming addicted to something. That's the way we were wired up. For millennia, our species coped with scarcity, so our physiological systems are geared to "finding more." If we fast-forward to the twenty-first century, we have more than enough of everything (information, material goods, freedom, government deregulations), and we don't know how to deal with such affluence.

PAM: It sounds as though you're not surprised by man's tendency toward addictive behaviors.

WHYBROW: From the standpoint of biology, addictive behaviors are entirely predictable. They shouldn't be a surprise to anyone. What we should focus on now is how we can offset our addictions in the seductive consumer world that we have created. We can't go back to the eighteenth century, but we can adapt to an environment of affluence by finding ways to restrain our appetites and to benefit our long-term health.

PAM: Do you think that there's more of a problem with addiction today?

WHYBROW: Historically, specific rates of addiction are very difficult to measure. But history does tell us that humans have always been predisposed to addictive behavior, especially when challenged by affluent circumstance. It's not so much that we're more addicted now than we ever were. It's that in the industrialized world, the general population is more exposed to addictive circumstance, which is abundance.

PAM: You write that we need to be more aware of how we spend our time.

WHYBROW: Time is the currency that we're really working with. It's not money. Our time is the only thing that we truly own. The problem is that the market has become dominant especially in the U.S. We now spend a disproportionate amount of our precious time in the pursuit of money and material goods, which supposedly will make us happy and content. In that pursuit, we're making ourselves sick in not eating well and depriving ourselves of sleep. It's a blindsided vision where immediate reward obscures the future advantages of staying healthy. Californians wish they could spend more time staring out at the ocean and enjoying the beach. Well, that's exactly what people were doing before the Europeans arrived a couple of hundred years ago.

PAM: You're a member of Slow Food, and in your book you explain that one strategy that could help integrate into our lives, in order to help us better cope with our Fast New World, would be to return to a focus upon the family and eating together.

WHYBROW: Yes. People can back away from the daily frenzy by creating a sane moment around mealtimes. In Slow Food, not only do people savor the quality of the food they're eating, they also appreciate the relationships they build with local producers and the moments they spend with their friends preparing the food and sharing it around the dinner table. The idea of Slow Food is that people thrive on the attachments forged around the dinner table. The Slow Food movement seeks a convivial, reflective way of life.

PAM: Studies show that we're not as happy today as we were in the 1930s, during the Depression.

WHYBROW: We know two things—that a subjective sense of happiness doesn't escalate with money: happiness cuts off at a certain point. Secondly, in a small community, small things generate a sense of happiness and contentment. If you're very poor, you're probably not going to be very happy. But if you're very rich, you also tend not to be very happy. There's some evidence to show that children from affluent families ($150,000+) have a much more difficult time in life than children from families with a median income (approximately $50,000). Studies show that material affluence does not breed happiness in children.

PAM: Historically, families have always relied on a strong, closely-knit community. Since about the middle of the twentieth century, it seems as though we've lost our sense of community.

WHYBROW: Humans crave interactions with family, friends and community, and we're losing these very precious connections. Attachment to others is the antidote to craving for more. Today, people are more concerned about themselves than about others. After a couple of generations of such thinking, it's difficult to know how we can return to our sense of sharing in community. And yet it is the give-and-take of community interaction that makes us strong

PAM: In Miriam Weinstein's book *The Surprising Power of Family Meals*, she cites studies that show that children who ate more family meals were less likely to develop addictions and, overall, grew up to be more successful in life.

WHYBROW: The challenge is to let people know about the simple value of the family meal. We need to relearn the advantages of returning to this important tradition. I try to motivate people to eat wholesome meals by pointing out to them that in eating pre-cooked fast food, they are in danger of destroying their own health. Through an awareness that we are damaging ourselves, we may slow down long enough to return to this very important tradition.

PAM: When it comes to how food affects our health, why are millions of people still ignoring all of the warning signs?

WHYBROW: Given all the distractions out there, it's difficult for people to change their priorities and focus more time on the importance of the family meal and nutritious foods. The culture does not promote such behavior. You don't see ads on TV showing people enjoying a wholesome, home-cooked family meal. People are characterized as in a hurry, so eating processed foods, such as breakfast cereal, frozen fries, or take-out chicken makes sense. Forty-five percent of Americans do not eat their meals sitting around a table. Indeed, as families we spend more time driving around in a car together than they do eating around a table. The family meal is dying unless we decide to bring it back. But it's essential to do so: the alternative is not healthy.

PAM: Marketers want to develop customers for life and, using a great deal of advertising, market highly addictive foods to our children. In a country where very little seems to be regulated, we need to do more to protect our children from these food ads.

WHYBROW: In most industrialized countries, marketing to children is highly restricted. It's not in the U.S. Here, we market almost anything to children, except alcohol or cigarettes. Where does social responsibility lie? Failing individual responsibility some sort of regulatory system must be put in place. For example, hockey players first rebelled against wearing helmets, but then, when helmets became mandatory, the players were happy to comply. They were *relieved* that they could wear a helmet as a defense against injury. So at times, regulation is good. There are ways in which regulation, which is sanctioned as a social good, can help things change. In a free society, we have perpetrated the myth that there is nothing as important as personal freedom. But personal freedom can also be a license to destroy oneself.

PAM: This is what you call the "dark side" of the free market.

WHYBROW: Right. We must be wise as opposed to foolish. At the moment, we're being shortsighted and foolish. America is the great Enlightenment experiment. Unfortunately, a certain amount of complacency has set in, and we now believe that it's the perfect experiment. But with most experiments, by definition, one must inspect progress to see whether or not it's working. The lessons we are learning from our American experiment are that some things are unhealthy. We can't continue following the quintessentially American lifestyle of self-indulgence. If we do then we'll soon collapse under our own weight. We're already seeing that happen.

PAM: So you're saying that we're failing at our own experiment?

WHYBROW: Yes.

PAM: You talk about controlling the mania we see in society today. In your book, you describe the cycles of mania, where, in the affluent times of the dot-com era, in the 1990s, many lived in a euphoric state of blind self-interest. Eventually, that bubble burst, and we woke up from the mania of the

1990s to find ourselves full of depressive self-doubt. The "crash" if you will.

WHYBROW: I use the term *mania* as a metaphor. For example, people who have manic depression, for the first few cycles, will not accept the fact that they are ill because they enjoy the frenzy—it's too precious to them. You see that in the American experiment. We consider the manic frenzy extraordinarily pleasurable and valuable: you can have a bigger and bigger house, you can have a larger and larger car, more and more of everything you want. The myth of the American dream is that you can have it all. Just mortgage the future: everything will be perfect. The reality is that we are living in a frenzied state. Environmental concerns, the price of oil, the collapse of our health care system, etc., may help us realize that our behavior needs to change.

PAM: We need to redefine the American dream. In your book, you write that 78% of Americans believe that they're going to strike it rich and reach fame and fortune. This unrealistic dream can cause people to make bad decisions. You say that the American dream is "tarnished," and that as we scramble to obtain this dream, we work long hours, deprive ourselves of sleep and don't eat properly.

WHYBROW: George Carlin put it well: "To believe in the American dream, you have to be asleep." The cultural myth is that we each can reach fame and fortune. And because it does happen to a few people, millions are working way too hard and are consequently making themselves sick.

PAM: We're living in an affluent time, and you call it the paradox of prosperity. We're paying a heavy price for this prosperity.

WHYBROW: Yes. It's the first time there has been mass wealth in the world. Relative to their ancestors, even the poor have many material goods. They, too, are constantly seduced into buying more. They go out on a limb financially, to the point where they are mortgaging a future that cannot be sustained. Consider the subprime housing crisis. We have been using the family home as an ATM, buying homes that they couldn't afford and gambling on a rise in the real estate to finance an inflated lifestyle. And then came a catastrophic intervention with the global financial crisis.

PAM: So the Fast New World is an intoxicating vicious cycle. Marketers exploit the fact that humans are insatiable beings. What kind of solutions do you suggest to your patients to motivate them to escape from this vicious cycle?

WHYBROW: People can start by taking a close look at their economic situation. Fifty percent of Americans have a net worth of less than $25,000. Seventy percent of Americans do not pay off their credit cards every month (the average balance is between seven to nine thousand dollars). And they are paying huge interest (between 15-40%). Consumers are seduced by the instant gratification they feel from buying goods they don't necessarily need. Because of their shortsightedness, millions of consumers are living beyond their means. Some are beginning to recognize this. If you search online, you can find groups of people involved in the "simplicity movement." These groups provide people with the support they may need to help get off the treadmill. As their name suggests, they do this by simplifying their lives, and usually greater contentment is the result.

PAM: So we must return to our senses so that we can control the mania.

WHYBROW: That's right. We'd all be better off if we could establish some sort of rationality behind what's going on in society today. If we use our intelligence, mankind has the ability to adapt to almost any environment. So, hopefully, we can find some sanity in this very manic world. We need a return to common sense.

PAM: Thank you, Dr. Whybrow. You have shared some remarkable insights into several factors that are contributing to our addictive behaviors.

INTERNET ADDICTION

> Unhealthy dependencies begin early in the lives of American children, including constant reliance on television, the Internet and video games. Aside from their own debilitating effects on children's lives, these early dependencies bespeak the possibility of additional addictions later on in the child's life. Few children, even those who use alcohol and drugs regularly, show the clinical symptoms of addiction. Yet many of them have experienced addictive involvements that they could subsequently transfer to drugs, alcohol, gambling, or the other dependencies that we fear most. [405]
>
> —Stanton Peele, PhD, JD, *7 Tools to Beat Addiction*

> Everything we create has a potential impact on our lives and everything good has to have a dialectic, or opposite, position. The Internet is no exception . . . there are many potential problems with the Internet: safety concerns, abuse, workplace issues, child protection, compulsive shopping, gambling, effects on marriage and Internet addiction are among the areas that we can now recognize.[406]
>
> —David Greenfield, PhD, *Virtual Addiction*

New inventions make us all feel better. We yearn for the newest, biggest color TV, the fanciest cell phones, cameras, radios, MP3s, iPods and so on. The most up-to-date gadgets grab our attention, making us race to buy the first one. Unfortunately, our feverish desire for the latest, greatest inventions has caused society to fall victim to its own inventions.

One of our newest inventions, the Internet, has a great deal of positive things to offer. An individual can gain access to a tremendous amount of positive information and entertainment. People can even meet a future spouse. But as with many things in life, the Internet has a dark side. Millions of Internet users have become too involved with the virtual world, neglecting their lives in the real world.

For more than a century, the media has been used to manipulate our behavior. The telegraph, telephone, television and other forms of media have been used to brainwash and control the human race, robbing us of our free will. Under the hypnotic spell of the television or the Internet, for example, people are no longer in control of their own emotions.

Media scientist Marshall McLuhan warned us about the powers of the media. When he coined the phrase *the medium is the message*, Professor McLuhan was warning us that the media have the ability to control how we think and feel. What he meant was that the medium is more important than the message itself.

The introduction of different forms of media has replaced our most traditional form of communication, speech, which involves the benefits of personal contact. The paradox of having so many new forms of communication available to us today is that while they have broadened our world, they have also isolated man from the community. The Internet is no exception. David Greenfield, PhD, who is featured in the next interview, calls this phenomenon the "Internet paradox," namely, *in order to expand your world, you have to nearly isolate yourself.*[407]

The telephone: speech without walls.
The phonograph: music without walls.
The photograph: museum without walls.
The electric light: space without walls.
The movie, radio and TV: classroom without walls.[408]

—Marshall McLuhan, PhD, media scientist

Invented in the 1840s, the telegraph fed into human beings' curiosity about what is going on around them. After the invention of the telegraph, we began living at a more rapid pace. Subsequently, the world accepted newer, upgraded forms of communication, such as the telephone, phonograph, radio and motion pictures. Eventually, entrepreneurial inventors were able to develop an elaborate, "upgraded" version of the telegraph—the television. When televisions became popular in the 1950s, the communications industry again developed some radical changes, taking on an entirely new dimension. Today, the telegraph of the nineteenth century has evolved into the "super telegraph," or the computer, a very sophisticated medium that is able to disseminate a very elaborate Morse code. Samuel F. B. Morse could not have predicted that his invention, which started out with signals running through cables along railroad tracks, could have developed into such an important and widespread system of communication.

INTERNET AND VIDEO GAME MANIA

- According to the Entertainment Software Association, "the average gamer is now 33 years old, devotes 7.5 hours a week to playing and has been at it for 12 years . . . . That adds up to six months of gaming."[409]
- Sales of video games topped $9 billion last year, challenging movies as American's favorite past-time.[410]
- 62% of Internet addicts are logging on to porn sites. However, 46% of non-addicts are also visiting porn sites.[411]
- About 20% of general Internet users make contact with and/or meet someone they are conversing with online.
- Nearly 50% of Internet addicts make contact with and/or meet each other in person.
- 31% of Internet addicts have had a real-time sexual relationship with someone they met online.[412]

According to Dr. David Greenfield, author of *Virtual Addiction*, up to 6% of Internet users meet the criteria for a "serious compulsive addictive problem," and another 4% have "mild to moderate problems."[413] He defines addiction as an activity that could have a negative consequence on a person's life, including social isolation and withdrawal, depression, family separation, marital problems or reduced job performance.[414]

Children are especially vulnerable to the lure of the Internet. If children are not properly supervised, they can encounter inappropriate content, such as pornography or violent games. If you are concerned about whether your child may be abusing his/her time online, Dr. Greenfield suggests watching for these warning signs:

1. Spending excessive or increasingly greater amounts of time online
2. Ignoring their other responsibilities
3. Decreasing grades or poor work performance

4. Frequent absences from school or job
5. Ignoring real-time friends in favor of new online relationships
6. An unwillingness to talk about what they're doing online
7. Increased irritability and social isolation
8. Changes in mood, particularly depression
9. Less interest in activities they were previously involved in
10. Meeting or telephoning new people they met online[415]

Dr. Greenfield also warns that when you look forward to playing a computer game more than to doing anything else, or lie about your use of video games, there may also be a problem.

Like marijuana, speed or Ritalin, when a person is playing video games, dopamine production in the brain increases. The change in brain chemistry is an indication that playing video games is addictive. Children can become addicted to elevated levels of dopamine and can have a very difficult time concentrating on anything without being stimulated by video games.

With the increased popularity of gaming, about 10% of players admit to overuse.[416] In China, Internet and gaming addiction has become such a problem that the Beijing Military Region Central Hospital has been turned into an officially licensed treatment center for compulsive gamers and Internet users. The patients include people who have a hard time distinguishing between the real world and virtual worlds. A Chinese teenager, Xiao Yi, was so addicted to video games, "he would sometimes play for two days straight, even skipping food or sleep."[417] Distraught, the thirteen-year-old eventually jumped to his death. In his suicide note, he explained that "he was going to another world to meet the game's characters."[418] In the United States, a couple was so obsessed with the Internet and video games that they left their babies starving and suffering other health problems.[419]

Interestingly, one area that has psychologists concerned is the increased incidence of sex addiction. Now that the Internet has opened the floodgates in the area of sex sites, people are being exposed to sexual experiences they would otherwise not encounter. It is really no wonder that this sexual overstimulation is contributing to yet another addiction. Because sex addicts are very secretive, it is difficult to determine the rate of this disorder. It has been estimated that approximately 6% of the population between the ages of 18 and 35 may suffer from sex addiction,[420] and some psychologists believe that the incidence of this condition is on the rise.[421]

Sex addiction is just as destructive as any addiction, as it can certainly destroy marriages and relationships. Like other addicts, people who are obsessed with sex can live with a great deal of shame and guilt. There are several theories about the reasons sex addiction is on the rise, but psychologists theorize that exposure to certain forms of media, including Internet sex sites and television, could be one explanation. Television and marketing thrive on the "sex sells" mantra. In the 2005 study, "Sex on TV 4," funded by the Kaiser Family Foundation, the number of sexual scenes on television has nearly doubled since 1998.[422] The study found that 70% of all shows include some sexual content and that these shows average five sexual scenes per hour, compared with 56% and about three scenes per hour in 1998.[423] According to the study, program types that would most likely include sexual material are the following:

- Movies (92%)
- Sitcoms (87%)
- Dramas (87%)
- Soap operas (85%)
- Reality shows (28%)[424]

Just as with other any form of media, individuals need to use the Internet and video games responsibly. Unless we learn to adjust to everything our Fast New World has to offer, relationships, careers and families will continue to suffer.

DAVID GREENFIELD, PhD

Dr. David Greenfield is founder of the Center for Internet and Technology Addiction (www.virtual-addiction.com) and is director of the Healing Center, LLC. Dr. Greenfield's research, writing and clinical work on Internet and Technology Addiction and Behavior have appeared on CNN, ABC News, CBS News, Fox, NBC, *Good Morning America* and *The Today Show*. His work has been featured in *U.S. News and World Report*, *BusinessWeek*, *Newsweek*, *People*, *The Washington Post*, *The Wall Street Journal*, *Time*, *Forbes* and many other popular publications. He is recognized as one of the world's leading authorities on Internet and cyber psychology, including its use and abuse, and is author of the book *Virtual Addiction*, as well as several professional articles and book chapters on Internet and computer addiction and the impact of this technology on human behavior. Dr. Greenfield is a fellow and past president of the Connecticut Psychological Association and is assistant clinical professor of psychiatry at the University of Connecticut School of Medicine. He maintains his home and clinical practice in Connecticut and conducts research, training, consultation and lectures throughout the world on the Internet and digital media technology. Dr. Greenfield may be contacted by e-mail at drdave@virtual-addiction.com or 860-561-8727.

* * *

PAM: It's been over 10 years since you wrote your book *Virtual Addiction*. At that time, you were already warning us about the potential abuse of our time on the Internet. Is the problem worse today?

GREENFIELD: Because more people are using the Internet, the problem does appear to be worse. Increasing accessibility (through portable devices like laptops, cell phones, PDAs and wireless technology) has increased the "abusability" of the Internet. In my practice, for example, I see a lot of people who are dealing with gaming addictions or Internet sex addictions. Initially, people didn't realize that the Internet was addictive. About 10 years ago, with the help of ABCNews.com, just prior to publishing my book,

I did a study with 18,000 people about Internet addiction. The study showed that about 6-8% use the Internet in a compulsive or addictive manner. Even though there are more people using the Internet today, that percentage is still about the same.

PAM: Can you describe the differences between abusing the Internet and using the Internet for information? How can one tell if someone is addicted to the Internet?

GREENFIELD: If spending too much time on the Internet is creating an imbalance in their lives, then that's a good sign. If you spend 30 minutes, an hour or even three hours a day on the Internet, you probably don't have a problem. But if you come home from work and spend 4, 8, 10, or 12 hours a day on the Internet and ignore your wife and kids, then there's a problem. Or, if you overuse the Internet at work, you may be ignoring your job. In my practice, I see a lot of people who get caught or even arrested for downloading illegal images at work.

PAM: You're not quick to label the excessive use of the Internet as an addiction.

GREENFIELD: The media and the press like the word *addiction*. I prefer to use the term *compulsive Internet use* or *pathological Internet use*. There really isn't a good label out there that can be agreed upon. The term *Internet addiction* has become the popular conceptualization of the phenomenon. When you compare it to gambling or other behavioral-based addictions, it does have a lot of features that look like addiction. People even report experiencing tolerance and withdrawal symptoms.

PAM: When you refer to withdrawal, are you referring to symptoms such as depression?

GREENFIELD: Yes. But the more time people spend on the computer (in an extreme sense), the more isolated they are and, therefore, the more vulnerable they are to depression. About half the patients I see are suffering from this problem. I see the problem manifest itself in many different forms, but mostly I see the negative impact that this behavior has on peoples' lives.

PAM: What are the most common forms of Internet addiction?

GREENFIELD: There are three areas that people tend to abuse on the Internet: (1) information—that includes texting and emailing, (2) gaming—electronic gaming, multi-user games and (3) sex—pornography and cybersex.

PAM: In your book, you say that about 62% of heavy Internet users are turning to Internet porn?

GREENFIELD: Yes. Among the heavy Internet users, about 62% of them turn to Internet porn. In the U.S., porn is a $14 billion-plus industry. In terms of availability, it's a virtual epidemic. The Internet was built around porn. It was a perfect medium for pornography. It really drove the early years of the development of the Internet.

PAM: Would you say, then, that addiction to the Internet has contributed to pornography addiction?

GREENFIELD: Yes. Because of the ease of access or availability of porn on the Internet, we have a whole slew of people who have become addicted to pornography who probably would not be were it not for the Internet. Porn has been around for a very long time, and the Internet has allowed much easier access to it. The Internet is a perfect medium for pornography.

PAM: If someone is neglecting their family or their career, do family members typically intervene and bring the individual to a therapist like you?

GREENFIELD: The people who usually intervene are the mother, father or spouse. Sometimes an employer, or even the law, can intervene as well. If the Internet has had a negative impact on someone's life, he/she may come and see me on their own, but this is rare and usually it's only after he/she has experienced a traumatic event.

PAM: You mentioned gaming. Children and adults are spending enormous amounts of time playing Internet games.

GREENFIELD: Not only is gaming easy to access on the Internet, it's a very inexpensive way to spend your time. Gaming has become the social connecting point for children. Many kids meet in cyberspace (online). I call it the Malt Shop of the Millennium. Several decades ago, kids used to meet in the malt shop. Then they started to meet at the mall. Now they hang out in cyberspace.

PAM: Some people actually dream about the games, or even believe that they are the characters in the game.

GREENFIELD: Children can become obsessed with the gaming characters and take on their roles in their own lives. It can be very stimulating for people to play out those roles in real life. Instead of creating their own fulfilling lives, they live vicariously through the roles of the characters of these online games. This is nothing new. For a very long time now, people have been emulating the lives of the characters they watch on TV or in the movies or read about in books or magazines.

PAM: How much abuse is going on in the area of texting?

GREENFIELD: The most popular area of communication abuse is texting. If kids are texting during class, or employees are texting during work, then there's a problem. Texting itself is probably not much different from when we were teenagers and talked on the phone for hours. So one could argue that it may not be a problem. In some respects, it's less of a concern for me. But many people are texting, and it's interfering with their ability to perform at work or at school. It can interfere with a major component of life, work, school, health, legal status, financial status, relationships.

PAM: You compare Internet addiction to gambling. You say that people become powerless and that they're not managing their time when they're overly involved with the Internet. They may think they've been on the Internet for one hour, when in fact they've been on for four hours.

GREENFIELD: That's right. We call it "dissociation." Universally, people tend to lose track of time and space online. When you lose track of time and space, that makes what you're doing "psychoactive." If we're drawn to an activity or a substance that makes us feel good (alcohol, drugs, gambling, etc.), in part it's because it makes us lose track of time and space. It creates the right environment to change consciousness. Like gambling, sex, emailing, etc., the whole Internet functions on a "variable ratio reinforcement schedule." So every once in awhile, you're going to get what you want online. You're going to get the e-mail you want or the score or the connection or the sex site or whatever. And when the brain gets intermittent or variable reinforcement, it's highly responsive to that. Every time you get a "hit," you elevate your dopamine. What you're getting addicted to is not the behavior per say, it's the elevation in dopamine. Other neurotransmitters are also probably being elevated. But dopamine seems to be the main one. It's the "feel good" neurotransmitter.

PAM: For decades now, researchers and media scientists have referred to the television as a very addictive medium. I suppose the Internet is just another medium that can be very addictive.

GREENFIELD: I don't think that the Internet makes people addicted. It's how the content makes them feel, especially if the content is very stimulating, such as porn, gaming, gambling or even information. Some people may find that they can't stop using it on their own. They need someone to block their access or install filters or software and switches that shut it off. For example, if someone's on for an hour, then the Internet will shut itself off. I work with a technical person who goes to the homes of my clients and will install these gadgets.

PAM: Regardless of the potential risks involved in abusing one's time on the Internet, you say that you're not entirely against its use.

GREENFIELD: Not at all. I think it's a great technology. I use it. I just think that it's a very powerful technology. I may even abuse it myself from time to time. Like television, the Internet can be an incredible time waster—it can defeat hours of your life without any return. What makes the Internet much more potent than television is that there's instant gratification for whatever it is you're looking for and there are no boundaries. If you watch television or a movie, it ends and then you're done watching. The Internet isn't like that. If you go online to do research, you can be there for hours.

PAM: Several decades ago now, the media scientist Marshall McLuhan recommended that if we wanted to avoid being brainwashed by television, we should turn it off.

GREENFIELD: The media can be used as mind control. It can very easily be used as a tool to brainwash people. The Internet is no different than television, it's just a higher tech version of it.

PAM: With our attention shifting to forms of media such as television and now the Internet, it seems as though we're losing our sense of community.

GREENFIELD: The Internet has replaced our community. It can give us an artificial sense of belonging to something that is much bigger. It's similar to the feeling we get when we are a part of a true community. Some people actually believe that they feel a similar sense of community through the use of the Internet.

PAM: Some families have been torn apart because a family member has become addicted to the Internet. What do you do to try and help these families?

GREENFIELD: They need to turn off the computer. If the problem is happening with a child or teenager, it's important to remove the computer from their bedroom. Putting a computer in a child's room is like putting sugar in a child's hand and telling them not to eat it. That's true of TV as well. If the problem involves an adult, just removing the machine doesn't solve all the problems.

PAM: As we've expanded our world on the Internet, we seem to have isolated ourselves from humanity.

GREENFIELD: Some compulsive Internet users are isolated, but some are also reporting that they feel more connected. In some ways, they *are* more connected through their use of the Internet. There can be a degree of social connection through the Internet. Community organizations, special interest groups, chat rooms, etc. There's nothing wrong with this type of use. The issue is, do they have a sense of community in the rest of their lives? One could make the argument that any community is better than none. My belief is that the Internet is not going to make the world a better place. There is something important about physical proximity and community in terms of where you live and work. Although it makes the world a smaller place, I don't know that it produces the same level of intimacy and connection that we would see—like knocking on your neighbor's door to say hi. Today, people are much more likely to e-mail someone in China than they are to knock on their neighbor's door. People are craving intimacy, connection and community.

The fact that intimacy may be easier to obtain online than it is in real life probably speaks volumes about the way our culture has developed.

PAM: Are you noticing that people are losing social skills as they spend more time using these technologies?

GREENFIELD: Absolutely. That's very well documented. On the other hand, it can help people who are disenfranchised, or who have social anxiety or poor social skills, or geographic or physical limitations or even financial ones. It can open doors for some individuals. So I think there can be a very positive side to Internet use. On the other hand, video games and Internet porn can certainly hamper people's social skills.

PAM: In your book, you offer advice to parents regarding the importance of monitoring their children's use of the Internet.

GREENFIELD: It's very important for parents to monitor their children's use of the Internet. As mentioned previously, children can become obsessed. The Internet can be very stimulating. Instead of supporting extended use of the Internet, parents should instead be encouraging their children to participate in social relationship activities such as baseball, hockey, dance, etc. The skills that they learn in these activities are invaluable. You can't gain these skills online.

PAM: So you're getting these compulsive users to replace their time online with fulfilling real-life activities?

GREENFIELD: Yes. I get them off the computer and encourage them to find other more fulfilling activities to do. Like improving themselves by developing a skill, volunteer work, hobby or spending time with friends and family. Getting them out into the world to experience a truer sense of community than the artificial sensations received from the Internet.

PAM: Do you think that we are more prone to addiction now than ever before in the history of mankind?

GREENFIELD: Yes, I do. I believe that, overall, there are more substances that are addictive; therefore, there are more addictions. Not just to drugs and alcohol, but to gambling, sex, food, media, etc. Sixty percent of Americans are obese. Food addiction is probably a bigger problem than Internet addictions because it's costing billions of dollars in health care-related costs and quality of life issues.

PAM: Historically, we've learned that prohibition doesn't work. Banning addictive substances or the Internet wouldn't necessarily increase the quality of our lives.

GREENFIELD: Declaring a war on drugs is ludicrous. What we have to declare a war on is an unhealthy lifestyle. Drugs are only one aspect of it. The problem isn't the supply of drugs, any more than it's a supply of Internet or TV or food. If you want to look at what's really killing us, just walk up and down the aisles of the food store. The stuff we're consuming is killing us. Ninety percent of the foods we're eating are artificially flavored or colored and are filled with other additives.

PAM: I'm glad to hear you acknowledge the importance of eating wholesome foods. Ultimately, what you're saying is that in order to prevent or reverse addictive tendencies, it's important to find balance in all areas of your life.

GREENFIELD: Yes. It's important to find balance and prioritize your life. Balance would be believing that a Friday night family dinner is as important as going out with your friends. We need to recognize the inherent value in the events that contribute to the overall quality of our lives.

PAM: Kids find family dinners boring because they are so stimulated by what they see on TV or the Internet.

GREENFIELD: That's correct. All of the technology has increased the threshold for what stimulates them. On the other hand, kids want to be heard and they want the stimulation of having family dinners. If they're given the opportunity, they can also come alive at family dinners. But if they're not given that opportunity, then they're going to turn toward what I call their "digital distraction."

PAM: With regard to Internet addiction, what could happen in the future? Will things get worse or better?

GREENFIELD: I wish I could tell you that it was going to a good place, but it's not. I think we're going to see a continued proliferation of the technology as it becomes cheaper, faster, more constant, more available and more affordable. I don't think it's going to be the end of civilization. I think that eventually we'll learn to try and balance our time on the Internet the way we're trying to balance our time watching TV.

PAM: Thank you for taking the time to share your insights with me today. Given the increase in problems with Internet and video game addiction, I know you are a very busy man!

SECTION IV
AMERICA'S OTHER DRUG PROBLEM

For decades, both the public and physicians thought the pharmaceuticals were looking out for the health and welfare of society and never challenged what the industry claimed. Now everyone is starting to wise up to an industry [that] is hugely profitable and driven, obsessed with making more profits and to do that by any means it can, even if it means stretching laws, stretching ethics.[425]

—Arnold Relman,
Professor Emeritus of Medicine at Harvard Medical School

The internal documents we've found through discovery show what a total sham these antidepressants are. The science is bought and paid for. Experts are willing to sell their names and their souls. The whole thing's been an amazing web of lies and fraud.[426]

—Karen Barth Menzies,
A Los Angeles lawyer who is
perhaps the leading antidepressant
litigation attorney in the world

John P. A. Ioannidis, an epidemiologist at Tufts University School of Medicine in Boston, examined the most frequently cited clinical studies published in the top three medical journals between 1990 and 2000 to see how well researchers' initial claims held up against subsequent research. His findings, published in the JAMA, show that the key claims of nearly one-third (14 out of 49) of the original research studies . . . were either false or exaggerated.[427]

—Jeanne Lenzer, *Discover Magazine*

To rely on the drug companies for unbiased evaluations of their products makes about as much sense as relying on beer companies to teach us about alcoholism.[428]

—Dr. Marcia Angell,
Former Editor-in-Chief
of the *New England Journal of Medicine*

Spending more money on mainstream health care is not improving the quality of our lives, nor is it increasing the quality of health care we receive. According to a study published by *Health Affairs*, U.S. states with higher Medicare spending have lower-quality health care. The authors concluded that "the negative relationship we found between spending and quality and the factors that drive it are of *immediate concern*"[429] (emphasis added).

When it comes to our conventional health care system, people are slowly beginning to realize that they are not getting a good deal. Throughout North America, individuals are increasingly turning to alternative solutions. One-third of Canadians say that the current health care system is not meeting their needs. Seventy percent of Canadians have become disillusioned about prescription medications and believe that they are being prescribed more often than necessary;[430] the majority of Canadian adults (71%) say that they are seeking out alternative solutions by turning to natural health products.[431]

In the United States about half of all adults use some form of dietary supplement, at a cost of $23 billion a year.[432] According to a survey conducted by the National Institutes of Health, 38% of American adults have opted for complementary and alternative medicine.[433] Another survey, conducted by Harris Poll (2005), revealed that 35% of Americans who were prescribed drugs did not take them because they wanted to save money and another 28% left their drugs on the medicine shelf because of "painful or frightening side effects."[434]

The hope is that nutritional medicine would become the rule, not the exception. Today, relatively few conventional health care practitioners are integrating nutritional protocols into their clinics. With almost 85% of us dying from chronic disease, conventional health care practitioners have no choice but to start integrating nutritional medicine into their practices.

JOHN ABRAMSON, MD

> The drug companies are no more responsible for our health
> than the fast food industry is responsible for the quality of
> our diet. Part of their job is to convince us that they care
> about our health . . . . It's time for the American people to
> demand that their politicians stop being driven by the drug
> money that runs the campaigns and stand up to these drug
> companies so that the American people can benefit from the
> best of medical science.[435]
>
> —John Abrahmson, MD

John Abramson, author of the book *Overdosed America: The Broken Promise of American Medicine* and clinical instructor at Harvard Medical School, worked as a primary care doctor for over 20 years. He was a Robert Wood Johnson Fellow at Case Western Reserve University, studying research design, statistics, epidemiology and health policy. During the 1990s, as he became increasingly aware of the declining quality of health care, he began "researching the research." He discovered that the clinical studies presented in even the most respected medical journals were often biased by drug and medical device company sponsorship. Dr. Abramson's goal is to restore the basic mission of medicine, offering patients the most effective and efficient health care possible. Dr. Abramson now serves as an expert to plaintiffs' attorneys in litigation involving the pharmaceutical industry and as the executive director of health management for Wells Fargo Health Solutions.

Dr. Abramson's Web site is www.overdosedamerica.com.

* * *

PAM: Since Guylaine Lanctôt wrote her book *The Medical Mafia*
            in 1995, it seems as if there's more corruption going on
            today in the pharmaceutical industry.
ABRAMSON: There was a hearing recently about an antipsychotic drug
            called Zyprexa, which is getting prescribed to children
            off-label. Zyprexa has some very serious side effects, including
            weight gain, diabetes and lipid disorders. The hearing was

about whether there should be a class-action lawsuit against Eli Lilly, the pharmaceutical company that manufactures the drug. The judge ruled that there was enough evidence of fraudulent marketing on the part of Eli Lilly to allow the case to go forward as a class-action lawsuit. We hear about racketeering* in the mafia. Well, there was enough evidence of racketeering on the part of Eli Lilly to allow for a RICO (*Racketeer Influenced and Corrupt Organizations*) charge to go before a jury. The plaintiffs are suing for about $5 billion (the judge's decision to allow the case to go forward is currently under appeal). Now that Eli Lilly is facing RICO charges in federal court, the term *medical mafia* is no longer an outsider's critique of the pharmaceutical industry.

PAM: I have seen how the foster care system uses children as guinea pigs by giving them all sorts of medications.

ABRAMSON: You're being far too kind. To say that they were being used as guinea pigs suggests that there was some plan to derive knowledge from the unknown risks that the foster children were being exposed to. I think that that is an unrealistically optimistic view as to what was going on. A more realistic view is that they weren't being used as guinea pigs, but rather were being used as objects of potential profit. Children, in particular, are defenseless about this because parents' or states' desire to do the best for the children leads people to trust the apparent authorities and the apparent authoritative view on these issues, which is usually dominated by the pharmaceutical industry itself.

PAM: People don't realize that social workers, doctors, teachers, etc., are blindly following orders from a system run by pharmaceutical companies. These companies are only interested in making a profit and are not working for our best interest.

ABRAMSON: The American Law Institute, which is a very prestigious non-partisan legal oversight organization, declared that the

---

*   Profiting from illegal business activities, such as bribery, fraud or intimidation.

primary function of a corporation is to maximize its profits and to return those profits to its shareholders. Anyone who thinks that the pharmaceutical industry's primary responsibility is to the health of the public is naïve to the point of irresponsibility. People must learn that the pharmaceutical companies' primary responsibility is to maximize their profits and return those profits to their shareholders. If people don't believe me, then read the *Wall Street Journal* or the *New York Times* business pages. The drug companies invest a tremendous amount of money in public relations efforts in order to fool us into believing that their mission is about improving our health. Anybody who thinks that the drug companies' primary responsibility is anything other than maximizing their profits probably should believe in Santa Claus or the tooth fairy as well. As P. T. Barnham said, "There's a sucker born every minute."

PAM: Millions of people are taking antidepressant drugs, yet the research shows that not only do these drugs not work, they also have some very serious side effects. In this case, the cure is worse than the disease.

ABRAMSON: There's no evidence that there's a positive effect on feelings of sadness from antidepressant drugs in other than major depression. The majority of people taking antidepressants are mildly depressed and don't get any improvement. When they come off these drugs, they experience symptoms of withdrawal. It's especially been identified with the anti-anxiety drug Paxil.

PAM: They trust that doctors know what they're doing and that they're reading the literature.

ABRAMSON: That's part of the problem. The doctors have been reading the literature. The article in the *New England Journal of Medicine* showed that there were 74 studies of antidepressants, of which 38 were positive and 36 were negative. Of the 38 positive studies, 37 were published as independent articles. Of the 36 negative studies, three were published accurately as independent articles. So doctors who are reading the literature are getting the wrong information.

PAM: In order to protect themselves, patients need to learn that the studies that are published in major journals are bought and paid for by the companies who are selling the drugs. Therefore, it is very common for studies to be inaccurate.

ABRAMSON: The evidence is clear. If you look at the highest quality studies, the odds are 5.3 times greater that commercially funded studies will conclude that the sponsor's drug is the treatment of choice, compared to non-commercially sponsored studies of exactly the same drugs. Doctors are expected to practice evidence-based medicine, but more often than not, they're practicing "infomercial-based medicine."*

PAM: The more patients learn about such blatant conflicts of interest, the more they will spend time asking doctors questions. Doctors don't seem to like patients asking too many questions . . .

ABRAMSON: Doctors get angry for a number of reasons. One is that the patient is taking up too much time. Another is that the patient may be asking questions about their condition from a standpoint that the doctor is not familiar with. In essence, the doctor and patient could be coming from two different paradigms. When you get into these paradigm conflicts, it's very hard to find a way to communicate that's going to bridge the gap between paradigms.

PAM: Given all the conflicts of interest in the scientific literature, the phrase *independent research* doesn't seem to mean much anymore. Where can people find unbiased information about prescription drugs?

ABRAMSON: The Therapeutics Initiative in British Columbia is one of the greatest resources of all, and it's funded by public money (BC Ministry of Health through a grant to the University of British Columbia). Please support them. They've come

---

*   For an excellent article on this subject, refer to Glen I. Spielmans and Peter I. Parry. "From Evidence-based Medicine to Marketing-based Medicine: Evidence from Internal Industry Documents." *Bioethical Inquiry*, January 21, 2010. http://freepdfhosting.com/ebaef05bfe.pdf

under fire from industry. They do the best drug research of
them all. Another good source is www.worstpills.org. We're
seeing some progress out there. We're seeing some critical
voices, but we need to see more.

PAM: Overall, is the situation with our health care system getting
better or worse?

ABRAMSON: I think things will get much worse before they get better.
For example, Canada does not allow direct-to-consumer
(DTC) prescription drug advertising and is at risk for
having DTC advertising because the media conglomerate,
CanWest Global, is challenging the charter, claiming that
freedom of commercial speech is being constrained, because
they are not allowed to make money by running DTC ads
for prescription drugs. If DTC ads are allowed in Canada,
then, like the U.S., there will be more pharmaceutical
influence in the government.

PAM: The children are most at risk. In the U.S., one million
children have been diagnosed as being bipolar. Millions
more have been diagnosed with attention deficit disorder
(ADD) or attention deficit hyperactivity disorder
(ADHD). Rather than educating parents about diet and
lifestyle, doctors are prescribing extremely toxic drugs to
control their symptoms. What's going to happen to the
children?

ABRAMSON: There's a polarity between medical approaches offered by
medical doctors and those offered by alternative practitioners.
The vast majority of "mental health problems" are really
problems in living. Their symptoms are really alarms that
are set off by the children that say, "Help, I'm trapped in an
environment that won't let me develop to my potential."
Instead of heeding the alarm, the child is treated as ill and
medicated. It's analogous to when you smell smoke in the
kitchen, and instead of dealing with the smoke, you take
the battery out of the smoke detector.

PAM: For the parents, they may not have the time to help. They're
too busy. So medication is the only answer for them.

ABRAMSON: Parents are very busy. And they have to trust what the
authorities in society are saying. When that authoritative
voice has been compromised by the drug industry, there's

very little to counterbalance the parents' belief in that authority. One way to protect your child would be to find a physician who is not quick to prescribe drugs. After trying non-pharmacological approaches first, if your physician then prescribes a drug as a last resort, you'd be more likely to trust that opinion.

PAM: We've seen an enormous increase in health problems since shifting toward a high-carbohydrate, low-fat diet.

ABRAMSON: Yes. I agree. I would put that in the problems-in-living category. When you subsidize corn farmers and are producing 500 calories of corn syrup, when they didn't eat it 40 years ago, you're going to create problems that go beyond obesity.

PAM: How can people protect themselves from the propaganda put out by the pharmaceutical industry?

ABRAMSON: I'm not an expert in evolutionary biology, but as a species, we spent 99.5% of our time in existence as humans in hunter-gatherer groups of 40-60 people. In that context, cultural cohesion confers a strong survival benefit. We're hardwired to participate in a belief system that is supported by the authorities. If you watch a pack of wolves, you'll even find social hierarchy. Industry propagandists exploit the fact that, as a species, we are hardwired to conform to the group. I don't have a solution to counter their marketing tactics. Before things can change, we need a critical mass of people to come forward and do something to force these companies to clean up their acts.

PAM: The *New York Times* exposed the fact that Dr. Joseph Biederman accepted $1.6 million from the pharmaceutical industry for his help in promoting the use of Zyprexa for children diagnosed with bipolar disorder. How on earth could a patient ever trust a doctor who is getting paid by the pharmaceutical company? This is scandalous!

ABRAMSON: The psychiatrists receive a lot of money from the drug industry, and they will continue to propagate the view that medications should be used very liberally and off-label. Those financial relationships aren't going to stop. Vermont passed a law that said psychiatrists had to disclose how much money they were getting from the drug industry. A

recent study in Vermont revealed that in 2006, the average
payment to psychiatrists was about $45,000—an increase
of about 120% over the average payment of about $20,000
in 2005.[436] The pharmaceutical companies don't hand
this money out randomly. It gets handed out to doctors
in the program. Doctors might get gifts or benefits, but
it will be in proportion to their writing prescriptions for
the drugs that are manufactured by the companies that are
their benefactors. The drug companies know who's writing
what prescriptions, and they hand out rewards based upon
that knowledge. So it's not a direct kickback for prescribing
the drug, but if you're with the program, then you're more
likely to get these benefits.

PAM: Millions of people are in a state of disbelief about the
              corruption and conflicts of interest going on in the
              pharmaceutical industry. For those willing to question
              what's going on, I tell them to learn how to follow the
              money.

ABRAMSON: That's true, but that's not nearly enough. I spend a lot of
              time doing work for lawyers in litigation. I'm involved in the
              CanWest Global litigation in Canada, and I get to see a lot of
              confidential documents. I can tell you that there's no possible
              way for people who don't have access to confidential corporate
              documents to come close to following the money. You can
              see the very tip of the problem, but there's no possible way
              to understand the extent to which corporations are willing to
              hide and misrepresent the truth in order to sell their drugs. It
              makes your hair stand on end.

PAM: Unbelievable! Do doctors actually make money each time
              they prescribe a drug?

ABRAMSON: No, but they get paid for seeing patients and you can see a
              patient for a medication visit a lot more quickly than you
              can for a patient who is there for a therapy visit. So the
              doctor can then do more visits.

PAM: I heard recently that there are more students at my local
              university on antidepressants than there are on birth
              control.

ABRAMSON: I hear that up to 30% of undergraduates at high-caliber
              universities are on antidepressants. These people are not

suffering from major depression. When I was in college, it was called an identity crisis. It wasn't a medical problem.

PAM: There's a pill for every ill. Which means more profits for the drug industry.

ABRAMSON: That's what it's all about.

PAM: And it's based upon very clever marketing. Why do you say that the medical system is in a state of crisis?

ABRAMSON: It's in a state of crisis because the science and the overall approach is driven by profit, rather than by the desire to optimize people's health most effectively.

PAM: Relative to what we spend on health care, how do we rate compared to other countries?

ABRAMSON: Our health is improving, but health is improving far less rapidly than health in other countries that are spending half as much money.

PAM: That's the paradox that you speak about.

ABRAMSON: That's right.

PAM: Are you getting a lot of opposition from the medical community or pharmaceutical industry for exposing your findings about the conflicts of interest and/or lack of care patients are getting, despite the trillions of dollars we're spending on health care?

ABRAMSON: There's resistance that comes from all institutions that have a stake in maintaining the credibility of commercially distorted medical information. That ranges from the pharmaceutical industry, organizations dependent upon pharmaceutical industry money and so on.

PAM: Even very reputable medical journals have been influenced by pharmaceutical dollars.

ABRAMSON: Any companies that are dependent upon drug company money are beholden to drug company interests. No institution is too prestigious to bend its mission so that their funding from the drug industry isn't threatened.

PAM: How do you feel about socialized health care?

ABRAMSON: For half the cost of health care, Canadians are healthier than Americans.

PAM: Given the high cost of health care and the overall poor health of Americans, then, is it an unsustainable system?

ABRAMSON: In the U.S., there's tension between private and public interests. There is a role for private interests (i.e., private drug companies), and there's a role for public interests, but the problem is that we're out of balance. The private interests (drug and other medical industries) are paid for their services whether or not those services actually improve our health. In other words, they should be paid relative to their products' improvement of our health. And when you consider all the money we're spending on health care and look at how sick we are, they don't deserve to be making huge profits. We need to balance private and public interests. It's not that one should triumph over the other, but that there should be a balance and the determination of where that balance is ought to be the public good.

PAM: So the private interests have lost sight of the public good?

ABRAMSON: No. Remember, it is the job of the private sector to generate as much profit as it can. Claiming that the private sector is out of control is like blaming a two-year-old for bad behavior, when the fact is, the parents haven't set limits. What we need is governmental action that sets appropriate regulatory and statutory limits to protect the integrity of science. The private interests should only be able to make a profit by serving the public interest.

PAM: You mean, by getting results?

ABRAMSON: Right. They should only make money if they're getting results. That's where we're out of balance. You can earn money by convincing people that you got results but not really having results.

PAM: It's good public relations.

ABRAMSON: Yes. I call it counterfeit knowledge. Counterfeit knowledge is a lot more valuable than counterfeit dollar bills.

PAM: So you're saying that with better regulations, we may be able to develop a more sustainable health care system?

ABRAMSON: Right. We need a health care system whose undisputed primary purpose is to optimize the public's health most effectively and efficiently. Our health care system could operate using both public and private interests. It's different for each country. In Canada, you'll see less private interest and more public. In the U.S., we'll see more private than public. That's okay. As long as the goal is to optimize the public's health.

PAM: What will happen to the FDA?

ABRAMSON: The FDA needs to be revamped. The only reason it hasn't been revamped is it's serving the vested interests. Senator Grassley just cosponsored a bill to revamp the FDA, and it won't happen because the drug industry has too much power. It's simply a matter of money, power and politics.

PAM: Do you think, then, that the solution will lie in grassroots efforts?

ABRAMSON: Absolutely! We're in deep trouble. We all have a moral obligation to become politically active on this issue. There's a way to become an activist in a way that is consistent with your personal style. It may mean talking to your neighbor, it may mean talking to people in the grocery store, it may mean writing op-ed pieces, it may mean becoming a researcher. We all have ways to communicate to other people, and the time is now.

PAM: If people do nothing, what will happen?

ABRAMSON: There's no time to waste. Our health and our economy are both in danger. We're in a crisis. We have an obligation to speak out. We have to be smart and informed in order to protect our own health and the health of our families. If not, our health will deteriorate. Our kids will be drugged. We'll have very serious side effects. Our sexual lives will be compromised by all the drugs.

PAM: Can we leave on a positive note? Other than becoming an activist, what can people do to protect themselves from the corruption going on in the medical mafia?

ABRAMSON: The Institute of Medicine says that 70% of our health is determined by the decisions we make surrounding our diet and lifestyle. In other words, 70% of our health is in our own hands. The more we can do to improve our diets and lifestyle, the better off we will all be.

PAM: Thank you for sharing your time with me today. I appreciate all of the work you are doing.

SECTION V
PREVENTING FUTURE ADDICTS

There has been a real increase in teenagers and young adults who display episodes of manic-like symptoms such as insomnia, excessive energy, racing thoughts, grandiose ideas about themselves, irrational and outrageous behaviors, extreme irritability, paranoia and psychosis. However, in my three and one-half years of intensive psychiatric training in the 1960s, I saw only one case of a young person suffering from these symptoms. In the following years through approximately 1990, I saw few other cases. Yet nowadays I evaluate many teens and young adults with manic-like symptoms in my medical and forensic practice.[437]

—Peter Breggin, MD, *Medication Madness*

There is an epidemic of depression in every industrialized nation in the world. "It's a paradox; the wealthier we get, the more depressed young people get.[438]

—Martin Seligman, PhD,
Fox Leadership Professor of Psychology, 2006
Positive Psychology Summit, University of Pennsylvania

In this section, we will discuss what else we can do to help keep our children happy, healthy and addiction-free. In addition, Dr. Natasha Campbell-McBride and Dr. Scott Shannon will speak about their successes in treating children with mental disorders using nutritional approaches.

A loving, nurturing home is not enough to protect our children from developing mental disorders, trying drugs, or developing addictions. With countless drugs available legally and illegally, it has become virtually impossible to protect our kids from using mood-altering substances. Many kids will experiment with drugs during their youth. Most, however, come to their senses by the time they reach their early 20s and modify their behavior accordingly. If we hope to prevent them from developing addictions, we need to ensure that their nervous systems are properly nourished. As we have seen, a strong nervous system will support a joyful, balanced mental state, reducing the chances that an individual will develop addictions.

We are into the third and fourth generations of children eating a diet high in processed foods. Doctors and researchers have predicted that, because of their unhealthy lifestyle, this generation of kids may not live as long as their parents.[439] In addition, about 20% of our children are struggling with mental disorders. In 2005, 3.2 million children and teens were treated for depression in the United States. This is more than double the number from the previous five years.[440] If children are having a tough time coping now, what will the future be like? Will they have the mental strength to cope with such stressors as career, family and aging parents? Will their nervous systems be so weak that they will have to turn to drugs to help them cope?

Today's baby boomers grew up at a time when playing outdoors was the norm. They had boundless energy. They got plenty of fresh air and sunshine. They were polite and respected their elders. They were curious and eager to learn. They jumped out of bed in the morning, excited about the day's possibilities. They were happy to help others. They offered little (if any) resistance to doing their chores or homework. And they ate three square meals a day, never questioning what they were being fed.

Unfortunately, today, things have changed. Millions of children are tired, lethargic, disrespectful and/or lack the attention span to learn properly. Perhaps the worst habit they have developed is their propensity for manipulating adults into feeding them what they want. Unlike any other generation before us, today's children dictate to their parents what they will or will not eat. When kids know they are in control over what they can eat, invariably they choose to eat junk food.

Before this situation can change, parents need to learn where this behavior is coming from. Clever marketing has set our children up for developing poor eating habits. Furthermore, our busy lifestyles have undermined the family meal—a tradition that may even help reduce the chances of your children developing addictions.

The Importance of Family Meals

> More than two thousand years ago, the Greek philosopher Epicurus wrote: "We should look for someone to eat and drink with before looking for something to eat and drink, for dining alone is leading the life of a lion or wolf."[441]

—Miriam Weinstein, *The Surprising Power of Family Meals*

With our busy lifestyles, it may be a pipe dream to consider sitting down to a family meal. But this tradition does offer long-term health benefits for children as they enter adulthood. For children ages 3-12, family meals are the single strongest predictor of better achievement scores and fewer behavioral problems.[442] According to Carolina A. Miranda, "Studies show that the more often families eat together, the less likely kids are to smoke, drink, do drugs, get depressed, develop eating disorders and consider suicide and the more likely they are to do well in school, delay having sex, eat their vegetables, learn big words and know which fork to use."[443]

Compared to teens who have family dinners twice a week or less, teens who have dinner with their families five or more nights a week are
- 32% likelier never to have tried cigarettes,
- 45% likelier never to have tried alcohol and
- 24% likelier never to have smoked pot.[444]

Sitting down to eat family meals may be an unrealistic goal, but even if we have a busy life, it is still important to plan properly and eat three square meals per day.

Marketing to Kids

As children grow up, it is crucial to protect them from unscrupulous marketers who spend billions of dollars to con us into buying substandard, industrially processed foods. For several years now, Big Food has been targeting our children in order to increase its bottom line. According to Marion Nestle, PhD, MPH, author of *Food Politics*, "since 1994, American companies have introduced about 600 new children's food products; half of them have been candies or chewing gums and another fourth are other types of sweets or salty snacks."[445] Think about it. If these companies were truly interested in our children's welfare, they would be producing less, not more of the very foods that are compromising their health.

Big Food spends billions of dollars annually to convince, not just parents, but now children as well, to buy their fake "phood." Dr. Nestle writes that "companies support sales of "kids' foods," with marketing budgets totaling an estimated $10 billion annually."[446] In 2004, a marketing expenditure of $22.2 million led to the sale of $139.8 million of Cheez-It crackers for Kellogg. McDonald's spent $528.8 million to support $24.4 billion in sales.[447] Companies spend about $229 million per year advertizing sugary breakfast cereals to children (some breakfast cereals marketed to children are more than half sugar by weight), but a significant number of adults (58%) also consume them.[448]

Today, marketers have developed advertising campaigns that are specifically designed to convince our children to nag their parents into buying junk food. Pester Power is one very sophisticated marketing strategy, which is designed to get children to nag their parents into purchasing items they might not otherwise buy. Think about how many times you have gone shopping and surrendered to your child's nagging you into buying some sort of sugary or salty snack (potato chips, energy drink, soda pop, candy bar and so on). If your child had not seen an advertisement for that given product, it is highly unlikely that he/she would have nagged you about it in the first place. Marketers understand that it is far more effective to convince children to manipulate their parents into buying junk food than it is to convince the parents themselves. In fact, according to Dr. Nestle, "marketers explicitly attempt to undermine family decisions about food choices by convincing children that they, not adults, should control those choices. Indeed, children now routinely report that they and not their parents, decide what to eat."[449]

Not only do children nag their parents to buy junk food, they are also lining up to spend their own money on the stuff. In 1989, American children ages 4-12 years spent $6.1 billion. By 2002, children in the same age group spent a whopping $30 billion. What on earth are these children buying? One-third of their direct purchases were for sweets, snacks and beverages, followed by toys and apparel.[450] Since 1980, children have doubled their caloric intake of soft drinks, which now account for more than 10% of calories consumed. Even some parents are feeding their babies 1,200-2,000 calories per day from soft drinks alone.*

As adults, we must all be careful to set good examples for our children. When children see their parents eating junk food, naturally they want to mimic their role models. Monkey see, monkey do. The only way we can prevent marketers from negatively influencing our children is by showing them how to eat properly.

Carbohydrate-Addicted Kids

Kids are loading up on refined carbohydrates in the form of breads, breakfast cereals, cookies, cakes, candy bars and other sweets. Not only are they bringing these foods from home, they are buying them right at school. The World Health Organization has blamed these highly processed foods on causing many of the chronic health problems we see today, including diabetes, heart disease, cancer and obesity.[451] Regardless, children's role models—parents, athletes, celebrities, teachers, principals, doctors and politicians—are still eating them. What many people may not realize is that refined carbohydrates are highly addictive; therefore, it is really no wonder that people are not able to give them up.

In 1997, Rachael Heller, PhD and Richard Heller, PhD, wrote the book *Carbohydrate-Addicted Kids*. The Hellers explain that we can literally become addicted to carbohydrates. Carbohydrate addiction has been classified as a "true" addiction and that victims get caught in a vicious "carbo cycle"—excessive amounts of carbohydrates lead to abnormally high insulin levels, which lead to more intense carbohydrate cravings. This leads to more frequent and/or more concentrated intake

---

*   Keep in mind that many of the beverages parents are buying contain both
      caffeine and sugar.

of carbohydrates (especially, simple sugars), which, in turn, leads to blood sugar problems.[452]

If you are concerned that your child may be addicted to carbohydrates, here is a list of signs and symptoms you could watch for:

- A focus on starchy foods, junk food, snack foods or sweets (often to the exclusion of other foods)
- A desire to snack rather than eat whole, balanced meals
- Swings in energy levels, moods, ability to concentrate or motivation
- Unexplained outbursts of anger or periods of withdrawal
- Heightened emotionality, including sensitivity, crying, insecurity or clinging
- Weight problems or incidents of uncontrollable eating[453]

Americans of all ages are eating so many carbohydrate-rich snacks—three times as many as they consumed only a decade ago—that food addiction is becoming the rule rather than the exception. And so are the weight-related, psychological, physical and emotional problems that go along with it.

Carbohydrate-rich snacks consist of starches, snack foods, junk food and, most of all, sugar, sugar, sugar. It has been estimated that the average American consumes six hundred calories from sweets each day, not including fruits and other natural sources of sugar . . . . It is no coincidence that, at the same time, . . . mood, learning and behavioral problems have hit an all-time high. Our children are drowning in a flood of carbo-rich foods that are making them overweight, unfocused, undermotivated, hyperactive and overly mood-responsive.[454]

—Rachael Heller, PhD and Richard Heller, PhD,
Carbohydrate-Addicted Kids

Sugar is not the only carbohydrate that is addictive. Since *all* carbohydrates raise blood glucose levels, thereby increasing insulin, then theoretically the overconsumption of any carbohydrate could lead to a carbohydrate addiction. They believe that the excessive amounts of carbohydrates in our diet may be increasing our risk for developing chronic diseases, such as heart disease, stroke, diabetes, high blood pressure, obesity and cancer. In his book *Trick and Treat*, Barry Groves, PhD, explains that there are many neurological illnesses associated with eating too many carbohydrates.[455] According to Dr. Groves, "nearly one out of every five pediatric patients with type-2 diabetes has a brain-development disorder, psychiatric illness or behavioral disorder."[456] Children who consume too many carbohydrates also "have a propensity for problems that include a range of behavior, mood and learning disabilities. Some have been diagnosed as having ADD or ADHD."[457]

Rhymes with orange (105945) © Hilary B. Price. King features syndicate.

As we have seen, switching to traditional foods, which include adequate amounts of animal fat and protein, along with some complex carbohydrates, will help stabilize blood sugar levels and in turn resolve cravings, behavioral, emotional and cognitive problems.

Sleepyheads

Sleep deprivation is not just a health concern among adults but adolescents as well. Chronic sleep deprivation is now common among our youth—25% of adolescents report that they get six or fewer hours of sleep per night.[458] According to the National Sleep Foundation 2006 Sleep in America poll, only 9% of high school students are getting the optimal nine hours of sleep on school nights.[459] Those who are sleep deprived report greater mood disturbances, including feeling nervous or tense, feeling unhappy, sad or depressed and feeling hopeless about the future, have trouble getting along with their family, feeling cranky and irritable, too tired to exercise and consumed two or more caffeinated beverages each day.

Among our youth, lack of sleep is associated with serious health problems such as an increased risk of depression and substance abuse:

- Researchers at the University of Texas Health Science Center, in Houston, found that 24% of the adolescents surveyed met diagnostic criteria for chronic insomnia.[460] Adolescents with chronic insomnia had a two to five-fold increased risk for more physical and psychological health problems, difficulties with interpersonal relationships and more problems with daily activities.[461]
- In a 2008 study published in the journal *Sleep*, adolescent insomnia symptoms were found to be associated with depression, suicide ideation and attempts and the use of alcohol, cannabis and other drugs such as cocaine.[462] In this study, insomnia was reported by 9.4% of the adolescents. According to principal investigator and lead author of the study, Brandy M. Roane, MS, a doctoral student at the University of North Texas, "adolescents with insomnia are more prone to developing mental disorders, specifically depression."[463] Results of the study indicate that adolescents who had insomnia were 2.3 times more likely to develop depression in early adulthood than adolescents without insomnia.
- A 2007 study in China showed that high school students who slept less than eight hours per night were more likely to smoke or drink.[464]

Jodi Mindell, PhD, co-chair of the National Sleep Foundation task force, professor of psychology at St. Joseph's University and associate director of the sleep center at the Children's Hospital of Philadelphia, points out that "any time an adolescent is being evaluated for depression, sleep should be in the equation."[465] Since caffeine can interfere with sleep, it only stands to reason that parents and health care practitioners should eliminate caffeine from a child's diet, especially if they are experiencing sleep problems or depression.

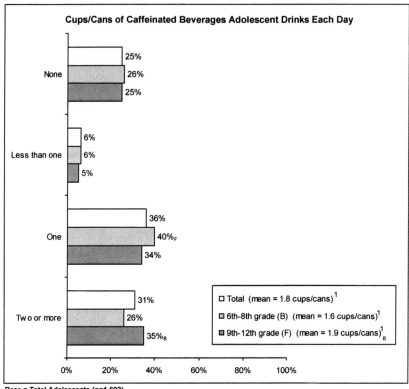

Cups/Cans of Caffeinated Beverages Adolescent Drinks Each Day

None: 25% / 26% / 25%
Less than one: 6% / 6% / 5%
One: 36% / 40%F / 34%
Two or more: 31% / 26% / 35%B

□ Total (mean = 1.8 cups/cans)[1]
□ 6th-8th grade (B) (mean = 1.6 cups/cans)[1]
■ 9th-12th grade (F) (mean = 1.9 cups/cans)[1]B

0%   20%   40%   60%   80%   100%

Base = Total Adolescents (n=1,602)
[1]Base = Those adolescents who drink at least one cup/can of caffeinated beverage each day
Don't know/Refused = 2%
Letters indicate significant differences at the 95% confidence level.
C25

Used by permission of the National Sleep Foundation, 2006 Sleep in America Poll

Interestingly, according to Dr. Mindell, caffeine is not the only thing interfering with children's sleep. Today, our children are exposed to more electronic devices than any other generation. When these electronic devices are in their bedroom, they could interfere with their sleep. Children with four or more items reported about 30 minutes less sleep than those with fewer devices.[466]

In a 2007 poll conducted by the Sleep Council, nearly 25% of teenagers between the ages of 12 to 16 admitted that they fell asleep while watching TV, listening to music or with other electronic gadgets running.[467] "This is an incredibly worrying trend. What we are seeing is the emergence of Junk Sleep—that is sleep that is of neither the length nor quality that it should be in order to feed the brain with the rest it needs to perform properly at school," said Dr. Chris Idzikowski of the Edinburgh Sleep Center.[468]

Age	Number of electronic devices in bedroom
11-12	2
17-18	4

About 97% of adolescents have at least one electronic device in their bedroom. As children get older, they tend to have more electronic devices in their bedroom. 2006 Sleep in America Poll, National Sleep Foundation

In order to make sure that children are not being distracted from getting enough sleep, Dr. Mindell recommends that adolescents forgo caffeine, regularize sleep schedules and take electronic devices such as electronic music and video game devices, television, cell phone, telephone, computer, Internet access out of their bedroom.

We must take proactive steps now in order to ensure that our children grow up to enjoy optimal mental and physical health. It is important to teach our children how to use electronic devices responsibly. In addition, children need to avoid stimulants such as caffeine, obtain adequate amounts of high-quality sleep and appropriate amounts of fresh air, sunshine and exercise.

Can Schools Help?

According to a March 2008 article in the online Independent, Britain may actually be the "unhappiest place on earth" for children. Education editor Richard Garner notes the "welter of evidence highlighting the fragile states of mind of many of the country's seven million primary and secondary school pupils," while reporting that British teachers had called for an independent Royal Commission to discover the reasons behind the widespread anxiety and unhappiness among the nation's children.[469]

—Gina Stepp, *Childhood: The New Age of Anxiety*

If children are not able to obtain wholesome foods at home, then perhaps our schools should help out. After all, school officials, teachers, principals and politicians are obligated to protect our children. We are well aware of the health problems associated with smoking and forbid students from smoking in school. If teachers and principals are supposed to be protecting our children, why is it that they allow them to buy or consume refined carbohydrates, sugary drinks, juice and caffeinated beverages at school?

With skyrocketing rates of obesity, diabetes, attention deficit disorder (ADD) and attention deficit hyperactivity disorder (ADHD), it is time for government officials to take a close look at school food to see what changes can be made to better nourish our children.

Prior to WWII, the British were known for their robust physical and mental health. Sir John Boyd Orr was a Scottish teacher, doctor, biologist and politician who, in 1949, received the Nobel Peace Prize for his scientific research into nutrition and his work as the first director-general of the United Nations Food and Agriculture Organization (FAO). Basically, Boyd Orr recommended a diet high in animal fat or Britain's standard fare—breakfasts of eggs and fatty bacon fried in lard, dripping (the fat from the Sunday joint), was saved to have on bread and toast, full-cream milk and butter.

"In the 1920s, Sir John Boyd Orr conducted a number of studies which compared growth rates of children in fee-paying schools with those in the state run schools. He found that those from wealthier backgrounds were significantly taller than their poorer peers. After examining their relative diets and changing constituents, Boyd Orr proved conclusively that children of the socially deprived, who lived on a largely carbohydrate diet of bread and potatoes, benefited from a diet supplemented with full-cream milk . . . . Boyd Orr concluded that the food intake of half the British population was seriously deficient in a number of what he called 'protective constituents' which were necessary for good health. Chief amongst these were foods of animal origin.

In the late 1930s he proposed that the British people should drink more milk and eat more dairy produce and meat. The British government . . . recommended that milk consumption should be doubled and introduced free school milk. The British Medical Association advised that the population should consume 80% more milk, 55% more eggs, 40% more butter and 30% more meat. And later, with the advent of television advertising, the government sponsored its own 'go to work on an egg' campaign."[470]

—Barry Groves, PhD,
Trick and Treat: How 'Healthy Eating' Is Making Us Ill

Historically, school food was considered a way to make sure children were eating nutritious and wholesome foods that they may not have been getting at home. In her book *School Feeding: Its History and Practice at Home and Abroad*, written in 1913, Louise Stevens Bryant wrote that "studies of the home diets of children, particularly those who are underfed, have shown that they are deficient in protein and fat . . . . The reason is that meat, fish, milk, eggs . . . are more expensive than bread, coffee and canned foods."[471] Considered an expert in school feeding, Ms. Bryant emphasized the importance of animal fats and animal protein in school lunch programs: "This is because fats and protein, being largely animal foods, are the most expensive kinds and are therefore bought sparingly by the vast majority of families."[472] She believed that it was the lack of the nutrient-dense animal fats and animal proteins that contributed to juvenile degeneracy, inattention, fatigue, listlessness, poor attendance and mental disability. When animal fats and animal protein were included in school food programs, she noted that mental disability was not only preventable but, in many cases, curable. School officials also noticed improvements in manners, conduct, mental ability and attendance. Overall, the children had a brighter manner and keener interest in their work.

For proper growth and development, children need animal fats. Since dairy products are an excellent source of animal fats, vitamins and other important nutrients, one way to ensure that they receive adequate amounts of nutrition is through the consumption of whole milk, cream and butter. Research indicates that children who drink milk have higher intakes of specific nutrients and better overall nutritional status than non-milk drinkers.[473] Unfortunately, rather than drinking milk, our children are drinking everything from coffee to sugary drinks such as energy drinks, pop and juice. Even with all of the growing health concerns surrounding obesity, consumption of sugary drinks and fruit juices has been steadily increasing over the last decade.[474]

By providing children with sugary drinks and juice, schools are sending the wrong message to children about what constitutes a healthy drink. One way to ensure that children get the nutrients they need is to provide them with whole milk rather than the soft drinks (juice, energy drinks, pop) and low-fat milk we see in the schools today.

Nutri-Washing

Removing processed foods and vending machines may be one step to help improve the quality of school food, but is it going to be enough? Are these new healthy school food initiatives really going to be providing healthy foods? Unfortunately, they will probably still promote the consumption of a high-carbohydrate, low-fat diet. Many new "healthy" school initiatives include margarine, plant-based oils, low-fat dairy products, juice or soy foods. Typical healthy school food initiatives also promote the consumption of plenty of fruits and vegetables—not that this is a bad idea, but it still ignores the importance of animal protein and animal fat. Therefore, as well intentioned as these initiatives may seem, children will still be missing many crucial nutrients.

In order to optimize their nutritional intakes, children should be consuming high-fat dairy products, including whole milk, butter and cheese. Ideally, dairy products should be in their natural form, unpasteurized and from local, pastured sources. These foods are critical to the development of their brain, bones and endocrine system. According to a recent report from the U.S. Preventive Services Task Force (USPSTF), U.S. Department of Health and Human Services, children who follow diets low in animal fats are at risk for malnutrition:

- Getting kids to eat low-fat diets is a popular trend among health conscious individuals; however, the *USPSTF* not only found lack of effectiveness, but evidence for harm.
- Lower fat intake is associated with lower levels of calcium, zinc, magnesium, iron, phosphorus, vitamin E, vitamin D, vitamin A, vitamin B12, vitamin B6, folic acid and niacin (B3).[475]

To make matters worse, some of the healthy school food initiatives may also promote the consumption of soy foods. According to Kaayla Daniel, PhD, author of *The Whole Soy Story*, there are hundreds of epidemiological, clinical and laboratory studies that link soy to:

- Malnutrition
- Digestive distress
- Thyroid dysfunction
- Cognitive decline

- Reproductive disorders
- Infertility
- Birth defects
- Immune system breakdown
- Heart disease
- Cancer[476]

In Asia, people consume small amounts of soy, and the soy that they do eat is traditionally prepared through fermentation. Along with these soy foods, they consume a significant amount of animal foods such as pork, fish and fowl. If you are interested in consuming soy products, do not eat large amounts and make sure they are made from certified organic soybeans and that the product is fermented through traditional methods (i.e., miso, natto, tempeh).

In our schools, efforts are underway to teach children how to grow food and prepare meals from scratch. At Northwestern Secondary School in Stratford Ontario, Paul Finkelstein has incorporated a culinary program where children have access to a greenhouse, garden, full kitchen facility and their own café. His culinary program has become so popular that it has caught the attention of the Food Network (to catch a glimpse into their culinary classes, you can watch for the television show entitled *Fink*). In Berkeley, California, Alice Waters has a similar program called *The Edible Schoolyard*. And in England, the government has recently announced that they will be integrating culinary programs in their schools, making cooking classes compulsory for children ages 11-14 by 2011. In order to achieve their goal, the government will be training over 800 cookery teachers and building teaching kitchens.

Healthy school initiatives are only a small step in the right direction. If they are truly sincere about properly nourishing our children, they need to start feeding our children the nutrient-dense foods, which kept our ancestors healthy for generations. This includes adequate amounts of animal foods—hopefully high in fat!

In addition to living in such a chaotic world, today's children are exposed to more nutrient-deficient processed foods and drinks than any other generation. Unlike any other generation before, they are consuming enormous amounts of caffeinated beverages, which further destabilizes their biochemistry. In order to help support their nervous system, we need to find better ways to cope in our Fast New World. One way to do this is to slow down and return to basics when it comes to what we eat. As we will see in the following interviews with Dr. Natasha Campbell-McBride and Dr. Scott Shannon, teaching families to return to healthy eating habits can help stabilize a child's mental state in our terribly destabilizing world.

Helping Kids with Mood and Behavior Problems

NATASHA CAMPBELL-MCBRIDE, MD

> We live in the world of unfolding epidemics. Autistic Spectrum Disorders, Attention Deficit Hyperactivity Disorder (ADHD/ADD), schizophrenia, dyslexia, dyspraxia, depression, obsessive-compulsive disorder, bipolar disorder and other neuro-psychological and psychiatric problems in children and adults are becoming more and more common.
>
> Children with these conditions are often diagnosed as being depressed and as they grow up they are more prone to drug abuse or alcoholism than their typically developing peers. When we start examining the patients with these so-called mental conditions, we find that they are also physically ill. Digestive problems, allergies, eczema, asthma, various food intolerances and immune system abnormalities are universally present amongst them . . . . I have yet to meet a child or an adult with autism, ADHD/ADD, dyspraxia, dyslexia, schizophrenia, bipolar disorder, depression, or obsessive-compulsive disorder who does not have digestive abnormalities.[477]
>
> —Natasha Campbell-McBride, MD,
> *Journal of Orthomolecular Medicine*

Natasha Campbell-McBride is a medical doctor, neurologist and nutritionist. After curing her own son of autism, she has committed her entire practice to helping children and adults with digestive problems, mood disorders, mental illness and learning disabilities. At her clinic in Cambridge, England, she has successfully treated thousands of children with learning disabilities, autism, dyspraxia, dyslexia, depression and schizophrenia, as well as adults with digestive and immune system disorders. She is the author of *Gut and Psychology Syndrome* (2004) and *Put Your Heart in Your Mouth* (2008).

Dr. Campbell-McBride has discovered that children struggling with Gut and Psychology Syndrome or GAPS (discussed below) experience digestive problems, asthma, eczema, allergies, thrush, bed-wetting, malnutrition and/or chronic cystitis. These children tend to develop other problems such as autism, ADHD/ADD, dyslexia, dyspraxia (clumsiness), learning, behavioral or social problems. As they age, their symptoms can deteriorate into problems with substance abuse, depression, obsessive-compulsive disorder, manic depression or schizophrenia.

Dr. Campbell-McBride's Web sites are www.gaps.me and www.medinform.co.uk.

* * *

PAM: As you point out in your seminars, children with poor eating habits and bad digestion develop behavioral problems. One of the consequences of their bad digestion is that they develop food addictions. Your concern is that when they reach adulthood, they can develop substance abuse problems.

DR. NATASHA: We have a big problem with addictions in general. Everybody knows about drug, alcohol and nicotine addictions, but very few people know about food addictions. We have addictions to various foods, including addictions to sugar, wheat or junk foods, including soft drinks. These foods disrupt our metabolism, damage gut flora and compromise brain function.

PAM: Based upon the work you are doing, these food addictions can be very damaging.

DR. NATASHA: Food addictions can be quite insidious. If an individual is allergic to a certain food, he or she may react with behavioral symptoms. These symptoms can be immediate or delayed. Addictive foods can cause someone to go into the typical cycle of displaying inappropriate behaviors (aggression, overexcitement, anxiety, panic attack, depression, etc.). Then, because they're addicted to that food, they crave that food again and their inappropriate behavior returns.

PAM: In your book *Gut and Psychology Syndrome*, you explain that childhood behavioral symptoms are really signs of malnutrition and toxicity. These symptoms include autism, learning disabilities, attention deficit disorder (ADD), attention deficit hyperactivity disorder (ADHD), dyspraxia, dyslexia, etc. As we age and the body becomes more toxic and more malnourished, these symptoms can lead to depression, obsessive-compulsive disorder, manic depression, schizophrenia. The symptoms can worsen as we age.

DR. NATASHA: The root of these conditions is Gut and Psychology Syndrome (GAPS)—a term I have coined which encapsulates everything from autism to schizophrenia to addiction. Right from birth, these children have not acquired a normal mixture of bacteria or gut flora because their parents have compromised gut flora. The pathogens developing in their digestive tract digest food in their own way, producing all sorts of toxic substances (including gases). These toxins are absorbed into the bloodstream and get distributed around the body and can enter the brain. Some of these toxins have an addictive nature. They have the chemical structure of opiates, which have an adverse effect on the neurotransmitters in the brain. The effect of these toxins on the brain will manifest itself as autism or hyperactivity, dyspraxia or dyslexia or another combination of behavioral and learning problems, which do not fit into any diagnostic box.

PAM: I see a lot of kids who may not fit into those diagnoses, but they display milder symptoms.

DR. NATASHA: The largest group of children affected by GAPS are those who haven't been diagnosed. These are the children who have some behavioral, learning and social abnormalities. They can't learn quite properly. They can't quite fit into society properly. They're fussy eaters. They may find it difficult to learn at school.

PAM: Can you explain how children and adults can become addicted to certain foods?

DR. NATASHA: Some of the toxins which enter the brain damage the brain, but some give it the pleasure signal. So the brain wants more. The child gets stuck in the vicious cycle of craving the very foods that damage him or her. As these foods feed the abnormal flora in the gut, this flora produces more toxins to feed the addiction.

PAM: What are the typical foods that children become allergic to?

DR. NATASHA: These foods are usually the starchy, stodgy, sweet processed foods—made out of sugar, flour, soy, vegetable oils, etc.

PAM: So in order to restore the good flora in the digestive tract, it would be important to stop eating these foods.

DR. NATASHA: That's right. They need to eliminate all the foods that feed that vicious cycle of craving and dependency. Millions of so-called "normal" children are finicky eaters, which is one of the major symptoms of GAPS. We can't just dismiss this symptom by saying, "Oh, he'll grow out of it." Or, "He doesn't like the food." Quite often, these children have a mild case of Gut and Psychology Syndrome, and they can display some behavioral abnormalities and some physical symptoms, including asthma, eczema or allergies. These are the children who get through their childhood undiagnosed, and then when they reach adulthood, they are more vulnerable to substance abuse. These are the children who react inappropriately to cannabis or marijuana developing a psychotic reaction. Unfortunately, what follows is the diagnosis of schizophrenia with a lifetime of psychiatric institutions and drugs. All these children need is to change their diet and heal their gut.

PAM: I think our ancestors would be rolling over in their graves if they saw how kids manipulated their parents into giving them what they want to eat. It's incredible what marketing has done to ruin kids' diets and turn them into fussy eaters. A hundred years ago, children ate what they were given, and it was usually three wholesome meals per day.

DR. NATASHA: Absolutely. And they liked what they were given. They had normal biochemistry in the body. Their systems hadn't been ruined by antibiotics, vaccinations and processed foods. They weren't exposed to things that could upset the balance in their gut flora.

PAM: Not to mention the fact that they didn't have the advertizing that we see today.

DR. NATASHA: Exactly. If you look at Dr. Weston A. Price's photographs of the faces of children and adults in primitive cultures, they look extremely healthy.

PAM: In your practice, you can probably see the physical degeneration in the faces of the children you see (cavities, crooked teeth, narrow jaws). As Dr. Price pointed out, the degeneration we see in our faces today is a sign of physical and mental degeneration within our bodies. Our ancestors didn't have chronic diseases at the rates we see today, and for the most part, they had beautiful facial structures and didn't have cavities or crooked teeth.

DR. NATASHA: Yes. In my practice, I can see the physical abnormalities and not only in their faces and their mouths. Children look malnourished. They have dark circles under their eyes. They are either obese and overweight or too small and underweight. They're pale, pasty looking. They have narrow jaws, crooked teeth, cavities, acne, brittle hair. It's difficult to find healthy looking children nowadays.

PAM: I see kids with brittle hair, and it doesn't look like a genetic trait. It looks like they're malnourished.

DR. NATASHA: Brittle hair is related to poor nutrition. Hair is a storage site for nutrients such as minerals and amino acids. GAPS children and adults haven't got enough of the essential nutrients which can build healthy hair.

PAM: How do parents react when they learn that they've been poisoning their child with highly processed foods?

DR. NATASHA: I see a lot of tears. But the vast majority of our patients are motivated and are very compliant with the program.

PAM: Are there any individuals who make excuses not to follow the program?

DR. NATASHA: In the majority of cases, by the time patients come to see me, after they've tried everything else with no success, they're willing to follow the diet. They've overcome denial, pessimism.

PAM: Do you see a lot of children with sleep disorders?

DR. NATASHA: The majority of children with GAPS have sleep disorders. They can't settle down, they're too wired to fall asleep. And when they do fall asleep, they can't stay asleep and wake up several times during the night crying. They have nightmares. Or, they're bed wetters.

PAM: Does it concern you to see so many doctors who make colic in babies out to be a normal part of infancy?

DR. NATASHA: Yes. Colic is *not* normal. Because so many children are colicky, doctors are normalizing this condition. Colic has never been normal and never will be normal. It is a clear sign of abnormal gut flora developing in the child.

PAM: We have an "auto brewery" in our gut. The imbalance in our gut flora produces some very toxic chemicals. Can you explain how these toxins adversely affect our neurotransmitters and their cofactors, such as vitamin B6?

DR. NATASHA: The auto brewery syndrome refers to the overgrowth of yeasts in the digestive tract. It was discovered and described for the first time in Japan. A doctor noticed that he had patients who appeared to be drunk even though they hadn't consumed any alcohol. This condition interfered with their work lives, family lives and social life. Testing found that these people had an overgrowth of yeast in their digestive systems. Yeast consumes simple sugars (glucose) as its food and convert them into alcohol through a biochemical process called alcoholic fermentation. These people have their own little brewery in their digestive tract. Every piece of bread, every teaspoon of sugar, breakfast cereal, any form of simple carbohydrate, will be converted into alcohol. When the alcohol gets to the liver, the first step in neutralizing this alcohol is the production of a very toxic chemical called acetaldehyde. It's an extremely harmful chemical, and it likes to attach itself to various proteins. By attaching to these proteins, it occupies the receptor sites where neurotransmitters, enzymes, hormones (thyroid, adrenal), vitamins and other nutrients would normally need to attach themselves in order to fulfill their functions. Because their working sites are occupied by acetaldehyde or some other toxin, then they cannot fulfill their function. That's called a functional deficiency.

PAM: People may believe they are deficient in, say vitamin B6, but if acetaldehyde is interfering with its receptor site, then the vitamin won't appear to be doing its job.

DR. NATASHA: That's right. An individual may have a perfectly normal amount of a particular vitamin in the bloodstream, but this vitamin can't work because its working site is occupied by acetaldehyde. This is one of the reasons we see an epidemic of hypothyroidism (low thyroid). People have the symptoms of low thyroid, but when we test them for the production of thyroid hormones (i.e., thyroxin, T3, T4, etc.), the majority of them have perfectly normal production. Their thyroid can be producing normal levels of hormones, but these hormones can't fulfill their functions because when they arrive at the working sites, these sites are occupied by acetaldehyde or some other toxin. As a result, they have all the typical symptoms of low thyroid—they gain weight, they become lethargic, mood changes, depression, skin problems, hair loss, poor temperature control, etc. Some of the most studied functional deficiency syndromes are vitamin B6, vitamin B12, thyroid hormones—all of which are connected to the auto brewery syndrome.

PAM: Dr. Abram Hoffer and other doctors who practice orthomolecular (nutritional) medicine recommend that patients with schizophrenia remove dairy and wheat from their diets. For some, this dietary change can help eliminate symptoms. If someone has mood problems, is it a good start to remove dairy and wheat?

DR. NATASHA: Absolutely! But I would go much further than that. The majority of patients notice that simply removing dairy and wheat isn't enough to help them recover. The reason for that is the fact that in an unhealthy gut most proteins are not digested properly and as a result absorb partially digested. The majority of dietary proteins are not researched very well yet, apart from gluten and casein. It has been discovered that in an unhealthy gut they turn into toxins called gluteomorphines (from gluten grains) and casomorphines (from dairy), which in their biochemical structure are similar to opiates. In that form, when they are absorbed they can act on the brain in the same way as a shot of morphine or heroin.

PAM: Morphine and heroin act more like depressants on the body. So these compounds must make people feel pretty dopey.

DR. NATASHA: Yes. After eating bread or a glass of milk, GAPS people can become very dull minded. Like drug addicts. Many researchers have looked into this, and they have come to the same conclusions. The gluten-and casein-free diet was born based upon this research. This diet removes all grains that contain gluten and all dairy that contain casein. Removing those two toxins out of the equation helps, but it's not enough. Those are only two toxic substances out of hundreds that are produced by abnormal gut flora and absorb into the blood stream through the damaged gut wall.

PAM: So the real solution is to repair the digestive system so that
            foods are broken down properly and individuals don't react
            any longer?

DR. NATASHA: Absolutely! The real solution is to concentrate on the
            digestive system so that you remove the pathogenic flora and
            replace it with beneficial flora so that you can heal and seal the
            gut lining. In GAPS people, the gut lining gets damaged and
            becomes like a sieve. Anything can leak through—partially
            digested proteins, bits of foods, microbes, toxins, etc.—and it
            disrupts the immune system. All of these toxins are distributed
            throughout the body and cause all sorts of symptoms. Not
            just mental symptoms, but all sorts of physical problems as
            well (arthritis, chronic fatigue, fibromyalgia, skin reactions
            and so on).

PAM: I'm looking forward to your next book, *Gut and Physiology
            Syndrome*, where you will be describing how your diet can
            help with physical illnesses as well, including type 1 diabetes.

DR. NATASHA: Type 1 diabetes is an autoimmune condition, and it is
            strongly connected to celiac disease—about 60% of children
            with type 1 diabetes have celiac disease. That's just another
            very clear indication that something is very wrong with their
            digestion. Because their gut lining is damaged and is like a
            sieve, all sorts of proteins do not get digested properly before
            they're absorbed. Instead, they are absorbed into the system
            in a partially digested form. Consequently, the immune
            system doesn't recognize these partially digested particles as
            food and starts producing antibodies against them. Because
            many of these proteins that we eat are similar to the proteins
            in our own body, a particular antibody then develops against
            a particular food protein, which cross-reacts to proteins in the
            pancreas (in the Langerhans cells which produce insulin in
            the pancreas). These antibodies start attacking the pancreas
            and start destroying the little islets that produce insulin. So
            the child can't produce insulin. In a nutshell, that's how type
            1 diabetes develops.

PAM: And type 1 diabetics are also moody, depressed, prone to
            addiction, etc.

DR. NATASHA: The type 1 diabetic patients aren't just dealing with
            diabetes. They all have behavioral problems, social problems,

learning problems. As I mentioned, the majority of them also have celiac disease. They may have asthma, eczema, etc. They're usually very pale, and look malnourished.

PAM: You say that 90% of a successful treatment depends upon diet. And you recommend a diet that focuses on animal protein and animal fats.

DR. NATASHA: The diet that I recommend is based upon the Specific Carbohydrate Diet (SCD), which was specifically developed to heal and seal the gut lining. The diet also encourages the growth of beneficial bacteria and removes pathogenic flora from the gut. I had to slightly restructure the Specific Carbohydrate Diet because I noticed that many people weren't interpreting the diet properly and were not getting the results they wanted. In other words, if parents succumb to the fact that their child is a fussy eater, many of them try to replace the sweet, starchy, stodgy foods which their child would accept with sweet foods that are allowed on the SCD diet. So they start feeding the child with SCD desserts made with almonds and honey, while the child is still stuck in that vicious cycle of dependency and craving.

PAM: What do you call the diet you recommend? And how is it different from SCD?

DR. NATASHA: I have restructured this diet and call it the Gut and Psychology Syndrome Diet. We concentrate on substances that heal and seal the gut lining. We focus on the child's food addictions so that we can help break inappropriate eating habits in children.

PAM: Carbohydrates are okay, but not as essential as protein and fat. As Dr. Weston A. Price studied, the animal fats kept our ancestors healthy for millennia.

DR. NATASHA: Absolutely. I agree 100% with the Weston A. Price Foundation. Fats are one of the most essential parts of our nutrition. We cannot live without them. We have to rely on natural sources of fats, without changing or altering them too much. That's why minimally processed fats, which are naturally occurring in meat, butter, ghee, cream, coconut oil, etc., are essential for us to eat. Considering that the brain is largely a fatty organ, it is essential to have a high-fat diet.

PAM: By saying a high-fat diet, do you mean a diet high in *animal fats*?

DR. NATASHA: That's right. High animal fat, particularly arachidonic acid (AA) which only comes from animal fats such as butter, ghee, pork fat, lamb fat, beef fat, poultry fat and fish.

PAM: I'm glad you mentioned fish. After all, fish has the reputation as being the ultimate brain food.

DR. NATASHA: It is essential for us to eat fish. Many of our ancestors subsisted mainly on fish. Over the last one hundred years, we've overfished our oceans, or we've introduced unreasonable regulations so fish has become a delicacy and is very expensive. Most of us don't eat enough fish. Fish is also an excellent source of cholesterol, which is also essential for rebuilding the brain structure.

PAM: Low cholesterol can contribute to depression, and yet there's a tremendous amount of pressure from the pharmaceutical industry to put children on statin drugs.

DR. NATASHA: That's absolutely awful. Putting children on statin drugs in order to reduce their cholesterol would be devastating for their physical and mental development.

PAM: If statins reduce cholesterol and low cholesterol contributes to depression, then these kids could end up turning toward addictions.

DR. NATASHA: Absolutely. If this policy is set in place, we are going to see lots of victims. In the first place, this policy is based upon a faulty theory, which has been proven conclusively to be wrong. I explain the history of the diet-heart hypothesis in my book *Put Your Heart in Your Mouth*. It is a myth that saturated fat and cholesterol cause heart disease. Since the diet-heart hypothesis was proposed in 1953, a lot of time, money and energy has gone into proving this hypothesis to be right, instead the research has proven that this hypothesis is wrong. Over the last 50 years, a huge commercial and political machine was built around this hypothesis. Despite the fact that they know that this hypothesis is wrong, these powers are making billions of dollars on marketing the idea that fat and cholesterol cause heart disease. Once people find out that this hypothesis is wrong, the commercial interests have a lot to lose. So they do their best to keep the faulty diet-heart hypothesis alive for as long as they can.

Cholesterol is one of the most essential substances in our bodies. We can't live without it. Twenty-five percent of blood cholesterol is consumed by our brain—the brain is particularly hungry for cholesterol, particularly, the myelin sheath. A major source of cholesterol is oily fish. The highest level of cholesterol is found in caviar (fish eggs), the next best source is cod liver oil. One of the reasons why people benefit from cod liver oil has to do with the fact that it contains a lot of cholesterol. For example, people with multiple sclerosis (MS) need a lot of cholesterol and do very well on cod liver oil.

PAM: You wrote your first book about gut health and then you wrote a book about saturated fats and cholesterol. It seems as though the two subjects are as different as night and day.

DR. NATASHA: I had to write the *Put Your Heart in Your Mouth* book because patients were worried about all of the animal fats and cholesterol rich foods I recommend in the Gut and Psychology Syndrome Diet. They're worried about developing heart disease. I've had to explain to hundreds of people that cholesterol has nothing to do with heart disease, and I thought it would be easier to get them to read about it in a book.

PAM: To help heal and seal the gut, you also recommend bone broths.

DR. NATASHA: Absolutely. In order to heal and seal the gut, you need several things—you need to feed the gut lining properly; you need collagen, gelatin, glucosamine, amino acids and all of these substances can be found in meat and bone broth. I recommend that people drink meat and bone broth every day with their meals. In order to drive out the pathogens and introduce the healing bacteria, they also must have probiotics in the form of probiotic foods and therapeutic strength probiotics.

PAM: What probiotic-rich food do you recommend?

DR. NATASHA: I recommend kefir, yogurt and other varieties of soured milk as well as lacto-fermented vegetables such as sauerkraut. Some people ferment coconut water, kvass and other lacto-fermented vegetables.

PAM: What kind of responses do you receive from your patients?

DR. NATASHA: Mostly excellent. In more than 90% of my patients, we see great improvements. Some people respond very quickly whereas with others, it may take more time. I have seen lots of children recover from autism. I have seen children with type 1 diabetes able to lower their dose of insulin or even manage without insulin altogether. I have even seen children recover from epilepsy.

PAM: People with damaged brains can turn toward addictions as they enter into adulthood. A damaged gut can lead to a damaged brain. Therefore, if you can help children heal and seal their guts, then hopefully you will help prevent them from developing addictions later in life.

DR. NATASHA: That's right. As we treat the children, we can prevent them from developing addictions. It's very common to find people suffering with mental illnesses such as schizophrenia who also have drug addictions. We want to do a study putting schizophrenic patients on the GAPS diet, but we couldn't get government support.

PAM: Any last thoughts that you'd like to share with us?

DR. NATASHA: I don't believe that there's anybody that's beyond help. No matter how young, no matter how old, no matter how severe—if you want to recover, it can be achieved. I see absolute miracles every day. It's wonderful!

PAM: Your book is a tremendous resource. Do you speak to people who have been able to get their child well after reading your book?

DR. NATASHA: Absolutely! I speak to people who were able to get their child well after they read my book. These people give me the most delight! They read my book and did all the work themselves. I take my hat off to them!

PAM: Well, I take my hat off to you! Thank you for all of the great work you are doing to help our children!

SCOTT SHANNON, MD

Scott Shannon is a child psychiatrist and leads the first university-based Integrative Child Psychiatry Clinic in the United States at the University of Colorado Children's Hospital in Denver, Colorado. He is the author of the book *Please Don't Label My Child* (2007).

Dr. Shannon is concerned about the many children he sees today who are just not fitting in to society. He notices that too many of them are not as happy as they should be. Many are not doing well at school and are suffering socially. Rather than exploring the social, nutritional and environmental reasons why children are demonstrating so many behavioral and emotional problems, millions of children are being labeled and treated as having medical conditions. Thanks to Dr. Shannon's clinical experience using nutritional and alternative treatment approaches in his practice, he has been helping children recover from attention deficit disorder (ADD), attention deficit hyperactivity disorder (ADHD), depression, anxiety, bipolar disorder, etc. He hopes that his work will help inspire parents, teachers and other doctors to break free of the doctor-diagnosis-drug cycle so that children can lead full, healthy lives naturally, without toxic pharmacological agents.

For more information about his work, visit his Web site www.wholeness.com.

*   *   *

PAM: What types of changes are you seeing in our children compared to, say, 25 years ago when you started practicing medicine?

SHANNON: The number of kids with unstable mood problems has escalated dramatically. A couple of decades ago, it was rare to see kids with bipolar disorder or volatile or aggressive behaviors. It was rare to have anyone other than a child psychiatrist treat these problems. Now the problems are so common, I find schoolteachers making the diagnosis. Child psychiatrists cannot handle the load, and pediatricians are expected to handle 2 or 3 psychiatric medications in six-year-olds. Again, twenty years ago, this was not happening. Recent studies show that the incidence of pediatric bipolar disorder in outpatient clinic settings increased forty-fold in a ten-year period! I'm aghast by that! It's happening across the U.S.

PAM: About a million children are diagnosed as being bipolar.

SHANNON: Yes. And I'm very concerned about that. I'm also very concerned about the number of kids who are being diagnosed as being hyperactive and placed on stimulant medications. Back in the 1970s, we had a few hundred thousand kids identified and treated as hyperactive, and now it's estimated that 4 million kids would meet the criteria for ADHD and 3 million are on stimulants.

PAM: Do you ever see children who are suffering with mild cases of anxiety or depression?

SHANNON: To some degree. Nationally, the numbers are in the 8 to 10% range for anxiety disorders in kids. I think it's a very undiagnosed and underappreciated problem because our society is getting more complicated, competitive and aggressive. Kids are struggling to cope.

PAM: Two of the first symptoms of starvation are anxiety and depression.

SHANNON: When I see this trend of more and more kids who are doing worse today, I think one of the common factors is poor nutrition. Across the board, our intake of omega-3 essential fatty acids has fallen. Kids are eating more trans fats or hydrogenated oils, which impair the metabolism of the omega-3 essential fatty acids to make the EPA and DHA that the kids need to build brains. I've also seen a pervasive magnesium and zinc deficiency, which also impairs the body's ability to produce essential fatty acids for the child's brain. When we talk about starvation, the key thing that concerns me as a holistic psychiatrist is brain nutrition. I focus on how well kids provide nutrients for their brains.

PAM: What is more remarkable is that when you do give the child the correct nutrition, their behavior improves. I know a woman whose son was a B student. As soon as she stopped feeding him boxed cereal for breakfast in the morning and started feeding him a more "bacon and egg" style breakfast, his marks went from Bs to As. She couldn't believe how much calmer and more focused he was just by changing his breakfast!

SHANNON: Sometimes, behavior is directly adversely affected by poor blood sugar metabolism. When kids are eating a high-carbohydrate diet, often with lots of sweets, their blood sugar goes up and peaks by 9:00 a.m. Then by ten thirty, their blood sugar is falling, and it's hard for them to focus their attention or stay awake. Eating a high-protein diet will help level off their blood sugar and may be the answer for many of these kids.

PAM: Millions of kids are following a high-carbohydrate diet, and they have terrible mood swings or poor focus. They can be very grumpy and irritable. I don't think it's normal to see so many kids suffering with irritability and bad moods. I would think that what is normal would be for kids to be optimistic and cheerful. Has the norm changed?

SHANNON: I think there are several factors that come together to disrupt children's behaviors. Some of what's going on could be because of a combination of things, including poor nutrition or sleep deprivation. Studies show that if kids are deprived of at least 30 minutes of sleep, their performance falls and they become more irritable and testy. Over the last 30 to 40 years, Americans are sleeping less. If we're staying up till midnight watching TV or playing video games online, then we're not focusing on real-time activities with family and friends, nor are we focusing on preparing healthy meals.

PAM: I hate to see the norms change so dramatically. Society and medicine are normalizing PMS, menopause, precocious puberty, etc. And I'm afraid our children are going to take the brunt of this—they may normalize behavioral problems such as oppositional defiant disorder (ODD) or attention deficit disorder (ADD). They may normalize outbursts of rage.

SHANNON: Kids are more symptomatic, and as a result, doctors are very quick to label them. I'm not as concerned about the labels as I am about the fact that parents and kids have lost the ability to self-regulate, and as a whole, society has lost the ability to know what factors are important and how to take care of ourselves. Parents and kids are heavily influenced by commercial interests—they may actually believe that a boxed cereal is the perfect breakfast. We've lost the ability to monitor, manage and self-regulate.

PAM: In her book *The Surprising Power of Family Meals: H o w Eating Together Makes Us Smarter, Stronger, Healthier and Happier*, Miriam Weinstein cites studies which show that children who ate the most meals with their families tended to eat better, performed better at school, had fewer emotional problems and were less likely to adopt risky behaviors such as smoking, drug or alcohol abuse.

SHANNON: And the converse is that if they're not eating a family meal, then they're eating fast food or junk food, which can contribute to brain starvation. If they're eating family meals, then hopefully, they're eating wholesome foods, which are more likely to feed the brain properly.

PAM: Research out of England illustrates that children who eat processed foods with commercial additives became hyperactive.

SHANNON: I encourage parents to reduce their intake of processed foods. The easiest way to do this is to encourage them to eat more protein.

PAM: By eating more protein, they'd be consuming fewer carbohydrates and would be better able to control their blood sugar.

SHANNON: That's right.

PAM: What are the typical symptoms you see with hypoglycemia (poor blood sugar control)?

SHANNON: Poor concentration, irritability, depressed mood, explosive temper, anxiety.

PAM: So you can warn parents that if their child is displaying these symptoms, they may be able to help improve their child's behavior by increasing their protein and decreasing carbohydrates in their diet.

SHANNON: When I see a child who has mood issues, anxiety or poor concentration, I encourage parents to put their kids on a high-protein diet. This is one of the simple things parents can do. I also get them to remove caffeine and soda out of their diets. I reduce the amount of sugar in their diets. I get them to eat more protein and less processed foods. Those are simple steps that most parents can understand. Intuitively, they know these changes will help their kids.

PAM: Sugar is addictive. If a child is addicted to sugar, could this lead to other addictions?

SHANNON: There's a close link between sugar metabolism and addictions, particularly alcoholism. Alcohol is a two-carbon compound broken down from a simple sugar. People who have mood histories often have alcoholism histories in their families. I see a close relationship with that. People who have a family history of addiction tend to move either toward alcoholism or sugar. Again, I encourage these people to get on to a high-protein diet, which helps them get away from that addictive tendency.

PAM: Dr. Stanton Peele, author of *Addiction-Proof Your Child*, is more concerned about the legal drugs than he is about illegal drugs. Both legal and illegal drugs are addictive.

SHANNON: As we put more and more kids on stimulant medicine, there's a concern. Whether we use stimulant medication or antidepressant medication, my concern is, are we teaching our kids to self-regulate? Or moving them away from that? Addiction is just one example of self-regulation gone awry.

PAM: I see kids lining up to get their coffee at local cafés. We're also teaching kids that it's okay for them to alter their brain chemistry at very young ages.

SHANNON: Yes. They are. Altering brain chemistry is a pervasive cultural message that is hard to avoid. That's why we're seeing a stronger move to medicate kids for any or all kinds of problems. Our societies' preferred response to deal with mood problems is to alter the pharmacology rather than manage the root issues.

PAM: Caffeine can cause anxiety and depression.

SHANNON: Yes. I've cured many kids suffering with anxiety or ADHD by getting them off their caffeinated beverages.

PAM: That's wonderful news! Some parents are pulling their hair out trying to manage kids with behavior issues, and if they could simply remove caffeine from their diets, I'm sure they'd have more peace in their lives if they could see their child calm down after removing caffeine from their diets. The answers can be simpler than they realize.

SHANNON: The problem can be that the parent is drinking 4 or 5 cups of coffee a day or even diet pops so they're having problems themselves.

PAM: Dr. Biederman was paid $1.6 million by the pharmaceutical industry to help promote the drug Zyprexa to children—a drug that wasn't approved for children.

SHANNON: Psychiatry has been compromised by the commercial influence of the pharmaceutical companies. At this point it's hard to draw a line between the pharmaceutical companies and the leaders in psychiatry because they're so interwoven not just in their finances but in the way they think and how they make their money. I think psychiatry has fallen by the wayside.

PAM: Thank goodness for doctors like yourself and Dr. Abram Hoffer and other nutritional psychiatrists who are bringing integrity to your profession.

SHANNON: At the very least, doctors need to learn that pharmaceutical drugs are not the only options and that there are natural solutions which can help these kids. Unfortunately, our research isn't as broad as it should be. Some of that is because the pharmaceutical industry has a stranglehold on the researchers. We shouldn't just be looking at the weight of the evidence, which is distorted by the wealth of the pharmaceutical companies. We need to look at the risk-benefit ratios. I think that's what could move this to a different direction. The risk-benefit ratios, when working with kids' diet, sleep, exercise, nutrition, home life, etc., is much different than the risk-benefit ratios of putting them on drugs like Zyprexa.

PAM: What types of testing do you perform?

SHANNON: I look at zinc, iron levels, vitamin D, thyroid and we check for lead. In isolated cases, I may do more in-depth nutritional testing. I try and keep it simple. I want to keep the parents empowered so that they can understand what's going on with their child. Doing a thousand dollars worth of testing moves parents out of a position of control or empowerment. I haven't seen the benefit from that. Not only is it cheaper and more cost-effective for the parents, but I think parents can more easily understand what to do to help their child get well if I keep things simple.

PAM: You've had enough clinical experience to see a pattern and to see what works to help these kids get well. For example, you see results by getting kids to eat three or more wholesome meals per day, which include protein and you see results when they take fish oil.

SHANNON: Yes. And I use other supplements that get great results as well. The ones I commonly use are vitamin C, B complex, fish oil, inositol, SAM-e, St. John's wort.

PAM: And you use acupuncture, emotional counseling.

SHANNON: Yes. We have a very complete holistic program.

PAM: It sounds like you're giving children and their families hope so that they can go on to have fulfilling lives.

SHANNON: That's my goal!

PAM: You must be getting a lot of positive feedback from your patients.

SHANNON: It's very rewarding work. I enjoy what I do.

PAM: We need more psychiatrists like you! What is your vision for the future of psychiatry?

SHANNON: Here in Denver, at the Colorado Children's Hospital and at our Integrative Child Psychiatry Clinic, I see a lot of positive changes and feel very hopeful for the field of psychiatry. We are even seeing more interest with residents, fellows and medical students.

PAM: Thanks to doctors like you, I think we can turn this situation around. Thank you for your time. Keep up the great work!

CONCLUSION

It takes an extraordinary intelligence to contemplate the obvious.

—Alfred North Whitehead, Philosopher (1861-1947)

It is evident that the deterioration in the quality of our food over the last one hundred years has contributed to the epidemic of physical and mental health problems we are seeing today. We all know that food affects how we feel, both physically and mentally—when we go without food, we can feel cranky and irritable; when we eat junk food, we can feel tired and listless; when we eat healthy food, we have energy and focus. What many people may not fully understand is that specific nutritional deficiencies can adversely affect mood, behavior and cognitive function. Pharmaceutical drugs and talk therapy are inadequate treatments if there are nutritional deficiencies that need to be addressed.

Nearly everyone is addicted to something—whether it is street drugs, prescription drugs, nicotine, caffeine, sugar, gambling, work, power, control, rage, shopping, hoarding, sex, video games, television and so on. Before we can recover from our addiction epidemic, society needs some sort of an intervention. The recent economic downturn may have given us all the wake-up call we needed. Millions of us have been forced into re-evaluating our priorities, causing us to focus more on our needs over our wants. In order to successfully recover from our addiction epidemic, we must return to basics, strengthening our families and communities. So that we have the proper building blocks to support our nervous system another significant step in our recovery program will be the return to real food.

Medical doctors and public health officials could also help reduce rates of addiction by warning society about the consequences of eating nutrient-deficient foods and teaching about benefits of eating nutrient-dense foods. As they start educating people about sound nutritional principles, medical doctors could avoid putting them on potentially addictive mood-altering drugs in the first place.* Not only

---

*   Unless, of course, the drug is absolutely necessary.

would this effort reduce health care costs, it would improve the quality of our lives.

One of my goals in writing this book was to provide readers with enough information to prevent themselves and their children from developing addictions. In addition, I wanted to provide helpful resources for anyone currently struggling with addiction. Now that we are seeing epidemic rates of addiction, we have no choice but to face this problem and look for *effective* treatment solutions. With rates of depression expected to increase, we must also talk about prevention. We talk about preventing cancer. We also need to talk about preventing mental disorders such as depression. Unless we improve our mental health, rates of addiction will continue to skyrocket. Substance abuse is already our number one health problem. We cannot afford to sit back and allow this epidemic to get worse.

APPENDIX

NON-PHARMACEUTICAL BRAIN REPAIR RESOURCES

Alliance for Addiction Solutions
www.allianceforaddictionsolutions.org

Charles Gant, MD, PhD, ND
www.charlesgantmd.com

David and Merlene Miller
www.miller-associates.org

Lifestream
www.lifestream-solutions.com

Safe Harbor
www.alternativementalhealth.com

Hypoglycemia Association of Australia
www.hypoglycemia.asn.au

Community Addiction Recovery Association (CARA International)
2230 Loma Vista Drive
Sacramento, CA 95825
916-485-2272
www.carasac.org
CARA is dedicated to improving recovery outcomes by providing education and services that integrate mind and body to support biochemical repair.

Residence

Bridging The Gaps
423 Cork Street
Winchester, Virginia 22601
540-535-1111
www.bridgingthegaps.com
(also has outpatient program)

InnerBalance Health Center
2362 East Prospect Road, Suite B
Fort Collins, CO 80525
970-225-2623
www.innerbalancehealthcenter.com

Total Health Recovery Program
Santa Fe, New Mexico
505-310-1340
www.totalhealthrecoveryprogram.com

Semi-residential

Health Recovery Center
3255 Hennepin Ave. S
Minneapolis, MN 55408
612-827-7800 or 800-554-9155
www.HealthRecovery.com
Founder Joan Mathews-Larson, PhD, author of *Seven Weeks to Sobriety*, is a pioneer in the biochemical repair and restoration of the brain and body. The orthomolecular model for addictions treatment is based on pure science. Comfortable detoxing with multiple IVs, extensive lab work to identify and repair damage, and bio-restoration that stops cravings, and ends depression and anxiousness, individual therapy, low stress teaching groups. This is not a 12-Step Program. Over 75% success rate.

Outpatient

Recovery Systems
147 Lomita Drive, Suite D
Mill Valley, CA 94941
415-383-3611
www.moodcure.com/consult.html
This is Julia Ross's outpatient clinic near San Francisco, where she and her staff provide assessment, nutritional therapy for detox and long-term recovery, and help in creating whatever holistic program is needed for recovery, combining psychological, spiritual, and nutritional components.

Excel Treatment Program
1660 South Albion Street, Suite 420
Denver, CO 80222
303-782-0599
www.exceltreatment.com
Excel offers amino acid intravenous treatment for the repair of genetic addiction, clinical acupuncture for environmental addictions, group alcohol and drug education classes, group alcohol and therapy classes, individual therapy, relapse prevention groups, monitored U.A.'s, antabuse and naltrexone distribution for court sanctioned alcohol treatment, and also provides in-house prescriptions including liver blood profile workups.

N.O.R.A. (National Organization for Recovering Alcoholics)
Alternative Addiction Treatment Center
422 Pagosa St. Suite #13
P.O. Box 5364
Pagosa Springs, CO 81147
970-264-4816 or 888-788-7348
http://noraa.org/
The treatment program uses a ten-day intravenous drip of all natural amino acids prescribed by a Doctor and administered by a Registered Nurse.

William Hitt Center Avenida Paseo Bursatil 406, Suite 403
Tijuana, B.C. 22320
Mexico
U.S. toll-free: 888-671-9849
Mexico: 664-683-17 88
www.williamhittcenter.com
Restoration and rebalancing of normal neurotransmission in the brain through IV amino acids.

MULTI-MEDIA ADDICTION RESOURCES FEATURING MEMBERS OF THE ALLIANCE FOR ADDICTION SOLUTIONS

Howard Jamison's Web site offers a variety of interviews and seminars featuring therapists in the addiction field, including members of the Alliance for Addiction Solutions.

www.jamisonmedia.com
www.addictionsolutionsource.com

Burton Goldberg's DVD, *Addiction: Getting the Monkey Off Your Back*, features interviews with recovering addicts and members of the Alliance for Addiction Solutions.

www.burtongoldberg.com

ACUPUNCTURE RESOURCES FOR DETOX AND RECOVERY

Brumbaugh, Alex G. *Transformation & Recovery: A Guide for the Design and Development of Acupuncture-Based Chemical Dependency Treatment Program*. Stillpoint Press, 1994.

Mitchell, Ellinor R. *Fighting Drug Abuse with Acupuncture: The Treatment That Works*. Pacific View Press, 1995

National Acupuncture Detoxification Association (NADA). www.acudetox.com

ALTERNATIVE HEALTH PHYSICIAN GROUPS

American Association for Naturopathic Physicians
www.naturopathic.org

International Society for Orthomolecular Medicine
www.orthomed.org

The Institute for Functional Medicine
www.functionalmedicine.org

Complementary and Alternative Medicine Specialists Connect (Canada)
www.CAMSpecialistsConnect.com

Holistic Health Research Foundation of Canada
www.holistichealthresearch.ca

American College for Advancement in Medicine
www.acam.org

American Holistic Medical Association
www.holisticmedicine.org

American Association for Health Freedom
www.healthfreedom.net

American Academy of Environmental Medicine
www.aaem.com

LABORATORIES/TESTING

Great Plains Laboratory
www.greatplainslaboratory.com

Genova Diagnostics
www.genovadiagnotics.com

Diagnos-Techs
www.diagnostechs.com

To diagnose mineral imbalances and heavy metals using Hair Tissue Mineral Analysis (also referred to as tissue mineral analysis) contact **Analytical Research Labs**
www.arltma.com/HairAnalysis.htm

IMPORTANT TRADITIONAL FOODS RESOURCES

Weston A. Price Foundation
www.westonaprice.org
The goal of the Weston A. Price Foundation is to restore nutrient-dense traditional foods to the human diet through education, research and activism. In order to achieve their goal, the foundation supports accurate nutrition instruction, organic and biodynamic farming, pasture feeding of livestock and community-supported farms. For audiovisual recordings of their annual conference, Wise Traditions, visit www.fleetwoodonsite.com.

Price-Pottenger Nutrition Foundation
www.price-pottenger.org
The Price-Pottenger Nutrition Foundation, a non-profit educational organization, is a clearinghouse for information on healthful lifestyles, ecology, sound nutrition, alternative medicine, humane farming and organic gardening.

SUPPORT GROUPS FOR SUSTAINABLE AGRICULTURE

Eat Wild
www.eatwild.com
Eatwild.com is an excellent source for safe, healthy, natural and nutritious grass-fed beef, lamb, goats, bison, poultry, pork and dairy products.

Slow Food
www.slowfood.com
The association's activities seek to defend biodiversity in the food supply, reinforce the importance of taste and link producers of excellent foods to consumers through events and initiatives.

Acres USA
www.acresusa.com
Acres USA offers a publication, Web site and annual conference that support and educate farmers and consumers about sustainable agriculture.

Local Harvest
www.localharvest.org
This Web site will help you find farmers' markets, family farms and other sources of sustainably grown food in your area, where you can buy produce, grass-fed meats and many other goodies.

Sustainable Table
www.sustainabletable.org
Sustainable Table promotes and educates consumers about making healthy food choices that support a sustainable system.

Farmers' Markets
www.ams.usda.gov/farmersmarkets
A national listing of farmers' markets.

Alternative Farming Systems Information Center, Community-Supported Agriculture
http://www.nal.usda.gov/afsic/csa/
AFSIC provides national farm databases to help you find a local CSA.

National Resources Defense Council
http://www.nrdc.org/health/foodmiles/
NDRC offers a great tool on their Web site that helps you determine what fruits and vegetables are in season in your state.

Eat Well Guide: Wholesome Food from Healthy Animals
www.eatwellguide.org/About.cfm
The Eat Well Guide is a free online directory of sustainably raised meat, poultry, dairy and eggs from farms, stores, restaurants, inns and hotels and online outlets in the United States and Canada.

Organic Consumers Association
www.organicconsumers.org
OCA is building a national network of consumers promoting issues such as food safety, organic agriculture, fair trade and sustainability.

Organic Center for Education and Promotion
www.organic-center.org

The goal of the Organic Center for Education and Promotion is to generate credible, peer—reviewed scientific information concerning verifiable benefits of organic farming.

Community Involved in Sustaining Agriculture
www.buylocalfood.com
CISA is dedicated to sustaining agriculture and promoting the products of small farms.

Ecological Farming Association
www.eco-farm.org
Eco-Farm is working to support the strengthening of the soil, protecting air and water and encouraging diverse ecosystems and economies.

National Campaign for Sustainable Agriculture
www.sustainableagriculture.net
The National Campaign for Sustainable Agriculture includes a diverse partnership of individuals and organizations supporting environmentally sound, profitable, healthy, humane and just food and agricultural systems.

FoodRoutes
www.foodroutes.org
The FoodRoutes Find Good Food map can help you connect with local farmers so that you can find the freshest, tastiest food possible. On their interactive map, you can find a listing for local farmers, CSAs and markets near you.

National Farmers Union
www.nfu.org
National Farmers Union is working to protect and enhance the economic well-being and quality of life for family farmers and ranchers and their rural communities. They believe that consumers and producers can work together to promote local, safe food.

GETTING HEALTHY FOODS INTO THE SCHOOLS

National Farm to School
www.farmtoschool.org
Farm to School programs are becoming increasingly popular all over the United States. These programs connect schools with local farms in order to provide healthy meals in school cafeterias, improve student nutrition and support local small farmers.

Farm to College
www.farmtocollege.org
This site offers information about farm-to-college programs throughout North America collected by the Community Food Security Coalition.

Sustainable Food in Schools
www.sustainabletable.org/schools/dining
If you do not approve of the food being served in your or your child's cafeteria, you can do something about it. This site includes guidelines on what to do, how to do it and examples of successful efforts that have already been initiated in the United States.

INFORMATION ABOUT FACTORY FARMING

The Meatrix
www.themeatrix.com
An entertaining video animation about factory farming and links about what you can do about it.

Global Resource Action Center for the Environment
www.gracelinks.org
www.factoryfarm.org
The GRACE Factory Farm Project (GFFP) works to create a sustainable food production system that is healthful and humane, economically viable and environmentally sound.

Beyond Factory Farming
www.beyondfactoryfarming.org
Beyond Factory Farming is a coalition of citizens' organizations from all across Canada that share a vision of livestock production for health and social justice. Their mission is to promote livestock production that supports food sovereignty, ecological, human and animal health, as well as sustainability, community viability and informed choice.

ENVIRONMENTAL ISSUES

Environmental Working Group
www.ewg.org
EWG specializes in environmental investigations. They have a team of scientists, engineers, policy experts, lawyers and computer programmers who examine data from a variety of sources to expose threats to your health and the environment and to find solutions.

GLOSSARY

acetylcholine—An excitatory (stimulating) neurotransmitter associated with memory, mental alertness, learning ability and concentration.

amino acid—A building block of protein. Examples of some important amino acids include tryptophan, phenylalanine, tyrosine, methionine and glutamine.

amphetamine—A mood-altering drug known to produce increased wakefulness and focus in association with decreased fatigue and appetite. It is related to methamphetamine.

attention deficit hyperactivity disorder (ADHD)—A neurodevelopmental disorder (mostly in boys), primarily characterized by the co-existence of attention problems and hyperactivity, with each behavior occurring frequently together.

autism—A disorder of neural development characterized by impaired social interaction and communication and by restricted and repetitive behavior

axon—The long extension from a neuron that transmits outgoing signals to other cells.

bipolar disorder—A mental disorder characterized by episodes of mania and depression

catecholamines—A group of compounds with active roles in the sympathetic and parasympathetic nervous systems. This group includes adrenaline (also known as epinephrine) which is a hormone secreted by the adrenal gland and noradrenaline (also known as norepinephrine). Effects include blood vessel constriction and increase in blood pressure and increased heart rate.

cholesterol—A fatty waxy substance made by the body and also found in some foods.

cortisol—An important hormone secreted by the adrenal glands. It is also known as "the stress hormone" because it is released in higher levels during the fight or flight stress response. Cortisol influences or regulates several stress related changes in the body including blood sugar (glucose) levels, immune responses, anti-inflammatory actions, blood pressure, heart and blood vessel tone and contraction, central nervous system activation and fat, protein and carbohydrate metabolism.

dendrite—Branches that connect nerve cells (neurons) with one another. A neuron can have up to 20,000 dendrites networking with other neurons.

dopamine—An excitatory (stimulating) neurotransmitter commonly associated with mood, energy and focus.

dyslexia—Impaired ability to learn to read and write.

dyspraxia—Impaired movement. Lack of coordination. Clumsiness.

ecstasy (3,4-methylenedioxymethamphetamine, or MDMA)—One of the most widely used recreational drugs in the world. Has a tendency to induce euphoria, a sense of intimacy with others and diminish anxiety and depression.

endocannabinoids—Naturally occurring, marijuana-like compounds.

endorphins and enkephalins—Naturally occurring, morphine-like neurotransmitters associated with pleasure, euphoria and pain relief.

epinephrine (adrenaline)—An excitatory (stimulating) neurotransmitter associated with motivation, drive, energy and the fight-or-flight stress response. Produced by the adrenal glands, it is also classified as a hormone (a chemical messenger produced by the glands of the endocrine system).

fibromyalgia—A medical condition characterized by chronic widespread pain throughout the body. Some other symptoms include debilitating fatigue, sleep disturbance and joint stiffness.

formaldehyde—A neurotoxic chemical used in manufacturing and chemical industries, and as a preservative by anatomists, embalmers and pathologists. Being exposed to formaldehyde may increase the risk of developing leukemia and brain cancer.

gamma-aminobutyric acid (GABA)—An inhibitory (calming) neurotransmitter associated with relaxation.

glutamate—Is the most common neurotransmitter in the brain. It is a stimulating (excitatory) brain chemical. Glutamate can be neurotoxic, and it has therefore been implicated as a potential contributor to certain neurodegenerative disorders such as Alzheimer's disease.

Haldol—An older antipsychotic medication used in the treatment of schizophrenia, acute psychotic episodes and delirium.

homocysteine—Homocysteine is an amino acid formed in the body through a process in the brain called methylation. Elevated homocysteine is a significant risk factor for several diseases, including depression, cognitive decline, dementia, Alzheimer's, schizophrenia, bipolar disorder, birth defects, diabetes, osteoporosis, macular degeneration, heart disease and cancer.

hypoglycemia—Low blood sugar levels or unstable blood sugar level due to insulin resistance, usually due to the overconsumption of empty calories such as sugar, sweetened beverages or juice.

hypothyroidism—A glandular disorder resulting from insufficient production of thyroid hormones.

insulin—A hormone made by certain cells of the pancreas. Insulin controls the amount of sugar in the blood by moving it into the cells, where it can be used by the body for energy.

insulin resistance—The body's inability to respond to and use the insulin it produces. Insulin resistance may be linked to obesity.

iodine insufficiency—A micronutrient deficiency that is linked to hypothyroidism.

lactalbumin—An important protein found in the milk of many mammals.

lupus—A chronic, autoimmune disorder characterized by periodic episodes of inflammation of and damage to the joints, tendons, other connective tissues and organs, including the heart, lungs, blood vessels, brain, kidneys and skin.

macular degeneration—Age related macular degeneration (AMD) is a medical condition that results in a loss of vision in the center of the visual field (the macula) because of damage to the retina.

methylation—Methylation helps to make, break down and balance brain chemicals (neurotransmitters), build neurons (nerve cells) and protect your brain from damage.

neuron—Also known as a nerve cell. The fundamental role of a neuron is to convey information both electrically and chemically. Neurons exist throughout the body, but are highly concentrated in the brain.

neurotransmitter—Chemical messengers produced by nerve cells to communicate and control almost every function of your body. They are made from amino acids or peptides. Some of the major neurotransmitters include serotonin, dopamine, acetylcholine and norepinephrine.

norepinephrine—An excitatory (stimulating) neurotransmitter with dual roles as a hormone and a neurotransmitter. Also known as noradrenaline. Precursor to epinephrine (adrenaline).

obsessive-compulsive disorder (OCD)—An anxiety disorder marked by the presence of obsessions and compulsions severe enough to interfere with the activities of daily life.

opioid—Opioids are natural or synthetic chemicals that have opium-like effects similar to morphine, though they are not derived from opium. Examples include endorphins or enkephalins produced by body tissues or synthetic methadone. Morphine, Vicodin, OxyContin and related drugs are often included in this category.

orthomolecular medicine—Orthomolecular medicine is a form of complementary and alternative medicine that seeks to prevent or treat diseases with nutrients prescribed as dietary supplements or derived from diets.

peptide—Two or more amino acids (the building blocks of proteins) that are chemically linked to each other.

phytic acid—A compound found naturally in plant cells, especially in seeds, grains and legumes.

psychotropic drug—A drug that affects the mind and psychology of an individual.

pyroluria—A genetic blood disorder that creates by-products during hemoglobin synthesis, which bind to zinc and B vitamins and cause deficiency symptoms of these nutrients.

receptor sites—The docking port for neurotransmitters located in the membrane of a neuron. Receptor sites are specific for different kinds of neurotransmitters.

schizophrenia—A psychiatric diagnosis denoting a persistent, often chronic, mental illness variously affecting behavior, thinking and emotion.

serotonin—A neurotransmitter associated with mood, sleep, dreaming, appetite, etc.

synapse—The gap between the dendrite and the neuron to which the dendrite connects. Neurotransmitters move from one neuron to another across this gap.

RECOMMENDED READING

Abrahamson, E. M. and A. W. Pezet. *Body, Mind & Sugar.* New York: Pyramid Books, 1974.

Abramson, John. *Overdosed America: The Broken Promise of American Medicine.* New York: Harper Perennial, 2005.

Allan, Christian B. and Wolfgang Lutz. *Life without Bread: How a Low-Carbohydrate Diet Can Save Your Life,* New York: McGraw Hill, 2000.

Beasley, Joseph D. and Susan Knightly. *Food for Recovery: The Complete Nutritional Companion for Recovering from Alcoholism, Drug Addiction and Eating Disorders.* New York: Crown Publishers, 1994.

Bennett, Connie and Stephen Sinatra. *Sugar Shock.* New York: Penguin, 2007.

Braly, James and Ron Hoggan. *Dangerous Grains.* New York: Avery, 2002.

Braverman, Eric R. *The Healing Nutrients Within.* 3rd Edition. Laguna Beach: Basic Health Publications, 2003.

—. *Younger You: Unlock the Hidden Power of Your Brain to Look and Feel 15 Years Younger.* New York: McGraw-Hill, 2007.

Breggin, Peter. *Medication Madness: The Role of Psychiatric Drugs in Cases of Violence, Suicide and Crime.* New York: St. Martin's Griffin, 2009.

Brownstein, David. *Salt Your Way to Health.* West Bloomfield, MI: Medical Alternatives Press, 2006.

—. *Overcoming Thyroid Disorders.* 2nd Edition. West Bloomfield, MI: Medical Alternative Press, 2008.

—. *Iodine: Why You Need It, Why You Can't Live Without It.* 4th Edition. West Bloomfield, MI: Medical Alternatives Press, 2009.

Campbell-Douglass II, William C. *Eat Your Cholesterol*. Panama: Rhino Publishing, 2003.

—. *The Raw Truth about Milk*. Revised and Expanded Edition. Panama: Rhino Publishing, 2007. (This is the updated version of *The Milk Book*.)

Campbell-McBride, Natasha. *Gut and Psychology Syndrome—Natural Treatment for Autism, Dyspraxia, ADD, Dyslexia, ADHD, Depression and Schizophrenia*. Cambridge: Medinform, 7th Reprint May, 2007. (Originally published 2004.)

—. *Put Your Heart in Your Mouth*. Cambridge: Medinform, 2007.

Cass, Hyla and Patrick Holford. *Natural Highs: Feel Good all the Time*. New York: Avery, 2002.

Chaitow, Leon. *Amino Acids in Therapy: A Guide to Therapeutic Application of Protein Constituents*. Rochester, VT: Healing Arts Press, 1988.

Challem, Jack. *The Food-Mood Solution: All-Natural Ways to Banish Anxiety, Depression, Anger, Stress, Overeating and Alcohol and Drug Problems—and Feel Good Again*. Hoboken, NJ: John Wiley & Sons, 2007.

Challem, Jack, Burton Berkson and Melissa Diane Smith. *Syndrome X: The Complete Nutritional Program to Prevent and Reverse Insulin Resistance*. Hoboken, NJ: John Wiley & Sons, 2000.

Cherniske, Stephen. *Caffeine Blues: Wake Up to the Hidden Dangers of America's #1 Drug*. New York: Warner, 1998.

Daniel, Kaayla T. *The Whole Soy Story*. Washington, DC: New Trends Publishing, 2005.

DesMaisons, Kathleen. *Potatoes Not Prozac*. New York: Fireside, 1999.

—. *Little Sugar Addicts: End Mood Swings, Meltdowns, Tantrums and Low Self-Esteem in Your Child Today*. New York: Three Rivers Press, 2004.

Dufty, Bill. *Sugar Blues*. New York: Warner, 1975.

Enig, Mary G. *Know Your Fats: The Complete Primer for Understanding the Nutrition of Fats, Oils and Cholesterol.* Silver Spring, MD: Bethesda Press, 2003.

Erdman, Robert. *The Amino Revolution.* New York: Fireside, 1987.

Fallon, Sally. *Nourishing Traditions: The Book That Challenges Politically Correct Nutrition and the Diet Dictocrats.* Washington, DC: New Trends Publishing, 2001.

Gant, Charles and Greg Lewis. *End Your Addiction Now: The Proven Nutritional Supplement Program That Can Set You Free.* Garden City Park, NY: Square One, 2010.

Gedgaudas, Nora. *Primal Body—Primal Mind.* Portland, OR: Primal Body—Primal Mind Publishing, 2009.

Gittleman, Ann Louise. *Why Am I Always So Tired?* San Francisco: Harper, 1999.

Greenfield, David. *Virtual-Addiction: Help for Netheads, Cyberfreaks and Those Who Love Them.* Oakland, CA: New Harbinger Publications, 1999.

Groves, Barry. *Natural Health and Weight Loss.* London: Hammersmith Press, 2007.

—. *Trick and Treat: How 'Healthy Eating' Is Making Us Ill.* London: Hammersmith Press, 2008.

Heller, Richard F. and Rachael F. Heller. *Carbohydrate-Addicted Kids.* New York: HarperCollins, 1997.

Hoffer, Abram. *Vitamin B3 & Schizophrenia: Discovery, Recovery, Controversy.* Kingston, Ontario: Quarry Health Books, 1998.

—. *Orthomolecular Treatment for Schizophrenia.* Toronto: The International Schizophrenia Foundation, 2007.

—. *Mental Health Regained.* Toronto: The International Schizophrenia Foundation, 2007.

Hoffer, Abram and Jonathan Prousky. *Naturopathic Nutrition.* Toronto: CCNM Press, 2006.

Hoffer, Abram and Harold Foster. *Feel Better, Live Longer with Vitamin B-3.* Toronto: CCNM Press, 2007.

Holford, Patrick, David Miller and James Braly. *How to Quit without Feeling S**t.* London: Piatkus, 2008.

Hyman, Mark. *The UltraMind Solution.* New York: Scribner, 2009.

Katz, Sandor Ellix. *Wild Fermentation.* White River Junction, VT: Chelsea Green Publishing, 2003.

Kendall-Reed, Penny and Stephen Reed. *Stress Solution.* Toronto: Robert Rose, 2004.

Ketcham, Katherine, William F. Asbury, Mel Schulstad and Arthur P. Ciaramicoli. *Beyond the Influence: Understanding and Defeating Alcoholism.* New York: Bantam, 2000.

MacFadden, Bernarr. *The Miracle of Milk: How to Use the Milk Diet Scientifically at Home.* Bedford, MA: Applewood Books, 1924.

Mathews-Larson, Joan. *Depression-Free Naturally: 7 Weeks to Eliminating Anxiety, Despair, Fatigue and Anger from your Life.* New York: Ballantine, 1999.

—. *Seven Weeks to Sobriety.* New York: Ballantine, 1997.

Milam, James and Katherine Ketcham. *Under the Influence: A Guide to the Myths and Realities of Alcoholism.* New York: Bantam, 1984.

Milkman, Harvey and Stanley Sunderwith. *Craving Ecstasy: The Consciousness and Chemistry of Escape.* Lexington, MA: Lexington Books, 1987.

Miller, David and Kenneth Blum. *Overload: Attention Deficit Disorder and the Addictive Brain.* Kansas City, MO: Andrews and McMeel, 1996.

Miller, Merlene and David Miller. *Staying Clean and Sober.* Orem, UT: Woodland, 2005.

Mueller, L. Ann and Katherine Ketcham. *Eating Right to Live Sober.* New York: Signet, 1986.

—. *Recovering: How to Get and Stay Sober.* New York: Bantam, 1987.

Olsen, Gwen. *Confessions of an RX Drug Pusher.* Lincoln, NE: iUniverse, 2005.

Peele, Stanton. *Seven Tools to Beat Addiction.* New York: Three Rivers Press, 2004.

—. *Addiction-Proof Your Child: A Realistic Approach to Preventing Drug, Alcohol and Other Dependencies.* New York: Three Rivers Press, 2007.

Petralli, Genita. *Alcoholism: The Cause and the Cure.* Santa Cruz, CA: Alternative Approaches to end Alcohol Abuse, 2008.

Pfeiffer, Carl C. *Nutrition and Mental Illness: An Orthomolecular Approach to Balancing Body Chemistry.* Rochester, VT: Healing Arts Press, 1997.

Planck, Nina. *Real Food: What to Eat and Why.* New York: Bloomsbury Publishing, 2006.

Plesman, Jurriaan. *Getting Off the Hook: Treatment of Drug Addiction and Social Disorders through Body and Mind.* Sydney, NSW: Shepson Printing, 1986 (available online through Google Books).

Porter, Charles Sanford. *Milk Diet as a Remedy for Chronic Disease.* West Bend, WI: God's Whey, 2005 (Originally published in 1905).

Price, Weston A. *Nutrition and Physical Degeneration.* 6th Edition. Los Angeles: Keats Publishing, 1998.

Prousky, Jonathan. *Anxiety: Orthomolecular Diagnosis and Treatment.* Toronto: CCNM Press, 2006.

Robinson, Jo. *Pasture Perfect: The Far-Reaching Benefits of Choosing Meat, Eggs and Dairy Products from Grass-Fed Animals.* Vashon, WA: Vashon Island Press, 2004.

Ross, Julia. *The Mood Cure.* New York: Penguin, 2002.

—. *The Diet Cure.* New York: Penguin, 2000.

Sahley, Billie J. and Katherine M. Birkner. *Heal with Amino Acids and Nutrients.* San Antonio, TX: Pain and Stress Publications, 2005.

Schachter, Michael B. *What Your Doctor May Not Tell You About Depression.* New York: Warner, 2006.

Schlosser, Eric. *Fast Food Nation: The Dark Side of the All-American Meal.* New York: HarperCollins, 2002.

Schmid, Ron. *Traditional Foods Are Your Best Medicine.* Rochester, VT: Healing Arts Press, 1997.

—. *The Untold Story of Milk.* Washington, DC: New Trends Publishing, 2003.

Shannon, Scott. *Please Don't Label My Child.* New York: Rodale, 2007.

Smith, Melissa Diane. *Going against the Grain: How Reducing and Avoiding Grains Can Revitalize Your Health.* New York: Contemporary Books, 2002.

Taubes, Gary. *Good Calories, Bad Calories.* New York: Knopf, 2007.

Weinstein, Miriam. *The Surprising Power of Family Meals: How Eating Together Makes Us Smarter, Stronger, Healthier and Happier.* Hanover, NH: Steerforth Press, 2005.

Wilson, James L. *Adrenal Fatigue: The 21st Century Stress Syndrome.* Petaluma, CA: Smart Publications, 2001.

Wright, Jonathan V. and Lane Lenard. *Why Stomach Acid is Good for You.* New York: M. Evans and Company, 2001.

Yudkin, John. *Sweet and Dangerous.* New York: Bantam, 1979. (Originally published 1972.)

ENDNOTES

1   Robert Hercz. "Rat Trap." *The Walrus*, January 29, 2008.
2   Julia Ross. "Preventing Relapse by Successfully Treating Substitute Addictions." Presentation at the Community Addiction Recovery Association (CARA) Conference, 2007.
3   John Hoffman and Susan Froemke, eds. *Addiction: Why Can't They Just Stop?* (New York: Rodale, 2007), p. 17.
4   Oliver James. "Selfish Capitalist Lectures." January 17 and March 1, 2008. http://www.selfishcapitalist.com/selfish_multimedia.html, or here: http://video.google.ca/videosearch?q=oliver+james&hl=en&emb=0&aq=f#q=oliver%20james&hl=en&emb=0&aq=f&start=10.
5   Constance Horgan. 2001. "Substance Abuse: The Nation's Number One Health Problem." Key Indicators for Policy Series—Update. Schneider Institute for Health Policy, Heller School, Brandeis University.
6   Constance M. Horgan. "Substance Abuse: The Nation's Number One Health Problem." Key Indicators for Policy Series Update. Schneider Institute for Health Policy, Heller School, Brandeis University, 2001.
7   Constance M. Horgan. 1995. "Cost of Untreated Substance Abuse to Society." *The Communiqué*, Spring, 1995.
8   "Sobering Facts on the Dangers of Alcohol." *NY Newsday*, April 24, 2002.
9   Barbara A. Ray, Ph.D. "A Conceptual Model for Measuring Substance Misuse and Abuse through the Life Cycle: The Importance of Recovery" and "Death Rates, Substance Abuse by Older Adults: Estimates of Future Impact on the Treatment System." Substance Abuse and Mental Health Services Administration. http://www.oas.samhsa.gov/aging/chap2.htm
10 Jacqueline Fowler Byers and Susan V. White, eds. *Patient Safety* (New York: Springer, 2004), 257.
11 Hoffman & Froemke, eds., 2001, p. 25.
12 H. Harwood. 2000. "Updating Estimates of the Economic Costs of Alcohol Abuse in the United States: Estimates, Update Methods and Data Report." Prepared by the Lewin Group for the National Institute on Alcohol Abuse and Alcoholism; "Understanding Drug Abuse and Addiction." NIDA InfoFacts, National Institute on Drug Abuse. http://www.drugabuse.gov/Infofacts/understand.html

13   "Substance Abuse and Recovery, Helping Break the Chains of Addiction." Department of Health and Human Services. http://innovationincompassion. hhs.gov/changing_lives/targeting_substance_abuse.html

14   Joseph Hibbeln, M.D. Interview by Cory SerVaas and Patrick Perry, "Fats for Mental Health." *Saturday Evening Post*, March 1, 1999. http://www. ect.org/fats-for-mental-health/#more-401

15   R. C. Kessler, P. Berglund, O. Demler, et al. 2005. "Lifetime Prevalence and Age-Of-Onset Distributions of DSM-IV Disorders in the National Co-Morbidity Survey Replication." *Archives of General Psychiatry*, Vol. 62: pp. 593-602.

16   Robert Whitaker. Interview by Terry Messman, "Psychiatric Drugs: An Assault on the Human Condition." *Street Spirit*, August 2005. http:// www.thestreetspirit.org/August2005/interview.htm

17   "The Numbers Count: Mental Disorders in America." National Institute of Mental Health, 2008. http://www.nimh.nih.gov/health/publications/ the-numbers-count-mental-disorders-in-america/index.shtml; "The World Health Report 2004: Changing History, Annex Table 3: Burden of Disease in Dalys by Cause, Sex and Mortality Stratum in Who Regions, Estimates for 2002." Geneva: The World Health Organization, 2004.

18   "The Numbers Count," 2008.

19   "Community Mental Health Services Block Grant Program." Substance Abuse and Mental Health Services Administration (SAMHSA), U.S. Department of Health and Human Services (HHS). http://mentalhealth. samhsa.gov/publications/allpubs/KEN95-0022/

20   Rahul K. Parikh, M.D. "Health for Hard Times." *Salon*, December 22, 2008. http://www.salon.com/env/vital_signs/2008/12/22/recession_health/ index.html?source=newsletter

21   Campbell Brown. "No Bias, No Bull." CNN, March 16, 2009. http:// transcripts.cnn.com/TRANSCRIPTS/0903/16/ec.01.html; "Stress in America." American Psychological Association, October 7, 2008, p. 3.

22   C. Brendan Montano, M.D. 2003. "New Frontiers in the Treatment of Depression." *Medscape*, September 29, 2003. http://cme.medscape. com/viewarticle/462198; C. J. Murray and A. D. Lopez, eds. *The Global Burden of Disease: A Comprehensive Assessment of Morbidity and Disability from Disease, Injuries and Risk Factors in 1990 and Projected to 2020*. Cambridge, MA: Harvard University Press, 1996; Martin Prince et al. 2007. "No Health without Mental Health, Global Mental Health 1." *Lancet*, Vol. 370 (No. 9590): pp. 859-877. DOI:10.1016/ S0140-6736(07)61238-0.

23 Candace B. Pert, Ph.D. *Molecules of Emotion: Why You Feel the Way You Feel* (New York: Touchstone, 1997), p. 299.

24 Barbara A. Ray, Ph.D. "A Conceptual Model for Measuring Substance Misuse and Abuse through the Life Cycle: The Importance of Recovery" and "Death Rates, Substance Abuse by Older Adults: Estimates of Future Impact on the Treatment System." Substance Abuse and Mental Health Service Administration (SAMHSA). http://www.oas.samhsa.gov/aging/chap2.htm

25 "Management of Substance Abuse: The Global Burden." World Health Organization. http://www.who.int/substance_abuse/facts/global_burden/en/index.html

26 Ibid.

27 "Society Shoulders Cost of Mopping Up Alcohol Messes." *Great Falls Tribune*, November 22, 1999. http://www.gannett.com/go/difference/greatfalls/pages/part11/mess.html; H. Harwood. 2000. "Updating Estimates of the Economic Costs of Alcohol Abuse in the United States: Estimates, Update Methods and Data Report." Prepared by the Lewin Group for the National Institute on Alcohol Abuse and Alcoholism; "InfoFacts: Understanding Drug Abuse and Addiction." National Institute on Drug Abuse. http://www.drugabuse.gov/Infofacts/understand.html

28 Michael Gossop. *Living with Drugs*. 6th Edition. (Hampshire, England: Ashgate, 2007), p. 61.

29 A. H. Mokdad, J. S. Marks, D. F. Stroup and J. L. Gerberding. 2004. "Actual Causes of Death in the United States, 2000." *Journal of the American Medical Association,* Vol. 291: pp. 1238-1245.

30 David Nutt, Leslie A King, William Saulsbury and Colin Blakemore. 2007. "Development of a Rational Scale to Assess the Harm of Drugs of Potential Misuse." *Lancet,* Vol. 369: pp. 1047-1053.

31 "Alcohol, Tobacco Worse than Pot, Ecstasy: Study." *Associated Press*, March 23, 2007. http://www.cbc.ca/health/story/2007/03/23/alcohol-tobacco.html

32 James Sexton, Ph.D. *Aldous Huxley's Hearst Essays* (New York: Garland Publishing, 1994), p. 20.

33 "Fact Sheet: Prescription Drug Abuse—A DEA Focus." U.S. Drug Enforcement Administration. http://www.usdoj.gov/dea/concern/prescription_drug_fact_sheet.html

34 "New CASA Report: Controlled Prescription Drug Abuse at Epidemic Level." Drug Rehabilitation Services. July 7, 2005. http://www.drug-rehab.ca/prescription-drugs-addiction.htm; "Under the Counter: The Diversion and Abuse of Controlled Prescription Drugs in the U.S." Center on Addiction and Substance Abuse (CASA), 2005.

35 Marshall Allen and Alex Richards. "Rising Use of Painkillers Taking Deadly Toll." *Las Vegas Sun*, July 7, 2008. http://www.lasvegassun.com/news/2008/jul/07/rising-use-painkillers-taking-deadly-toll/

36 Benedict Carey. "Brain Enhancement Is Wrong, Right?" *New York Times*, March 9, 2008. http://www.nytimes.com/2008/03/09/weekinreview/09carey.html?_r=3&sq=adderall&st=nyt&oref=slogin&scp=1&pagewanted=all

37 James E. Lessenger, M.D. and Steven D. Feinburg, M.D., M.P.H. 2008. "Abuse of Prescription and Over-the-Counter Medications." *Medscape*, April 3, 2008. http://www.medscape.com/viewarticle/570574_1

38 "Overdose Deaths on the Rise, CDC Says." *LA Times*, January 26, 2008. http://articles.latimes.com/2008/jan/26/local/me-drugs26

39 Jay Cohen, M.D. 2002. "Over Dose: The Case against the Drug Companies, Part I." http://articles.mercola.com/sites/articles/archive/2002/02/06/overdose-part-one.aspx; L. Bowman. "51% of U.S. Adults Take 2 Pills or More a Day, Survey Reports." *San Diego Union-Tribune*, January 17, 2001, A8.

40 Cohen, 2002.

41 "Global Market for Pharmaceuticals Worth Over $1 Trillion by 2013." PharmaLive, June 11, 2008. http://www.pharmalive.com/News/index.cfm?articleid=548154&categoryid=10

42 "National Survey on Drug Use and Health, National Findings." Department of Health and Human Services. Substance Abuse and Mental Health Services Administration (SAMHSA). Office of Applied Studies, 2006. http://www.oas.samhsa.gov/nsduh/2k6nsduh/2k6Results.pdf; Laxmaiah Manchikanti, M.D. and Angelie Singh, B.S., B.A. 2008. "Therapeutic Opioids: A Ten-Year Perspective on the Complexities and Complications of the Escalating Use, Abuse and Nonmedical Use of Opioids." *Pain Physician*, Issue 11: pp. S63-S88. http://www.painphysicianjournal.com/crrent_issue_vw.php?journal=42&code=983&issue=past_issue

43 Richard Monastersky. "Some Professors Pop Pills for an Intellectual Edge." *The Chronicle*, April 25, 2008. http://chronicle.com/free/v54/i33/33a00102.htm

44 Ibid.

45 Ibid.

46 Peter Breggin. "Psychiatric Drug Dependence (Addiction) and Withdrawal Reactions." http://www.breggin.com/index.php?option=com_content&task=view&id=48&Itemid=66

47 Toby Burwell and Randall Stith (directors). *Making a Killing: The Untold Story of Psychotropic Drugging*. Documentary. Citizens Commission on Human Rights, 2008.

48 "Almost Half of Americans Use at Least One Prescription Drug, Annual Report on Nation's Health Shows." Centers for Disease Control and Prevention, National Center for Health Statistics, Department of Human Health Services, December 2, 2004. http://www.cdc.gov/nchs/pressroom/04news/hus04.htm

49 G. I. Papakostas. 2007. "Limitations of Contemporary Antidepressants: Tolerability." *Journal of Clinical Psychiatry*, Vol. 68 (No. 10): pp. 11-17; Mark Hyman, M.D. *The UltraMind Solution* (New York: Scribner, 2009), p. 14.

50 "Manufacturing Addiction: The Over-Prescription of Benzodiazapines and Sleeping Pills to Women in Canada." British Columbia Center of Excellence for Women's Health. http://www.bccewh.bc.ca/publications-resources/documents/manufacturingaddiction.pdf

51 Alisha Wyman. "Prescription Drug Abuse Rising among Youth." *Union Democrat*, June 13, 2008. http://www.uniondemocrat.com/2008061392825/News/Local-News/Prescription-drug-abuse-rising-among-youth

52 Leonard J. Paulozzi, M.D., M.P.H. "Trends in Unintentional Drug Overdose Deaths." CDC Congressional Testimony, March 12, 2008. http://www.cdc.gov/Washington/testimony/2008/t20080312a.htm; Leonard J. Paulozzi, M.D., M.P.H. "Trends in Unintentional Drug Poisoning Deaths." National Center for Injury Prevention and Control. Centers for Disease Control and Prevention, October 24, 2007. http://www.hhs.gov/asl/testify/2007/10/t20071024a.html

53 Wyman, 2008.

54 Manchikanti and Singh, 2008.

55 Ibid.

56 "Leger Survey Reports 84% of Ontario Physicians Feel Patients May Be Addicted to Prescription Painkillers." CNW Group, September 3, 2008. http://www.newswire.ca/en/releases/archive/September2008/03/c7803.html; "Suboxone Research." Leger Marketing, August 12, 2008. http://www.legermarketing.com/documents/spclm/080812ENG.pdf

57 "Leger Survey," 2008.

58 Peter Breggin. *Medication Madness: The Role of Psychiatric Drugs in Cases of Violence, Suicide and Crime* (New York: St. Martin's Griffin, 2009), p. 34.

59 Damien Cave. "Legal Drugs Kill Far More than Illegal, Florida Says." *New York Times*, June 14, 2008. http://www.nytimes.com/2008/06/14/us/14florida.html?partner=rssnyt&emc=rss

60 Hsiang-Ching Kung, Ph.D., et al. 2008. "Deaths: Final Data for 2005." National Vital Statistics Reports. Centers for Disease Control, Vol. 56 (No. 10): p. 10. http://www.cdc.gov/nchs/data/nvsr/nvsr56/nvsr56_10.pdf

[61] T. J. Moore, M. R. Cohen and C. D. Furberg. 2007. "Serious Adverse Drug Events Reported to the Food and Drug Administration, 1998-2005." *Archives of Internal Medicine*, Vol. 167: pp. 1752-1759. http://www.ismp.org/pressroom/PR20070910_1.pdf

[62] Gary Null, Ph.D., Carolyn Dean, M.D., N.D., et al. "Death by Medicine." GaryNull.com, December, 2003. http://www.garynull.com/pix/DeathbyMedicine_march09bf2Faloon.pdf; J. Lazarou, B. H. Pomeranz and P. N. Corey. 1998. "Incidence of Adverse Drug Reactions in Hospitalized Patients: A Meta-Analysis of Prospective Studies." *Journal of the American Medical Association*, Vol. 279 (No. 15): pp. 1200-1205; D. C. Suh, B. S. Woodall, S. K. Shin and E. R. Hermes-De Santis. 2000. "Clinical and Economic Impact of Adverse Drug Reactions in Hospitalized Patients." *Annals of Pharmacotherapy*, Vol. 34 (No. 12): pp. 1373-1379.

[63] Claudia Kalb. "When Drugs Do Harm." *Newsweek*, April 27, 1998. http://www.newsweek.com/id/92265/page/1

[64] Paulozzi, 2008.

[65] Dave Parks. "Too Little Treatment, Too Many Addicts." *The Birmingham News*, July 8, 2007.

[66] J. Colliver, W. Compton, J. Gfroerer and T. Condon. 2006. "Projecting Drug Use among Aging Baby Boomers in 2020." *Annals of Epidemiology*, Vol. 16 (No. 4): 257-265. http://shsfaculty.swan.ac.uk/MichaelAdams/DualDiagnosis/Gerwyn%20Panes%2031.01.08/drug%20use%20baby%20boomers.pdf

[67] Mike Males. "This Is Your Brain on Drugs, Dad." *New York Times*, January 3, 2007. http://www.nytimes.com/2007/01/03/opinion/03males.html

[68] "More Middle-Age Americans Dying from Drug Overdose." National Center on Addiction and Substance Abuse, Columbia University, April 20, 2006. http://www.jointogether.org/news/headlines/inthenews/2006/addiction-increasingly-seen.html

[69] Males, January 2007.

[70] Mike Males. "This Is Your (Father's) Brain on Drugs." *New York Times*, September 17, 2007. http://www.nytimes.com/2007/09/17/opinion/17males.html?pagewanted=print

[71] "More Middle-Age Americans Dying," 2006; Richard A. Sherer. 2006. "Drug Abuse Hitting Middle-Aged More than Gen-Xers." *Psychiatric Times*, Vol. 23 (No. 4). http://www.psychiatrictimes.com/display/article/10168/49331#

[72] Males, January 2007.

[73] Ibid.

74   Ibid.

75   Sherer, 2006.

76   Ibid.

77   Ibid; Colliver et al., 2006.

78   "A Guide for Developing a Substance Abuse Awareness Program for Older
     Adults." Central East Addiction Technology Transfer Center, District of
     Columbia, Department of Health, 2006. http://newsroom.dc.gov/show.
     aspx?agency=doh&section=2&release=12843&year=2006&file=file.
     aspx%2frelease%2f12843%2f06_seniorguide-final.pdf

79   "Bush Vows to Wipe Out Prescription-Drug Addiction among Seniors."
     The Onion, August 22, 2001. http://www.theonion.com/content/
     node/28266

80   Samuel P. Korper, Ph.D., M.P.H. and Ira E. Raskin, Ph.D. "Substance Use
     by Older Adults: Estimates of Future Impact on the Treatment System."
     Substance Abuse and Mental Health Services Administration. http://www.
     oas.samhsa.gov/aging/chap1.htm

81   "Guide for Developing a Substance Abuse Awareness Program for Older
     Adults." U.S. Department of Health, 2006.

82   Males, January 2007.

83   Ibid.

84   Donna Leinwand. "Prescription Drugs Find Place in Teen Culture." *USA
     Today*, June 13, 2006. http://www.usatoday.com/news/health/2006-06-
     12-teens-pharm-drugs_x.htm

85   Ibid.

86   Benedict Carey. "Bipolar Illness Soars as a Diagnosis for the Young." *New
     York Times*, September 4, 2007. http://www.nytimes.com/2007/09/04/
     health/04psych.html

87   "Study Questions Use of Newer Antipsychotic Drugs in Children."
     News-Medical.Net, September 16, 2008. http://www.news-medical.
     net/?id=41500

88   Bryan Flagg. "$4 Million Spent on Antipsychotics for NH Kids in 2007:
     Should We Demand the State to Seek Damages and Criminal Prosecution?"
     North Country News, May 5, 2008. www.northcountrynewsnh.com

89   "InfoFacts: Prescription and Over-the-Counter Medications." National
     Institute on Drug Abuse. http://www.nida.nih.gov/Infofacts/PainMed.
     html

90   "Teen Abuse of Prescription Pills Holds Steady." *Associated Press*, February
     15, 2007. http://www.msnbc.msn.com/id/17153831/

91   "New CASA Report," 2005.

92 "Teen Abuse of Prescription Pills Holds Steady," 2007.

93 Leinwand, 2006.

94 National Youth Anti-Drug Media Campaign. http://www.theantidrug. com/pdfs/resources/teen-rx/Prescription_Abuse_brochure.pdf

95 Stanton Peele, Ph.D., J.D. *Addiction-Proof Your Child: A Realistic Approach to Preventing Drug, Alcohol and Other Dependencies* (New York: Three Rivers Press, 2007), p. 85.

96 "Rank Order—Life Expectancy at Birth." CIA World Factbook, 2006. www.cia.gov/cia/publications/factbook/rankorder/2102rank.html.

97 "National Health Expenditure Projections, 2007-2017." http://www.cms. hhs.gov/NationalHealthExpendData/Downloads/proj2007.pdf

98 John Abramson. "Guest Opinion: Americans Spend Most on Health Care, But Are Least Healthy." *Tucson Citizen*, November 16, 2006. http://www. tucsoncitizen.com/daily/local/32737.php

99 Aldous Huxley. *Brave New World* (Middlesex, England: Penguin, 1966), pp. 52-53.

100 Joseph D. Beasley, M.D. and Susan Knightly. *Food for Recovery: The Complete Nutritional Companion for Recovering from Alcoholism, Drug Addiction and Eating Disorders* (New York: Crown Publishers, 1994), p. 43.

101 James Braly, M.D. and Patrick Holford. *Hidden Food Allergies* (Laguna Beach: Basic Health, 2006), p. 83.

102 Nora Gedgaudas. *Primal Body—Primal Mind* (Portland: Primal Body—Primal Mind Publishing, 2009), p. 29.

103 S. B. Eaton, et al. 1997. "Paleolithic Nutrition Revisited: A Twelve-Year Retrospective on Its Nature and Implications." *European Journal of Clinical Nutrition*, Vol. 51 (No. 4): pp. 207-216.

104 Jared Diamond. "The Worst Mistake in the Human Race." *Discover*, May 1987. http://www.environnement.ens.fr/perso/claessen/agriculture/ mistake_jared_diamond.pdf

105 Christian B. Allan, Ph.D. and Wolfgang Lutz, M.D. *Life without Bread* (New York: McGraw Hill, 2000), p. 190.

106 Ibid.

107 Diamond, 1987.

108 James Braly, M.D. and Ron Hoggan, M.A. *Dangerous Grains* (New York: Avery, 2002), p. 24.

109 Diamond, 1987.

110 Braly and Hoggan, 2002, p. 146.

111 Allan and Lutz, 2000, p. 136.

[112] Brian M. Berman, M.D. and David B. Larson, M.D., M.P.H., eds. 1994. "Alternative Medicine: Expanding Medical Horizons." A Report to the National Institutes of Health on Alternative Medical Systems and Practices in the United States. Prepared under the auspices of the Workshop on Alternative Medicine, Chantilly, VA, September 14-16, 1992. (Washington, DC: U.S. Government Printing Office, Superintendent of Documents, 1994), p. 210.

[113] Courtney Van de Weyer. "Changing Diets, Changing Minds: How Food Affects Mental Well-Being and Behavior." Sustain, Winter 2005, p. 77.

[114] Sarah Murray. "The World's Biggest Industry." Forbes, November 15, 2007. http://www.forbes.com/2007/11/11/growth-agriculture-business-forbeslife-food07-cx_sm_1113bigfood.html

[115] Eric Schlosser. Fast Food Nation: The Dark Side of the All-American Meal (New York: HarperCollins, 2002), p. 120.

[116] Laura Shapiro. Something from the Oven (New York: Viking, 2004), p. 45.

[117] Ibid., pp. 46-47.

[118] Van de Weyer, 2005, p. 78.

[119] Adam Voiland. "10 Things the Food Industry Doesn't Want You to Know." U.S. News, October 17, 2008. http://health.usnews.com/articles/health/2008/10/17/10-things-the-food-industry-doesnt-want-you-to-know.html?PageNr=1

[120] "Diet, Nutrition and the Prevention of Chronic Disease." WHO Technical Report Series, #916, Geneva, 2003. http://whqlibdoc.who.int/trs/WHO_TRS_916.pdf

[121] Fiona MacRae. "Junk Food Is Causing Famine Symptoms." Daily Mail, May 6, 2007. http://www.dailymail.co.uk/news/article-453099/Junk-food-causing-famine-symptoms.html

[122] John Tintera, M.D. "What You Should Know about Your Glands." Adrenal Metabolic Research Society/Hypoglycemia Association Inc., Ashton, MD. This article was first published in Woman's Day, February 1958. Dr. Tintera was a pioneer in the use of adrenal cortex extract for the treatment of hypoglycemia, allergies, fatigue and adrenal exhaustion. http://www.westonaprice.org/archive/tintera.html

[123] Z. Stanga et al. 2007. "The Effect of Nutritional Management on the Mood of Malnourished Patients." Clinical Nutrition, Vol. 26 (No. 3): pp. 379-382. http://linkinghub.elsevier.com/retrieve/pii/S0261561407000350

[124] Leah M. Kalm and Richard D. Semba. 2005. "They Starved So That Others Could Be Fed: Remembering Ancel Keys and the Minnesota Experiment." Journal of Nutrition, Vol. 135 (No. 6): pp. 1347-1352. http://jn.nutrition.

org/cgi/content/full/135/6/1347#B15; W. Quigley. "Conchies' Tests at U Disclose—Many in Europe Must Starve." *St. Paul Dispatch*, July 26, 1945.

125 Allan and Lutz, 2000, p. 46.

126 Gary Taubes. *Good Calories, Bad Calories* (New York: Knopf, 2007), p. 393.

127 Loren Cordain, et al. 2000. "Plant-Based Subsistence Ratios and Macronutrient Energy Estimations in Worldwide Hunter-Gatherer Diets." *The American Journal of Clinical Nutrition*, Vol. 71 (No. 3): pp. 682-692. http://www.ajcn.org/cgi/reprint/71/3/682?maxtoshow=&HITS=80&hits=80&RESULTFORMAT=1&andorexacttitle=and&andorexacttitleabs=and&andorexactfulltext=and&searchid=1&FIRSTINDEX=420&sortspec=relevance&resourcetype=HWCIT

128 Barry Groves. *Trick and Treat: How'Healthy Eating' is Making Us Ill* (London: Hammersmith Press, 2008), p. 211.

129 Beasley and Knightly, 1994, p. 53.

130 http://www.hypoglycemia.asn.au/

131 Ibid.

132 Pert, 1997, p. 298.

133 Kathleen DesMaisons, Ph.D. *Little Sugar Addicts: End Mood Swings, Meltdowns, Tantrums and Low Self-Esteem in Your Child Today* (New York: Three Rivers Press, 2004), p. 193.

134 Imre Loefler, M.D., F.R.C.S. 2005. "No Sweet Surrender." *British Medical Journal*, Vol. 330 (No. 7495): p. 853. doi:10.1136/bmj.330.7495.853-a

135 Connie Bennett and Stephen Sinatra, M.D. *Sugar Shock* (New York: Berkley Books, 2007), p. 137.

136 Taubes, 2007, p. 118.

137 Her Web site is: www.nancyappleton.com.

138 R. J. Anderson, et al. 2001. "The Prevalence of Comorbid Depression in Adults with Diabetes: A Meta-Analysis." *Diabetes Care*, Vol. 24 (No. 6): pp. 1069-1178.

139 J. Goldman, et al. 1986. "Behavioral Effects of Sucrose on Preschool Children." *Journal of Abnormal Child Psychiatry*, Vol. 14 (No. 4): pp. 565-577.

140 L. Christensen, et al. 1985. "Impact of a Dietary Change on Emotional Distress." *Journal of Abnormal Psychology*, Vol. 94 (No. 4): pp. 565-579.

141 K. Krietsch, et al. 1988. "Prevalence, Presenting Symptoms and Psychological Characteristics of Individuals Experiencing a Diet-Related Mood-Disturbance." *Behavior Therapy*, Vol. 19 (No. 4): pp. 593-604.

142 F. Lechin et al. 1992. "Effects of an Oral Glucose Load on Plasma Neurotransmitters in Humans." *Neurophychobiology,* Vol. 26 (Nos. 1-2): pp. 4-11.

143 C. Anderson and J. A. Horne. 2006. "A High-Sugar-Content, Low-Caffeine Drink Does Not Alleviate Sleepiness but May Worsen It." *Human Psychopharmacology,* Vol. 21 (No. 5): pp. 299-303.

144 Kay Sheppard. *Food Addiction: The Body Knows* (Deerfield Beach, FL: HCI, 1993), 52; Robert LeFever, M.D. and Marie Shale, Ed.D. 1991. "Brain Chemistry: Combinations of Foods in the Blood Trigger Effects Very Similar to Alcohol." *Employee Assistance,* Vol. 3 (No. 8): pp. 30.

145 Rachael F. Heller and Richard F. Heller. *The Carbohydrate Addict's Diet* (New York: Dutton, 1991), p. 23.

146 Allan and Lutz, 2000, p. 212.

147 Ibid., p. 138.

148 Ibid.

149 Alissa Hamilton. "Nudging Nudge into the Supermarket." Email from www.foodforethought.com, November 4, 2008.

150 Devra First. "Secrets of Orange Juice." *Boston Globe,* February 22, 2009. http://www.boston.com/bostonglobe/ideas/articles/2009/02/22/qa_with_alissa_hamilton/

151 Ibid.

152 J. Murdoch Ritchie. "The Xanthines." In *The Pharmacological Basis of Therapeutics,* eds. L. S. Goodman and A. Gilman. New York: Macmillan, 1970, pp. 358-370; Edward M. Brecher and editors. "The Consumers Union Report on Licit and Illicit Drugs. Caffeine: Recent Findings." *Consumer Reports,* Chapter 22, 1972. http://www.drugtext.org/library/reports/cu/CU22.html

153 DesMaisons, 2004, pp. 97-98.

154 Elizabeth Scott, M.S. "Caffeine, Stress and Your Health: Is Caffeine Your Friend or Your Foe?" *About.com,* November 1, 2007. http://stress.about.com/od/stresshealth/a/caffeine.htm?

155 Bennett Alan Weinberg and Bonnie K. Bealer. *The World of Caffeine: The Science and Culture of the World's Most Popular Drug* (New York: Routledge, 2001), p. xi.

156 R. Gregory Lande, D.O., F.A.C.N. "Caffeine-Related Psychiatric Disorders." eMedicine.com, June 21, 2007. http://www.emedicine.com/med/TOPIC3115.HTM#ref1

157 David Yew, M.D. and Jeffrey T. Laczek, M.D. "Toxicity Caffeine." eMedcine.com, December 17, 2007. http://www.emedicine.com/emerg/TOPIC949.HTM#Multimediamedia1

[158] M. A. Lee, P. Flegel, J. F. Greden and O. G. Cameron. 1988. "Anxiogenic Effects of Caffeine on Panic and Depressed Patients." *American Journal of Psychiatry,* Vol. 145: pp. 632-635; G. L. Clementz and J. W. Dailey. 1988. "Psychotropic Effects of Caffeine." *American Family Physician,* Vol. 37: pp. 167-172; J. P. Boulenger, T. W. Uhde, E. A. Wolff III and R. M. Post. 1984. "Increased Sensitivity to Caffeine in Patients with Panic Disorders—Preliminary Evidence." *Archives of General Psychiatry,* Vol. 41: pp. 1067-1071; M. S. Bruce and M. Lader. 1989. "Caffeine Abstention in the Management of Anxiety Disorders." *Psychological Medicine,* Vol. 19: pp. 211-214.

[159] Michael B. Schachter, M.D. *What Your Doctor May Not Tell You about Depression* (New York: Warner Wellness, 2006), p. 43.

[160] Yew and Laczek, 2007.

[161] "Children Increasingly Consuming Caffeine." National Drug Strategy Network. *NewsBriefs,* May-June 1998. http://ndsn.org/mayjun98/caffeine.html

[162] Ibid.

[163] "Caffeinated energy drinks may present serious health risks, scientists say." *The Daily Star,* September 25, 2008. http://www.dailystar.com.lb/article. asp?edition_id=1&categ_id=1&article_id=96292

[164] Alexander Schauss, Ph.D., F.A.C.N. *Nutrition and Behavior* (New Canaan, CT: Keats Publishing, 1980), p. 17.

[165] Beasley and Knightly, 1994, p. 55.

[166] F. Lifshitz and N. Moses. 1989. "Growth Failure: A complication of dietary treatment of hypercholesterolemia." *American Journal of Diseases of Children,* Vol. 143: pp. 537-542.

[167] A. S. Wells, N. W. Read, J. D. E. Laugharne and N. S. Ahluwalia. 1998. "Alterations in mood after changing to a low-fat diet." *British Journal of Nutrition,* Vol. 79 (No. 1): pp. 23-30.

[168] M. F. Muldoon, S. B. Manusk and K. A. Matthews. 1990. "Lowering cholesterol concentrations and mortality: A quantitative review of primary prevention trials." *British Medical Journal,* Vol. 301: pp. 309-314.

[169] L. Wardle, P. Rogers, P. Judd, et al. 2000. "Randomized trial of the effects of cholesterol-lowering dietary treatment on psychological function." *American Journal of Medicine,* Vol. 108: pp. 547-553; M. J. Kretsch, M. W. K. Green, A. K. H. Fong, N. A. Elliman and H. L. Johnson. 1997. "Cognitive effects of a long-term weight reducing diet." *International Journal of Obesity,* Vol. 21: pp. 14-21; M. W. Green and P. J. Rogers. 1995. Impaired cognitive functioning during spontaneous dieting. *Psychosomatic Medicine,* Vol. 25: pp. 1003-1010.

170 L. Christensen and S. Somers. 1996. "Comparison of Nutrient Intake among Depressed and Nondepressed Individuals," and "DISCUSSION: The Increased Carbohydrate Consumption Is Consistent with the Carbohydrate Cravings Characteristic of the Depressed and May Relate to the Development or Maintenance of Depression." *International Journal of Eating Disorders*, Vol. 20: pp. 105-109.

171 P. J. Rogers. 2001. "A Healthy Body, a Healthy Mind: Long-Term Impact of Diet on Mood and Cognitive Function." *Proceedings of the Nutrition Society*, Vol. 60: pp. 135-143.

172 Groves, 2007, p. 252.

173 William Campbell-Douglass II. *Eat Your Cholesterol* (Panama: Rhino Publishing, 2003), p. 53.

174 Professor John Yudkin. "Fat Is the Most Valuable Food Known to Man." http://www.second-opinions.co.uk/fat-not-protein.html; John D. Speth and Katherine A. Spielmann. 1982. "Energy Source, Protein Metabolism and Hunter-Gatherer Subsistence Strategies." *Journal of Anthropological Archaeology*, Vol. 2: pp. 1-31; D. Noli and G. Avery. 1988. "Protein Poisoning and Coastal Subsistence." *Journal of Archaeological Science,* Vol. 15: pp. 395-401.

175 Taubes, 2007, p. 11.

176 Ibid., p. 11.

177 Ibid., p. 69.

178 Sally Fallon. *Ancient Dietary Wisdom for Tomorrow's Children*. Mercola. com, p. 6.

179 Weston A. Price. *Nutrition and Physical Degeneration*. 6th Edition. (Los Angeles: Keats Publishing, 1998), p. 24.

180 Ibid., p. 27.

181 Ibid., p. 47.

182 Vilhjalmur Stefansson. "Adventures in Diet, Part 2." *Harper's Monthly Magazine*, December 1935. http://www.biblelife.org/stefansson2.htm

183 Ibid.

184 Ibid.

185 Ibid.

186 Groves, 2008, p. 57.

187 G. T. Wrench, M.D. *The Wheel of Health: A Study of a Very Healthy People*. London: C.W. Daniel Co. Ltd., 1938. http://journeytoforever.org/farm_library/Wrench_WoH/WoHToC.html

188 Ibid.

368   PAM KILLEEN

189   Adam Campbell. "The Cure for Diabetes." *Men's Health Magazine*, November 20, 2006. http://www.menshealth.com/cda/article.do?site=M ensHealth&channel=health&category=other.diseases.ailments&conitem= 4a935e4e40fae010VgnVCM20000012281eac____

190   Taubes, 2007, pp. 329-330.

191   Estelle Hawley, Ph.D. and Grace Carden, B.S. *The Art and Science of Nutrition* (St. Louis: The CV Mosby Company, 1944), p. 309.

192   Allan and Lutz, 2000, p. 5.

193   Ibid., p. 7.

194   N. Saleem Basha. "Role of DHA in Proper Gestation and in Development of Good Intellectual & Visual Acuity of Fetus." http://ezinearticles. com/?Role-of-DHA-in-Proper-Gestation-and-in-Development-of-Good-Intellectual-and-Visual-Acuity-of-Fetus&id=1705476

195   Groves, 2007, p. 137.

196   J. R. Hibbeln and N. Salem, Jr. 1995. "Dietary Polyunsaturated Fats and Depression: When Cholesterol Alone Doesn't Satisfy." *American Journal of Clinical Nutrition*, Vol. 62: pp. 1-9; P. W. Lavori, M. Warshaw, G. Klerman, T. I. Mueller, A. Leon, J. Rice, et al. 1993. "Secular Trends in Lifetime Onset of Mdd Stratified by Selected Sociodemographic Risk Factors." *Journal of Psychiatric Research*, Vol. 27: pp. 95-109; Felicity Lawrence. "Omega-3, Junk Food and the Link between Violence and What We Eat." *The Guardian*, October 17, 2006. http://www.guardian. co.uk/politics/2006/oct/17/prisonsandprobation.ukcrime/print

197   Janice K. Kiecolt-Glaser, Martha A. Belury, Kyle Porter, David Q. Beversdorf, Stanley Lemeshow and Ronald Glaser. 2007. "Depressive Symptoms, Omega-6: Omega-3 Fatty Acids and Inflammation in Older Adults." *Psychosomatic Medicine*, Vol. 69 (No. 3): pp. 217-224. PSY.0b013e3180313a45.

198   Joseph Mercola. "More Proof Good Fat Helps You Drop Weight." Mercola.com, May 24, 2005. http://articles.mercola.com/sites/articles/ archive/2005/05/24/good-fats-part-two.aspx

199   Mary Enig, Ph.D. and Sally Fallon. *The Oiling of America*. Weston A. Price Foundation. http://www.westonaprice.org/knowyourfats/oiling.html

200   Their Web site is: http://www.health.bcu.ac.uk/physiology/ Pharmacology01.htm.

201   "Alzheimer's Disease: Unraveling the Mystery." National Institute on Aging. http://www.nia.nih.gov/Alzheimers/Publications/UnravelingtheMystery/ Retrieved from Wikipedia on July 21, 2009. http://en.wikipedia.org/wiki/ File:Chemical_synapse_schema.jpg

[202] K.-P. Su. 2009. "Biological Mechanism of Antidepressant Effect of Omega-3 Fatty Acids: How Does Fish Oil Act as a 'Mind-Body Interface'?" *Neurosignals*, Vol. 17: pp. 144-152.

[203] R. J. Wurtman, M. Cansev, T. Sakamoto and I. H. Ulus. 2009. "Administration of Docosahexaenoic Acid, Uridine and Choline Increases Levels of Synaptic Membranes and Dendritic Spines in Rodent Brain." *World Review of Nutrition and Dietetics*, Vol. 99: pp. 71-96.

[204] U. N. Das. 2008. "Folic Acid and Polyunsaturated Fatty Acids Improve Cognitive Function and Prevent Depression, Dementia and Alzheimer's Disease—But How and Why?" *Prostaglandins, Leukotrienes and Essential Fatty Acids*, Vol. 78 (No. 1): pp. 11-19.

[205] Kenneth J. Bender. 1998. "Dietary Fatty Acids Essential for Mental Health." *Psychiatric Times*, Vol. 15 (No. 12).

[206] A. Tanskanen, J. R. Hibbeln, J. Hintikka, K. Haatainen, K. Honkalampi and H. Viinamaki. 2001. "Fish Consumption, Depression and Suicidality in a General Population." *Archives of General Psychiatry*, Vol. 58: pp. 512-513; K. M. Silvers and K. M. Scott. 2002. "Fish Consumption and Self-Reported Physical and Mental Health Status." *Public Health Nutrition*, Vol. 5 (No. 4): pp. 27-431.

[207] Marianne Haag. 2003. "Essential Fatty Acids and the Brain." *Canadian Journal of Psychiatry*, Vol. 48 (No. 3). http://thedyslexiashop.co.uk/pdfdocuments/haag.pdf. Adrian S. Dobs and Daniel Edelstein. *Wild-Type Food in Health Promotion and Disease Prevention*. Totowa, NJ: Humana Press, January 23, 2008. http://www.springerlink.com/content/u100xm2161w16r61/; Marlene P. Freeman, M.D. 2006. "Omega-3 Fatty Acids; Evidence Basis for Treatment and Future Research in Psychiatry." *Journal of Clinical Psychiatry*, Vol. 67: p. 12. http://www.biovita.fi/suomi/pdf/APA_2006.pdf; A. L. Stoll, W. E. Severus, M. P. Freeman, S. Rueter, H. A. Zboyan, A. Diamond, et al. 1999. "Omega-3 Fatty Acids In Bipolar Disorder." *Archives of General Psychiatry*, Vol. 56: pp. 401-412; Malcolm Peet. "Dietary Omega-3 Fatty Acids in Relation to Depression and Schizophrenia." 2007-05-09. http://www.fhf.org.uk/meetings/inquiry2007/2007-05-09_peet.pdf

[208] T. A. Dolecek and G. Grandits. 1991. "Dietary Polyunsaturated Fatty Acids and Mortality in the Multiple Risk Factor Intervention Trial (MRFIT)." *World Review of Nutrition and Dietetics*, Vol. 66: pp. 205-216.

[209] Their Web site is: http://www.hc-sc.gc.ca/dhp-mps/prodnatur/applications/licen-prod/monograph/mono_fish_oil_huile_poisson-eng.php.

[210] Fran McCullough. *The Good Fat Cookbook* (New York: Scribner, 2003), p. 45.

[211] D. F. Hebeisen, F. Hoeflin, H. P. Reusch, E. Junker and B. H. Lauterburg. 1993. "Increased Concentrations of Omega-3 Fatty Acids in Milk and Platelet Rich Plasma of Grass-Fed Cows." *International Journal for Vitamin and Nutrition Research*, Vol. 63 (No. 3): pp. 229-233; Gillian Butler, et al. 2008. "Fatty Acid and Fat Soluble Antioxidant Concentrations in Milk from High- And Low-Input Conventional and Organic Systems: Seasonal Variation." *Journal of the Science of Food and Agriculture*, Vol. 88: pp. 1431-1441.

[212] C. J. Lopez-Bote, et al. 1998. "Effect of Free-Range Feeding on Omega-3 Fatty Acids and Alpha-Tocopherol Content and Oxidative Stability of Eggs." *Animal Feed Science and Technology*, Vol. 72: pp. 33-40.

[213] Eric Schlosser. "Fast-Food Nation: Meat and Potatoes (Part II)." *Rolling Stone Magazine*, Issue 794, September 3, 1998. http://www.mcspotlight. org/media/press/rollingstone2.html

[214] Chris Masterjohn. 2008. "The Pursuit of Happiness: How Nutrient-Dense Animal Fats Promote Mental and Emotional Health." *Wise Traditions*, Vol. 9 (No. 4): pp. 14-24; Reza Zolfaghari and A. Catharine Ross. 2003. "Recent Advances in Molecular Cloning of Fatty Acid Desaturase Genes and the Regulation of Their Expression by Dietary Vitamin A and Retinoic Acid." *Prostaglandins Leukotrienes and Essential Fatty Acids*, Vol. 68 (No. 2): pp. 171-179.

[215] Neil J. Mann, Leeann G. Johnson, Glenda F. Warrick and Andrew J. Sinclair. 1995. "The AA Content of the Australian Diet Is Lower than Previously Estimated." *Journal of Nutrition*, Vol. 125: pp. 2528-2535.

[216] Natasha Campbell-McBride. *Gut and Psychology Syndrome.* 7th Reprint. (Cambridge: Medinform, 2007), p. 179; Groves, 2008, p. 380; J. D. Laugharne, et al. 1996. "Fatty Acids and Schizophrenia." *Lipids*, Vol. 31 Suppl: pp. S163-165.

[217] J. R. Burgess, L. Stevens, W. Zhang, L. Peck. 2000. "Long-Chain Polyunsaturated Fatty Acids in Children with Attention-Deficit Hyperactivity Disorder." *American Journal of Clinical Nutrition*, Vol. 71 (1 Suppl): pp. 327S-30S; J. R. Chen, S. F. Hsu, C. D. Hsu, L. H. Hwang and S. C. Yang. 2004. "Dietary Patterns and Blood Fatty Acid Composition in Children with Attention-Deficit Hyperactivity Disorder in Taiwan." *Journal of Nutritional Biochemistry*, Vol. 15 (No. 8): pp. 467-472.

[218] Norman Salem, Jr. 1989. "Alcohol, Fatty Acids and Diet." *Alcohol Health and Research World*, Vol. 13 (No. 3): pp. 211-218.

219   Y. Kiso. 2006. "AA Improves Brain Function and Sleep in Elderly People." *Bio Ind*, Vol. 23 (No. 7): pp. 14-18.

220   Sally Fallon and Mary Enig, Ph.D. "Comments on the Report of the 2005 Dietary Guidelines Advisory Committee." Weston A. Price Foundation, September 27, 2004. http://westonaprice.org/federalupdate/testimony/comments_dietaryguidelinesrep.pdf

221   J. Tong, P. P. Borbat, J. H. Freed and Y. K. Shin. 2009. "A Scissors Mechanism for Stimulation of Snare-Mediated Lipid Mixing by Cholesterol." *Proceedings of the National Academy of Sciences of the U.S.A.*, Vol. 106 (No. 13): pp. 5141-5146.

222   Fallon and Enig, 2004.

223   Chris Masterjohn. "Learning, Your Memory and Cholesterol." July 2005. http://www.cholesterol-and-health.com/Memory-And-Cholesterol.html

224   Their Web site is: http://faculty.washington.edu/chudler/ms.html.

225   Chris Masterjohn. "Cholesterol—Nature's Life Giving Substance." http://www.cholesterol-and-health.com/Functions-Of-Cholesterol.html

226   Eric Braverman. *The Healing Nutrients Within*. 3rd Edition. (Laguna Beach: Basic Health Publications, 2003), p. 37.

227   T. Oishi and S. Szabo. 1984. "Tyrosine Increases Tissue Dopamine Concentration in the Rat." *Journal of Neurochemistry*, Vol. 42: pp. 894-896; W. T. Chance, T. Foley-Nelson, J. L. Nelson and J. E. Fischer. 1990. "Tyrosine Loading Increases Dopamine Metabolite Concentrations in the Brain." *Pharmacology Biochemistry and Behavior*, Vol. 35 (No. 1): pp. 195-199.

228   A. J. Gelenberg, J. D. Wojcik, J. H. Growdon, A. F. Sved and R. J. Wurtman. 1980. "Tyrosine for the Treatment of Depression." *American Journal of Psychiatry*, Vol. 137 (No. 5): pp. 622-623; C. Gibson and A. Gelenberg. 1983. "Tyrosine for the Treatment of Depression." *Advances in Biological Psychiatry*, Vol. 10: pp. 148-159.

229   J. Eisenberg, G. M. Asnis, H. M. van Praag, et al. 1988. "Effect of Tyrosine on Attention Deficit Disorder with Hyperactivity." *Journal of Clinical Psychiatry*, Vol. 49: pp. 193-195; F. W. Reimherr, P. H. Wender, R. D. Wood, et al. 1987. "An Open Trial of L-Tyrosine in the Treatment of Attention Deficit Disorder, Residual Type." *American Journal of Psychiatry*, Vol. 144: pp. 1071-1073; R. D. Wood, F. W. Reimherr, P. H. Wender, et al. 1985. "Amino Acid Precursors for the Treatment of Attention Deficit Disorder, Residual Type." *Psychopharmacology Bulletin*, Vol. 21: pp. 146-149.

230   Braverman, 2003, p. 57.

231   A. Neumeister, N. Praschak-Rieder, B. Hesselmann, O. Vitouch, M. Rauh, A. Barocka and S. Kasper. 1998. "Effects of Tryptophan Depletion in Fully

Remitted Patients with Seasonal Affective Disorder during Summer." *Psychological Medicine*, Vol. 28: pp. 257-264.

232 S. N. Young. 1986. "The Clinical Psychopharmacology of Tryptophan." In R. J. Wurtman and J. J. Wurtman, eds. *Food Constituents Affecting Normal and Abnormal Behaviors* (New York: Raven Press, 1986), pp. 49-88; J. Thomson, H. Rankin, G. W. Ashcroft, et al. 1982. "The Treatment of Depression in General Practice: A Comparison of L-Tryptophan, Amitriptyline and a Combination of L-Tryptophan and Amitriptyline with Placebo." *Psychological Medicine*, Vol. 12: pp. 741-751; R. J. Wurtman, F. Hefti and E. Melamed. 1980. "Precursor Control of Neurotransmitter Synthesis." *Pharmacological Reviews*, Vol. 32: pp. 315-335.

233 M. aan het Rot, D. S. Moskowitz, G. Pinard, et al. 2006. "Social Behaviour and Mood in Everyday Life: Effects of Tryptophan in Quarrelsome Individuals." *Journal of Psychiatry and Neuroscience*, Vol. 31: pp. 253-262.

234 L. Booij, W. Merens, C. R. Markus, et al. 2006. "Diet Rich in Alpha-Lactalbumin Improves Memory in Unmedicated Recovered Depressed Patients and Matched Controls." *Journal of Psychopharmacology*, Vol. 20: pp. 526-535; C. R. Markus, B. Olivier and E. H. de Haan. 2002. "Whey Protein Rich in Alpha-Lactalbumin Increases the Ratio of Plasma Tryptophan to the Sum of the Other Large Neutral Amino Acids and Improves Cognitive Performance in Stress-Vulnerable Subjects." *American Journal of Clinical Nutrition*, Vol. 75: pp. 1051-1056.

235 J. L. Weihrauch and Y.-S. Son. 1983. "Phospholipid Content of Foods." *Journal of the American Oil Chemists Society*, Vol. 60 (No. 12): pp. 1971-1978.

236 Parris Kidd. *PhosphatidylSerine: Nature's Brain Booster.* 2nd Edition. (St. George, UT: Total Health, 2007), p. 4.

237 S. W. Souci, E. Fachmann and H. Kraut. *Food Composition and Nutrition Tables.* Stuttgart: Medpharm Scientific Publishers, 2008. Adapted from Wikipedia. Retrieved on May 13, 2009.

238 James Braly and Patrick Holford. *The H-Factor Solution* (Laguna Beach: Basic Health Publications, 2003), pp. 194-195.

239 Schachter, 2006, p. 135.

240 Elizabeth M. Haney, M.D. 2007. "Screening for Lipid Disorders in Children and Adolescents: Systematic Evidence Review for the U.S. Preventive Services Task Force." Agency for Healthcare Research and Quality, U.S. Department of Health and Human Services, HRQ Publication No. 07-0598-EF-1, p. 28, tables on pp. 150-154. http://www.ahrq.gov/clinic/uspstf07/chlipid/chlipidsyn.pdf

[241] Hector M. Burton, Jr. 1988. "What Are the Psychiatric Manifestations of Vitamin B12 Deficiency?" *Journal of the American Geriatrics Society,* Vol. 36: pp. 1105-1112; H. Murck. 2002. "Magnesium and Affective Disorders." *Nutritional Neuroscience,* Vol. 5: pp. 375-389.

[242] Mark Hyman, M.D. *The UltraMind Solution* (New York: Scribner, 2009), pp. 141-143.

[243] Ibid., p. 143.

[244] Jeremy E. Kaslow, M.D., "Copper/Zinc Imbalance." http://www.drkaslow. com/html/zinc-copper_imbalances.html

[245] Ann Louise Gittleman. *Why Am I Always So Tired?* (San Francisco: Harper, 1999), p. 35.

[246] Ibid.

[247] Kathryn R. Simpson. *The Women's Guide to Thyroid Health* (Oakland, CA: New Harbinger, 2009), p. 8.

[248] Schachter, 2006, p. 166.

[249] M. Krajčovičová-Kudláčková et al. 2003. Iodine Deficiency in Vegetarians and Vegans. *Annals of Nutrition and Metabolism,* Vol. 47 (No. 5): pp. 183-185.

[250] M. Raeder, et al. 2007. "Associations between Cod Liver Oil Use and Symptoms of Depression: The Hordaland Health Study." *Journal of Affective Disorders,* Vol. 101 (Nos. 1-3): pp. 245-249.

[251] Sally Fallon and Mary Enig, Ph.D. "Vitamin A Saga." Weston A. Price Foundation. http://www.westonaprice.org/basicnutrition/vitaminasaga.html

[252] L. B. Dixon, M. A. Winkleby and K. L. Radimer. 2001. "Dietary Intakes and Serum Nutrients Differ between Adults from Food-Insufficient and Food-Sufficient Families: Third National Health and Nutrition Examination Survey, 1988-1994." *Journal of Nutrition,* Vol. 131 (No. 4): pp. 1232-1246.

[253] Fallon and Enig, "Vitamin A Saga."

[254] Ibid. and I. W. Jennings. *Vitamins in Endocrine Metabolism.* Springfield, IL: Charles C. Thomas Publisher, 1970.

[255] William Rea, M.D. "Chemical Sensitivity." Vol. 1 (Boca Raton, FL: CRC Press, 1992), p. 245.

[256] D. J. Armstrong et al. "Vitamin D Deficiency Is Associated with Anxiety and Depression in Fibromyalgia." 2007. *Clinical Rheumatology,* Vol. 26 (No. 4): pp. 551-554; M. Berk et al. 2007. "Vitamin D Deficiency May Play a Role in Depression." *Medical Hypotheses,* Vol. 69 (No. 6): pp. 1316-1319; W. J. Hoogendijk et al. "Depression Is Associated with Decreased 25-Hydroxyvitamin D and Increased Parathyroid Hormone Levels in Older Adults." 2008. *Archives of General Psychiatry,* Vol. 65 (No.

5): pp. 508-512; John Cannell, M.D. "Vitamin D and Depression." http://www.vitamindcouncil.org/depression.shtml

[257] Ed Edelson. "Vitamin D Vital for the Heart." *US News & World Report*, December 1, 2008. http://health.usnews.com/articles/health/healthday/2008/12/01/vitamin-d-vital-for-the-heart.html; John H. Lee, et al. 2008. "Vitamin D Deficiency: An Important, Common and Easily Treatable Cardiovascular Risk Factor?" *Journal of the American College of Cardiology*, Vol. 52: pp. 1949-1956; "Vitamin D Deficiency Drains $9 Billion from Canadian Health Care System." *Vitamin D Society*, Press Release, October 31, 2007. http://www.newswire.ca/en/releases/archive/October2007/31/c2359.html

[258] "Vitamin D Important in Brain Development and Function." *Science Daily*, April 23, 2008; J. C. McCann, B. N. Ames. 2008. "Review Article: Is There Convincing Biological Or Behavioral Evidence Linking Vitamin D Deficiency to Brain Dysfunction?" *FASEB Journal*, Vol. 22: pp. 982-1001. http://www.sciencedaily.com/releases/2008/04/080421072159.htm

[259] John Cannell. "The Vitamin D Connection." http://www.vitamindcouncil.org/health/autism/vit-D-connection.shtml

[260] E. Puchacz, W. E. Stumpf, E. K. Stachowiak and M. K. Stachowiak. 1996. "Vitamin D Increases Expression of the Tyrosine Hydroxylase Gene in Adrenal Medullary Cells." *Molecular Brain Research*, Vol. 36 (No. 1): pp. 193-196; C. H. Wilkins, Y. I. Sheline, C. M. Roe, S. J. Birge and J. C. Morris. 2006. "Vitamin D Deficiency Is Associated With Low Mood And Worse Cognitive Performance In Older Adults." *American Journal of Geriatric Psychiatry*, Vol. 14 (No. 12): pp. 1032-1040; D. J. Armstrong, G. K. Meenagh, I. Bickle, A. S. Lee, E. S. Curran and M. B. Finch. 2007. "Vitamin D Deficiency Is Associated with Anxiety and Depression in Fibromyalgia." *Clinical Rheumatology*, Vol. 26 (No. 4): pp. 551-554.

[261] http://www.vitamindcouncil.org/depression.shtml

[262] F. M. Gloth III, W. Alam and B. Hollis. 1999. "Vitamin D vs Broad Spectrum Phototherapy in the Treatment of Seasonal Affective Disorder." *Journal of Nutrition Health & Aging*, Vol. 3 (No. 1): pp. 5-7.

[263] A. T. Lansdowne and S. C. Provost. 1998. "Vitamin D3 Enhances Mood in Healthy Subjects during Winter." *Psychopharmacology (Berlin)*, Vol. 135 (No. 4): pp. 319-323.

[264] Gloth, Alam and Hollis, 1999, pp. 5-7.

[265] Patrick Holford, David Miler and James Braly. *How To Quit without Feeling S**t* (London: Piatkus, 2008), p. 42.

[266] "Nutrition Fact Sheet: Folate." Northwestern University. http://www.feinberg.northwestern.edu/nutrition/factsheets/folate.html

[267] Adapted from "Nutrition Fact Sheet: Folate." Northwestern University. http://www.feinberg.northwestern.edu/nutrition/factsheets/folate.html

[268] L. Allen. "How Common Is Vitamin B-12 Deficiency?" 2009. *American Journal of Clinical Nutrition,* Vol. 89, (No. 2), pp. 693S-696S; Milly Ryan-Harshman and Waldi Aldoori. 2008. "Vitamin B12 and Health Canadian Family Physician." Vol. 54 (No. 4): pp. 536-541; N. Dali-Youcef and E. Andrès. 2009. "An Update on Cobalamin Deficiency in Adults." *Quarterly Journal of Medicine,* Vol. 102 (No. 1): pp. 17-28.

[269] Sally Fallon and Mary Enig, Ph.D. "Vitamin B12: Vital Nutrient for Good Health." Weston A. Price Foundation. http://www.westonaprice. org/basicnutrition/vitaminb12.html; H. Curtius, et al. 1982. Short Communications Tetrahydrobiopterin: Efficacy in Endogenous Depression and Parkinson's Disease. *Journal Neural Transmission,* Vol. 55: pp. 301-308; R. Leeming, et al. 1982. Tetrahyudrofolate and hydroxycobolamin in the management of dihydroptridine reductase deficiency. *Journal of Mental Deficiency Research,* Vol. 26: pp. 21-25.

[270] http://www.westonaprice.org/basicnutrition/vitaminb12.html

[271] C. J. M. Van Tiggelen, et al. 1984. "Vitamin B12 Levels of Cerebrospinal Fluid in Patients with Organic Mental Disorder." *Journal of Orthomolecular Psychiatry,* Vol. 12 (No. 4): pp. 305-311; R. Deana, E. Vincenti and A. Donella Deana. 1977. "Levels of Neurotransmitters in Brain of Vitamin B12 Deficient Rats." *International Journal for Vitamin and Nutrition Research,* Vol. 47: pp. 119-122.

[272] M. Okawa, et al. 1990. *Sleep,* Vol. 13: pp. 1-23.

[273] B. W. Penninx, et al. 2000. "Vitamin B(12) Deficiency and Depression in Physically Disabled Older Women: Epidemiologic Evidence from the Women's Health and Aging Study." *American Journal of Psychiatry,* Vol. 157 (No. 5): pp. 715-721; A. Coppen and C. Bolander-Gouaille. 2005. "Treatment of Depression: Time to Consider Folic Acid and Vitamin B12." *Journal of Psychopharmacology,* Vol. 19 (No. 1): pp. 59-65; Hvas Anne-Mette, Juul Svend, Bech Per and Nexø Ebba. 2004. "Vitamin B6 Level Is Associated with Symptoms of Depression." *Psychotherapy and Psychosomatics,* Vol. 73 (No. 6): pp. 340-343; J. W. Stewart, et al. 1984. "Low B6 Levels in Depressed Outpatients." *Biological Psychiatry,* Vol. 19 (No. 4): pp. 613-616; Coppen and Bolander-Gouaille, 2005, pp. 59-65; P. S. Godfrey, B. K. Toone, M. W. Carney, T. G. Flynn, T. Bottiglieri and M. Laundy. 1990. "Enhancement of Recovery from Psychiatric Illness by Methylfolate." *Lancet,* Vol. 336: pp. 392-395; N. Dimopoulos, C. Piperi, A. Salonicioti, et al. 2007. "Correlation of Folate, Vitamin B12 and Homocysteine Plasma Levels with

Depression in an Elderly Greek Population." *Clinical Biochemistry,* Vol. 40 (Nos. 9-10): pp. 604-608. [PubMed: 17320847.]; Tolmunen, et al., 2003, pp. 3233-3236; Godfrey, et al., 1990, pp. 392-395. [PubMed: 1974941.]; Adams, et al., 1974, pp. 516-517; I. R. Bell, J. S. Edman, F. D. Morrow, et al. 1992. "Brief Communication: Vitamin B1, B2 and B6 Augmentation of Tricyclic Antidepressant Treatment in Geriatric Depression with Cognitive Dysfunction." *Journal of the American College of Nutrition,* Vol. 11 (No. 2): pp. 159-163; H. Doll, S. Brown, A. Thurston and M. Vessey. 1989. "Pyridoxine (Vitamin B6) and the Premenstrual Syndrome, A Randomized Crossover Trial." *Journal of the Royal College of General Practitioners,* Vol. 39, pp. 364-368.

274   D. Mischoulon and M. Fava. 2002. "Role of S-adenosyl-L-methionine in the Treatment of Depression: A Review of the Evidence." *American Journal of Clinical Nutrition,* Vol. 76 (No. 5): pp. 1158S-61S; A. Williams, et al. 2005. "S-Adenosylmethionine (SAMe) as Treatment for Depression: A Systematic Review." *Clinical and Investigative Medicine,* Vol. 28 (No. 3): pp. 132-139.

275   Coppen and Bolander-Gouaille, 2005, pp. 59-65.

276   Agency for Healthcare Research and Quality. 2002. "S-Adenosyl-L-Methionine for Treatment of Depression, Osteoarthritis and Liver Disease." Evidence Report/Technology Assessment: Number 64. http://www.ahrq.gov/Clinic/epcsums/samesum.htm

277   Allan and Lutz, 2000, p. 90.

278   Ibid; Mann, et al. 1998. "The Effect of the Diet on Homocysteine in Healthy Male Subjects." *Netherlands Journal of Medicine,* Vol. 52 (Suppl.): p. S10.

279   Mark Easton, ed. *The Happiness Formula: The Recipe for Happiness.* Documentary. London: BBC Two, 2006.

280   "U.S. Farms: Numbers, Size and Ownership." Structure and Finances of U.S. Farms: 2005 Family Farm Report. Economic Research Service, USDA. http://www.ers.usda.gov/publications/EIB12/EIB12c.pdf?

281   "The Case for Local and Regional Food Marketing." Farm and Food Policy Project, May 2007, p. 3. http://www.farmandfoodproject.org/documents/uploads/The%20Case%20for%20Local%20&%20Regional%20Food%20Marketing.pdf; Helena Norberg-Hodge, Todd Merrifield and Steven Gorelick. *Bringing the Food Economy Home: Local Alternatives to Global Agribusiness.* Bloomfield, CT: Kumarian Press, 2002.

282   Charles Benbrook, Xin Zhao, Jaime Yáñez, Neal Davies and Preston Andrews. "New Evidence Confirms the Nutritional Superiority of Plant-Based

Organic Foods." The Organic Center for Education and Promotion, March 2008. http://www.organic-center.org/reportfiles/Nutrient_Content_SSR_Executive_Summary_FINAL.pdf; and, Charles Benbrook. "Elevating Antioxidant Levels In Food Through Organic Farming And Food Processing". The Organic Centre for Education and Promotion, January 2005. www.organiccenter.org/science.antiox.php?action=view&report_id=3

[283] David Brownstein. *Salt Your Way to Health* (West Bloomfield, MI: Medical Alternative Press, 2006), p. 75.

[284] Donald Davis. 2009. "Declining Fruit and Vegetable Nutrient Composition: What Is the Evidence?" *HortScience,* Vol. 44: pp. 6-223.

[285] Natasha Campbell-McBride, *Gut and Psychology Syndrome* (Cambridge: Medinform, UK, 2004), p. 49.

[286] Melissa Diane Smith, *Going against the Grain* (New York: Contemporary Books, 2002), p. 96; C. Hallert, et al. 1982. "High Levels Of Pyridoxal 5'-Phosphate in the Cerebrospinal Fluid of Adult Celiac Patients." *American Journal of Clinical Nutrition,* Vol. 36: pp. 851-854.

[287] M. Gobbetti, C. Giuseppe Rizzello, R. Di Cagno and M. De Angelis. 2007. "Sourdough Lactobacilli and Celiac Disease." *Food Microbiology,* Vol. 24 (No. 2): 187-96.

[288] Sally Fallon. *Nourishing Traditions* (Washington, DC: New Trends Publishing, 2001), p. 452.

[289] C. A. Lowry, et al. 2007. "Identification of an Immune-Responsive Mesolimbocortical Serotonergic System: Potential Role in Regulation of Emotional Behavior." *Neuroscience,* Vol. 146 (No. 2): pp. 756-772.

[290] Natasha Campbell-McBride. "Autism in Children and Probiotics." SPEACH, July 2001. http://www.scribd.com/doc/3738715/Autism-In-Children-And-Probiotics-by-Dr-Natasha-CampbellMcBride-

[291] Campbell-McBride, 2004, p. 43.

[292] Ibid., p. 45.

[293] Natasha Campbell-McBride. 2007. "Gut and Psychology Syndrome: The GAPS in our Medical Knowledge." *Wise Traditions,* Vol. 8 (No. 4): pp. 13-23.

[294] Sandor Ellix Katz. *Wild Fermentation* (White River Junction, VT: Chelsea Green Publishing, 2003), p. 5.

[295] Charles Stanford Porter, M.D. *Milk Diet as a Remedy for Chronic Disease* (West Bend, WI: God's Whey, 2005), p. 203.

[296] K. H. Steinkraus, ed. *Handbook of Indigenous Fermented Foods.* New York: Marcel Dekker, Inc., 1995; Andre G. van Veen and Keith H. Steinkraus. 1970. "Nutritive Value and Wholesomeness of Fermented Foods." *Agricultural and Food Chemistry,* Vol. 18 (No. 4): p. 576.

[297] S. Salminen, C. Bouley and M.-C. Boutron-Ruault, et al. 1998. "Functional Food Science and Gastrointestinal Physiology And Function." *British Journal of Nutrition,* Vol. 80 (Suppl. 1): pp. 147-171; R. H. Frohlich, M. Kunze and I. Kiefer. 1997. "Cancer Preventive Impact of Naturally Occurring, Non-nutritive Constituents in Food." *Acta Medica Austriaca,* Austria; P. A. Barrett, E. Beveridge, P. L. Bradley, et al. 1965. "Biological Activities of Some Alpha-Dithiosemicarbazones." *Nature,* Vol. 206 (No. 991): pp. 1340-1341; M. Tolonen, M. Taipale, B. Viander, J.-M. Pihlava, H. Korhonen and E.-L. Ryhanen. 2002. "Plant-Derived Biomolecules in Fermented Cabbage." *Journal of Agricultural and Food Chemistry,* Vol. 50 (No. 23), pp. 6798-6803. DOI: 10.1021/jf0109017

[298] H. S. Gill. 1998. "Stimulation of the Immune System by Lactic Cultures." *International Dairy Journal,* Vol. 8: pp. 535-544; H. S. Gill. 1999. "Potential of Using Dietary Lactic Acid Bacteria for Enhancement of Immunity." *Dialogue,* Issue 32, pp. 6-11; J. W. Lee, J. G. Shin, E. H. Kim, H. E. Kang, I. B. Yim, J. Y. Kim, H. G. Joo and H. J. Woo. 2004. "Immunomodulatory and Antitumor Effects In Vivo by the Cytoplasmic Fraction of Lactobacillus casei and Bifidobacterium longum." *Journal of Veterinary Science,* Vol. 5 (No. 1): pp. 41-48.

[299] Nora Gedgaudas. Primal Body—Primal Mind (Portland, OR: Primal Body—Primal Mind Publishing, 2009), p. 71.

[300] Thomas McPherson Brown. "Check Your Stomach for Sufficient Hydrochloric Acid." http://www.rheumatic.org/hcl.htm. Also see: Henry Pleasants, Jr. M.D. Associate Editor. *Three Years of HCL Therapy.* W. Roy Huntsman: Philadelphia, PA, 1935. http://www.arthritistrust.org/Books_&_Phamplets/Three%20Years%20of%20HCl%20Therapy.pdf

[301] S. Hossein Fatemi. *Neuropsychiatric Disorders and Infection* (Abingdon, England: Taylor & Francis, 2005), Preface, p. xv.

[302] Ibid., Foreword, p. xiii.

[303] Eric R. Braverman, M.D. *The Edge Effect: Reverse or Prevent Alzheimer's, Aging, Memory Loss, Weight Gain, Sexual Dysfunction and More* (New York: Sterling, 2004), p. 184.

[304] John Cannell, M.D. *The Vitamin D Newsletter,* June/July 2006. www.vitamindcouncil.com/newsletter/2006-june-july.shtml

[305] P. T. Liu, et al. 2006. "Toll-Like Receptor Triggering of a Vitamin D-Mediated Human Antimicrobial Response." *Science,* Vol. 311 (No. 5768): pp. 1770-1773. Epub 2006 Feb 23.

[306] Ron Seely. "Hazardous Homes Part II: Household Products That May Be Harmful." *Coulee News,* January 9, 2008.

307 Nicholas Ashford and Claudia Miller. *Chemical Exposures: Low Levels and High Stakes.* 2nd Edition. (New York: John Wiley & Sons, 1988), p. 93.

308 Marla Cone. "EPA Is Faulted as Failing to Shield Public from Toxins." *LA Times*, July 13, 2005. http://www.commondreams.org/headlines05/0713-03.htm

309 Pamela Reed Gibson, Ph.D., "An Introduction to Multiple Chemical Sensitivity and Electrical Sensitivity." The Environmental Illness Resource. http://www.ei-resource.org/articles/multiple-chemical-sensitivity-articles/an-introduction-to-multiple-chemical-sensitivity-and-electrical-sensitivity/

310 M. C. Alavanja, J. Hoppin and F. Kamel. 2004. "Health Effects of Chronic Pesticide Exposure: Cancer and Neurotoxicity." *Annual Review of Public Health*, Vol. 25: pp. 155-197.

311 R.N. Golden, B.N. Gaynes, R.D. Ekstrom, et al. 2005. "The Efficacy of Light Therapy in the Treatment of Mood Disorders: A Review and Meta-Analysis of The Evidence." *American Journal of Psychiatry*, Vol. 162: pp. 656-662.

312 M. aan het Rot, D. S. Moskowitz and S. N. Young. 2006. "Exposure to Bright Light Is Associated with Positive Social Interaction and Good Mood over Short Time Periods: A Naturalistic Study in Mildly Seasonal People." *Journal of Psychiatric Research*, Vol. 42 (No. 4): pp. 311-319; M aan het Rot, C. Benkelfat, D. Boivin and S. N. Young. 2008. "Bright Light Exposure during Acute Tryptophan Depletion Prevents a Lowering of Mood in Mildly Seasonal Women." *European Neuropsychopharmacology*, Volume 18 (No. 1), pp. 14-23; "Dose Of Summer Sun Good For You—And Others." Canadian Institutes of Health Research, July 2007. http://www.cihr-irsc.gc.ca/e/34335.html

313 "Light Cafe to Beat the Winter Blues." BBC News, January 6, 2006. http://news.bbc.co.uk/2/hi/health/4595626.stm

314 Daniel M. Landers. "The Influence of Exercise on Mental Health." *PCPFS Research Digest*, Series 2, Number 12. Arizona State University. http://www.fitness.gov/mentalhealth.htm

315 C. B. Taylor, J. F. Sallis and R. Needle. 1985. "The Relation of Physical Activity and Exercise to Mental Health." *Public Health Reports,* Vol. 100 (No. 2): pp. 195-202. http://www.pubmedcentral.nih.gov/picrender.fcgi?artid=1424736&blobtype=pdf; F. Dimeo, M. Bauer, I. Varahram, G. Proest and U. Halter. 2001. "Benefits from aerobic exercise in patients with major depression: a pilot study." *British Journal of Sports Medicine*, Vol. 35: pp. 114-117; Landers, http://www.fitness.gov/mentalhealth.htm; Daniel Landers and Steven Petruzzello. 1994. "State Anxiety Reduction and

Exercise: Does Hemispheric Activation Reflect Such Changes?" *Medicine & Science in Sports & Exercise*, Vol. 26 (No. 8): pp. 1028-1035. http://www.acsm-msse.org/pt/re/msse/abstract.00005768-199408000-00015.ht m;jsessionid=Ly1QxLMFCq11w2JDhSmhhQmTbPryGhG90TyXN9vFl j8vKQSXsYV5!691622333!181195628!8091!-1

316   Margie Patlak. "Your Guide to Healthy Sleep." National Institutes of Health, National Heart, Lung and Blood Institute, Department of Health and Human Services, November 2005, p. 2. http://www.nhlbi.nih.gov/health/public/sleep/healthy_sleep.pdf

317   N. Tsuno, A. Besset and K. Ritchie. 2005. "Sleep and Depression." *Journal of Clinical Psychiatry,* Vol. 66 (No. 10): pp. 1254-1269. [PubMed: 16259539.]

318   Patrick Holford, David Miller and James Braly. *How to Quit without Feeling S**t* (London: Piatkus, 2008), p. 200.

319   Ibid., p. 203; N. J. Pearson, et al. 2006. "Insomnia, Trouble Sleeping and Complementary and Alternative Medicine: Analysis of the 2002 National Health Interview Survey Data." *Archives of Internal Medicine*, Vol. 166: pp. 1775-1782. http://archinte.ama-assn.org/cgi/content/abstract/166/16/1775

320   Rich Thomaselli. 2009. "Pharma Benefits from Surge in Sleep-Aid, Antidepressant Prescriptions." *Advertising Age*, March 9, 2009. http://adage.coverleaf.com/advertisingage/20090309/?pg=8

321   Anne M. Holbrook. 2004. "Treating Insomnia: Use of Drugs Is Rising Despite Evidence of Harm and Little Meaningful Benefit." *British Medical Journal*, Vol. 329 (No. 7476): pp. 1198-1199.

322   Stephanie Saul. "Sleep Drugs Found Only Mildly Effective but Wildly Popular." *New York Times*, October 23, 2007. http://www.nytimes.com/2007/10/23/health/23drug.html?ref=science

323   T. Field, M. Hernandez-Reif, M. Diego, S. Schanberg and C. Kuhn. 2005. "Cortisol Decreases and Serotonin and Dopamine Increase Following Massage Therapy." *International Journal of Neuroscience*, Vol. 115 (No. 10): pp. 1397-1413. [PubMed: 16162447]

324   R. J. Leo and J. S. Ligot, Jr. 2007. "A Systematic Review of Randomized Controlled Trials of Acupuncture in the Treatment of Depression." *Journal of Affective Disorders,* Vol. 97 (Nos. 1-3): pp. 13-22. [PubMed: 16899301.]

325   T. W. Kjaer, C. Bertelsen, P. Piccini, et al. 2002. "Increased Dopamine Tone during Meditation-Induced Change of Consciousness." *Brain Research, Cognitive Brain Research*, Vol. 13: pp. 255-259.

326   Robert L. Spencer and Kent E. Hutchinson. "Alcohol, Aging and the Stress Response." *Alcohol Research and Health*, Winter 1999. http://findarticles.com/p/articles/mi_m0CXH/is_4_23/ai_63506636/

327 Their Web site is: www.cabinetoffice.gov.uk.

328 Mark Pendergrast. *Uncommon Grounds: The History of Coffee and How It Transformed Our World* (New York: Basic Books, 1999), pp. 16-17.

329 Barry Groves. *Natural Health and Weight Loss* (London: Hammersmith Press, 2007), p. 42.

330 Gary Langer. "Poll: What Americans Eat for Breakfast." ABC News, May 17, 2005. http://abcnews.go.com/GMA/PollVault/story?id=762685

331 Francine Segan. "Ivy League School's Dining Halls Get A for Effort." *Milwaukee Marketplace*, September 13, 2005. http://www.milwaukeemarketplace.com/story/index.aspx?id=355415

332 Groves, 2007, p. 40.

333 Melinda Beck. "Skipping Breakfast Can Break Your Diet—Fast." *Wall Street Journal*, September 9, 2005.

334 Ross, 2002, p. 156.

335 Ibid., 147.

336 Ross, 2002, p. 161.

337 R. E. Kleinman, S. Hall, H. Green, et al. 2002. "Diet, Breakfast and Academic Performance in Children." *Annals of Nutrition and Metabolism*, Vol. 46 (No. 1): pp. 24-30. [PubMed: 12428078.]; J. A. Fulkerson, N. E. Sherwood, C. L. Perry, D. Neumark-Sztainer and M. Story. 2004. "Depressive Symptoms and Adolescent Eating and Health Behaviors: A Multifaceted View in a Population-Based Sample." *Preventive Medicine*, Vol. 38 (No. 6): pp. 865-875. [PubMed: 15193910.]; A. Allgower, J. Wardle and A. Steptoe. 2001. "Depressive Symptoms, Social Support and Personal Health Behaviors in Young Men and Women." *Health Psychology*, Vol. 20 (No. 3): pp. 223-227. [PubMed: 11403220.]

338 "Food, Nutrition, Physical Activity and the Prevention of Cancer: A Global Perspective." American Institute for Cancer Research, 2007, p. 24.

339 Terry L. Neher, D.D.S., CCDC III. "Altered (Chemical) States: A Practical Look at Brain Chemistry and Addiction," *Professional Counselor*, March/April 1991.

340 Joseph D. Beasley, M.D. and Susan Knightly. *Food for Recovery: The Complete Nutritional Companion for Recovering from Alcoholism, Drug Addiction and Eating Disorders* (New York: Crown Publishers, 1994), p. 52.

341 Cheryle Hart, M.D. and Mary Kay Grossman, RD. *The Feel Good Diet.* (New York: McGraw-Hill, 2006), p. 22.

342 Ross, 2002, p. 59; L. Gohler, et al. 2000. "Reduction of Plasma Catecholamines in Humans During Clinically Controlled Severe Underfeeding." Clinics of Physical Medicine and Rehabilitation, University

Hospital Charite, Humboldt University, Berlin, Germany. *Preventive Medicine*, Vol. 30 (No. 2): pp. 95-102.

343 Kathleen DesMaisons, Ph.D. *Little Sugar Addicts: End Mood Swings, Meltdowns, Tantrums and Low Self-Esteem in Your Child Today* (New York: Three Rivers Press, 2004), p. 25.

344 Bruce Wilshire. *Wild Hunger: The Primal Roots of Modern Addiction* (Lanham, MD: Rowman and Littlefield, 1998), p.102.

345 Ross, 2002, p. 55.

346 Neher, 1991.

347 Joel Robertson, Ph.D. *Peak-Performance Living* (San Francisco: Harper, 1996), p. 18.

348 Ibid; Schachter, 2006, p. 60.

349 Ibid., p. 59.

350 Robertson, 1996, p. 29; Schachter, 2006, pp. 60-61.

351 Ibid., pp. 29-30.

352 Schachter, 2006, p. 62.

353 Neher, 1991.

354 Eric R. Braverman, M.D. *The Edge Effect: Reverse or Prevent Alzheimer's, Aging, Memory Loss, Weight Gain, Sexual Dysfunction and More* (New York: Sterling, 2004), p. 31.

355 Ross, *The Mood Cure* (New York: Penguin, 2002), p. 25; Gottfried Kellerman, Ph.D. Prepublication Research Data on 2200 Subjects and Controls Given Urinary Neurotransmitter Level Testing at Parmasan Labs, Minneapolis, 1996-2002.

356 Robertson, 1996, pp. 23-24; Schachter, 2006, pp. 57-58.

357 Neher, 1991.

358 Robertson, 1996, pp. 30-31; Schachter, 2006, pp. 58-59.

359 Robertson, 1996, pp. 30-31.

360 Robertson, 1996, p. 27

361 Terry l. Neher, D.D.S., CCDC III. "Neuronutrient Therapy: A Study in Stabilizing the Stress of Recovery." *Professional Counselor*, August 1993, p. 53. http://209.180.175.75/becalmd/therapy.htm

362 Marc Siegel. "'The Cleaner' Does a Fair Job of Depicting Drug Addiction and Recovery." *LA Times*, July 28, 2008.

363 Caroline Jean Acker. *Creating an American Junkie: Addiction Research in the Classic Era of Narcotic Control* (Baltimore: The Johns Hopkins University Press), 2002, page 182.

364 Charles Gant, M.D., Ph.D. and Greg Lewis, Ph.D. *End Your Addiction Now: The Proven Nutritional Supplement Program That Can Set You Free* (New York: Warner, 2002), p. 7.

365 Katherine Ketcham, William Asbury, et al. *Beyond the Influence: Understanding and Defeating Alcoholism* (New York: Bantam, 2000), page 158.

366 Ibid., p. 165.

367 Ibid., p. 168.

368 Terry L. Neher, D.D.S., CCDC III. "Neuronutrient Therapy: A Study in Stabilizing the Stress of Recovery." *Professional Counselor*, August 1993, p.53. http://209.180.175.75/becalmd/therapy.htm

369 Stanton Peele, Ph.D., J.D. *Addiction-Proof Your Child: A Realistic Approach to Preventing Drug, Alcohol and Other Dependencies* (New York: Three Rivers Press, 2007), pp. 190-191.

370 http://www.whale.to/v/kalokerinos2.html

371 James R. Milam and Katherine Ketcham. *Under the Influence: A Guide to the Myths and Realities of Alcoholism* (New York: Bantam, 1984), pp. vi-vii.

372 Ross, 2002, p. 267; Raymond Brown, Ph.D., Kenneth Blum, Ph.D., et al. 1990. "Neurodynamics of Relapse Prevention: A Neuronutrient Approach to Outpatient DUI Offenders." *Journal of Psychoactive Drugs*, Vol. 22 (No. 2): pp. 173-187.

373 Beasley and Knightly, 1994, pp. 10-11.

374 Eric Braverman, MD. *The Healing Nutrients Within*. 3rd Edition. (Laguna Beach: Basic Health, 1997), page 3

375 Ibid.

376 John Hoffman and Susan Froemke. eds. *Addiction: Why Can't They Just Stop?* (New York: Rodale, 2007), p. 57.

377 http://www.allianceforaddictionsolutions.org/services-programs/nutrition

378 Carolyn Reuben. "CARA Model of Brain Repair at the Sacramento Drug Court." *Townsend Letter*, January 2007. http://www.townsendletter.com/Jan2007/CARA0107.htm

379 Jill Smith et al. 2007. "Low-Dose Naltrexone Therapy Improves Active Crohn's Disease." *American Journal of Gastroenterology*, Vol. 102 (No. 4): pp. 820-828.

380 Carolyn Dean. *Death by Modern Medicine* (Belleville, Ontario: Matrix Verité, 2005), p. 274.

381 Joseph D. Beasley, M.D. and Susan Knightly. *Food for Recovery: The Complete Nutritional Companion for Recovering from Alcoholism, Drug Addiction and Eating Disorders* (New York: Crown Publishers, 1994), p. 53.

382 Sally Fallon and Mary Enig, Ph.D., *The Skinny on Fats*. Weston A. Price
     Foundation. http://www.westonaprice.org/knowyourfats/skinny.html
383 Julia Ross. *The Mood Cure* (New York: Penguin, 2002), p. 8.
384 Ibid., p. 7.
385 Ibid., p. 8.
386 Katherine Ketcham, William Asbury, et al. *Beyond the Influence:
     Understanding and Defeating Alcoholism* (New York: Bantam, 2000), pp.
     291-292.
387 Peter Whybrow, Ph.D. *American Mania: When More is Not Enough* (New
     York: W. W. Norton, 2005), back cover.
388 Caroline Jean Acker. *Creating an American Junkie: Addiction Research in the
     Classic Era of Narcotic Control* (Baltimore: Johns Hopkins University Press,
     2002), p. 7.
389 Mark Easton, ed. *The Happiness Formula: The Politics of Happiness*.
     Documentary. London: BBC Two, 2006.
390 Whybrow, 2005, p. 3; Robert E. Lane, *The Loss of Happiness in Market
     Democracies* (New Haven: Yale University Press, 2000), pp. 26-31.
391 "Pre-war Britons 'were happier.'" BBC News, September 1, 2005. http://
     news.bbc.co.uk/2/hi/uk_news/wales/4203686.stm
392 John De Graaf, David Wann and Thomas Naylor. *Affluenza: The All-Consuming
     Epidemic* (San Francisco: Berrett-Koehler Publishers, 2001), p. 109.
393 "Antidepressant Helps Alleviate Compulsive Shopping Disorder, Stanford
     Researchers Find." *Science Daily*, July 17, 2003. http://www.sciencedaily.
     com/releases/2003/07/030717090529.htm
394 "Dopamine Provides Shopper's High." UPI, December 11, 2005. http://www.
     upi.com/Odd_News/2005/12/11/Dopamine_provides_shoppers_high/
     UPI-46891134357034/
395 Jennifer Michael Hecht. *The Happiness Myth: Why What We Think Is Right
     Is Wrong* (New York: HarperCollins, 2007), p. 169; M. T. Bardo and L.
     P Dwoskin. "Biological Connection Between Drug and Novelty Seeking
     Motivational Systems." In *Motivational Factors in the Etiology of Drug
     Abuse*, ed. R.A. Bevins and M.T. Bardo (Lincoln: University of Nebraska
     Press: 2004), pp. 127-158.
396 Hecht, 2007, p. 169.
397 Mary Tanneeru. "9/11 Trauma Persists Five Years Later." CNN, September
     11, 2006. http://www.cnn.com/2006/US/09/08/911.overview/index.html
398 Tara Parker-Pope. "This Is Your Brain at the Mall: Why Shopping Makes
     You Feel So Good." *Wall Street Journal*, December 6, 2005, p. 1.

399 De Graaf, Wann and Naylor, 2001, pp. 13-16.
400 Ibid., p. 153.
401 Whybrow, 2005, p. 133.
402 "An Interview with Dr. Peter Whybrow." http://www.peterwhybrow.com/books/americanmania/interview.html
403 Whybrow, 2005, p. 229.
404 http://www.slowfood.com/about_us/eng/mission.lasso
405 Stanton Peele, Ph.D., J.D. *Seven Tools to Beat Addiction* (New York: Three Rivers Press, 2004), p. 234.
406 David Greenfield, Ph.D. *Virtual-Addiction: Help for Netheads, Cyberfreaks and Those Who Love Them* (Oakland, CA: New Harbinger Publications, 1999), p. 196.
407 Greenfield, 1999, p. 12.
408 Terrence Gordon, ed. *Understanding Media: The Extensions of Man* (Berkeley, CA: Gingko Press, 2003), p. 380.
409 "The Today Show." NBC, March 1, 2008.
410 Ibid.
411 Greenfield, 1999, p. 213.
412 Ibid., p. 28.
413 Ibid., p. 8.
414 Ibid.
415 Ibid., p. 188.
416 NBC, 2008.
417 "China Tackles Rise in 'Internet Addiction.'" CTV.ca News, December 29, 2005. http://www.ctv.ca/servlet/ArticleNews/story/CTVNews/20051228/china_internetaddiction_20051228/20051228
418 Ibid.
419 "Parents Neglect Starved Babies to Feed Video Game Addiction." *Associated Press*, July 14, 2007. http://www.foxnews.com/story/0,2933,289331,00.html
420 Emily Payne. "Is Sex Addiction Really That Bad?" *The London Paper*, September 4, 2008. http://www.thelondonpaper.com/cs/Satellite/london/love/article/1157154961736?packedargs=suffix%3DArticleController
421 "Net Sex Addiction on the Rise." BBC, May 6, 2000. http://news.bbc.co.uk/2/hi/science/nature/738699.stm
422 "Number of Sexual Scenes on TV Nearly Double Since 1998." Press Release, Kaiser Family Foundation, November 9, 2005.
423 Ibid.
424 Dale Kunkel, et al. "Sex on TV 4." The Henry J. Kaiser Family Foundation, 2005, p. 45.

http://www.kff.org/entmedia/upload/Sex-on-TV-4-Full-Report.pdf
425   Robert Lusetich. "Busting Big Pharma." *The Australian News*, December 16, 2004.
426   Ibid.
427   Jeanne Lenzer. "Wonder Drugs That Can Kill." *Discover Magazine*, June 20, 2008.
428   Jay Cohen, M.D. 2002. "Over Dose: The Case Against the Drug Companies, Part I." http://articles.mercola.com/sites/articles/archive/2002/02/06/overdose-part-one.aspx; M. Angell. 2000. "The Pharmaceutical Industry—To Whom Is It Accountable?" *New England Journal of Medicine*, Vol. 342: pp. 1902-1904.
429   Katherine Baicker and Amitabh Chandra. "Medicare Spending, the Physician Workforce and Beneficiaries' Quality of Care." *Health Affairs*, April 7, 2004. http://content.healthaffairs.org/cgi/reprint/hlthaff.w4.184 v1?maxtoshow=&HITS=10&hits=10&RESULTFORMAT=&fulltext=spending%2C+quality&andorexactfulltext=and&searchid=1&FIRSTINDEX=0&resourcetype=HWCIT
430   "Current Health Care System Not Meeting Needs for a Third of Canadians: More than Half Open to Trying Alternative and Natural Therapies before a More Traditional Approach." Canadian Health Reference Guide, July 15, 2008.
431   "Baseline Natural Health Products Survey among Consumers." Survey Conducted for Health Canada by Ipsos Reid, March 2005. http://www.hc-sc.gc.ca/dhp-mps/alt_formats/hpfb-dgpsa/pdf/pubs/eng_cons_survey-eng.pdf
432   Tara Parker-Pope. "Vitamin Pills: A False Hope?" *New York Times*, February 16, 2009. http://www.nytimes.com/2009/02/17/health/17well.html?_r=2&scp=3&sq=vitamins&st=cse
433   "According to a New Government Survey, 38% of Adults and 12% of Children Use Complementary and Alternative Medicine." National Institutes of Health, Press Release, December 10, 2008. http://nccam.nih.gov/news/2008/121008.htm
434   "Prescription Drug Compliance a Significant Challenge for Many Patients, According to New National Survey." Harris Interactive, Press Release, March 29, 2005. http://www.harrisinteractive.com/news/allnewsbydate.asp?NewsID=904
435   John Abramson. Interview by Ellen Kagan, 12/01/05. http://overdosedamerica.com/articles.php

436 "Pharmaceutical Marketing Disclosures." Report of Vermont Attorney General William H. Sorrell, June 26, 2007. http://www.atg.state.vt.us/ upload/1182891672_2007_Pharmaceutical_Marketing_Disclosures_ Report.pdf

437 Peter Breggin, M.D. "Psychiatry Makes War on 'Bipolar Children.'" *Huffington Post*, May 23, 2008. http://www.huffingtonpost.com/ dr-peter-breggin/psychiatry-makes-war-on-b_b_103337.html

438 Craig Lambert. "The Science of Happiness, Psychology explores humans at their best." *Harvard Magazine*, August 2007.

439 "Doctors Fear Ontario Children May Not Live as Long as their Parents." Ontario Medical Association, October 4, 2005. www.oma.org/Media/ news/pr051004.asp and *New England Journal of Medicine*, 2005 Mar; Vol. 352 (No. 11): pp. 1138-1145.

440 D. Brent. 2005. "Is the Medication Bottle for Pediatric and Adolescent Depression Half-Full or Half-Empty?" *Journal of Adolescent Health* Vol. 37 (No. 6):431- 433.

441 Miriam Weinstein. *The Surprising Power of Family Meals: How Eating Together Makes Us Smarter, Stronger, Healthier and Happier* (Hanover, NH: Steerforth Press, 2005), 60.

442 S. L. Hofferth. 2001. "How American Children Spend Their Time." *Journal of Marriage and the Family*, Vol. 63: pp. 295-308.

443 Carolina A. Miranda. "The Magic of the Family Meal." *Time* (Canadian Edition), June 12, 2006, p. 30.

444 Weinstein, 2005, p. 35.

445 Marion Nestle. 2006. "Food Marketing and Childhood Obesity—A Matter of Policy." *New England Journal of Medicine*, Vol. 354 (No. 24): pp. 2527-2429. http://content.nejm.org/cgi/content/full/354/24/2527

446 Ibid.

447 Ibid.

448 Maggie Fox. "Some U.S. Cereals More than Half Sugar: Report." *Reuters Health News*, October 1, 2008. http://www.reuters.com/article/ healthNews/idUSTRE49096420081001; "Better Cereal Choices for Kids." *Consumer Reports*, November 2008. http://www.consumerreports. org/health/healthy-living/diet-nutrition/healthy-foods/breakfast-cereals/ overview/breakfast-cereals-ov.htm

449 Nestle, 2006.

450 "Food and Beverage Marketing to Children." Toronto Board of Health, February 8, 2008; J. B. Schor. *Born to Buy: The Commercialized Child and the New Consumer Culture*. New York:

Scribner, 2004. http://www.toronto.ca/legdocs/mmis/2008/hl/bgrd/backgroundfile-11151.pdf

451 "Diet, Nutrition and the Prevention of Chronic Disease." WHO Technical Report Series, #916, Geneva, 2003. http://whqlibdoc.who.int/trs/WHO_TRS_916.pdf

452 Richard Heller and Rachael Heller. *Carbohydrate-Addicted Kids* (New York: HarperCollins, 1997), p. 270.

453 Ibid., p. 47.

454 Ibid., p. 39.

455 M. Hadjivassiliou, et al. 1996. "Does Cryptic Gluten Sensitivity Play a Part in Neurological illness?" *Lancet,* Vol. 347: pp. 369-371.

456 L. E. Levitt Katz, et al. 2005. "Neuropsychiatric Disorders at the Presentation of Type 3 Diabetes Mellitus in Children." *Pediatric Diabetes,* Vol. 6: pp. 84-89; Groves, 2008, pp. 371-372.

457 Heller and Heller, 1997, p. 117.

458 Caroline Cassels. 2008. "Insomnia Chronic and Common among U.S. Adolescents." *Medscape,* March 28, 2008. http://www.medscape.com/viewarticle/572125; R. E. Roberts, et al. 2008. "Chronic Insomnia and Its Negative Consequences for Health and Functioning of Adolescents: A 12-Month Prospective Study." *Journal of Adolescent Health,* Vol. 42: pp. 294-302. http://www.ncbi.nlm.nih.gov/pmc/articles/PMC2488408/

459 "2006 Sleep in America Poll." National Sleep Foundation. Prepared by WBS Market Research, p. 8.

460 Cassels, 2008; Roberts, et al., 2008.

461 Cassels, 2008.

462 Brandy M. Roane and Daniel J. Taylor. 2008. "Adolescent Insomnia as a Risk Factor for Early Adult Depression and Substance Abuse." *Sleep,* Vol. 31(10):1351-1356.

463 "Adolescent Insomnia Linked to Depression and Substance Abuse during Adolescence and Young Adulthood." Press Release, American Academy of Sleep Medicine, October 1, 2008. http://www.eurekalert.org/pub_releases/2008-10/aaos-ai092908.php

464 Xianchen Liu, M.D., Ph.D. 2007. "Sleep Deprivation Can Lead to Smoking, Drinking." [Smoking & Drinking Can Also Lead to Sleep Deprivation—A Two Way Street]. Research abstract presented at SLEEP 2007, the 21st Annual Meeting of the Associated Professional Sleep Societies (APSS) in Westchester, Illinois. American Academy of Sleep Medicine (2007, June 14). "Sleep Deprivation Can Lead To Smoking, Drinking."

ScienceDaily. Retrieved October 23, 2008. http://www.sciencedaily.com / releases/2007/06/070612075012.htm

465 Lynne Lamberg. 2006. "Sleep-Deprived Teens Report Stress, Mood Disorders." *Psychiatry News,* Vol. 41 (No. 10): p. 41. http://pn.psychiatryonline.org/cgi/content/full/41/10/41-b

466 Ibid.

467 "'Junk sleep' damaging teenagers' health." *Reuters,* August 28, 2007. http://www.reuters.com/article/technologyNews/idUSL2854227920070828

468 Ibid.

469 Gina Stepp. "Childhood: The New Age of Anxiety." *Vision,* May 27, 2008. http://www.vision.org/visionmedia/article.aspx?id=5452

470 Groves, 2008, p. 57.

471 Louise Stevens Bryant. *School Feeding: Its History and Practice at Home and Abroad* (Philadelphia: J. B. Lippincott Co., 1913), p. 252.

472 Ibid., 244.

473 C. Ballew, S. Kuester and C. Gillespie. 2000. "Beverage Choices Affect Adequacy of Children's Nutrient Intakes." *Archives of Pediatrics and Adolescent Medicine,* Vol. 154: p. 1148; S. A. Bowman. 2002. "Beverage Choices of Young Females: Changes and Impact on Nutrient Intakes." *Journal of the American Dietetic Association,* Vol. 102 (No. 9): 1234-1239; J. S. Volek, A. L. Gomez, T. P. Scheett, et al. 2003. "Increasing Fluid Milk Favorably Affects Bone Mineral Density Responses to Resistance Training in Adolescent Boys." *Journal of the American Dietetic Association,* Vol. 103 (No. 10): 1353-1356.

474 Y. Claire Wang, Sara N. Bleich and Steven L. Gortmaker. 2008. "Increasing Caloric Contribution from Sugar-Sweetened Beverages and 100% Fruit Juices among U.S. Children and Adolescents, 1988-2004." *Pediatric,* Vol. 121 (No. 6): pp. e1604-e1614. http://pediatrics.aappublications.org/cgi/reprint/121/6/e1604

475 Elizabeth M. Haney, M.D. "Screening for Lipid Disorders in Children and Adolescents: Systematic Evidence Review for the US Preventive Services Task Force." Agency for Healthcare Research and Quality, U.S. Department of Health and Human Services, July 2007. HRQ Publication No. 07-0598-EF-1 Page 28, Tables pp 150-154. http://www.ahrq.gov/clinic/uspstf07/chlipid/chlipidsyn.pdf

476 http://www.wholesoystory.com/

477 Natasha Campbell-McBride. 2008. "Gut and Psychology Syndrome." *Journal of Orthomolecular Medicine,* Vol. 23 (No. 2): pp. 90-94.

INDEX

A

ABC News, 132, 274, 381
Abrams, H. Leon, 72
Abramson, John
Overdosed America: The Broken Promise of American Medicine, 286
accumbens, 63
acetaldehyde, 120, 316
acetylcholine, 94, 141, 346
Acres USA, 338
Acudetox, 244
Adderall, 34, 42-43
addiction, 23-24, 27-28, 40-41, 59, 146-48, 178-81, 183-85, 201-3, 209-11, 215-16, 218-20, 227-28, 233-37, 244-45, 326-27, 355-58
Addiction Prevention and Recovery Administration (APRA), 41
Addiction-Proof Your Child (Peele), 327
addictive environment, 24-25, 262
ADL (activities of daily living), 92
Adrenal Fatigue: The 21st Century Stress Syndrome (Wilson), 61
adrenal glands, 49, 60, 98, 110, 213
adrenaline, 60, 66, 137, 181-83
adverse drug reactions (ADRs), 38, 360
Affluenza: The All-Consuming Epidemic (de Graaf, Wann, and Naylor), 260
Alabama Department of Forensic Sciences, 39
Alcohol and the Addictive Brain (Blum), 149
Alcoholics Anonymous (AA), 147, 214
Allan, Christian, 77, 110
Allen, Johnny, 248
Alliance for Addiction Solutions, 9, 152, 159, 202, 208, 333, 336
Alternative Farming Systems Information Center (AFSIC), 339
American Dietetic Association (ADA), 55, 389
American Health Network, 210

American Law Institute, 287
American Mania: When More Is Not Enough (Whybrow), 262
American National Institutes of Health, 127
American Psychiatric Association (APA), 176
American Psychological Association, 27, 356
ammonia, 120
Analytical Research Labs Inc., 99
Anderson, Karsen, 74
Angel, Lawrence, 51
Appleton, Nancy
Lick the Sugar Habit, 63
arachidonic acid (AA), 79, 86, 189, 320
Archives of Internal Medicine, 38, 360, 380
Armelagos, George, 51
Paleopathology at the Origins of Agriculture, 50
Armour, 101
Armstrong, Bruce, 63
attention deficit disorder (ADD), 42, 90, 206, 290, 306, 312, 323, 325
attention deficit hyperactivity disorder (ADHD), 26, 42, 180, 234, 290, 306, 312, 323, 343

B

Bardo, Michael, 260
Barnham, P. T., 288
Batmanghelidj , F.
Your Body's Many Cries for Water and Water: Rx for a Healthier Pain-Free Life, 116
Beasley, Joseph
Food for Recovery: The Complete Nutritional Companion for Recovering from Alcoholism, Drug Addiction and Eating Disorders, 151, 349, 362, 381, 383
Beijing Military Region Central Hospital, 272

CPSIA information can be obtained at www.ICGtesting.com
Printed in the USA
BVOW082150221012

303607BV00001B/8/P